These
United States

These "Colored" United States

African American Essays from the 1920s

EDITED BY TOM LUTZ
AND
SUSANNA ASHTON

RUTGERS UNIVERSITY PRESS
New Brunswick, New Jersey

Library of Congress Cataloging-in-Publication Data

These "colored" United States : African American essays from the 1920s
/ edited by Tom Lutz and Susanna Ashton.
     p.   cm.
   Includes index.
   ISBN 0-8135-2305-2 (cloth : alk. paper).—ISBN 0-8135-2306-0
(pbk. : alk. paper)
   1. Afro-Americans–Social conditions—To 1964. I. Lutz, Tom.
II. Ashton, Susanna, 1967– .
E185.6.T44 1996
973'.0496073—dc20   95-52258
                                          CIP

British Cataloging-in-Publication information available

To our families

CONTENTS

ACKNOWLEDGMENTS

We would like to thank the University of Iowa Department of English for the research money that seeded this project, the reference and interlibrary loan staffs at the University of Iowa libraries, the reference staff at the Schomberg Center for Research in Black Culture, the University of Southern California's Doheny Library, and the Los Angeles Public Library. The work of Theodore Kornweibel, Jr., was indispensable to us, as was that of Daniel Borus. The suggestions of Kevin Gaines, who read the manuscript at an early stage, were extremely valuable. We would also like to thank Linda Bolton, Eileen McWilliam, Mary Moran, and Laurie Winer for their help and suggestions; Leslie Mitchner and Carole Brown for their editorial assistance; and each other for our hard work and dedication.

These "Colored"
United States

TOM LUTZ

Introduction: Diversity, Locality, and Ideology in "These 'Colored' United States"

In the introduction to his monumental two-volume collection of African American essays, *Speech and Power* (1992), Gerald Early claims that the essay was the genre that informed the coming of age of black writing in the 1920s. Whether or not this is true, the essay was clearly the dominant genre in those magazines in which the renaissance of African American literature was nurtured. *These "Colored" United States* brings together essays originally published between 1923 and 1926 in one of those magazines, *The Messenger*. Along with *Opportunity* and *The Crisis,* and a handful of white magazines, *The Messenger* published the work of a loosely knit group of poets, painters, novelists, and other thinkers and artists centered in Harlem in the 1920s, a group now known as the Harlem Renaissance. But although Harlem was home to *The Messenger* and much of its audience, it was a national magazine and national and international in its interests, as these essays attest. Written by a highly diverse and eclectic group of African American writers, these essays were and are unique in offering a state-by-state overview of "colored" life, a snapshot of each state's culture, society, history, economics, and even geography from the perspective of its African American citizens. Cultural nationalists and assimilationists, capitalists and socialists, separatist followers of Marcus Garvey and integrationist officers of the NAACP, modernists and traditionalists, radicals and conservatives, as well as a few writers so idiosyncratic that none of these labels fit, these authors collectively convey a sense of the diversity of African American intellectual and cultural opinion in the 1920s. Their essays represent an unexamined chapter in African American cultural history and provide a unique overview of African American social and cultural thought during what was a crucial decade for race relations in the United States.

The 1920s have long captured America's historical imagination. Its nickname, the Roaring Twenties, has helped cement a picture of a nation under the sway of speakeasies, flappers, movies, modernism, and rapidly replaced fads and fashions, from bobbed hair to frenetic dances to flagpole sitting. And people in the 1920s, whether they felt the time to be liberating or frightening, very often found themselves flooded with a sense that theirs was a decade in which all was changing, all was new. While isolationists, fundamentalists, and other traditionalists did their best to push a "return to normalcy," as Warren G. Harding's 1920 presidential campaign slogan put it, the decade continued to be one of cultural experiment and innovation.

For white culture this often included imbibing large quantities of African American culture.

Many African Americans, too, felt the lure and promise of opportunity and change, and sometimes a corresponding trepidation. More than at any time since the era of Reconstruction immediately following the Civil War, many African Americans in the 1920s saw significant possibilities for individual and racial advance. The economic disruption caused or accelerated by the Great War, along with the example of European openness toward color difference, reported by many returning servicemen, had profound effects on attitudes of Americans both white and black. Many editorialists and activists argued that, as Kelly Miller wrote, "the Negro will emerge from this war with a double portion of privilege and opportunity." W.E.B. Du Bois wrote a series of articles in *The Crisis,* the official magazine of the NAACP, during and immediately after the war arguing that the industrial and military opportunities and experiences offered by the war would be good for individuals and for the race, giving a "new, clear vision of the real, inner spirit of American prejudice" and, equally important, new, lucrative skills to black workers. The majority of printed opinions during the war followed this general line, even if, as George Schuyler suggested, many who publicly expressed patriotic opinions actually believed that German rule would not have been any worse than white American rule. In the few years following the armistice in 1919, what wartime optimism existed was severely damaged by a serious economic downturn, growing unemployment, the ominous resurgence of the Ku Klux Klan, and race riots in many large and medium-sized cities. But however we might evaluate the losses and gains for African Americans during these years, there is no disputing the magnitude of the changes.

The Great Migration, which began before the war and was accelerated by it, saw over a million African Americans move from southern farms to northern, midwestern, and western cities. This vast movement permanently altered life in all regions of the country for whites and blacks alike. Having come in search of economic opportunity, many southerners found not just new livelihoods but new ways of living, and perhaps most important, there emerged on a national scale a new sense of "Negro" culture. The mingling of northern and southern, middle and working class, native and foreign, urban and rural people caused many to reconsider the meaning of their common African ancestry, both its extent and limits. Blues and jazz flourished in the bars and dance halls of New York, Chicago and other cities, and the newly founded "race labels" distributed the new music to African American consumers across the nation. Whites also listened to jazz, and all-black musicals were widely performed to both white and black audiences, the most visible success being Blake and Sissle's Broadway hit *Shuffle Along* in 1921. In the 1920s African American culture was in vogue, as historian David Levering Lewis has put it (following Langston Hughes), and the effect was to give both white and black America a sense of the distinctive modern culture of African

Americans. The publishing of African American novelists, poets, and essayists, the launching of new magazines and newspapers, and the noticeable growth of a middle class of doctors, lawyers, and entrepreneurs all helped establish an often contested but nonetheless real sense of accomplishment and identity.

The cultural center of these changes was Harlem. Harlem had been a fashionable neighborhood of Manhattan in the 1880s, but the well-to-do moved out as successive waves of immigrants arrived. During the war, African Americans moved into central Harlem in great numbers, making it the largest black urban center in the world by the late 1920s. A melting pot of the African diaspora, Harlem was home, not just to native northeasterners and emigrant southerners, but to immigrants from the West Indies as well, with a few new arrivals from Africa. The various cultural traditions of these very different groups found expression and cross-pollinated with each other, especially in popular cultural forms and the arts. Of the African American cultural phenomena of the period, the Harlem Renaissance has received the most attention from literary and cultural historians. Now at the center of the canon of African American literature, Langston Hughes, Countee Cullen, Jessie Redmon Fauset, Angelina Grimké, Charles Johnson, Claude McKay, Nella Larsen, Zora Neale Hurston, Jean Toomer, and numerous other artists were announced as the voice of the "New Negro." The African American magazines *Opportunity, The Crisis,* and *The Messenger* were the most important outlets for these writers, along with white magazines such as *The Nation* and *American Mercury.* As Alain Locke, whose collection *The New Negro* (1925; originally published in *Survey Graphic*) put the renaissance group on the cultural map, wrote in his introduction to that volume, the "significant achievement" and "abundant promise" of these artists pointed toward the eventual equality of the races, of "the Negro's . . . full initiation into American democracy."

But whatever the hoped-for changes in the politics of the race, the Harlem Renaissance was primarily an artistic movement, and the renaissance group placed much more emphasis on cultural and artistic achievement than did many other African American writers and activists in the decade, including many who wrote in these same magazines. For those of the latter group, the primary goal was economic advance, with the knowledge that for the majority of African Americans, the kind of aesthetic polemics that engaged the Harlem Renaissance writers had little vital import. An editorial in *The Messenger* in 1919, for instance, took Du Bois to task for giving music and art precedence over economics and politics. But even for those writers and editors whose prime interest was economic advancement, the cultural achievements of the Harlem group and others remained an important sign of increasing equality between the races.

There was little agreement among African American polemicists about how to effect true equality. In the pure size of its audience and in the amount of news coverage it received, the populist utopian movement led by Marcus Garvey, also based in Harlem, for a time dwarfed any other single group. Garvey, an immigrant from Jamaica, founded the United Negro Improvement Association (UNIA) to promote race pride and black capitalism. Claiming he was "the equal of any white man," Garvey spread his message of equality through separatism to a largely working-class audience. He had at least a half million followers by the mid 1920s (he claimed to have six million), and through his newspaper, *The Negro World,* he preached for black patronage of black business and for the creation of a black nation in Africa to which African Americans should emigrate. He began a shipping line, the Black Star Line, that was to be used to raise money for and finally effect this mass emigration but that later in 1920s went bankrupt. Garvey was always controversial, perhaps never more than when he made tentative alliances with the Ku Klux Klan on the grounds that they, too, believed in race purity and that they were more likely than other whites to help in the planned expatriation to Africa. He was arrested on charges of mail fraud (in connection with the Black Star Line), convicted, and deported, after which the movement declined. At its height, the UNIA was a powerful populist movement, and as such was watched anxiously by whites and zealously opposed by African American integrationists who disagreed with the movement's separatist message.

Garvey's utopian separatism was anathema to those involved with the National Association for the Advancement of Colored People, for instance. The NAACP, which issued its tenth annual report as the decade opened, was committed to a policy of full equality as soon as possible. With members and officers drawn primarily from the growing black middle class and their white middle-class allies, the association was growing quickly and had demonstrated its clout by winning several important court cases during the war. The journal of the organization, *The Crisis,* was edited by W.E.B. Du Bois, who, although he was to live another forty-five years, was already an elder statesman of the movement. Many young activists, both Garveyites and socialists, considered Du Bois one of the "old guard," out of touch with the new realities of the black masses. Many southern and northern whites, as well as some conservative blacks, still saw in Du Bois the fire-breathing radical who demanded immediate equality and had dared to pick fights with the more conservative Booker T. Washington as early as 1903. At that time Du Bois's voice seemed, for all his Harvard education and solid academic achievements, a radical one to most Americans. He advocated equality of opportunity, of justice, and of education—all of the equality granted by the Constitution. To those at the turn of the century who considered the black race inferior, and even to those comfortable with the gradualist and accommodationist policies advocated by Washington, Du Bois often seemed like a hotheaded youth, too impatient with the realities of race. But the NAACP, which merged from the Du Bois–inspired Niagara Movement, had managed in little more than a decade to move Du Bois's program of equality from the margins to the center, however contested, of the national debate and of middle-class American opinion.

The national headquarters of the NAACP was in New York City, but from early on the group's strategy for establishing national equality was carried out on a state-by-state basis, with each individual chapter acting on whichever local injustice it viewed as most pressing. In Boston, for example, the local branch spent a great deal of money and effort lobbying against the 1915 screenings of the viciously racist D. W. Griffith film *The Birth of a Nation*. The Washington, D.C., chapters fought hard for equality in hiring procedures and employment for federal government workers. Many of the contributors to "These 'Colored' United States" were deeply involved in both the national and local NAACP chapters, and some, like Robert W. Bagnall and William Pickens, built their careers upon researching, recognizing, and battling problems of racial inequality on a state-by-state basis. Bagnall, for instance, organized many local chapters across the country, not just for the local work they could accomplish, but also because they were intrinsic components of national clout.

When it was founded by A. Philip Randolph and Chandler Owen in 1917, *The Messenger* differed sharply in its views from the NAACP's *Crisis* and the Urban League's *Opportunity,* calling itself "The Only Radical Negro Magazine in America." As its historian, Theodore Kornweibel, Jr., has written in *No Crystal Stair: Black Life and The Messenger, 1917–1928* (1975), *The Messenger* involved itself in all of the important debates in the 1920s, and as such is a particularly useful window on the period. The masthead slogan was soon replaced with "A Journal of Scientific Radicalism," but this slight modification did not stop it from being deemed "insolently offensive" by the Red-baiting attorney general A. Mitchell Palmer. Randolph and Owen were committed socialists during the war, and unlike many leftists in America, who were silenced by anti-Red hysteria, anticommunist riots, and the infamous Palmer raids of 1919, they continued to argue their brand of radicalism through the early 1920s, as Randolph did for some time thereafter.

The magazine itself, however, remained considerably less constant. Langston Hughes in his memoir *The Big Sea* (1940) remembers the three main outlets for Negro writing in the 1920s as "*Crisis, Opportunity,* and the *Messenger*—the first two being house organs of inter-racial organizations, and the latter being God knows what." Owen left in the early 1920s to take a position in Chicago, and Randolph began to spend more time organizing labor and less time running the magazine, which was left to the day-to-day direction of George Schuyler, an iconoclast with (at that time) a less obvious political agenda. Always running on inadequate funds, the magazine attempted to expand circulation by broadening its appeal, and by the mid 1920s the masthead read, "The World's Greatest Negro Monthly." More probusiness articles appeared, along with more apolitical cultural pieces, and more nondidactic fiction and poetry. In the last year of its life, from late 1927 to mid 1928, the masthead subtitle was "New Opinion of the New Negro," and this perhaps best sums up the magazine's editorial position while these essays were run. "New Negro" opinion ran the gamut from politically radical to pro-business, from cultural nationalism to cultural conservatism, and so did the essays in this series.

What the editors of *The Messenger* hoped to accomplish with the series is not entirely clear. The first eight essays in the series carried a blurb stating that "a brilliant representative from each State that has a goodly population of Negroes will speak out . . . and say to the world in plain language just what conditions they face." Many of the essays are just that, an attempt to make plain the legal, economic, and social conditions impinging on the lives of African Americans in the state. But such a progressive exposé was clearly not the intent of some of the writers, who opted, on the contrary, to detail, proudly and loudly, the sales and capitalizations of various black-owned businesses and the accomplishments of "Negro society," meaning middle-class "high society." Noah Thompson's essay on California reads like a chamber of commerce brochure, lauding the limitless business opportunities for and widespread successes of African Americans in the state. The unabashed celebration of bourgeois achievement was seen as a means of encouraging race pride and further material advancement, much like the pieces in the uplift journals of the previous generation (such as *The Colored American*) or the facile pro business boosterism common to mass-market magazines in the 1920s and satirized in Sinclair Lewis's *Babbitt* (1922).

Some of the writers resisted attempts to frame their work as either exposé or celebration. Toward the end of his tenure as editor of *The Messenger,* Wallace Thurman wrote, as an aside in his own essay on Utah, that "to write of "These Colored United States' is to be trying to visualize a phantom," because "the Negro . . . is a negative factor contributing nothing politically, historically, or economically. He only contributes sociological problems." There are cities in which the "Aframerican spirit manifests itself," according to Thurman, but "there are no Colored United States, *id est,* no state in the Union where the Negro has been an individual or vital factor." Obviously, many authors explicitly contradicted him. Robert W. Bagnall, for instance, applauded the significant achievements of Michigan's "Negro contingent" and predicted black would play an even larger role in Michigan's future. Alice Dunbar-Nelson depicts many different African American groups in Delaware that are neither "social problems" nor bourgeois paragons. Therefore, to write about the essay series "These 'Colored' United States" as a whole, while it may not be quite as difficult as trying to visualize a phantom, is a bit like trying to pin one down.

But if the editorial bias is impossible to locate, the inciting cause of the series is easy to discern. Ernest Greuning, the editor of *The Nation,* an important forum for new thought and commentary at the time, commissioned a series of essays titled "These United States." The essays, by the likes of Willa Cather (on Nebraska), Sinclair Lewis (on Minnesota), Theodore Dreiser (on Indiana), W.E.B. Du Bois (on Georgia), H. L. Mencken (on Maryland), and Dorothy Canfield Fisher (on Vermont), ran in that magazine from 1922 through 1925 and later appeared in book form, also edited by Gruening. One purpose of this series was to counteract the excessively cosmopolitan, urban, and largely pessimistic view of America that was the seeming consensus of New York's young intellectuals. Gruening hoped to provide a more balanced, less cynical picture of the state of the culture than theirs, one that, unlike the depressive denouncements common to radical and liberal critiques, looked to the strengths of the nation.

One view Gruening wanted to counteract was that presented in Harold Stearns's pessimistic, postwar collection of essays *Civilization in the United States* (1922). Stearns's collection was a manifesto against the status quo by the young, mostly disenchanted intellectuals of the day. The essays on art, literature, science, sex, the family, politics, and other arenas of social and cultural life all reached the same negative conclusions—the problem with civilization in the United States is that there is not enough of it and commercial culture is destroying what little of it there is, because the bourgeois ethic is hostile to art, fulfillment, and spirit. While far from alone in its dismissal of contemporary culture, Stearns's collection was undoubtedly one of the most influential critiques of the decade.

The collection was a major sally in the ongoing debate about the nature of civilization in the 1920s, a debate that had many causes and consequences, as Warren Susman and others have noted. World War I, with its vast carnage, had damaged the culture's faith in human progress, toned down its adulation of technology, and shaken its faith in civilization itself. If the seemingly most advanced civilizations in history could foster such savagery, the progress of civilization as an ideal was emptied of meaning. At the same time, the United States had emerged from the war as an undisputed world power, taking over from Europe the position of the world's leading civilization.

One important strand in the debate about civilization was that provided by a number of scientists and academics who took race and civilization as their subject. The teens and twenties saw a proliferation of popular and scholarly books and articles of "scientific racism," which among other things predicted the overthrow of Western civilization by the "darker races" if steps were not taken to prevent such a debacle. Madison Grant's *Passing of the Great Race* (1916), Lothrop Stoddard's *Rising Tide of Color* (1920) and *Revolt against Civilization* (1922), Charles Gould's *America: A Family Matter* (1920), Clinton Stoddard Burr's *America's Race Heritage* (1922), and Charles Conant Josey's *Race and National Solidarity* (1923) all argued that races with black, brown, red, or yellow skin are inferior to those with white skin, and that this was proven by the accomplishments of white civilization. They all held a Malthusian belief that increasing populations of "inferior" peoples would destroy the civilization whites had been developing for millennia. And they all (like Marcus Garvey) believed in race purity, since miscegenation, in their eugenicist view, could produce only offspring with at least some inferior characteristics. Post–World War I nativism also fueled the resurgence of the Ku Klux Klan, antiradical riots and legislation (since radical politics were seen as a European import), and moves to further restrict immigration. Political campaigns pitted urban and rural constituencies against each other, often invoking and manipulating nativist fears of blacks and immigrants. The prewar progressive attitude of cosmopolitan openness, as represented for instance by Randolph Bourne's well-known essay "Trans-National America" (1917), although never fully accepted, was further marginalized. A spate of popular books on Native Americans in the 1920s romanticized the "vanishing American," but the accent was on "vanishing." These books, like many stories about immigrants, such as O. E. Rolvagg's *Giants in the Earth* (1927), tended to be set in the past, nostalgically separated from the real life of the nation. Or, as in the best-selling, self-congratulatory autobiography of the immigrant editor of *Ladies' Home Journal, The Americanization of Edward Bok* (1920), they celebrated the replacement of identity and difference with "success" and conformity.

Both the intellectuals associated with Stearns and those associated with *The Nation,* on the other hand, tended to find such conformity stifling, deadening. One common complaint was that American society, under the sway of mass production and mass culture, was growing more and more standardized. Greuning repeats this criticism in his introduction to *The Nation* series: "Though centralization and regimentation may be a great convenience to administrators, they are death to variety and experiment and, consequently, in the end to growth." He hoped the series would instead ask, "What riches of variety remain?" and take account of the diversity of the country's citizens and regions. As has often been true in American culture, there was some hope that modern urban thought and culture could be recouped or redirected through a look to more provincial and traditional ways of life. But more important, Greuning saw in "diversity," in the "distinctive colors of life among its sections and climates and altitudes" the cultural wealth of the nation.

The Nation's decision to provide regional analyses as an antidote to the malaise of civilization had a long tradition. Regionalism in American culture has long been a response to the processes of industrialization and urbanization, whether in the form of frontier ideologies and other Western myths; agrarianism; or sometimes-pastoral, sometimes-populist "local color" stories and novels. Some of the essays in *The Nation* repeat these themes, and some are the essayistic equivalents of a week in the country away from the cares of the city. Willa Cather, for instance, provided a regionalist alternative to urban angst in her essay on Nebraska. Elizabeth Shepley Sargeant explicitly stated that the relationship between nature and culture in New Mexico is the opposite of that necessarily found in cities, and that this difference is the source of the state's beauty and value. But not all of

Greuning's authors agreed. Sinclair Lewis, Theodore Dreiser, H. L. Mencken, and others were as cynically negative in their evaluations as the Stearns group, finding in each of their states simply more standardization and homogenization, more banality and sterility. These authors pushed the series less toward a repudiation of Stearns's pessimism about civilization than toward a recapitulation of it.

It was this series in *The Nation* that prompted *The Messenger* to respond with "These 'Colored' United States." Having noticed immediately that African Americans were conspicuously absent from the survey of diversity in *The Nation,* except for the single case of Du Bois's essay on Georgia, the editors of *The Messenger* commissioned African American authors to write their own surveys of life in their respective states. *The Nation*'s essay on Illinois, for instance, ignores issues of race and ethnicity entirely, except for a brief mention of the race riots in Chicago in 1919. Like the rest of the essays in the series it seems completely unaware of the Great Migration. Charles S. Johnson's essay on Illinois in *The Messenger,* on the other hand, insists on the centrality of race and ethnicity to understanding Illinois. The racial and ethnic divisions within the state are so great, Johnson writes, that "only by the most reckless interpretation of statehood" can Illinois "be considered a sovereign unit." He points out that the Polish population of Chicago is larger than that of Warsaw, that it is the second-largest German city in the world, that its black population is larger than that of Nashville and twice as large as that of Savannah, and that its economic and social life have been determined by successive waves of immigrating Irish, Swedes, Canadians, Norwegians, Danes, Scotch, Swiss, Welsh, Belgians, Slavs, Italians, and African Americans. The rest of the state accounts for fewer people than Chicago, and though it is less racially diverse, writes Johnson, its culture is still marked by race. The entire history of the state in the nineteenth century centered on the question of slavery, Johnson argues, and race continues to control its destiny, as shown by the complete segregation of most towns in the state. The Ku Klux Klan had grown to 165,000 members, and race riots had occurred since the war not just in Chicago, but in East St. Louis, Springfield, and Herrin.

Not all of the essays in *The Messenger* so clearly address the shortcomings of those in *The Nation,* and even those that do avoid becoming simply tracts on the race issue. They are attempts to intervene in this important general debate about the state of American civilization, from the perspective of, and in the interests of, African Americans in the 1920s. Again, there was a great deal of variation among the individual authors. The essay series came into being because of this debate, but its authors did not always remain tied to the issues to which they were supposedly responding. Some kept the national debate at the fore, as in Thurman's Menckenesque essay on Utah, while others kept the form of the essays in *The Nation* while radically altering it to fit their polemics or pet projects. Still others seemed to reinvent the form completely.

The authors include some recognized as the foremost African American writers of the day, such as Thurman, Schuyler, Johnson, Dunbar-Nelson, Kelly Miller, Roy Wilkins, and E. Franklin Frazier. Some of the writers are known by specialists but not by many others, as in the case of Theophilus Lewis, who as a theater critic with no formal higher education got his publishing start in *The Messenger* and went on to become the theater critic for the Catholic monthly *America* for over twenty years. Although just starting out when he wrote his essay on Maryland, Lewis was the most important critic of African American theater in the middle of the century. Well known as an NAACP organizer and wartime bureaucrat, William Pickens demonstrates a passionate and consummate skill as a writer in his essay on Arkansas. Anita Coleman, a writer who won *The Crisis* short-story contest in 1925, at the height of the Harlem Renaissance and who has not been in print for over fifty years, provides here the essay on New Mexico and Arizona. Some of the pieces, like J. Egert Allen's astounding, ironic essay on the "sun-kissed folks" of Mississippi, are rhetorical tours de force, though Allen is better known as an educator than as an author. Some of the authors have been completely forgotten, as in the case of Mamie Francis, whose essay on New Jersey is nonetheless one of the most penetrating and sophisticated in the collection.

Some of the authors were among those lambasted personally in *The Messenger*'s more radical days, when the editors lashed out at any writers or public figures they found too conservative, politically or culturally—the NAACP and the so-called Old Crowd associated with the black colleges, the New Negro artists, and Garveyites had all felt the sting of the early *Messenger*'s wrath. But Kelly Miller, who wrote the essay on South Carolina, and other members of the Old Crowd published in this series, as did William Ferris, the former literary editor of Garvey's *Negro World,* who wrote the essay on Connecticut. Frazier, Miller, and Johnson all contributed both to this series and to *The New Negro,* a collection much more in tune with bourgeois aspirations than radical politics. Of course, by the early 1920s, the magazine had become much more eclectic than in the days when it ran satirical cartoons of Miller, Du Bois, and others. But its radical edge still prompted some authors to tailor their arguments accordingly. Frazier, a pivotal figure in the history of African American sociology, wrote the essay on Georgia here, and did so in counterpoint both to Du Bois's essay in *The Nation* and to his own contribution on Durham, North Carolina, in *The New Negro.* In that essay, Frazier celebrates the emerging black middle class of Durham, listing assets for black businesses and cheering for the "transformed Negro" with middle-class psychology and ideals, and ignoring all other parts of Durham society. In his *Messenger* essay, Frazier discusses urban and rural blacks and whites and the various relations and lack thereof among these classes. He gives a full historical overview and discusses the different psychologies of racism at work in these different groups. His *Messenger* essay presents, in other words, a less optimistic stance, and a considerably fuller view. And a similar difference can be seen in Miller's two contributions. His piece in *The New Negro* is purely celebratory, but in his *Messenger* essay he mixes praise and censure.

By the mid 1920s, essays on individual states appeared not just in *The Nation* and *The Messenger,* but in *The New Republic, American Mercury,* and elsewhere, and had begun to follow a common form, often beginning with geographical and climatological facts, moving to economic and demographic information, and then on to cultural discussion. Playing with this generic conflation of the geographical and the social, Francis writes in her introductory paragraph on New Jersey: "Aside from being the wettest state in the Union, it maintains a rather unique point of view toward the Negro Problem." Dunbar-Nelson remarks in her essay that "there is not much of Delaware, geographically." These and other essays comment on and play with other conventions of the genre as well, as did writers elsewhere, for example, William Carlos Williams, whose 1925 essay on Virginia was part spoof on the popularity of the form and part serious attempt at pushing the form forward.

Coleman writes about two states in which African Americans are largely an "unconsidered quantity," Arizona and New Mexico. "So far, in New Mexico, the Negro has not yet become a bone to gnaw in politics," she writes, in part because of their inconsequential numbers. Nonetheless, she shows the important place of African Americans in the histories of these places rarely associated with black America and, through her attention to Native American and Hispanic American histories and presences, the importance of the full range of American peoples in the construction of local and national identities. Like the other essays on western states, the Virgin Islands, and the Midwest, Coleman's essay is an important source for cultural historians eager to go beyond the bounds of urban history and southern ruralism. These essays are not exercises in provincialism or simple pluralism but reflect instead the complexity of African American relations to both African American and American nationalism.

Historians have been slow to study the interrelations between white and black intellectual culture in the United States, with the latter too often seen as either a self-contained and self-contextualizing field or as a purely derivative repetition of longstanding themes, however racially inflected. In their insistence on African American presence, in the way they address the invisibility of black life in the mainstream press, in their presentation of counternarratives to conventional histories of the nation and its regions, in their meditations on the meaning of modern progress and achievement for African American communities, and in their characteristic stylistic, thematic, and cultural concerns, these essays demonstrate the deep dialogue that structured African American culture in the 1920s. They help us to see the allegiances and disagreements among African American intellectuals as they engaged and debated with each other and mainstream discourses, and as they struggled, in many different ways, to define and reinvent the color line. In describing and encouraging the development of African American institutions of higher learning, business, literature, journalism, social science, activism, music, in their various relations to other American institutions, these essays bring alive the forgotten, vibrant diversity of American cultural life in the 1920s.

These "Colored" United States

NATHAN B. YOUNG

Alabama—
Like Miriam

VOL. 7, NO. 3, MARCH 1925

One of the oldest contributors to this series, Nathan B. Young was in his sixties when his articles on Alabama and Florida appeared in *The Messenger.* In his long career as an educator, Young was perceived as a dynamic and distinctly controversial public figure. As a champion of liberal arts education for African Americans, he was at the center of the raging argument among African American leaders and intellectuals like Booker T. Washington and W.E.B. Du Bois, who were wrestling with the question of what education could and should mean for African Americans.

Young was born amidst the chaos of the Civil War in Newbern, Alabama, on September 15, 1862. He was the son of a young woman who had been a slave and who later took care of her son by working as a tenant farmer. A true product of a "Reconstruction education," Young was taught entirely by white teachers, some of whom encouraged him to attend Talladega College and later Oberlin College, from which he received both a B.A. in 1888 and an M.A. in 1891. After graduation he was appointed principal of an Alabama high school, but left soon afterward to work under Booker T. Washington as head of the academic department at the famous Tuskegee Institute. Six years at Tuskegee did not fully convince him of the merits of industrial education, and he left to serve as professor of English and education at Georgia State College. Young then served as president of Florida Agricultural and Mechanical College for twenty-two years, where he was often embroiled in controversy as he pursued a policy of incorporating a liberal arts ethos into a vocational institution.

In the early 1920s, Lincoln University of Jefferson City, Missouri, recruited him as president. There his zeal for controversy led to his dismissal in the spring of 1927 and reappointment in the fall of 1929. Hostilities continued to rage, however, until the spring of 1931, when he was fired again, this time more decisively. For the next two years, Young continued to lecture for the Association for the Study of Negro Life and for the National Association of Teachers in Colored Schools. He died on July 19, 1933, in Tampa, Florida.

Young's highly mobile career from college reflects a tempestuous life's work, always impassioned and engaged. His essays on both Florida (signed Dr. N. B. Young) and Alabama (signed Nathan Ben

Young) reflect his educator's sense of how to organize and present information. The first half of the essay on Alabama reads like a section from a history textbook, the first half of the essay on Florida reads like a travel guide. They help point out the truly educational aspects of the essay series, providing readers with a sense of the history, culture, and geography of little-known parts of the country.

But the essays also demonstrate the unflinching gaze and uncensored talk that made Young a valuable and controversial spokesperson. "Florida: Our Contiguous Foreign State" features sardonic and wry humor to express what might otherwise be almost unfathomable horror. "Florida is making strenuous efforts to win the pennant in the lynching league for 1923. It came to the end of the first half with a *terrible* lead that Georgia and Texas may not be able to overcome." Florida has roots in the "racial catholicity" of Spanish culture, Young writes, but it has become unfortunately "Americanized." In a decade that touted the idea of "100% Americanism" and was outlawing the immigration of "unassimilable" peoples, this statement contained a severe, however ironic, critique. Florida, in fact, had become so mainstream in it racism, Young writes, that it is an exemplar of what is wrong with "these *Colored* United States."

Young's Florida essay was published just as he was assuming the presidency of Lincoln University in 1923. By his second year in the post he perhaps felt able to write more freely: his second essay for the series, "Alabama—Like Miriam," published sixteen months later, is considerably more layered and rhetorically adventurous. The enigmatic title refers to the biblical figure of Miriam, who was cursed with leprosy because she objected to the Ethiopian wife of Moses. Young uses the voice of a lecturing professor to mediate and deliver much of the introduction to the essay, creating a rhetorical distance that is reinforced by Young's regular reversion to heavy satire, punctuated with exclamation points. Young himself calls the essay a "ramble," but its ramblings are significant. In what might seem a nonsequitur, for instance, Young ends one paragraph with an image of a black miner walking down the street with a suitcase of dynamite and begins the next with the image of Birmingham rising from her sea of troubles.

Young also might seem to ramble in his convictions, sometimes appearing to be for amalgamation, sometimes against, sometimes for Booker T. Washington, sometimes against. But as he says, "All is not a paradox," and he manages to use these multiple opinions to construct a coherent, complex view of the state and its institutions (or, as the case may be, its lack of institutions, the "criminal negligence towards half her population"). His conclusion about Tuskegee is one such case: "Tuskegee has done and is doing a distinctive task, theories to the left, theories to the right, theories to the center volleying and thundering nevertheless." Young understands that all of the opinions surrounding a social fact give it its meaning. Rather than reduce these opinions and attitudes to a single interpretation, Young displays the contestations, the "volleying and thundering," that make up the culture of his time.

The essay remains playful, even if the humor is a bit grim. "If you recall the map of the Southern States Alabama has the shape of a coffin: however, a more favorable manner of depicting its topographic outline is to think of it as a sandwich, with Georgia and Mississippi great hunks of bread and Alabama the meat." The tinny humor he uses when depicting the Ku Klux Klan's parade through Birmingham does not belie the vividness of his description, and his other "light" touches are very barbed: "Colored Birmingham is a titan with a mediocre brain," and the "social inebriety" of Montgomerians is a tragic flaw, since it means that "colored Montgomery spends much of its potential force in a social outlet, never fully developing that pride and vision it possess."

His final assessment is that Alabama "deserves to its ownself a better way in life." While other writers saw hope or despair in their state, Young locates value in some sort of unrecognized merit. As in the case of Florida, Alabama is not just its own entity. Both are parts of the South and share its problems; both are parts of the United States and share the its problems. In Alabama and Florida, African Americans are "maltreated and cheated," Young writes, "cajoled and paroled with occasional justice even as his fellows of other states."

DR. YOUNG

Early Alabama History is rich in its problem of races. Like many other States it had the Indian to contend with. But the aborigines in Alabama were a stubborn lot. Tradition has it that when the wayworn Red Skin came to the territory and beheld its fertile lands and splendid streams, he stuck his spear in the earth, saying "Alabama," meaning "here we rest." Thus the motto of the State. In this land where Nature was so bountiful, the Indian did not give up the fertile fields and brimming rivers without tenacity and bloodshed. And so in 1855 lectured a Professor to the Historical Society at the University of Alabama.

"I may however remark," he began the close of his oration, "that the Red Men of Alabama, if properly reviewed, would be found to present more interesting facts and features, upon a more extended scale, than any other American Tribes. The peculiarities which had ever invested the character of the Indian with so much romantic interest, making him a chosen child of fable and of song, were here exhibited in bolder relief than elsewhere. In numbers; in their wide and terrific wars; in intercourse and traffic with the whites; in the mystery of their origin and migration; in the arts, rude though they were, which gradually refine and socialize man; in their political and religious forms, arrangements, and ceremonies; in manifestations of intellectual power, sagacity and eloquence; and all those strange moral phenomena, which mark 'the stoic of the woods, the man without a fear'—the native inhabitants of our soil surpassed all other primitive nations north of Mexico."

And then the erudite Professor injected a pregnant sentence which must have sparkled from his lips, for today it burns. Said he:

"Alabama emerged, like Miriam, from the Red Sea of her struggles, and now a new era of growth and prosperity began."

There is room for speculation as to the import of this remark of the Professor. Surely he knew what he was talking about, although the biblical allusion may have passed over the heads of his audience.

Did they or did they not recall the story of Miriam, sister of Moses, who "spake against Moses because of the Ethiopian woman whom he had married"—a Cushite? "And the Lord heard" and "came down in the pillar of the cloud" to rebuke Miriam for her murmuring against her brother for marrying a woman of color. In penalty, "behold, Miriam became leprous, white as snow" (one instance where white is not used in a comparison of angelic purity). Smitten with this plague as the result of her prejudice Miriam was quarantined for seven days while Moses besought the Lord to heal her. So when Miriam showed a change of heart she was cleansed of the leprosy.

By 1855 it was from the Indian harassment that "Alabama had emerged." In 1955 and some years thereto will Alabama be emerging like Miriam from the Red Sea of a prejudice more subtle than her early Indian hatred. In a manner it is a riddle of the Sphinx put to Alabama. Any attempt to sketch the State with anything better than a superficial scratching of the surface perforce pictures the "Red Sea of her struggles"—past, present, future.

In fact, in 1836 the Red Men had been shunted westward to reservations. They went in Indian resignation. But life ever substitutes a new problem. Black men, black women were being herded across the Chattahoochee from the east as the Creek and Choctaw were being driven westward across the Tombigbee and the Mississippi. Here was a different racial trait coming—Negro adaptiveness. If the Indians were drones, this black folk coming in under the yoke were worker bees a'right, and being such could not be killed out or driven off.

Permit the Professor to finish the lecture to the Historical Society.

"Go on, then, Gentlemen, energetically in your noble undertaking, consoled by the assurance that you are collecting the materials that shall illustrate and embellish the annals of your state, in the far-distant, when they shall receive the plastic touch and vivifying truth of some future Xenophon or Polybius, some Tacitus or Livy, who, like the Hebrew prophet, shall bid the dry bones—live!"

Plastic touch! Vivifying truth! Who can do such of Alabama—the South? Who dares the plastic touch, to vivify the truth! Not he or she who remains there!

Before the Indian moves from the scene, a bit of Alabama romance must be recited. It has a contrast value which will be needed later on.

In the early days of Mobile many Choctaws were close around. Into the town often came a young Choctaw girl who for her beauty was known as the "Fawn of Pascagoula." In the winter she peddled trinkets and lightwood and in her rounds had as a customer a young white soldier–lawyer, widely known for his handsome sway over feminine hearts. On each trip to his office with her wares the "Fawn of Pascagoula" had coyly smiled at this proud paleface until one day he had placed his fine physique between the Fawn and the door. (O relentless Mother Nature, why hast thou made sex impulse greater than race instinct?) "A kiss!" he demanded. When shall the truth be known? Was this Choctaw girl right? Or were her darker sisters to follow right?

"Stand off, Mister Howard," she exclaimed in better English than he had heard from her lips. "Me good friend to kind gentleman—but no love! She love young warrior who have heart and skin same color. The Fawn must marry her own people."

And so the passing of the first race problem in Alabama. By 1850 the Indians were across the Mississippi, except a few stragglers.

I I

The Civil War loomed. Alabama sizzled in hatred against the "highly incendiary" Northern Abolitionist. A Tuscaloosa grand jury returned a true bill against Robert G. Williams, editor of *The Emancipator* of New York, "for circulating within our State, pamphlets and papers of a seditious and incendiary character, and tending by gross misrepresentation, and illicit appeal to the passions, to excite to insurrection and murder our slave population."

Forthwith, Governor Gayle of Alabama demanded of Governor Marcey of New York the arrest of Williams until "I can dispatch an agent to conduct him to Alabama."

In his message to the Alabama Legislature that same year the Governor lambasted "Arthur Tappan and the infuriate demoniacs associated with him"—"that unless the Northern fanatics are prevented by timely measures from pursuing their made career"—"he who believes fanaticism can be put down by public opinion, has a very imperfect knowledge of human nature, and must be deaf to the lessons and admonitions of history—" and such bile he exhorted in a fashion that has clung to the South lo these seventy odd years since. Despite the progress the South has made, this type of groggy berating is still in vogue, save a few voices sounding in the last decade.

Of course, the editor of *The Emancipator* was not turned over to the Alabama agent. Is there any doubt as to what Alabama would have done with him?

The foregoing excerpts of ante-bellum Alabama would not be worth their space were it not that today the average, the masses, the holders of political power in the State spew this same brand of snuff.

The Civil War not only loomed, it arrived. The boom of a cannon on Goat Hill in Montgomery announced the conflict to Alabama. And the Civil War ended, leaving Alabama to the whims and passions of reconstruction. Sudden freemen, sullen rebels, mercenary Northerners, hasty adjusters, "forty acres and a mule," gilded ignorance and smouldering prejudice—such was the reconstruction mess of Alabama.

Today, look upon the outworn Capitol in Montgomery and recollect black Carraway of Mobile in there in 1867 demanding upon the Legislature "life imprisonment for any white man marrying or living with a black woman." Was there ever anything more Nordic, more of regard for white supremacy proposed in Alabama than that?

Reconstruction in Alabama was a monster three-ring circus. Some day, some future Xenophon besides Tom Dixon may "bid the dry bones—live!"

From that time until Washington crossed the Chattahoochee in 1895 to recite his soothing syrup simile "separate as the fingers, yet one as the hand" Alabama lay in a coma. This Atlanta speech was the inaugural that moved the Capitol of Alabama's hopes from Montgomery to Tuskegee.

Before judging Tuskegee one should first see it. The place has an impressive personality. Tuskegee has done and is doing a distinctive task, theories to the left, theories to the right, theories to the center volleying and thundering nevertheless.

Its founder, human himself and a keen student of human nature in others, made constructive headway against a current of criticism. His methods of procedure may have drawn question marks but not his accomplishment. No man has yet been right in everything. In his autobiography Washington refers to the Ku Klux of Reconstruction, concluding: "There are few places in the South now where public sentiment would permit such organizations to exist." A clean miss. Did his eternal eyes see crouched armed and ready those teachers and students on the night the hooded Klansmen paraded the highroad that skirts Tuskegee Institute? "Booker T. Washington walked that road last night," someone said the next morning. He may have, for the loosening of a pebble might have made itself heard around the world.

Today, a two million dollar Government hospital and a five million dollar endowed Tuskegee Institute are betrothed, some day to be wedded in the great University of the Southland. Subtract Muscle Shoals and the Coal and Iron Corporations and Tuskegee from Alabama and what is left is equivalent to the State of Mississippi.

III

If you recall the map of the Southern States Alabama has the shape of a coffin; however, a more favorable manner of depicting its topographic outline is to think of it as a sandwich, with Georgia and Mississippi great hunks of bread and Alabama the meat. And Alabama is the meat so far as nature's endowments are considered. Given the rightful strip of West Florida due her with a coast line from Mobile to the Chattahoochee River and you have as fine a State as Missouri for natural resources, as California for generous climate, as Pennsylvania for minerals, with a water power greater than many Niagara Falls. Who would not like to live and die in Alabama if there were no blight, no leprosy of prejudice rampant?

Man invents machines to save hand toil, and the machines turn and enslave the man. At the beginning of the nineteenth century came the fly shuttle and carding machine in the making of cloth, then the steam engine and power loom. Over in Georgia Eli Whitney schemed up the cotton gin and King Cotton ascended the throne. Only the boll weevil has challenged his throneship.

Today, in Alabama black laborers share the cotton fields with the mines and rolling mills and in various ways are slaves to the system, for in Alabama black laborers can and do make money, but it is a money with the purchasing value depreciated when solid American civic rights and privileges are desired.

Yet, this is a general Southern condition, not alone true of Alabama, but as well of her sister States in misery. The average American, it may be ventured, has the general picture of the South's criminal negligence towards half her population. Alabama is but a part of the picture, hardly any better or worse than Georgia, Florida, Louisiana or Mississippi in the main. Let this sketch be more of a sightseeing trip, which for the lack of space can only be a peep here and there. If only a whiff of that nature-kindled flame that sears beneath the crust or a tang of the bitter-sweet of a viand that is human flesh, if you can register these you will have partaken of Alabama.

IV

Alabama first breaks faith with her shibboleth of "white supremacy" in her towns. Troy, Eufaula, Tuscaloosa, Selma, Gadsden, and Demopolis. There one finds beautiful colored womanhood in its bud and flower. But one soon finds out also that a number of these golden-browns and bronze-creams are *demi-monde,* in many cases not to be seen on the street with men of their own color; one soon learns of families of color that are connected underground to some well-known white families, so that one soon has the anonymous feeling that the race problem "ain't what it's claimed to be."

Be careful here. In these towns not all is miscegenation; all is not a paradox; nor is it a matter of percentage. It is simply a condition you find, just as you find cotton growing in Mississippi and sugar cane in Louisiana.

The larger towns (for there is but one city in Alabama) are Mobile and Montgomery. Both are old. Mobile going back to the early French and Spanish settlements. Montgomery, first called New Philadelphia and founded by a Yankee, holds in prided memory its label "Cradle of the Confederacy."

Negro Mobile, like many other Southern towns, has a handful of grab-bag local leaders. The rank and file have no solidarity, no rigidity that makes itself felt. Mobile has a tinge of caste due to the foreign influence. In short, the Mobile Negro is not essentially the Alabama Negro. New Orleans, Louisiana; Mobile, Alabama; and Pensacola, Florida, so to put it, are three black-eyed, raven-haired sisters doing a fandango to a jazzed La Paloma.

On the other hand Negro Montgomery is a representative slice of Negro Alabama. Here there has always been some sort of captaincy, either a fearless preacher, a keen business man or a thoughtful educator. The Montgomerian has somewhere about him a spark of group pride. His short-coming has been a type of social inebriety. The ailment reaches way back, when Montgomery, the cotton center of the rich Black Belt, harbored the aristocrats and wealthy merchants whose slaves were not field hands and plantation equipage, but butlers, footmen, maids. So when ante-bellum Montgomery had its farfamed balls and soirees these servants echoed in follow-up affairs of their own. Southern hospitality in Montgomery has always had a crust of society on it; and today, colored Montgomery spends much of its potential force in social outlet, never fully developing that pride and vision it possesses.

V

The magic city Birmingham is a hybrid of Northern money and Southern "cussedness." Here are eighty thousand colored people with an "Emancipation Day Celebration" leadership, if any at all. Here are gathered citizens of color from every section of Alabama, many of whom are merely making their first stop between Chicago and Detroit and Cleveland. Here are twenty thousand children of color, brown, black, cream, pale, brown, brown, brown, hungry for schools that accommodate and inspire and truthfully and thoroughly teach. Here is the meanest Jim Crow street car system in the world. Here is a police force without an Irishman, not that it matters, and a white insurance company without a Caucasian policy holder, which does matter. Here the earning capacity of Negro laborers ranks high; and here the leading Negro-owned enterprises are barber shops. Colored Birmingham is a titan with a mediocre brain; it has financial and numerical power but no ambition; it has large churches where revivals draw and flourishing lodges where parades form, but there is no unity of purpose for the welfare of the Colored population.

It was in Birmingham that Harding spoke to a vast and mixed audience and after delivering a political harpoon saved his scalp by declaring "amalgamation there can not be," and it was in Birmingham that Sam Johnson landed in Big Rock jail and sent for his good pastor, who came, heard Sam's story and advised: "Why, Sam, they can't put you in jail for that; no sir, they can't." And it was in Birmingham, Alabama, that Sam Johnson answered both his good pastor and his good President, "but I'se in jail already!"

Coal and iron and steel and the by-products in fifty years have sprouted and grown here a hustling city. Office buildings tower like gigantic stalagmites wherein the farthest elevator from the front is labeled "For Freight and Colored," but is freely used by the whites; office buildings where so many offices have colored maids and office girls. Shade of the "Fawn of Pascagoula!" Naomi gives up her job in the old Penny Bank Building to work for a white doctor. Ruth is maid in a white lawyer's office and is the best dressed girl who struts down Eighteenth Street. Rebecca used to work in the twenty-three story building, but she doesn't have to work now! And all these are six and eight dollar a week jobs. The extra money . . . !

Just open your eyes and see. Don't try and think. Come along! In the street below there is a long parade in progress; it is certain to go around to Eighteenth Street and Fourth Avenue, where the Negro barber shops, white-owned movie houses and Greek cafes for colored are doing a rushing business. Notice there is a motorcycle squad from the police department leading the parade, followed by an electrical fiery cross. Three hundred automobiles are in line; traffic blocked, yellow street cars at a standstill, pedestrians silently watching from the curbing. The American flag passes, and then a sign the length of a limousine reading "For White Supremacy."

Don't think yet! A metallic alarm is in the air; it comes nearer and nearer, down the street that crosses the parade. There is confusion amid the watching crowd on the corner, but the parade goes solemnly on. The clanging alarm again, now growing dimmer and dimmer in its retreating terror. The fire department must get to the fire by another route—nothing must break the solemn parade! Come! There is a billboard that says Ringling's circus will parade these same streets next week, but there will not be so many clowns.

VI

All is not bad. There is too much human nature in Birmingham to be without redeeming qualities. The matter with Birmingham is that it is so young, so engaged in making money and growing bigger that it has not come to its thoughtful age. Take this piece of forewarning from one of its clear-visioned Anglo-Saxon citizens.

"I heard a public man recently argue with fine oratorical effect that God has climaxes everywhere: A climax in heaven, for the sun is king: a climax among the birds, for the eagle is king; a climax among animals, for the lion is king; and a climax among the peoples of the earth, for the Anglo-Saxon is king.

"As that stands alone there is a false note to it. The Anglo-Saxon is certainly at this time upon the throne, but it is a shallow and thoughtless man who would make it an occasion for boasting.

"The old Roman in his day said exactly the thing that we are prone to say now. But he forgot the processes and the purposes of his upliftment, and today is one with 'Nineveh and Tyre.' "

"Verily pride goeth before a fall and an haughty spirit before destruction. Germany erased the word service from her character and she 'fell as Lucifer fell.' "

> " 'Still stands thine ancient sacrifice,
> A broken and a contrite heart.' "

"If we can occupy our kingly place in that spirit, then all hell shall not prevail against us. If not, we, too, must take our place in the sad procession of the nations that are lost!"

And this from a white pulpit shortly after Birmingham came near as a feather's edge staging a Saturday night race riot that would have made Atlanta, Chicago and Tulsa mere pikers. Negroes around Birmingham use dynamite daily in the mines. On that particular night one ordinary fellow walked down Twentieth Street with a suit case of it!

Some day ruddy young Birmingham, capstone of Alabama, will emerge, like Miriam, from the Red Sea of her struggles and a new era will begin. Some day! And as Birmingham emerges, Alabama will emerge.

Down there, whenever the band strikes up "Dixie" there always follows the outbursts from the depths of rebel breasts a resounding "ALABAMA" that challenges the welkin. Alabama! Alabama! 'Tis a resonant and mouthful American word. It always heads the list, whether with "twenty-four for Underwood" or in the category of States. And in the dictionary there is close by a nefarious and nefandous relative, a fearful word, a Frankenstein destroyer of reason, and that word is—Amalgamation!

So endeth this ramble through a State that deserves to its ownself a better way in life. Alabama! Here we rest!

ANITA SCOTT COLEMAN

Arizona and New Mexico—the Land of Esperanza

VOL. 8, No. 7, SEPTEMBER 1926

Although not widely known today, during the 1920s and 1930s Anita Scott Coleman's name cropped up frequently on literary prize short-lists, alongside Countee Cullen and Langston Hughes. During the height of the Harlem Renaissance she regularly garnered awards from *Opportunity* and *The Crisis* for her poetry, short stories, and essays, sometimes under her pseudonym, "Elizabeth Stokes." Her volume of poetry, *Reason for Singing,* was published in 1948, and her work was featured in the anthologies of African American poetry *Ebony Rhythm* and *Negro Voices*. Biographical notes accompanying her work identify her variously as a former teacher, a manager of a Los Angeles boarding home for children, and a housewife. In the February 1927 *Crisis* she wrote, somewhat disingenuously, "Having been born in Guaymas, Mexico, and raised in New Mexico, I am a firm believer in the delightful possibilities of 'manaña.' At present there are four kiddies, a husband and a house to keep in order." Coleman does not appear in any standard biographical sources, and what little is known of her life is gleaned from the sparse and often elliptical, blurbs accompanying her magazine contributions. She apparently lived most of her adult life in California.

Coleman's *Messenger* essay on Arizona and New Mexico was quickly reprinted, with excerpts from it appearing in the black-run newspaper the *Albuquerque Southwest Review* in 1926. Coleman's consciousness of African American identity as distinctly local is worked out carefully in her essay. Arizona and New Mexico are places of staggering promise and "boundless space," and African Americans have lived in the region long before its current spatial boundaries. Her examination of Estevan, the slave she reports as guiding whites through the area in 1538, tellingly reveals a concern for establishing an identity and a racial sensibility not necessarily tied to a traditionally constructed national one. She portrays the southwestern states as reso-lutely diverse, marked by the complicated intersections of various Native American peoples, "Spanish-Americans," and African Ameri-cans. Her most famous poem, "American Negra," likewise chants out the mixture that makes the race: "I am Indian . . . I am Irish and Scottish and Welsch . . . I am Africa."

Her fiction, as in the story "Cross Crossings Cautiously," is often constructed paratactically and disjointedly, a technique she applies, considerably less successfully, to the essay. The essay is at times weak, in fact, and at times silly, as when, at the end of a long catalogue of the accomplishments of African Americans in the region, she adds: "And a black man was the first to fall before the deadly aim of Billy the Kid, in a gambling hall in Silver City."

Her treatment of the ambiguous roles African Americans have played in fighting and dying for the border of the United States is doubtless informed by her own position as a black immigrant from Mexico and shows the stresses and strains of multiple, contradictory, and yet overlapping racial, regional, and national identities. Nonetheless, she writes, "Here prevails for every man be he white or black a hardier philosophy—and a bigger and a better chance, that is not encountered elsewhere in these United States."

It is singular that most persons think of Arizona and New Mexico in unity. The fact is that Arizona was a part of New Mexico until 1863, when it was divided by Congress into a separate territory. Since each not so many years ago attained the status of Statehood, they have striven diligently, albeit amiably, to establish a distinct and separate individualism.

Yet for this once, we shall consider them as one.

Together they cover an area of 235,654 square miles, a boundless region of vast treasures.

Their mineral resources are limitless. Manganese, iron, coal, oil, zinc, copper, gold, silver, onyx and marble, meerchaum and turquoise, emeralds, sapphires, garnets and opals lie buried in level plains and rugged mountains.

Great stretches of timbered lands are protected in forest reserves, and one forest in Holebroke, Arizona, is so old, it is petrified, its trees but solid rock. The lower mountain ranges and hills are covered with stunted growth of pine, juniper, pinon, cedar, and oak. The rolling prairies are arrayed in the wonder vegetation of the Southwest—the cactus, the sagebrush, the mesquite, and the yucca.

Its surface is traversed by rivers. The greatest of these being the Rio Grande, the old reliable, of whom legend says: obligingly changed its course to suit the whim of "el Gringo"; cleaving the State of New Mexico from tip to toe as it wends its way to the Gulf. This and the Pecos and the Gila rivers along with their tributaries water extraordinarily fertile valleys; in which wonder apples, figs, apricots, grapes, wheat, corn, cotton, and alfalfa are produced. While the Colorado River in Arizona is that small and turbid stream which has wrought through centuries the mighty marvel of the Grand Canyon.

The animals and the insects of these States, like its arid vegetation, are unique. Here is the home of the Gila-monster, the vinegerone, the rattlesnake, the centipede, the tarantula and the nina de terra. The coyote and the prairie dog keep watch upon its plains, the fox and deer, the wolf and bear, sheep and mountain lions, and countless feathered "game," bestow upon their natal states the title: "The hunting ground of the United States."

Another natural resource is the climate. Rarely does the sun hide its face from these two states. Endless breezes lilt and sing as effective as an electric fan in summer and as bracing as a tonic.

Natural resources are the gifts of generous Nature, and industry is the outcome of man's manipulations of these gifts.

Since minerals are strewn in such lavish quantities, mining is an important occupation, the leading one in Arizona. Copper is yet being taken from "workings" bearing the scars and marks of the day when Spaniards conquered and enslaved the Indian, gave him the crude implements of the time and sent him chained into the bowels of the earth to delve for treasure. Later the white man came and conquered and so it is the Mexican miner rather than the Negro or the foreigner of the East who goes down and up the shaft, in and out the tunnel, down and down into endless pits in quest of minerals.

The vast stretches of grass grown plains give rise to the cattle industry, the greatest pursuit in the State of New Mexico. To all appearances and despite legend—cattle raising is an exclusive white man's trade. Mexican cowboys there are, and perhaps in a bygone day, the natives were large cattle owners—but today, one sees only the white cattleman. Occasionally one glimpses a Negro cowboy, or rather a Negro who has learned a lot about cattle; quite likely, he has often gone with cattle-trains into Kansas, Nebraska, Old Mexico to punch cattle—to prevent any of the packed cattle lying down, where they would be trodden to death beneath the hoofs of the others—on their long railway journey. But very few black men have ridden beneath the stars, singing cowboy chants to still the restless herds. And in no instance has a black American plied himself to the task of becoming one of the "big" cattlemen of the Southwest. Maybe, it is due to the side line of cattle rustling; which once upon a time accompanied cattle raising, most profitably, who knows?

In Arizona and New Mexico, man has aptly turned the climate into an industry. We have here the business of dispensing health to the health-seeker. The different chambers of commerce vie one with the other in advertisements of climate.

"Sunshine 365 days in the year," boasts New Mexico.

"Arizona—land of golden sunshine," acclaims Arizona.

Indisputably, these States offer the best in health giving "ozone" and revivifying sun-light. The sanatorium is the outstanding feature of many towns. But Tucson, in Arizona, and Silver City, in New Mexico, are favored spots. Prescott, in Arizona, and Ft. Bayard, in New Mexico, the latter the largest sanatorium of its kind in the country, both Veteran Bureau Hospitals, treat Negro patients. Besides these, there is no especial provision made for the Negro health-seeker. Several tentative efforts to establish a Negro sanatorium have fallen short. Yet, such an institution is a needed and certainly a humane project for an American Negro.

Again, the scenic wonders of these two States lures the tourist into their midst, while "big game" during the hunting seasons beguile the sportsmen, and so the trade of entertaining a traveling public becomes an important one.

Farming, a new and steadily growing project owing to the recently completed dams for the conservation of a bountious water supply enabling irrigation on larger scales, the climate, the productivity of soil, and the acreage for large crops holds forth a promise of vast reward for the inhabitants of these States. Likewise, farming, more than all its other industries swings wide its gates and cordially welcomes the Negro.

Cotton as an experiment. Cotton in the Maricopa valley and Mexican peon labor. Cotton in the Mesilla valley and Negro hands from the South. Cotton, a wonderful yield and experiment, becomes an established fact. With it all there are many Negroes in Phoenix and some scattered throughout the State. And mayhaps, Mexican peons will eventually return to Mexico. But in the Mesilla valley, Vado, a Negro town, is born. Jammed against the States' scenic highway, plodding its way to the high road of success.

As industry is dependent upon natural resources, population is dependent upon industry. It is seen, then, that industry in these States has held little promise for the Negro.

The inhabitants here are as striking as the plant and animals of Arizona and New Mexico. They are historically interesting. Consisting of fast dwindling tribes of Indians, living echoes of a by-gone day, remnants of a centuries-old civilization. The tatters of the Aztecs, cliff dwellers and the humble dwellers in Pueblos. And the Spanish-American or Mexican native, the first conquerors of Indians, plenteous whites, and essentially, it is the home of the half-breed, the inevitable outcome, where two or more races meet and mingle in an unaccustomed freedom.

While here and there are Negroes, like straggly but tenacious plants growing, nevertheless, though always in the larger towns. Becoming fewer and fewer, until in many or in all of the remoter hamlets and towns they are as sparse as rose bushes upon the prairies.

But all which the Negro has failed to give to the industry or to the population of Arizona and New Mexico, he has made amends for with the contribution to its history.

It is potent to recall that in 1538, Estevan, the Negro slave in the role of interpreter and guide to the Friar Marcos de Niza, was sent on ahead to spy upon the people and the strange lands they were entering, and send back reports to his peers. Thus, it was that Estevan the Negro was first to behold the wonders of the seven cities, and though he himself was killed, sent back the report:—"Advance, the find is worth it."

Negroes have fought and struggled over all the vast stretches that included the one time Indian Territory, the Panhandle, New Mexico and Arizona, throughout the years of Indian warfare. Most of the old settlers among Negroes in "these parts" are descended or related to a hoary-haired and fast-passing, honorably discharged, Indian war fighter, who thought wearily upon receiving his discharge that "here" was as good as "way back there" to settle down and rest after his long, arduous campaign.

And mingled with the tales of Indians on warpaths are the stories of heroism performed by avenging whites and all interwoven with these deeds are mingled the deeds of solitary Negroes.

In 1916 Negroes helped patrol the borders in New Mexico and Arizona, safeguarding the doorways through which Villa or a mightier foe might enter. That Villa did enter and raided Columbus, New Mexico, was no fault of theirs. Yet they it was, who rode out in to chaparral hard on the trail of the treacherous Villa, to their death in Carrizol.

Among the famous acts of outlawry are knit the acts of black men. Oft'times they have accompanied posses in the capture of dangerous bandits. And a black man was the first to fall before the deadly aim of Billy the Kid, in a gambling hall in Silver City.

Among famous frontier huntsmen are the names of Negroes. One George Parker was the best crack shot and the gamest bear hunter who ever followed a trail. He was also a lucky prospector and amassed a fortune in mines. As did his friend John Young, who still survives; who was at one time the richest Negro and one of the wealthiest mine owners in the territory of New Mexico.

Among the lowly and humble tasks, which likewise make history, are such deeds as this: In Roswell a town of tree lined streets, it is told that a Negro, an old pioneer, recently deceased, planted the trees which grace the City's streets.

Withal, the Negroes in these States are an isolated lot, yet in nearly all instances they are home owners. In the remote hamlets, if there be blacks at all, they seem a bit hazy concerning their relationship to the great hordes of Negroes beyond their confines. This is not true of the groups in larger towns.

One is almost persuaded to say, that the brains and the brawn of the Negro population is gathered in Albequerque. Negro enterprise of various sorts are here. Negro doctors and dentists reside here. Two churches are supported. The N.A.A.C.P. is represented—and it is the home of the *Southwest Review,* a Negro publication, edited by S. W. Henry.

Though the greatest outstanding feature of the Negro population is that in New Mexico, there are two exclusively Negro towns. Blackdom, sixteen miles south of Roswell and situated in the Chavis County oil area, and Vado, previously mentioned, a score of miles below Las Cruces.

So far, in New Mexico, the Negro has not yet become a bone to gnaw in politics. He is not legislated either pro or con, he is an unconsidered quantity, due to his inconsequential numbers. But what New Mexico may or may not do is evidenced in the fact that the influx of Negro children to Dona Ana County the center of the cotton activity were not allowed to attend the schools. Separate schools were immediately installed; also Roswell in Chavis County maintains a separate school system.

On the other hand, Arizona has made rigid laws concerning her Negro inhabitants. A rather funny one is eight Negro children in any community is a sufficient quota for instituting a Negro school.

Boiled down to finality—these States are the mecca-land for the seeker after wealth—the land of every man to his own grubstake—and what-I-find-I-keep.

And criss-crossing in and out through the medley of adventure stalk the few in number black folks. Often, it is only the happy-go-lucky, black gambler; again it is but the lone and weary black prospector—but ever and ever the intrepid, stalwart Negro homeseeker forms a small yet valiant army in the land of esperanza.

And over it all the joyous freedom of the West. The unlimited resourcefulness, the boundless space—that either bids them stay—or baffles with its vastness—until it sends them scuttling to the North, the South, and East, whence-so-ever they have come.

For here prevails for every man be he white or black a hardier philosophy—and a bigger and better chance, that is not encountered elsewhere in these United States.

WILLIAM PICKENS

Arkansas—a Study in Suppression

VOL. 5, No. 1, JANUARY 1923

Langston Hughes described William Pickens as "one of the most popular platform orators in America," and it was this tremendous public presence that escalated Pickens to field secretary of the NAACP in 1920, and in 1941 to the director of the Interracial Section of the Treasury Department's War Bonds Division, the agency charged with selling war bonds in African American communities. Born in Anderson, South Carolina, on January 14, 1881, but raised in Little Rock, Arkansas, Pickens "got away," as he put it, and went to Yale, where he won the nationally prestigious Ten Eyck oratorical prize. This prize, awarded him for a speech he delivered on the subject of Haiti, drew young Pickens to the attention of Booker T. Washington, who assisted him in obtaining a position as a classics instructor at Talladega College, in Alabama. Pickens taught classics, languages, and sociology at Talladega from 1904 to 1914 and at Wiley University in Texas from 1914 to 1915. He then taught at Morgan State College in Baltimore, Maryland, where he was later appointed dean and ultimately vice president. Pickens was a contributing editor to the Associated Negro Press for twenty years, and his weekly articles, stories, and poems eventually ran in more than a hundred African American newspapers and journals. *The Vengeance of the Gods* (1922) is probably the best known of his literary works.

He held complex political positions on issues such as Marcus Garvey's separatism and the accommodationist policies of Booker T. Washington, positions that caused him to be simultaneously denounced and praised by groups as disparate as the American Communist party and the Roosevelt administration. Pickens was accorded the dubious honor of a House Committee on Un-American Activities investigation in 1943, despite having been removed from his post at the NAACP in the previous year for failing to strenuously denounce prejudice within the armed forces. Pickens remained at his Treasury post until 1945, by which time over one billion dollars worth of bonds had been sold to African Americans.

His interest in the constructions and intersections of racial and regional identity figures, not only in his essay but also in his autobiography, *Bursting Bonds* (1923), which was advertised in *The Messenger*. The advertisement asks: "What happens when American WHITE

MEETS American BLACK in Europe?" "How does a black child grow up in a state like South Carolina or Arkansas?" "What is the plain experience, north, east, south, and west, of BEING AN AMERICAN NEGRO?" and somewhat enigmatically, "What is the meaning of LIFE IN TEXAS?" The advertisement then promises to answer these questions and 106 more in "this gripping life story." Pickens wrote his autobiography when he was forty-two; he died in 1954 at the age of seventy-three.

More virulent than any of the other essays in this often biting series, Pickens's treatment of Arkansas stands out as an exercise in fury and horror. After establishing that a state need be judged on its relationship "as an institution to its people and the relation of its people to each other," he then goes on to assess those relationships with devastating candor. "Indeed," he writes, "no good thing can be named which would be missing in the world today if Arkansas had never been created by river silt and an act of Congress." Pickens chides Arkansans for boasting loudly that there are only fourteen thousand foreigners, *as if it would not be a better state if outside civilization could invade it.*" Here he invokes a theme that is implicit in many of the essays, that is the relative poverty of American civilization and its denial of cultural complexity, this denial causing such poverty. The rhetorical pacing of Pickens's essay is bumpy yet effectively shocking as he moves from assessing Arkansas as "[ranking] 20th in the total output of its crops" to being "6th in the total output of its lynchings, and higher still in the horribleness of those murders." Less ironically, but equally effectively, he juxtaposes the treatment of African American women by white men with the supposed threat posed by African American men to white women. The "unmeasured misery" Pickens sees in Arkansas places the state not merely beyond the help of the federal government. In fact, Pickens writes, it "might just as well *not-have-been.*" Pickens seems to be continually adding levels of irony, as when he writes, "We are not of that breed of fatalists who affect to believe that every individual man and fly and frog are necessary parts of the cosmic scheme," mocking both the believers and revilers of the sanctity of life. But he also suggests in this passage that the "cosmic scheme" of these United States needs to be thoroughly discarded and reinvented.

"U-GAKH-PA," said the Sioux Indians, meaning "Down-stream-people"; and the French settler of the 18th century, in poor imitation of the sound, repeated, "Ar-kan-sas," which is pronounced *Ar-kan-saw.* In territorial days this section was known as "the Arkansas country," and the state that was later carved out of that territory was named Arkansas.

What is a state? Is it so many square miles, so many different kinds of mineral, breeds of hog, species of hardwood and types of factory? Do such statistics show the *character* of a state?—When asked what kind of man a given man is, we might as well answer by telling the number of buttons on his shirt, the color of his coat, the width of his parlor and the breed of cocks in his back yard. The character of a state is not its mountains of quartz, its acres of cotton and its prize Hereford bulls. It is rather the relation of that state as an institution to its people and the relation of its people to each other.

WHAT IS ARKANSAS?

What is Arkansas? It might satisfy some merely academic interest to know that Arkansas is in the middle of the United States; that its northern and western half is highland and mountains, and that its southeastern part is rich and flat alluvial Mississippi bottom land; that the boundary line between these highlands and this flat land represents the primordial shoreline of the Gulf of Mexico, and that the flat alluvium was washed down from the higher parts of the prehistoric continent, gradually filling out the great Mississippi valley and continuing today to push out into the Gulf at the deltas; that this inland country was early claimed by the French; that it was bought from Napoleon for a few million dollars, and that this particular state represents a very insignificant part of the investment; that the territory of "the Arkansas country" was rather artificially created in 1818, being carved out of Missouri and the neighboring wastes; that it was made a state in 1836; and that it has made no contribution to human civilization since.

Indeed no good thing can be named which would be missing in the world today if Arkansas had never been created by river silt and an act of Congress. There would simply be fewer lynchings, less peonage and slavery, many gallons less of "moonshine," and the world might have escaped the invention of two of its most murderous frontier weapons,—the Bowie knife and the Colt's pistol. Arkansas has been somewhat worse than a useless accident. We are not of that breed of fatalists who affect to believe that every individual man and fly and frog are necessary parts of the cosmic scheme. We believe with all our might that Nero, the World War and Arkansas might just as well *not-have-been*.

The real Arkansas that matters is the character of its people and their civilization. Why describe and estimate Arkansas by telling that it has cypress woods and gas? That it has 58 trees of commercial importance, with 14 species of oak? That it has exactly 27 minerals whose names begin with A, from Actinolite to Azurite; 15 beginning with B, from Barite to Brucite; a like number beginning with C, from Calcite to Carbonite; and at least one mineral to begin with any letter of the alphabet except X? These items are the accidental coincidences of the works of nature and of the alphabet-makers, and would have existed if Congress had divided this piece of land between Missouri and Mississippi.

A better symbol of Arkansas would be the picture of one of its county jails, product of its own civilization and still to be seen. The one in Garland County was built up like a pen out of great solid logs. Its only window was the tiny square opening in front, through which food and water were handed to the inmates. The victims were thrust into this dungeon from the top, after being led up a high stairway; they were let down on a ladder and the ladder was then drawn out, leaving them in a square wooden well, as it were, and less decently penned in than the hogs of the neighborhood. According to the records of Arkansas there was sometimes only standing room in these wooden Bastilles.

The best representation of the character of present-day Arkansas would be two sketches; one from the highlands where the poor whites live, and the other from any one of the large plantations on the alluvial plains, where live the great landowners and their Negro serfs and peons. The picture of "The Arkansas Traveler" has made familiar and famous the slatternly family and household, and the general unprogressiveness of the "po' white" of the hill country—the dirt-floor cabin, the coon-skin caps, the "moonshine" and the bevy of small children. The whole family might sleep in this one room, the older folk in rough beds attached to the corners of the cabin, and the swarm of smaller children in loft beds reached by a ladder. But it was such a home as this that Abraham Lincoln's indolent father first erected for his family in the wilds of Indiana. Only one Lincoln, however, might ever come out of such a nest. This type of human habitation in Arkansas has not yet been entirely superseded by the unpainted, rough-timbered two-and three-room houses that have sprung up with the growth of lumbering centers and factory towns. To one who has seen and moved among them, there is no exaggerating the lankiness, dirty carelessness and profanity of the tobacco-chewing men, and the sallow and Neolithic unloveliness of the pale, formless, long-necked and sametimes disheveled women.

In many localities these hill whites pride themselves on the fact that "no niggers are allowed" in their community. They have unreasonably, but very naturally, hated the Negro ever since the black slave labor and subsequent peonage were used by the wealthy whites to force the poorer whites off the fat lands into the barren hills. The poor free whites could not compete against the labor of black slaves and peons, and very humanly their resentment attacked the system that was used against them at its most innocent but most vulnerable part—the black race itself. The "Hill Billies," as they were called by the aristocratic whites, could not compete at farming against the great landowners who used black slave and semi-slave labor; and so nothing was left for them in the earlier days but to hunt, fish, trap, engage in the illicit manufacture of spirits, and "hate niggers." Mark Twain or some other wag has said that their only form of recreational exercise was "to sit on a fence and have a chill."

"POOR WHITES"

One of the worst evils of slavery was the degradation of these people; and this accounts for their undoubted backwardness today. With the coming of lumbering, factories and mining among them, they became the chief element of labor in these industries, and their material civilization was somewhat improved, for the great land barons found their black labor more profitable in cotton. Till this day these hill whites never reflect on the origin of their celebrated hatred for Negroes, and the traveler may still see signs like these: "Mister Nigger, don't let the sun go down on you," or "Nigger, read and run," with the waggish addition, "but if you can't read, run anyhow." When trainloads of colored people recently passed through this country, bound from the east to some great convention in Muskogee, Oklahoma, they had to shut the windows and pull down the shades to avoid the murderous missiles that are sometimes hurled especially at "a nigger in a Pullman." When some of these unfortunate whites visit a city like Hot Springs or Little Rock and see the splendid achievements of the handicapped but educated and well-to-do Negroes, it does not seem to lessen but to intensify their fear and hate. Perhaps this is due to the fact that every demagogue or anti-Negro politician who wants to carry an election, will rush into the hill counties and make any incoherent noise about "nigger domination" and the pressing need of "keeping the nigger in his place," which is always understood to be down and under. And so, just as the helpless blacks were used to drive out and degrade the poor whites, now the renascent power of these poor whites is being used in an effort to keep down the rising free Negro—and these poor white people have not read enough history to understand that they are again beating around in the same cycle: keeping themselves down and cheapening their own status as men and workers by serving as tools to the richer whites for keeping the latters' black labor under and cheap.

"RIVER BOTTOMS"

The companion-piece to this picture, in any series illustrating Arkansas, must be one of the plantations of the wealthy land barons, down in the river bottoms, a day's ride on the slow trains from the hill country. A single planter may own many thousands of acres and control everything in his county from the courts to the church revival seasons. Schools are not allowed to open when the children are needed in the fields; education cannot interfere with cotton; and a Negro church may be forbidden to open a revival to harvest in the sinners until after the crops are harvested. The present planter's grandfather acquired this land from the United States Government for nothing, and his father sent east to the poor states of the Carolinas and Georgia and induced Negro families to come west to the land of plenty and "make a fortune" (as Croesus was told by the oracle to go to war and "destroy a kingdom"). This is the origin of 99% of all the fortunes of all these planters. The Negro was induced by promise of higher wages and fabulous crop returns. The land-owner paid the railroad fares for the entire family, usually at greatly reduced rates granted by the railroad companies, the benefits of such reductions accruing only to the land-owner,—and the head of the Negro family in some little hamlet of South Carolina signed a contract that he and all his household would work for some unknown master in the river lands of Arkansas until these equally unknown transportation costs and all other debts were satisfied. As the planter had to furnish this family during the first year with "rations" and a cabin at the planter's own price, this debt could be so piled up by the time for the first "settlement" that the Negroes would be deeper in debt than on the day of their arrival. All the cotton raised by this black family would be sold by the planter at prices unknown to the usually illiterate peons, and then credited to the Negroes at whatever price the planter chose to fix. Even the bills of the plantation doctor, who was much needed during the first years of these unacclimated newcomers, were paid by the plantation-owner and charged with great profit against the accounts of the tenants and laborers. It is plain that such a Negro debt-slave might just as well try to lift himself over the fence by pulling at his own boot-straps as ever to get out of debt under such an arrangement, unless the planter had a better conscience than nine-tenths of mankind have. The only way many of these colored folk every got free again was to pack their goods clandestinely and steal away at night, and so add to the reputation of their race for "jumping its contracts." If they were caught before they got too far beyond the range of local jurisdiction, they were brought back and fined,—and the ignorant Negro considered the "justice of the peace" as the last court of appeal,— which it was in fact for him, as he had no money to employ lawyers or make bond, if indeed there was ever a lawyer in such a place that would oppose a great planter for a Negro peon.

All accounts were kept by the planter, and nothing was ever given to the tenants in writing; so that "settling time" meant only that the heads of the Negro families were to gather at the planter's house and hear each in his turn what the status of his debt was. Most of these peons did not know one Arabic figure from another, but they could be robbed of everything but their humor, and as they waited their turn, they would sarcastically sing the refrain:

> *"Nought's a nought*
> *An' figger's a figger:*
> *All fer de white man—*
> *None fer de nigger."*

"LEADING A DOG'S LIFE"

This epigrammatic rhyme expressed their humorous conception of the "figgering" legerdemain with which the white planter always came out ahead, with the Negroes still in debt.

The social morality in such a little land-barony does justice to its other marks of civilization. The planter and his sons and overseers were almost as free with the desirable-looking and unprotected Negro women as the old slave masters had been. There were to every wealthy white man's credit at least two families,—one white and small, the other colored and large. In so far as they were able, the Negroes, of course, imitated their "betters."

In spite of these handicaps in the thirty years beginning in the middle 80's, when many Negroes were carried west by this camouflaged slave traffic, at least a few of these colored folk and their descendants, by sheer grit and by one and another miracle, had managed by the time we declared war on Germany to become land-owners by splitting off small pieces from these baronial estates. A larger number were renters and share-croppers, most of them still in debt. The war boosted the prices of cotton fabulously, and these prices threatened to release these Negroes from debt and to deprive these planters of their bound labor and of their usurious mortgages. Then the inevitable happened: the planters very naturally sought to forestall this calamity,—by keeping the price down to the Negro who had to sell his cotton to them or thru them, while they in turn sold into the markets of the world and reaped the war profits. But by this time many of these Negroes could read, in spite of the poor schooling which they had been given, and they organized and began a perfectly lawful and nonviolent contention for the market prices. They hired white Arkansas lawyers to secure their charter and to help them in their suits for a just share of the profits. Then the planters took the next natural step of the desperate overlord: they fired on a perfectly peaceful meeting of this Negro farmers' organization assembled in a church, and then wired the powers-that-be, the governor and other state officers, that the Negroes were in insurrection! This governor, who held his office by virtue of the usual pledge to the hill people and the planters to "keep the Negro down," did not investigate or hesitate. He got together all the troops he could lay hands on and rushed down into the alluvial plains to make good. Hundreds of Negroes were shot down at sight, many while at work in the fields; large numbers were imprisoned and twelve were condemned to the electric chair. No white rioter was arrested, accused or molested by the state, altho white mobs, not only of Arkansas but of ruffians from the neighboring states, had poured in and held a carnival of death for days. The only white man arrested and mistreated was one of the lawyers whom the Negroes had employed to take their cases against the planters.—The twelve innocent men have not yet been electrocuted, but their cases are still pending in the courts, after a nation-wide fight in their behalf by white and colored people for nearly three years. (May, 1922).

ARKANSAS "PRESTIGE"

That is Arkansas! Why, then, should one think that he has described Arkansas by telling that it produces 3 billion feet of pine lumber in a single year,—that a certain one of its Hereford bulls, who bore the aristocratic title of Point Comfort XIV, won the Grand Championship of all bulldom in

1914,—or that the state grows six varieties of *useful nuts* in addition to the worse than *useless "nuts"* of its mediaeval-minded law-administrators? Arkansas ranks 20th in the total output of its crops, but it ranks 6th in the total output of its lynchings, and higher still in the horribleness of those murders. The state produced the largest nugget of zinc and the largest nugget of lead ever taken out of the ground; but also the largest and most murderous *riot against the helpless in the history of the whole South, and the most deliberately cruel burning of a human being (Henry Lowry) in the history of the world. Arkansas was the first Southern state to ratify the suffrage of women, but is also a leader among the states in denying equal citizenship of and kind to 38% of its most loyal people, men and women. It was first to pass a Bone Dry Law, and is foremost among those who oppose a law against lynching. It has the highest mountain west of the Alleghenies and east of the Rockies,—and in some years the highest homicide record in an even wider area. It boasts of 85,000 bales of cotton from 75,000 acres, but cannot boast of the semi-slave labor that produced it. Its people boast that they have fewer undertakers (not fewer deaths) to the population than any other state,—as if the Africans of the Congo and the Fiji Islanders could not make the same boast.* And we will leave it to the reader's sense to catch the humor in the two following boasts from an enthusiastic booster of "Ark'nsaw," who says: *"Arkansas has more pure bred swine than New York, Pennsylvania, California and Michigan,"* and as if that were not enough, he goes on: *"Arkansas offers ideal conditions for the raising of goats. It ranks second in goats. They are great land-clearers."*

THE RACE QUESTION

The state of Arkansas is inhabited by one and three-quarter millions of people, and it boasts at the top of its voice that among them are only 14,000 *foreigners, as if it would not be a better state if outside civilization could invade it.* They are opposed to immigration, although the inbreeding of their present ideals means backwardness. If you talk with an Arkansan about education in his state, you will find that he will endeavor to speak in general terms of the *whole body* and not to dissect it "along the color line." He will speak of a total school property of $20,000,000 and of an annual taxation for school purposes of $8,000,000, but you will have to find out for yourself that perhaps less than 10% of these sums is invested in the education of nearly 40% of the state's people.—*In Arkansas, as in the other Southern states, this question of the Negro is the skeleton in the closet,—the cancer in the system. And the discouraging feature in the present generation is, that most of the whites do not seem to realize that they and their children can never be much higher in civilization than they are willing for the blackest of their black people to become.* To many millions of perfectly law-abiding American citizens a trip on a "slow train thru Arkansas" is one of the horrors of life. On a Pullman car from St. Louis to Little Rock an educated and well-behaved young man was threatened with death by shooting because he occupied a berth on that train against the wishes of some "Arkansas fellers" who also had berths. The Pullman conductor and the conductor of the train, being also "fellers" of Arkansas, took the side of the gang and had a sheriff threaten the mistreated passenger with arrest when he reached the capital of the state. On another occasion a man was condemned to be hung in Arkansas because he and a woman were discovered kissing each other. Both parties were unmarried, and the man was convicted of "rape." The conscience-worried woman finally gathered a number of preachers and went to the governor and explained that she and this man had been intimate friends for 15 years and that they would have been married long before if it had been possible for them to marry in Arkansas. The governor refused to act, nevertheless, but much pressure by a few people of better conscience finally secured the intervention of a Federal court. How outrageous! and not the less outrageous because the victimized man in both these cases was black and the other parties white. Why, then, should Arkansas people boast that their state equals any state of the Union in the yield per acre of *lespedeza,* about which most men know nothing, while their state equals any and excels most in repressive laws and mediaeval customs?

WHERE NEGROES "GET OFF"

A few months ago a colored woman was awarded a judgment of only fifty dollars against a railroad company in Arkansas, for having been put off the train with her young child in the open country because she refused to go and take a seat in the smoker when the Jim Crow car was crowded out. She is a woman of culture and refinement, a teacher in college, and her husband is a college officer. She spent money and time in this suit against the road for a year. This judgment of fifty dollars by the court is a license to the railroads of Arkansas to do as they please with the rights and privileges of the colored population. Only very few of those who are so mistreated would ever dare enter suit under any circumstances, and to fine the railroads fifty dollars becomes a joke. *A court might as reasonably pretend to break up illicit whiskey selling by fining the bootlegger five dollars when it is proven that he sold a barrel of liquor,* even though they may catch him with only every tenth barrel! The small fine in the case of the gross mistreatment of a colored woman serves only one purpose: it sustains the law sufficiently so that in case the railroad should treat a white person in the same way, it could be fined and fined more heavily. And why did this woman object so strenuously to going into the men's smoker? The appearance of a lone colored woman among white men in Arkansas is the signal for indecent talk of all sorts. The gallant gentlemen immediately begin to insult her, by remarks to each other. "Do you talk like that before *ladies?*" one will ask clownishly, in order to elicit from another (as in minstrel shows) the reply: "Why, there h'ain't no *lady* in hyeah." Any colored woman who knows would rather be put off the train and take her chances in the wild woods. *There is great pretense in Arkansas, as in all the South, that white women are greatly in need of protection against Negro men, but it is known the world over that sex-imposition is by the strong against the weak. It never has yet been that the colored woman was half as safe in the proximity of white men as is the white woman in the midst of colored men in the South.*

Such is the character of the Arkansas of the present, one of the strongholds of the Ku Klux Klan and the home of the Ancient Concatenated Order of Hoo Hoo. *If in the first year of the 19th century the primeval gulf had rolled again up the valley of the Mississippi and covered the rich black plains to the original water line, nothing would be missing in the world today except Bowie knives, unmeasured misery and an unaccountable number of horrible homicides.*

NOAH D. THOMPSON

California: The Horn of Plenty

VOL. 6, NO. 6, JUNE 1924

Noah D. Thompson was born in Baltimore, Maryland, on June 9, 1874. After studying business at Greggs Business School in Chicago, he worked in Chicago as a general solicitor for U.S. Express Company before moving to Tuskegee, Alabama, where he worked as circulation director and assistant to the treasurer at Tuskegee Normal and Industrial Institute. Upon moving to California in 1911 he began the Noah D. Thompson Realty Company, which he continued to run while commencing a career as a journalist. He became a member of the editorial staff of the *Los Angeles Evening Express,* where he was noted for such achievements as attaining the capitalization of the word "Negro" in the Los Angeles press. (This was an ongoing issue in the 1920s. In the same issue of *The Messenger* Nora Newsome faulted the otherwise progressive Upton Sinclair for failing to "dignify by capitalization" a word "that connotes a particular race.") Thompson contributed articles for the *Los Angeles Times* and the *Chicago Defender* and also served as a correspondent to the *Japanese Daily News.* He served as the associate editor of *The Liberator* and was the business manager of *Opportunity* from 1927 to at least 1929. He was an active member of the NAACP. Congressman H. Z. Osborne proposed that Thompson be named minister to Liberia, and although Thompson's writings about California demonstrate that he was well suited for an ambassadorial position, this proposal never resulted in an appointment.

The almost comically overblown prose here sounds more like Thompson's real estate brochures than his journalistic copy. His glowing portrait of California, touched up with fatherly sternness (" 'free lunch counters' . . . have passed and gone forever") and what seems to be an awkward attempt at a breezy personal style ("Are these successful brethren selfish? I should say not!"), makes "California: The Horn of Plenty" oddly reminiscent of the gung-ho boosters satirized in Sinclair Lewis's *Babbit.* Yet Thompson's enthusiasm should not be belittled, for his idyllic portrait of a society free from prejudice and suffering had some basis in fact. In comparison with many other states, California had very little Klan activity. And though we may be embarrassed by the optimistic hard sell, it was a common and respectable way of representing a community at the time. There were real Babbitts and they did help build communities. That Thompson was proud that even the churches were run in a businesslike manner makes sense in a decade when the president of the United States could announce that the business of America is business.

Thompson's statistical portrait of African American life in California consists of small and manageable figures. There are two plastering contractors, ten public stenographers, one cartoonist, and thirty barber shops, "many of them with more than three chairs of the latest model." He points out that the three-story structure that will hold the Commercial Council of Los Angeles cost fifty-thousand dollars. But his sprightly valorization of the opportunities and technology that California could offer to hard-working African Americans is more than a simple-minded adherence to numbers. His rhetoric appeals quite concretely to the desires of a population that, at this point in the century, was highly mobile and motivated. People who might be considering a move west would indeed want to know about the business opportunities there. Furthermore, Thompson's reliance upon specifics is couched in accessible and comforting terms. He does not speak of the "many establishments" owned and operated by African Americans as some of the other essays do; rather, he relentlessly lists them ("1 tile contractor; 10 high-class dressmakers . . ."), searing the success into the mind of his readers. Thompson's essay features twenty-seven portrait photographs—more than any other essay—and succeeds in presenting a California brimming with good humor, promising numbers, and a successful population of African Americans. The numbers and the photographs are meant to accomplish the same purpose, to increase the visibility of the African American middle-class and encourage others to join it.

MR. THOMPSON

Seventy-three years ago, September 9, California's white star first blazed forth upon the field of navy blue in the tri-colored flag of these United States, thereby heralding an event of supreme importance, not only to our nation, but to the world at large. It was the morning star appearing at the dawn of a new day in this Western Empire, marking the beginning of the end of slavery on this troubled continent.

California's dramatic entrance into the Union as the sixteenth "Free State" broke the balance of power between the "free" and "slave territory," and turned our judicial scales in favor of an honest interpretation of that part of our Constitution that declares all men are created free and equal.

It had already been proclaimed upon the floor of the United States Senate that upon the decision of the slave question rests the destiny of the nation, and California's entrance into Statehood just at that time precipitated the great Civil War. With the flow of gold and silver from her rich mines, she gave the Union its financial strength to carry on the battle of freedom to a glorious and successful conclusion.

The design on California's State flag indicates that she's a "bear," but I am thinking that the horn of plenty would perhaps better typify this beautiful home of the setting sun, where flowers grow wild the year round, while it peacefully rests on the world's largest ocean and holds the key to the Western gate of the Western Hemisphere.

History records the heroic events leading up to and following California's admission into the sisterhood of these United States, and the romantic manner of her entrance into the Union is being retold on stage and screen in a way that should quicken the pulse of every lover of conquest, romance and beauty.

Great and glorious as has been California's part in the upbuilding of America, her future is destined to be of a transcendent greatness and a glory beyond the comprehension or imagination of her fondest admirers. As no other State, she is geographically situated to obtain the greatest advantage from the ever–increasing traffic in the trade and commerce of the world, while many world famous men and women of all nations are yearning to call her "home."

The physical make-up of California tends to make her peoples healthy, active and prosperous, while her unlimited resources of almost every conceivable kind are, for the most part, yet to be developed.

What about the colored brother in California? The answer must be written by none other than the brother himself, for his opportunities in the great "Bear State" are limited solely by his ability to succeed in whatever line of business or profession he may claim to know. Is he a success in New York, Mississippi, or wherever he may be while reading this article? Then he, if he cares to, can come to California and be a howling success, provided he brings with him something like the same determination to succeed that the "gold-rushers" from all parts of the world brought with them in 1849, about three years after Mexico lost her control of the one hundred and fifty-eight thousand, two hundred and ninety-seven square miles of territory, which ranks California as second in size of these United States. According to Delilah L. Beasley's "California History of Negro Trail Blazers," the colored brother was in that "rush" of the "days of '49," and he has been in every important California movement, before and since

A trio of big cities has California: San Francisco, Los Angeles and San Diego, that have recently become important world shipping ports, thereby increasing her opportunities to dispose of her vast stores of petroleum, lumber, cotton, fruits and vegetables. To those who would study her topography and various geological peculiarities, as well as her vast agricultural, horticultural and mining developments; her unsurpassed school systems; and last, but not least, her great motion picture industry, I cheerfully recommend the reading of "Beasley's History of Negro Trail Blazers of

California," and other reliable books on California that may be found in the reference room of any up-to-date public library.

From now on we will deal with the brother in Los Angeles. Los Angeles, the largest city in California, has a population far in excess of eight hundred thousand, about forty thousand of whom are Negroes, with perhaps less than one thousand adults who are native born. Some are wealthy, some are poor, and some are, oh, just so, so . . . which means, just about like they were back yonder, and just about like they would be in New York, New Albany or Old Africa. The wealthy have numerous opportunities greatly to improve their condition through work and thrift. As for the "just so, so's," they are contented to "rest in peace," while yet alive in this age of "jazz" and "go get 'em." Do you see what I mean?

Tourists of all nations come to California, particularly to Los Angeles, to play. Many of them see at once the innumerable opportunities here and remain to work and grow rich in health, wealth and intellect. Many colored brethren were among these tourists who came to play and remained to work, and as a result, Los Angeles has a large group of the brethren that are engaged in almost every trade, industry and profession.

Are these successful brethren selfish? I should say not! Within the last three months a few of them have organized a "Commercial Council" for the express purpose of encouraging members of their racial group, first, to study the conditions in California, and then combine their efforts to better the economic condition of the Negroes throughout the State. Already much valuable data has been gathered that will enable the brother better to see his opportunities and seize them. This data is available to every Negro who desires to come to California to work and live.

Besides having secured the location and perfected the plans (by a Negro architect) for a $50,000 three-story building, to be known as "the home of the Commercial Council of Los Angeles," this organization has already, through its Department of Statistics and Records, compiled a list that gives the name and location of 20 beauty and hair culture parlors; 10 public stenographers; 15 carpenters, painters and general contractors; 12 dry goods, notions and gents' furnishing stores; 5 second-hand furniture dealers; 12 auto accessories, repair shops and garages among them one that is said to be the largest and best-arranged of any west of St. Louis; 6 auto salesmen, two with their own well-filled display rooms; 1 high-class architect with million-dollar clients; 2 plastering contractors; 5 printers, with all the work they can do; 2 weekly newspapers, both owning linotype machines, one owned and managed by a woman; several monthly periodicals; one member of the State Legislature.

There are also 3 authors, 1 dramatist, 1 cartoonist, 30 moving picture actors regularly employed, one of whom is head of all and known in the industry as "the Will Hayes" of the group. Fifteen teachers in the public school system, one a woman principal (the schools in California are mixed); 1 school of photography; 3 wholesale candy manufacturers; 30

TOP ROW, LEFT TO RIGHT: Mrs. Fred'k. M. Roberts, wife of F. M. Roberts, mem. California Legislature; Miss Marion F. Carter, junior, Cal State Univ., Los Angeles, Cal.; Mme. Te-Outley, musical director, radio entertainer, Los Angeles, Cal.; Dr. Vada Somerville of Los Angeles, dentist. MIDDLE ROW, LEFT TO RIGHT: Miss Delia Beasley, author, Oakland, Cal.; Mrs. Clarence O. Jones, Grad. College Arts & Sciences, Ohio State Univ., Los Angeles, Calif.; Mrs. Eva Carter Buckner, social worker, poet, artist. BOTTOM ROW, LEFT TO RIGHT: Mrs. Azelie Palmer, Los Angeles, wife of J. W. Palmer, capitalist; Mrs. Theodora L. Purnell, Oakland, Cal., in business with her son, Lee Purnell, electric appliances, radio; Mrs. Katheryn Campbell Graham, vocal instructor, Los Angeles City Schools; Mrs. Marguerite Cox, prominent designer and milliner, Los Angeles, Cal.

TOP ROW, LEFT TO RIGHT: Mrs. Gertrude Chrisman, teacher in Foreign Opportunity Dept., Los Angeles City Schools; Mrs. Nellie M. Reed, probation officer of City of Los Angeles; Mrs. Flora E. Dorsey, engaged in catering business; Dr. Alice Watkins Garrott, associated with her husband, Dr. W. Garrott, in Los Angeles. MIDDLE ROW, LEFT TO RIGHT: Mrs. Sadie C. Cole of Los Angeles, clubwoman, Vice Pres. NAACP; Mrs. Martha L. Dodge of San Diego, Calif., wife of Chas. H. Dodge, currency accountant San Diego's largest bank; Mrs. Florence Anita Gordon of Los Angeles, Cal. & husband Dr. J. D. Gordon, prominent clergyman. BOTTOM ROW, LEFT TO RIGHT: Mrs. Emma K. Barnett of Los Angeles, Cal., wife of Atty. LeRoy Barnett, criminal lawyer; Mrs. Edith May Loving, wife of Mayor Walter H. Loving, Oakland, Cal.; Mrs. A. Bowers, Los Angeles, member firm Bowers-Bowers Druggists; Mrs. Nellie V. Conner, Los Angeles, Cal., member Conner & Johnson Undertakers.

UPPER LEFT: Mrs. John Howard Butler, firm of Hudson and Butler, Funeral Directors, San Francisco, Calif. LOWER LEFT: Mrs. Arthur L. Reese, treasurer and part owner with her husband of the Venice Boat and Canoe Co.; prominent in society and politics, Venice, Calif. CENTER: Mrs. Angelita Nelson, talented wife of Dr. Eugene C. Nelson of Los Angeles. RIGHT: Miss Bernice O. Ellis, "The Oklahoma Song Bird," a recent addition to the Los Angeles group.

barber shops, many of them with more than three chairs of the latest model; 15 cigar stores and shoe-shining parlors; 10 shoe repairing shops, several of which make custom shoes of a very high grade; 45 real estate and fire insurance agents, several having up-to-date offices with escrow departments; 3 funeral directors, with up-to-the-minute mortuaries and equipment; 1 fully-equipped hospital; 25 tailoring establishments, catering to all classes; 2 laundries; 25 groceries and meat markets; 15 express and transfer men, one with a storage and warehouse of which any city would be proud; 10 general merchandise dealers; 1 tile contractor; 10 high-class dressmakers, several of whom cater exclusively to the "moving picture trade"; 7 drug stores; 35 restaurants and cafes; 1 theatre; 15 bakeries and dairy lunch rooms; 15 sweet shops; 20 physicians, both sexes; 6 chiropodists, both sexes; 16 lawyers, one a woman practising in New York City; 30 professional musicians, entertainers and composers; 4 music shops; 10 small hotels; 20 rooming houses; 2 life insurance agents; 3 jewelers, and 10 taxicab owners.

This is just a partial list for Los Angeles, and does not include the *brethren* who are in business in San Francisco, Oakland, San Diego, in the valley districts, at the beaches and other California cities, where the very stars of heaven spell Opportunity! Opportunity!! for all who care to come and work and work and work and then work some more to achieve the success that is the reward for efficient work.

The personnel of the Commercial Council of Los Angeles does not include all of the successful Negro men and women of Los Angeles, but it does include, besides Dr. Eugene C. Nelson, its founder and president, a few men whose slightest nod of approval will suffice to cause the cashiers of their respective banks to honor your check or mine, regardless of whether the amount written thereon be in four, five or six figures.

Perhaps not the least in importance of the several purposes of the Commercial Council is the department that gets hold of the newcomer of their group for the purpose of helping him find a suitable place to live and work or open up business, if he is prepared, and then when he is here legally long enough (one year) see to it that he registers and votes for the individuals and principles that will be most beneficial to the entire group and the best interests of his community.

The California Development Company is another organization of the brethren, less than ten months old, that is acting as a stimulus to their kind in California and helping them to see their opportunity and grab it. Headed by Chandler Owen, "tourist lecturer" of New York City, and managed by Morgan G. Stokes, former "tourist" from Colorado, but now a permanent and successful business man of Los Angeles, the California Development Company has recently purchased a large apartment house building in the center of "the Harlem of Los Angeles," which is paying the "developers" a handsome income, while furnishing comfortable shelter for other "tourists" who are trying to decide which opportunity to seize and hold, " 'till death cuts 'em loose."

In the early part of this year (1924), prominent colored citizens of Los Angeles organized the Liberty Building and Loan Association for the purpose of assisting colored citizens in building homes. It operates under the building and loan laws of California, with an authorized guaranteed capital stock of $100,000.

Officers of the company are: Dr. Wilbur C. Gordon, president; C. S. Blodgett, first vice-president; George S. Grant, second vice-president; A. Hartley Jones, secretary-manager; Norman O. Houston, sales manager; Dr. Eugene C. Nelson, Albert Baumann and Frank A. Harvey, directors.

The recently formed Unity Finance Company, with a capital stock of $200,000, is a big step in the direction of a bank for the Negro community of Los Angeles. According to a recent survey of the Commercial Council, it was found that among the 50,000 colored residents of the city approximately $1,000,000 is carried in local banks. It was felt that this huge sum might just as well be at the disposal of progressive and dependable colored citizens in need of financial assistance.

Dr. Eugene C. Nelson is president; Elijah Cooper, vice-president; Dr. Alva C. Garrott, second vice-president; Charles E. Pearl, secretary; S.B.W.

May, treasurer; Eugene Johnson, T. J. Winston, Emery V. Crain, Paul R. Williams and F. M. Roberts, directors.

"Production," "Progress," "Active Life" are the mottoes that will soon hang upon the wall of every brother in California, if they follow the lead of the members of these organizations of active and progressive men and women.

California has many individual Negroes who own larger and perhaps better paying pieces of income property than any of the organizations mentioned, but it is the group combination idea which is fostered by these organizations with the hope that the brother will soon learn that it is the modern way of doing big things.

Churches? Oh, yes! We have them, more numerous than the grocery and the furniture stores combined. However, they are filling their niche in our scheme of group development," and several of them are progressive enough to own apartment houses and other income property and to give aid to the Commercial Council in their efforts to help the brethren find themselves and their opportunities, here and hereafter.

As I write this final word, an aviator away up in the air is writing, in letters each a mile long, so all may read, the word "Welcome." This invitation is cordially extended to all who choose to come to the Poppy-covered State of California. But, for the brother or anyone else who is merely a loafer or dreamer of the slouching, half-apologetic type, that word will quickly fade away into the gem-colored sky against which it is written, and he will find nothing, absolutely nothing in California for him save the salubrious climate, which alone will not suffice to sustain him in this age from which the "free lunch counters" and the "free transportation trains" have passed and gone forever.

WILLIAM H. FERRIS, A.M.

Connecticut: The Nutmeg State

VOL. 6, NO. 1, JANUARY 1924

William H. Ferris was born in New Haven, Connecticut, on July 20, 1874. After graduating from Hillhouse High School in New Haven in 1891 and from Yale University in 1895, he studied at Harvard Divinity School from 1897 to 1899 and then transferred to the graduate school to study journalism, receiving an A.M. in 1900. After a very public and varied career as a writer from the turn of the century through the 1920s, he fell out of the public eye, and died in 1941. The *Journal of Negro History* ran an obituary, explaining that Ferris had "died suddenly in obscurity . . . and his body saved from the Potter's Field" by his classmates at Yale. "Thus passed from this life a man whose career is difficult to estimate." According to the *JNH,* he failed as a teacher and as a preacher. He was a follower rather than a leader. Most of his acquaintances were disappointed with his achievements, given his abilities and preparation. The Yale classmates who arranged his funeral, however, published a notice claiming that Ferris had "a remarkable record of accomplishment; he was indeed a credit to his university and his country."

Contradictory and controversial, William H. Ferris was one of the few contributors to "These 'Colored' United States" who was a public supporter of Marcus Garvey. In his autobiography, the acerbic George Schuyler described Ferris as "a shabby little brown man with pockets ever bulging with newspapers and magazines, [who] had acquired his knighthood from Marcus Garvey." Ferris served as literary editor of Garvey's *Negro World* from 1919 to 1921, and he did in fact accept a Garveyite knighthood. In some circles, this accorded him the title of "Sir." In other circles, of course, it provoked ridicule. His Garveyite politics, however, were only part of Ferris's role among African American intellectuals of the time. He also became known for his temporary alliances with W.E.B. Du Bois, Monroe Trotter, and Booker T. Washington. He published in major national magazines and newspapers during all of these transformations. His two-volume work *The African Abroad; or, His Evolution in Western Civilization, Tracing His Development under the Caucasian Milieu* came out in 1913 and increased his national fame. This study was one of the first important texts to discuss not just the problems of African Americans but of the African diaspora more generally. Ferris also holds the distinction (along with

William Pickens, another *Messenger* writer) of having won the prestigious Ten Eyck Prize for oratory at Yale University.

The backlash against African Americans, "The anti-Negro wave
that has swept over the country like a pestilence," Ferris writes here, is
all too present in Connecticut. Ferris unfavorably compares the conditions of the 1920s with those of the late nineteenth century, and this
analysis, more than any other quality, makes this essay stand out
among the easy-progress polemics of the 1920s. He acknowledges "on
one hand educational and economic opportunity, political status and
freedom of residence on the part of the colored people, cordial and
pleasant relations between the races, and on the other hand a partial
barring of the colored people from swell hotels, restaurants and ice
cream and soda parlors." Ferris makes no attempt to bask in the
rhetoric of helpless contradictions, maintaining that the African
Americans of New Haven refuse to accept such contradictions. Rather
than present the wave of segregation only in terms of oppression,
however, Ferris hails the individual entrepreneurs who have used Jim
Crow as an incentive to creating black-only businesses and services.

The writing suffers from some poor editing: there are abundant mis-
placed modifying phrases, usage problems, and, most egregiously, paragraphs made up of non sequiturs. But within what might otherwise
seem like a desultory listing of random facts, individual sentence-long
portraits stand out, marking moments of wry and curious poignancy.
There is Joseph R. Robinson, the butler who "accumulated wealth to
the value of $50,000 and lost three-fourths of it by speculation." Or the
happier story of "another colored butler" who "was left $10,000 in the
will of his employer." Many authors in the series provide a litany of
prominent names, but Ferris's focused portrait of the janitorial staff of
Yale, the "heroes of the battle of Fort Wagner," or the "popular tonsorial artist" (a humorous term for a barber) make his list more informa-
tive and vivid. His story of the African American community of New
Haven as being largely dependent upon the employ and goodwill of the
white people at Yale offers not only an interpretation of the lifestyle of
New Havenites in the 1920s but also an image of Ferris in the 1890s: a
young African American student at Yale, both part of and distant from
his racially identified community.

In 1923 Ferris reviewed Harold Stearns's *Civilization in the United
States: An Inquiry by Thirty Americans* and hailed the work as a
harbinger of future American thought. The youth of the contributors
especially intrigued Ferris, and he saw in their attitudes forces that
were to "partly shape American thought and life in the next twenty
years." Ferris quotes Sterns, proclaiming that "whatever else American civilization is, it is not Anglo-Saxon, and . . . we shall never
achieve any genuine nationalistic self-consciousness as long as we allow certain financial and social minorities to persuade us that we are
still an English Colony." Ferris's regard for the Stearns's collection is

largely for its provocative nature, for its call for a radical reconsideration of America's cultural and racial makeup. In his review Ferris spends more time discussing the "Intellectual Life" essay and the "Science" section than the "Racial Minorities" essay, but his assessment of that section praised it for its candor in treatment of miscegenation. He praised Geriod Tanquary Robinson, author of the "Racial Minorities" section, for seeking to understand, rather than solve, race problems. Ferris's *Messenger* essay thus can be considered in the light of such appreciation for facts rather than prescriptions. And the specificity of Ferris's facts—as when he tells us that "John F. Shufford, the welder, . . . paid $8,000 cash for a Locomobile"—makes his essay a fascinating record of the times.

Mr. Ferris

New Haven and Hartford, the two largest cities in Connecticut, were settled about 285 years ago. The Plymouth Fathers who landed in Plymouth in 1616 and who located in Boston soon afterwards found the long winters and the cold northeast wind rather searching. It is reported that Indians came up to Boston and told of a country a few days' journey southward, where the winters were not so severe, where the scenery was beautiful and where a beautiful river flowed calmly by. They told of another beautiful place set in a basin between high hills with a river running from a sound into it. The first place is known as Hartford and the second as New Haven. Hooker was the moving spirit in the Hartford Colony and Theophilus Eaton in the New Haven Colony.

Both in size, wealth and number of famous residents, Hartford and New Haven easily overtop all other Connecticut towns. Inventors, the Colt's revolver, and insurance companies made Hartford a rich city. And Mark Twain, Harriet Beecher Stowe, Charles Dudley Warner, Rev. Horace Bushnell, Rev. Joseph Twitchell, General Joseph Hawley and Senator Morgan G. Bulkeley were her most illustrious citizens.

The Winchester Repeating Arms Company, the Sargent Company, the Candee Rubber Shop and the Strouse Adler Corset Company helped to swell the population and the wealth of New Haven, Connecticut. But she became famous chiefly because she was the seat of Yale University. And because of her picturesque elm trees, she was known as the City of Elms. The erection of high brick buildings close by the sidewalk and the setting up of trolley car overhead wires have caused scores of elm trees to be cut down, so that while New Haven has a population twice as large as she had thirty years ago, she only has half as many elm trees.

Besides famous scholars like Woolsey, Porter, Dwight, Hadley, Silliman, Thacher, Seymour, Lounsbury, Dana, Whitney, Gibbs, Fisher, Ladd and Sumner, the first four of whom served as presidents of and the latter ten as professors in Yale University, four other New Haven citizens attained international fame. These were Roger Sherman, one of the signers of the Declaration of Independence; Eli Whitney, the inventor of the Cotton Gin; Noah Webster, the compiler of a dictionary; and Donald G. Mitchells, known as "The Marvel," the author of "Dream Life," "Reveries of a Bachelor," "English Lands, Letters and Kings" and "American Lands and Letters."

Connecticut is a small state and is pre-eminently a manufacturing state. Waterbury, Derby, Shelton, Ansonia, Naugatuck, Torrington and Winsted on the Naugatuck River; New Britain, Bridgeport and South Manchester teem with mills and factories. Bridgeport became famous because she is and was the winter home of Peter Barnum's show and the home of the Remington Fire Arms Company. The famous Cheney Silk Mills are located in South Manchester. The Waterbury watch put Waterbury on the map. The towns along Long Island Sound between Greenwich and Green Farms, the Litchfield Hills and Simsbury are summer homes for many New York millionaires.

Connecticut is also famous for her nutmegs and grows a mild flavor tobacco. The cigars which have the Connecticut leaf with Havana wrapper will give the lover of the weed exquisite delight. East Granby, Rockville and Glastonbury are the tobacco centers. It is a wonderful sight to ride from Hartford to Rockville by trolley and look down into the valley on the north, before you enter Rockville and see what looks like a number of small lakes. But when you get nearer you see that the miniature lakes are only white nets, spread over the famous shade grown tobacco.

COLORED CONNECTICUT

The colored population of Bridgeport, Waterbury, Derby, Meridan, Ansonia, Norwich, New London and Middletown is not over large. Frequently there is some one colored man who stands out prominently in these towns. Mr. Burr of Norwich and Mr. Jeffries of Meridan were intelligent barbers who were identified with the anti-slavery movement and were forceful speakers. Mr. Tappan was a prominent citizen of Ansonia. Messrs. Gefford and Miller organized a realty company in Waterbury and purchased a few houses. Dr. Gibbs is a prosperous dentist of Bridgeport, Conn., Mrs. R. F. Tanner runs an Art and Craft Shop in Stamford, Conn.

In Hartford six colored men became very prosperous through working for rich white people. Jack Ross and Mr. Edwards took care of the lawns, furnaces and offices of wealthy people and became prosperous. Mr. Edwards' daughter won honors as a scholar. Joseph R. Robinson was a butler for a wealthy family, accumulated wealth to the value of $50,000 and lost three-fourths of it by speculation. Mr. Cephas Grant rose from the position of butler until he became the manager of the estate of his employer. Mr. Munsey became chief superintendent of two insurance buildings. And another colored butler was left $10,000 in the will of his employer.

Rev. Wheeler, who pastored the colored Congregational Church for many years; Rev. Wm. H. Harrod, now pastor of the First African Baptist Church of Philadelphia, who built a magnificent church on Albany Avenue; and Rev. Kimbell Warren, who developed the Union Baptist Church, were the most prominent colored preachers of Hartford, Conn. Rev. Dr. Jackson, pastor of Union Baptist Church, and Rev. R. C. Ball, the pastor of the Pearl St. A.M.E. Church, are the most prominent pastors at present.

Another colored young man, Professor Lawson, excelled as a pianist and organist, opened a studio and numbered among his pupils the children of Hartford's wealthiest citizens.

COLORED NEW HAVEN IN THE PAST

But it is in New Haven, Conn., that we find the remarkable examples of intellectual and financial progress. Today there are more prosperous and educated colored people in New Haven, Conn., than in all Connecticut. In fact the six thousand colored people in the City of Elms represent more wealth and intelligence than any other equally numerical group of colored people in the world. The influence that Yale University radiates, and the chance and opportunity New Haven has always given to colored men of brains, energy and character, as well as the type of colored men who settled in New Haven accounts for their remarkable progress.

The colored people of New Haven have been recruited from five sources: First, the free Negroes of the North, who have lived there since the days of the Revolutionary War. Secondly, the group of carpenters, blacksmiths and laborers who came from Newbern and Washington, N. C., before and after the Civil War. Thirdly, the waiters who came to work in the Yale Dining Hall in the closing days of the Nineteenth Century. Fourthly, the lawyers, physicians and dentists, who began to come in the closing days of the Nineteenth Century. And fifthly, the mechanics and laborers who came to work in the munition plants during the World War.

Before the Civil War, the colored people of New Haven had reached a high stage of intelligence and prosperity. In 1854, the colored people of New Haven, who numbered nearly 2,000, owned $200,000 worth of real estate, banks, and railroad stock, and had four Methodist churches, one Congregational church, one Episcopal church and one Baptist church. They had a literary society with a circulating library and four colored school houses.

Colored people in those days owned property on Webster Street, Dixwell Avenue, Bradley Street, Morocco Street, now called Oak Street, Cedar Street, Putnam Street, Carlisle Street, Howe Street, Edgewood Avenue, and West Chapel Street. Had they foreseen that in seventy years New

Haven would jump in population from 30,000 to 200,000 and that property would increase in value tenfold, fifteenfold and even twentyfold, and held on to the property, their descendants would now be rolling in the wealth.

Mr. Lyman then owned property on Ashman Street between Foote and Gregory Streets, and also owned part of Mill Rock and furnished rock for building. Some of the old colored residents were very philanthropic. Mr. Bias M. Stanley, a butler of the Suhetel family, left an estate of $10,000, two-thirds for church work and one-third for the education of the colored youth. The Goodman family lived near Portsea and Putnam Streets and left the Goodman fund to Yale University for the education of students to the ministry.

Mrs. Brewster left the house on Edgewood Avenue to Yale University. Mr. Charles McLynn, a colored carpenter for Yale University, bought it and remodeled it. Three colored men were very prominent in New Haven during the *ante bellum* days. These were Rev. Dr. Beamon, pastor of the Congregational Church, and an anti-slavery speaker, Mr. Lathrop, the pillar of the Congregational Church, and Mr. Creed, the popular caterer for Yale University.

COLORED NEW HAVEN SINCE THE CIVIL WAR

Lane, John Godette, Dave Fenderson, Anthony Skinner, Charles McLynn, Groves, Willis Bonner and Keyes were the skilled carpenters and blacksmiths who came to New Haven from Newbern and Washington, N.C., before, during and after the Civil War. They were joined by John Rosseby Alexander, an expert bricklayer, and by James Norcum, a carpenter from Virginia. They worked for the richest citizens and made good wages. Of this group, Lane, Skinner, Groves and Norcum accumulated considerable property. Then came Captain James Wilkins, Captain Thomas Griffin and Joseph Selsey, heroes of the battle of Fort Wagner. The first organized a colored military company, accumulated a small fortune as a bookmaker, invested it wisely in real estate and lost it speculating in Wall Street. The second developed into a polished orator and the third into a tonsorial artist. The brother of Captain Griffin, Joseph Griffin, became the popular tonsorial artist for Yale University and the New Haven aristocrats. Then there was Father Manning, an old patriarch, a ship builder of Fair Haven, one of whose sons, "Bill" Manning, became an expert carpenter, and two of whose sons, John and Edward Manning, graduated from Yale College. In those days, Dr. Creed, the son of Yale's popular caterer, had a lucrative practice, most of his patients being white. Two of Mr. Willis Bonner's sons also graduated from Yale. In those days the cooks, butlers and coachmen for the rich were colored, the headwaiters and chefs of the New Haven House, the Elliott House and the Hotel Tontine were colored. The stewards of the Yale University Club, the Country Club, the Ausantowie Club and the Colony Club were colored. The carpenters and janitors of Yale

University and custodians of the Secret Society Buildings were colored. The popular boxing teacher at Yale, Hannibal L. W. Silliman, was colored. Mr. Cooper, the janitor of the old Yale gymnasium, who invented the swimming tank, was colored. And Mr. Shells, who supervised the putting together of the bits of clay which made the figures of the Yale athletes on the Yale gymnasium look like they were chiseled out of a single block, was a colored man. Judson Saunders, Perry Davis, M. K. Holland and Charles Johnson have been trusted by Yale officials.

Of the colored headwaiters, Mr. Moses T. Rice accumulated a fortune of $100,000. Mrs. De Ladson, whose husband ran a restaurant, had $70,000 deposited in the savings bank when she died. Mr. Fleming was a popular caterer and restaurateur. For eleven years between 1889 and 1900 Mr. James Stewart was New Haven's most popular caterer and catered for the swell functions of Yale University.

Two organizers came to New Haven in those days: Rev. Albert P. Miller developed the Dixwell Avenue Congregational Church and made it the first colored Congregational church in the country to become self-supporting. Mr. Joseph P. Peaker in the years between 1896 and 1900 organized the State Sumner League and through his organization sent Rev. Dr. Jackson as United States consul to Cognacs, France.

COLORED NEW HAVEN TODAY

Today, there are seven colored churches in New Haven, Conn., one colored newspaper, two colored lawyers, four physicians, three dentists, two undertakers, a colored welder, a colored garage, one upholsterer, one grain store, three tailors, six proprietors of restaurants or boarding houses, five barber shops, three insurance agents, three real estate promoters, one electrical shop, one clerk in the Post Office, seven letter carriers, four teachers in the public schools, a clerk in the City Hall, a clerk in the library, one artistic sign painter, a drug store, over two score men who earn their living as skilled artisans, carpenters, bricklayers, blacksmiths, and battery men for stero-type companies, machinists, engineers, mechanicians, chauffeurs, and there are a few carting contractors. In Lawyer Harry Tolliver, they have an alderman. In Miss Hope they have a graduate of the Yale School of Music.

The *New Idea,* an attractive eight-page weekly, of which F. I. Smith is managing editor, is owned by a company of which F. I. McDaniel is president, G. F. Smith, secretary, and F. C. Lewis, treasurer. W. A. Holley is the proprietor of the large drug store and C. Franklyn Baker, head of the firm of Baker and Brown, the pioneer undertaker. Daniel Brown, Edward Howell, Tom Ewell and Mr. Ed Melton started the real estate promotion which is now being pushed by Mr. William Howard. Mr. Spears started the insurance work, which is now promoted by J. Lester Pugh. Mr. Brown has held his own as a restaurateur for several years. Frank Swan and Mr. Joseph

Peters have done well as carting contractors. Mr. Trippet, a Yale graduate, excels as an electrician, and Mr. Roston as a printer. Mrs. Eloise Day is also a pioneer. Rev. E. R. Goin, pastor of the Dixwell Avenue Congregational Church; Rev. H. O. Bowles, rector of St. Luke's Episcopal Church; Rev. J. B. Pharr, pastor of the Immanuel Baptist Church; Rev. S. G. Shottswood, pastor of Varick Memorial A.M.E. Zion Church; Rev. D. A. Christie, pastor of Bethel A.M.E. Church, Rev. J. H. White, pastor of St. Paul's Union A.M.E. Church, Rev. H. S. Rossin of the Seventh Day Adventist Church, and Rev. F. A. Toote of the African Orthodox Church, are the well-known pastors. Rev. Bowser, like Rev. Daniel Brown, resigned the pastorate of Bethel Church for more lucrative secular work.

The Odd Fellows own and control a magnificent building. A colored company headed by Dr. McGill owns a splendid hotel at Savin Rock, opposite the beaches. The colored people of New Haven and Waterbury own a splendid country club in Cheshire. Seven of New Haven's colored citizens have a large white patronage. These are: Dr. I. W. Porter, a genius in diagnosis, whose fame has spread over the country; Dr. Fleming, the dentist, who owns a $20,000 home; Lawyer George Crawford; James W. Stewart, the caterer; John F. Shufford, the welder, who paid $8,000 cash for a Locomobile; Miss Berry, who runs a dining hall for students; and Herman Scott, the dyer and cleaner. The aggregate wealth of the six thousand colored people of New Haven probably exceeds $1,000,000.

CLOSING REFLECTIONS

But while the present generation of New Haveners like the former generation has given capable and efficient colored men employment at lucrative wages, while it has patronized colored physicians, dentists, restaurateurs, caterers, welders, electricians, and truckmen, New Haven has been slightly influenced by the anti-Negro wave that has swept over the country like a pestilence. Colored people are not welcomed quite as cordially in the restaurants, ice cream parlors and soda water fountains downtown as they were a quarter of a century ago. They are not welcomed quite as cordially in Wilcox's restaurant at Savin Rock, where delicious shore dinners are served, as they were in days of yore. They have been barred from Mansfield Grove, a beautiful park on Long Island Sound. But, since they are prospering, since they live in fine homes which they own, since they own nearly fifty cars, since they have their own country club at Cheshire and their own hotel at Savin Rock, they are not disturbed by the rising segregation wave. Their main thought is centered on getting houses, lands, a bank account, and political influence.

So in New Haven, Conn., the observer can witness on the one hand educational and economic opportunity, political status and freedom of residence on the part of the colored people, cordial and pleasant relations between the races, and on the other hand a partial barring of the colored people from swell hotels, restaurants and ice cream and soda parlors. As an offset, colored people in the City of the Elms are beginning to develop hotels, restaurants and ice cream and soda parlors of their own where residents and visitors can be provided for. A year ago last November a party of friends motored from Boston to the Yale-Harvard game. After the game they wondered where they would eat and sleep, as they were dubious about white hotels and restaurants. The writer secured one splendid home where the ladies were cared for, another splendid home where the gentlemen were provided for, and a dining room where the whole party partook of an elaborate dinner. So the partial segregation in New Haven does not oppress the colored citizens. They are, for the most part, taking advantage of present opportunities and looking forward to the future with hope.

ALICE DUNBAR-NELSON

Delaware: A Jewel of Inconsistencies

Vol. 6, No. 8, August 1924 (first part)

Vol. 6, No. 9, September 1924 (second part)

Born in New Orleans, Louisiana, in 1875, Alice Dunbar-Nelson developed a career as author, editor, and activist, following a trajectory
distinctly different from most other contributors to "These 'Colored'
United States." Although known for her 1898 marriage to the celebrated poet Paul Laurence Dunbar, Dunbar-Nelson's own literary and
political work was well known before she ever met Dunbar. Her first
book, *Violets and Other Tales* (1895), published when she was only
twenty, had already garnered much critical attention. Many stories,
plays, novels, and essays followed, and her work became noted for its
exploration of racial issues, particularly as they pertained to Creole
culture, mulattoes, and the issues of "passing" and racial identity. *The
Goodness of St. Rocque and Other Stories* (1899) came out as a com-
panion volume to her husband's famous *Poems of Cabin and Field* and
yet reaped much attention in its own right as a major contribution to
the short-story tradition, especially that of African American women
writers.

After Paul Dunbar's death in 1906, Dunbar-Nelson taught high
school; pursued graduate studies at Cornell, Columbia, and the University of Pennsylvania; and tried academic writing (her article on Milton's
influence on Wordsworth was published in *Modern Language Notes* in
1909). With Robert J. Nelson she published the *Wilmington Advocate
Newspaper* from 1920 to 1922 and became increasingly involved in politics, heading the Delaware Crusaders for the Dyer Anti-Lynching Bill
(1922). Her work extended to women's clubs and feminist organizing,
and she became noted for her contributions to the suffrage movement
and education for African American girls. Serving as executive secretary of the American Inter-Racial Peace Committee from 1928 to 1931,
she traveled widely to lecture and to promote this Quaker committee,
raising national consciousness about civil injustice toward African
Americans, other race issues, and international relations.

With the Harlem Renaissance of the 1920s, Dunbar-Nelson's literary fame soared. She continued to write poetry, fiction, and social
commentary for *The Crisis, Opportunity,* the *Washington Eagle,* the
Pittsburgh Courier, and other leading periodicals of the early twentieth century. After her death in 1935, her work was largely forgotten,

but a recent revival of interest has caused much of it to be republished. Her diary has also been published and has received attention from historians and critics as a major contribution to lesbian studies. Her work is now included in all major anthologies of American literature.

Dunbar-Nelson was forty-nine years old when her essay on Delaware was published, and her status as a respected senior African American literary figure was likely recognized by *The Messenger,* which allocated more space to her lengthy two-part essay, on one of the country's smallest states than it did to any other article in the series. Her essay is laden with period details: the local NAACP chapters, for example, make certain that *The Birth of a Nation* and "pictures of like ilk" cannot be shown in Delaware. In another instance, she chronicles the painful passage of the School Code of 1917, which was proposed by Pierre duPont and once passed was credited with raising Delaware's ranking from thirty-seventh to seventh in national standards. And yet despite her eye for nuances and contradictions (her opening paragraph describes Delaware as "an absorbing topic" for whoever might be "interested in anomalies"), her analysis is significantly more conservative than that of many of her younger peers. "There are no extremes of poverty and wealth among the colored people, but all are comfortable and moderately well-to-do," she serenely states. She certainly deplores the fact that "restaurants and soda fountains . . . will not serve Negroes," but her assessments are fundamentally comparative, and she seems secure in her convictions that "there is no city in the country, no state in the Union where there is more complete amity between the races."

Dunbar-Nelson proudly chronicles both black and white achievements in her adopted state. Furthermore, she pays attention to the contributions made by women to Delaware, and not as just philanthropists of "club women," as they so often appear in other essays of the series. She hails Anna Jump Cannon, a white woman who was "the foremost woman astronomer in the country," and calls our attention to African American poet Phillis Wheatley's wartime residence in Wilmington. She even spends a whole paragraph discussing the contributions of Sally Shadd, an ex-slave who supposedly invented ice cream.

Unlike many of the illustrated essays, which featured photographs of businessmen, beautiful young girls, or society wives, Dunbar-Nelson provides cameos of five substantial women. Four of the five are educators and politically active, and the fifth, Eleanor Lee Murray, though listed simply as a "prominent social leader," has an expression suggesting that she was no idle socialite. The photographs reaffirm Dunbar-Nelson's argument that Delaware is a state of diverse achievement.

Dunbar-Nelson's depiction of the "Moors" of Delaware adds a layer to her analysis of racial difference. Supposedly descended from a shipwrecked Spaniard, under Delaware law the Moors were considered a separate race, neither, "white," nor "Negro," nor "immigrant." And although they were thus recognized by the legislature, they were socially and culturally segregated from the rest of Delaware, by prejudice and their own clannishness. This, Dunbar-Nelson suggests, may be a loss to the larger community. But their ability to defy easy racial categorization is also liberating, and allows them to be a self-determining group. That paradoxical combination, the defiance of and the acceptance of racial categories, as the Moors and Dunbar-Nelson's life and work attest, helps liberate human energies.

PART I

Delaware! The first state in the Union. Wilmington, which is one-half of Delaware, the first city of the first state. Delaware, little, but mighty. Delaware, next to the smallest state in the Union, but next to none in power. Delaware, one of the richest states in the Union, in proportion, and yet one of the poorest. Delaware, the home of the charter mill, and the whipping post, and yet the home of Methodism and blue laws. Delaware, which never ratified the civil war amendments to the constitution, but which sent the largest quota of soldiers to defend the Union cause of any state in the Union, in proportion to its population. Delaware, which believed in slavery, but refused to import slaves within its borders, and punished slave running, which flourished extensively in its counties and was one of the largest stations of the Underground Railroad. Delaware, which fought to abolish slavery, yet which refused Lincoln's proposition to be paid for its slaves, and split itself in two on the question of the Missouri Compromise. Delaware, which was at one time a part of the colony of New Amsterdam, or New York, at one time a part of Pennsylvania, and once almost a part of Maryland, and yet the first state in the Union to ratify the Constitution, and upon whose vote depended the ratification of the Declaration of Independence. DELAWARE! Surely an absorbing topic, an interesting and ever-vital subject, for the student, whether he be a historian, interest in anomalies, or a politician, interested in early statesmanship, or later political corruption.

There is not much of Delaware, geographically. Its extreme length is 96 miles, and it is 35 miles at its widest part, and 9 miles at its narrowest. It boasts 2,120 square miles and 1,356,800 acres. Wilmington, at the upper part of the state, is on the direct main line between the north and the south, halfway between Washington and New York. A splendid point of departure. Delaware, like Gaul, is divided into three parts, counties, if you will, or, as the wits have it, two counties at high tide, and three at low tide, and it is the only state in the Union which boasts a lovely curve for a boundary line. In laying out the boundaries, in an attempt to settle the riparian dispute between New Jersey and Delaware, the surveyor's compass slipped, with the result that the upper boundary of the little state is the arc of a circle, pushing up into Pennsylvania, changing the geography of New Castle county, and making an awkward little triangular patch of land upon which Delaware, Maryland and Pennsylvania encroach, giving rise to a dispute which took over a hundred years to settle. The people in that triangular patch were never sure whether they were Pennsylvanians, Marylanders, or Delawareans. It is part of a peninsula, formed by the Chesapeake and Delaware Bays and the ocean.

The Delaware River widens out here, and forms the Delaware Bay, and the state is partly bounded on the east by the bay, and partly by the Atlantic Ocean. Cape Henlopen's "jewelled finger, flashing out across the brine," winks howdy to the lighthouse at Cape May, just across they bay, and some day there will be a ferry between Cape May and Lewes, at Henlopen light. Not immediately; it has only been talked of for half a century, and it has only been since 1631 that Lewes was first settled by De Vries. Sussex County moves slowly with great projects. For the rest of the state, Pennsylvania and Maryland take care of the boundaries, and New Jersey, a stone's throw across the river and the bay—a fine place for the duPont powder mills, and chemical works, which have overflowed the limits of the state. The Mason and Dixon line cuts directly through the state—another unique feature—about five miles south of Wilmington, and the quaint stones marking the surveyor's work are carefully tended and protected from wind and weather. And there, in the geography of the state, you have its history, politics and sociological story, partly northern, partly southern, always individualistic.

As to its history, Delaware is rich in traditions and shrines. Settled, first by the Dutch, then by the Swedes, then part of old Peter Stuyvesant's demesne, then part of William Penn's domain, called "the three lower counties on the Delaware," named after Lord De La Warr, Sir Thomas West. Old Swedes' Episcopal Church, founded in 1699, is the oldest church in America in continuous use. Delaware was a strategic point in the Revolutionary War, and Washington and Lafayette passed many an anxious moment within its borders. The famed Caesar Rodney, whose ride, in point of far-reaching effects upon the nation, and dramatic climax, far exceeded the much-advertised ride of Paul Revere, made his famous journey of nearly 24 consecutive hours, in a blistering July heat, from Lewes, by way of Dover and Wilmington, to reach Independence Hall in Philadelphia, July 4, 1776, in order to cast the deciding vote on the Declaration of Independence, and thus save that document from oblivion. The first time the American flag was carried in battle was at the battle of Cooch's Bridge, September 3, 1777. Delaware, in the war of 1812, gave MacDonough, of naval fame, and it was in this war also that the duPont powder company sprung into prominence for its mighty shipments by way of the covered wagons to Lake Erie.

The duPont powder company, founded in 1802, by the sons of that Huguenot refugee, the friend of Hamilton and Jefferson, who had so large a part in framing the financial policy of the new nation, has not ceased to play a decisive part in the wars, finances, and politics of the nation. From 1812 to the last war, it has led a more or less exciting existence. The company was threatened by the Maryland Confederate troops, and mysterious explosions in all its works, both in the state and across the river, were frequent from 1914 to 1918. So prominent a part does the name duPont play in the story of the state, that Delaware has been referred to in high quarters as "the ward of a feudal family"—there being something like two hundred duPonts, of various clans. It is one of the remaining nine states which keeps the old English chancellorship, which same chancellorship, by the way, got some of that same feudal family into serious political trouble some few years ago.

Delaware is not only the home of the duPonts, many of whom have achieved national fame in history, science and politics; but of the Bancrofts, those famous Quakers, connected with John Bright, and no less stern in their abolitionist efforts; of Thomas Garrett, of Underground Railroad fame; of the Bayards, who hold a lien on statesmanship; the elder Bayard, descendant of the French chevalier, *"sans peur et sans reproche"*—ambassador, senator, secretary of state; of John M. Clayton, of the Clayton-Bulwer treaty fame; of Andrew Gray; and John Bassett Moore. Delaware was also the resting place of "Gas" Addicks, whose name was a symbol for political corruption, and whose efforts to ride into the United States senate through bribery kept the little state from March, 1905, to May, 1906, with only one Senator in Congress. Delaware is the home of the foremost woman astronomer in the country, Anna Jump Cannon, and also the birthplace of one of the most famous and beloved of American artists, Howard Pyle.

For the rest of it, the soil is so fertile that there are almost two crops a year; the climate so diversified that strawberries are to be picked in November in Sussex County, while skating is to be had in New Castle County; the people are most modern and most conservative, and while the Ku Klux Klan flourisheth mightily, the Negro holds the balance of power politically and has seen to it that Delaware was one of the first and one of the few states to forbid the showing of the "Birth of a Nation" or any such hate-stirring picture.

Delaware produces most of the leather which is made into the shoes which you and the rest of the nation wears, and invented vici, or glazed kid. All the pyralin products and fabrikoid products, of which the number is uncountable, were invented in Delaware, as well as smokeless powder, and most of the other death-dealing explosives. Once upon a time Delaware made matches for the whole world, and the "cracking match," or the match which makes a noise when struck, was invented in Wilmington with other perfections in matchmaking.

Your trolley cars are largely made in Wilmington, and your boats and ships, your iron bridges and—well, to enumerate the inventions and productions of the little state were tiresome. Suffice it to say, it is in reality the "diamond state," and Wilmington, from its setting on seven hills, the high facet, which catches the light of an approving nation.

As for the Negro in Delaware, he believes in his diamond state, and loves it, prospers when it prospers, sorrows when it is sad, and is loyal to a degree that is fine, if at times irritating. The Brandywine River, which flows through Pennsylvania, down through New Castle County, and into the Christiana at Wilmington, may be responsible for this. During Revolutionary times a British vessel with an anti-Volstead cargo was wrecked and sunk at the mouth of this river, hence its name. One who walks along the picturesque banks of this river, or drinks of its limpid water, can never leave Delaware, so the legend goes.

Just when the Negro first came to Delaware is a fact shrouded in mystery. There is no record of slave ships touching anywhere on its shores, but the proximity of the state of Maryland makes it possible that Negroes from Maryland filtered in across the border. Delaware is a part of the "eastern sho," by the way, and lays claim to Frederick Douglass. The Delmarva peninsula feels itself almost a separate state, and the Negroes of the peninsula are closely akin.

Although the slave system was in vogue from the beginning of the colony, it did not receive legal recognition until 1721, when there was passed an act providing for the trial of slaves by two justices and six freeholders. Delaware was influenced a great deal in her views by Pennsylvania, where slavery was generally opposed, though tolerated. In 1776 she attempted to stop the slave trade by constitutional enactment. This article of Delaware's was the first such in any state constitution. It was about this time, so says tradition, when refugees were fleeing from Boston, that Phillis Wheatley, with her newly wedded husband, Peters, fled to Wilmington, and for three years led a rather forlorn existence, returning to Boston after its evacuation by the British troops.

There was an Abolition Society in Wilmington as early as 1777, and in 1801 a school was established for the education of "the Blacks and people of color," taught on the first day of the week, by one of the members of the society, who instructed the pupils gratis in reading and writing and arithmetic. About twenty pupils began in this school, and by 1816, enough progress had been made to have a Negro teacher, capable of keeping the school up to the standard. A library had been added to the school by this time, and another academy for colored girls established, taught by Quaker women, who specialized in domestic arts for young colored girls.

In 1820 a Democratic statesman, one Caesar Rodney, not the one of the famous ride, but a younger relative, announced himself in the General Assembly of the state against slavery, and was successful in having resolutions adopted condemning the practice. The reactionary attitude of the whole country towards the black men, caused by Nat Turner's Insurrection, found expression in Delaware, however, for in 1831, the state passed a law

UPPER LEFT: Mrs. Cora M. Aiken, well-known educator, Wilmington, Del. UPPER RIGHT: Mrs. Emma Gibson Sykes, prominent socially and politically, Wilmington, Del. CENTER: Mrs. Sadie B. Waters, Bridgeville, Del., prominent educator. LOWER LEFT: Miss Edwina B. Kruse, Principal Emeritus of Howard High School of Wilmington, Del., great educator of Negro youth. LOWER RIGHT: Mrs. Eleanor Lee Murray, prominent social leader, Wilmington, Del.

limiting the franchise to white men, forbidding the use of firearms by free Negroes, and forbidding any more to come within the state. An act also provided that no congregation or meeting of free Negroes or mulattoes of more than twelve persons should be held later than twelve o'clock at night, except under the direction of three respectable white persons, who were to attend the meeting. It further provided that no free Negro should attempt to call a meeting for religious worship, to exhort or preach, unless he was authorized to do so by a judge or justice of the peace, upon the recommendation of five respectable and judicious citizens. It was not until 1863 that the General Assembly finally passed a positive measure to prevent the assemblages of colored persons for instruction and all other meetings, except for religious worship and the burial of the dead.

In 1850 we find that the free colored population of Delaware was 18,073, of which number 187 were in school. By 1860 the number had increased to 19,829, with only 250 in school. Yet that schooling seems to have been effective, for we find Mary Ann Shadd, of Delaware, who had gone to Canada, teaching and maintaining a splendid school there at Sandwich.

Lincoln University, first called Ashmun Institute, established in 1856 near Oxford, in Pennsylvania, just over the Delaware state border, owed its existence to the recommendation of the Presbytery of New Castle County, whose limits extended up into Pennsylvania, for that body decided to establish within its limits an institution for the "scientific, classical and theological education of the colored youth and the male sex."

At the outbreak of the Revolutionary War there were listed 8,887 slaves. This number had decreased, by manumission, at the beginning of the Civil War to 1861. No less an authority than Williams tells us that 2,317 of these slaves were enlisted in the Revolutionary War, and of that number 376 were in the militia. Certainly the Civil War found its quota of enlisted men who fought for the freedom of their brethren. No separate Delaware regiment is noted, but Maryland and Pennsylvania, and even the far off 54th and 55th Massachusetts, recruited their numbers for the little state, from the northern boundaries of New Castle County, to Laurel and Milton and Rehoboth, down in the ocean-washed Sussex land.

The Underground Railway flourished in Delaware, side by side with the most infamous slave running syndicate in the country, headed by Patty Cannon, of nefarious memory, who has been immortalized in Gail Hamilton's novel, "The Entailed Hat." Slaves passing through on their way to freedom, slaves slipping over the Maryland border, from the Chesapeake, only a few miles away; freedmen, traveling through the state on legitimate business; freedmen going about their own affairs from one part of the state to another, all were grist to Patty Cannon's mill. Frederick Douglass tells us, in his autobiography, that he did not breathe freely until he had passed through Delaware when making his famous dash for freedom. Patty Cannon was eventually condemned to death for an unusually brutal murder, but somehow escaped the gallows, wherefore sentiment will not allow Delaware to hand another woman, no matter what her crime. The latest murder in the state by a colored woman carried with it only imprisonment for life as its penalty.

The nefarious projects of Patty Cannon were offset by the wonderful work of Thomas Garrett, one of the most successful agents of the Underground Railway. He assisted nearly 3,000 slaves to escape. Finally he was convicted and fined so heavily that he lost all his property. When the auctioneer had knocked off his last piece of property to pay the fine, he said: "I hope you will never be guilty of doing the like again." Garrett, although penniless at the age of sixty, replied: "Friend, I have not a dollar in the world, but if thee knows a fugitive who needs a breakfast send him to me."

It is interesting to note that the Edgemoor Iron Works, which turns out some of the most famous iron construction in the country, was until very recently managed by Thomas Garrett's daughter, "the iron woman with the tender heart," her friends called her, in token of her many philanthropies.

The A.M.E. Church "points with pride" to Delaware as its home. Richard Allen, its founder, though born in Philadelphia, was reared and educated, albeit a slave, in Dover, Delaware, and it was he, with Absolom Jones, another Delawarean, born in Sussex County, who in 1794 started the Independent Free African Society, in Philadelphia, which eventually split into two factions, the one faction, headed by Allen, being the present A.M.E. Church, and the other, headed by Absolom Jones, who was made a regularly ordained Negro Episcopal clergyman, and began the now famous St. Thomas Episcopal Church, in Philadelphia, the first of such denominations among Negroes in the country.

Not content with these two religious pioneers, Delaware offers another founder of a church—Peter Spencer, of beloved fame, who founded the Union African Methodist Episcopal Church, in Wilmington, in 1813. Its branch churches are all over the United States, particularly the East, and Canada. We find these pioneers holding an annual conference in Philadelphia, as early as 1830, a year before the Nat Turner Insurrection. In the first Conference Delaware was represented not only by its clergyman, but a layman of the classic name of Shadd—Abraham D.—doubtless one of the descendants of that Shadd of the historic Chadd's Ford of Revolutionary fame.

Delaware Negroes are as famed in legend as in history. In Skinner's Myths and Legends of Our Own Land the story is told of a huge black Negro who suddenly appeared, no one knew from where, at the Battle of the Brandywine, armed only with an immense scythe. The battle was going badly for the American troops until the appearance of the Black Sampson, as the soldiers hailed him, who nonchalantly went through the British lines, mowing down the redcoats as if they were so much wheat. His courage and daring saved the day. The redcoats fled before the black reaper, and the American soldiers "took the victory." Black Sampson of Brandywine has been immortalized in a poem by Dunbar, and to their credit, be it said, practically every colored child in Delaware old enough to read knows it by heart.

The other legend dear to the hearts of colored Delawareans has it that ice cream was invented by a colored woman, again of the historic name of Shadd. Aunt Sallie Shadd was a freed woman, who had been bought by her husband. Shortly after the Revolution was over she opened a little ice cream parlor, we would call it nowadays, on the corner of Ninth and French Streets, Wilmington, on the present site of the largest colored church in the city. Here in a unique place—a platform built up and around a huge tree—Aunt Sallie served a delicious confection the like of which had not been previously known. It became the fashion for the elegantes of the town, natives and visitors, to stroll down to Aunt Sallie's, particularly on warm summer Sunday evenings, and watch the white-sailed vessels on the broad Delaware, while they enjoyed her cooling dish.

The fame of Aunt Sallie's delicious dainty spread to Philadelphia, and, so the story goes, no less a person than the charming Dolly Madison, sojourning in the capital of the nation, Philadelphia, heard of Aunt Sallie's famous dish, came down to Wilmington to taste, to admire, and to obtain the recipe from the old woman. So, though Dolly Madison is hailed as the inventory of ice cream, colored Delawareans will tell you that she obtained the recipe from Aunt Sallie Shadd, the founder of that famous Shadd family, afterwards so distinguished in Washington and elsewhere.

PART II

We have noted the agitation for education of the Negro in Delaware as far back as 1801—a year before the famous duPont powder mills were established. In 1866 the "Delaware Association for the Moral Improvement and Education of the Colored People" was incorporated, and schools for the freedmen were started all over the state. The Association imported from Connecticut a young girl, Edwina B. Kruse, who went about establishing schools in the rural districts under the auspices of the society. In 1869 a school for colored children was founded at Twelfth and Orange Streets, Wilmington, and named after Gen. O. O. Howard, who was present at the laying of the cornerstone. The Howard School is still there, no longer a two-room primary school, but an accredited high school, whose graduates have received degrees from every big college in the East, and have gone forth everywhere to teach and to practice medicine. In a few years this same young girl, born in Porto Rico of German and West Indian parentage, and educated in Massachusetts and Hampton, became principal of the school and brought it up from its low estate to the solid, splendid high school that it now is. At the fiftieth anniversary of the school, December, 1919, she was still principal, and one of the visitors who came to rejoice at the occasion was the daughter of Gen. Howard, now married to Joseph Bancroft, of another famous Delaware abolitionist family.

In 1875 a law was passed to tax colored people for their own schools. This proved a hardship, for the colored people of the state, being largely dependent upon agriculture as a means of livelihood, were very poor. But in 1881 a measure passed the assembly granting aid to colored schools, and in 1897 the State College for Colored Students was founded at Dover, the capital of the state—a Morrill Land Grant School, presumably, agricultural. It is at present the only other high school for colored children in the state, and is beginning to take its place with the other institutions worth while in the East.

But while education for the Negro flourished in Wilmington, where the public schools have always been co-equal with the white schools in equipment, expense, salaries of teachers and supervision, the condition of the rural schools, up to a few years ago, was pitiful in the extreme. State taxes went only a part of the way toward meeting the expense of Negro education, for owing to the code of 1875, two-thirds of the expense of the upkeep of the schools was obtained from the taxes of the colored people, in the hands of a colored board of trustees in each respective district. The result was an aggregation of ill-kept shacks in the rural districts taught by poorly paid, and hence poorly equipped teachers, who each year had to eke out the school term—raise it from six or seven months to eight, by rallies, entertainments, and other money-raising schemes.

When Pierre S. duPont came forward in 1917 with a proposition to raise Delaware's educational standard and bring her up from the thirty-seventh place in the educational roster of the states he was bitterly opposed by the farmers, who saw in his scheme an infringement of their ancient and honorable rights of working children on the farm; by the canning factories, of which there are legion, who foresaw in compulsory education a curtailment of the cheap child labor which has made the canning of tomatos and peas and crab meat profitable; by the illiterates, who forsaw a raise in taxes that would not benefit them directly; and by the demagogues, who raised the howl of white people being taxes to "educate niggers." Some few Negroes, over-persuaded by their white farmer neighbors, joined in the opposition, but the bulk of them saw in the proposed duPont gift to the state a chance for their own children to receive a decent education, and for their girls to have an opportunity to receive a living salary as teachers. The "School Code Fight" is classic. The local elections of 1918 and 1921 were fought out on this bitter point: should Delaware go on in her old way or have decent schools? Whether you were "for the school code" or against it split friendships of years. Pierre duPont proposed to give the state decent schools to the tune of four or five million dollars, without any string attached, and without asking for any reward, but he proposed so to amend and change the school law—the new code being the work of experts in law and education, working a year over its provisions—that the new buildings would be in the hands of the friends of education. The School Code finally prevailed in a modified way—even though a special session of the legislature had to be called to straighten things out—and the Negro was the beneficiary to the tune of a million and half, expended in schools, most modern and well equipped; a school year of 180 days, teachers among the best paid in the country, and a system that lifted Delaware from thirty-seventh to seventh place. Pierre duPont's gift to Negro education in Delaware is the greatest single gift by an individual to Negro education ever made in this country.

Pierre duPont is not to be confused, by the way, with his cousin, T. Coleman duPont, National Republican Committeeman from Delaware, hero of the so-called "Dirty Deal," by which a chancellorship was swapped for a senatorship, and rocked the state with Addick-like fumes. "T. C." does not mind, if it suits his purpose, benefiting politically by the votes of the Negroes, when they confuse the two duPonts and acclaim him, thinking that he is Pierre.

Delaware is probably the only state in the union where there is a separate and distinct race of colored people, other than the Negro. She rejoices in a race of people who call themselves Moors and are listed on the statute books as a separate race—a race of Moors. In some districts they have separate schools and churches, of the Methodist Episcopal persuasion, which are neither white nor colored. They claim descent from a Spanish Moor, who, according to tradition, was shipwrecked off the coast of Delaware at the mouth of the Indian River in Sussex County. This Moor married an Indian woman, so one legend goes, whose children in turn married Swedes. Another version has it that the Moor married an English woman and their children intermarried with Indians, and Swedes, and Negroes, the latter to an infinitesimal degree. The descendants are to be found all over the state, but concentrated largely in two sections—Indian River, near Milton, in Sussex County, and Cheswold, near Dover, in Kent County. They are a very beautiful people, ranging in type from extreme blonds of the Scandinavian type to swarthy Moorish or Indian looking people. The frame is always heavy, sturdy and often extremely tall. They are thrifty people, farmers largely, not much bothered about higher education, but having hefty bank accounts, devoted to the Methodist Church, prolific of progeny, marrying early in their own families once removed, because they are extremely clannish. Strangers and folks not Moors are regarded with suspicion. Except for their thrift and modernity they are strongly suggestive of the mountaineers of Tennessee and Kentucky. Where they maintain separate schools, and the State Board of Education recognizes their right to have separate schools, and in their churches, they insist upon people of their own race, or colored people, who look generally like them, for teachers or preachers, and where they send their children to colored schools or attend colored churches their vote is always preponderatingly in favor of light-skinned leaders.

But the younger generation frequently moves away and intermarries with others, and spreads over the Atlantic Coast, particularly to Philadelphia, and you have the Durhams, the Stevens, the Bolivars, the Carneys and scores of other leading families of the Quaker City, whose family names form the larger part of the inscriptions on Delaware Moorish tombstones.

Wilmington is the only city north of Mason and Dixon's line where the ante-bellum custom of celebrating Big Quarterly obtains to the present time. In slavery days, when the harvest was over and the winter work not yet begun, it was the custom to allow the slaves to visit each other and attend all-day services on the last Sunday in August. It was a great occasion and was made the most of by the Union A.M.E. Church, founded, as we have noted, by the Rev. Peter Spencer. The first recorded Big Quarterly was held in 1815, and has continued with infrequent interruptions until the present year, flourishing when even all other meetings of Negroes were legally banned.

The colored people came from all over Delaware, from the contiguous "eastern sho'," and even from southern Pennsylvania, and that part of Virginia which is on the peninsula. Their costumes were pathetic attempts to dress for the occasion—castoff finery from mistress and master—plug hats, linsey woolsey, homespun, calicoes and cottons, rubbing elbows with silks and satins and velvets of an earlier date. They came in ox cart, in mule cart, in better horse-drawn vehicles, on foot, by boat or by stage. The business of life centered around the grove of the church, where all-day services of singing and shouting, preaching and praying, vied with earnest, consistent, persistent and continuous eating—eating from the myriad food stands lining the main road, now French Street.

Until a comparatively recent date this picture had not changed, save for the loss of the picturesque ox cart. Sometimes as many as 30,000 visitors congested in three blocks of the wide street which was the camping ground. The crowd still comes on the last Sunday in August, and the city, white and colored, makes preparations for its reception, but the visitors motor from Pennsylvania and Maryland and Virginia and lower Delaware. The picturesque garb of old has gone the way of the quaint ox cart, but the singing and shouting and vending of ballads and food still persists. Visitors come from all parts of the peninsula and from nearby cities, to become themselves objects of curiosity and amusement to the townsfolk. The thrifty Wilmingtonian, who is fortunate enough to live in the vicinity of French, Ninth, Eighth and Walnut Streets, profits hugely by this one day. The devout ones go in and out the grove of the church, to pray and sing, but the eating goes on continuously. Hundreds of gallons of ice cream and soft drinks and lemonade are consumed. Hundreds of chickens and hams and doggies and rolls and loaves of bread find their way down the throats of the devout. Peanuts and popcorn, watermelon and deviled crabs, fried chicken and chicken potpie are consumed by the wagon load, and stoves set up on the sidewalk or in the edge of the grove send up a homelike odor of cabbage and ham and coffee steaming hot in the sunlight. This, mind you, on a street which is part of the Lincoln highway, in the heart of a city, one block from the municipal building and the principal skycrapers, two blocks from the post office and a few squares from the Pennsylvania railroad station. The street is roped off by the city fathers, so that joy may reign all day undisturbed by motors passing through from Washington to New York.

The end of a perfect Big Quarterly finds the Street and Sewer Department sweeping up tons of refuse from a space of four or five blocks; an army of singers and exhorters and ballad venders, too hoarse to whisper; railroad trains, boats and trolleys, piled with humanity, leaving the scene, and the outgoing auto roads congested with all kinds of vehicles, from the humble flivver to the lordly Packard, while the denizens of the neighborhood sit down in a pile of soiled dishes, and overturned booths, and soiled napery, to count the pile of shekels the gods have thrown their way.

Delaware is a state of anomalies, of political and social contradictions. We have noted its strange attitude in the Civil War, fighting for the Union cause, and rejecting the 13th, 14th and 15th amendments. It was Delaware, by the way, which held up the ratification of the suffrage amendment until it seemed as if the whole cause would be lost—until Tennessee came to the rescue and was the needed thirty-sixth state before the year was out. There are few states where the relations between the races is more amicable, and the commonwealth still shudders with horror when it recalls its one lynching, for which it punished the inciter of the deed, a Presbyterian clergyman, who suggested the lynching in a fiery sermon, by expelling him from its borders. Yet the lines between the two dominant races are more or less tightly drawn. That is not to say that there are separate street or railway cars or waiting rooms. No such thought has ever entered the heads of either race, but restaurants and soda fountains, except in rare instances, will not serve Negroes, nor will theatres admit them, save in one or two instances, and then only to the gallery. On the other hand there is never a public movement of any sort that does not have on its committee the names of one or more Negro citizens of good standing, and colored men and women are always consulted in all matters of public interest. There is never a public meeting to which the Negro is not bidden, nor a public entertainment at which the Negro is not represented. The attitude of the newspapers is conservative, and they are amenable to suggestions from the Negroes, while welcoming their news items. There is a strong desire on the part of newspapers and public officials to keep the relations between the races pleasant and unstrained, and a conservative desire to avoid trouble of all sorts. The Delaware Negro, by the way, has the reputation of being a "bad actor" when he gets started. Whether this has anything to do with the conservative attitude of the white citizenry, deponent sayeth not.

There are in the city five colored public schools, with a total of about seventy colored teachers, one of the schools, mentioned above, being a junior and senior high school. In the state the colored teachers number over three hundred. With the exception of one physician in Dover, all the medical men are concentrated in Wilmington, where there are seven. Pharmacists in the city of Wilmington are three, and one in Dover, a woman, Mrs. Cecie P. Henry, wife of Dr. W. M. Henry. Dentists in the lower part of the state, there are none at present, though one or two have moved away. In Wilmington there are three. Wilmington is one of the few cities in the country which has, at the same time, a colored physician on the Board of Health, Dr. J. B. Stubbs; a colored man on the Board of Education, Dr. H. Clay Stevens; and a colored man in City council, Dr. John O. Hopkins; four colored men and four colored women on the State Republican Committee, and about ten or twelve colored men and women on the City Republican Committee.

BUT—Delaware is the only state in the Union where a colored man may not practice law. There is no law against it, merely custom and maneuver. "A Negro lawyer!" said old Benjamin Nields, of legal fame, "Why, that's *a gentlemen's* profession!"

Also, Delaware never calls a Negro to a jury, except to serve on a coroner's jury of a Federal jury.

This combination of no Negro lawyers and no Negro jurymen has resulted in the *nolle prosse* of a number of cases where shrewd Negro malefactors have threatened to import their own counsel or to stand by their constitutional rights of being tried by their own peers.

There are no Negro policemen in the city of Wilmington. Some constables there may be in the rural districts, but somehow even if a Negro passes the preliminary examination in the city he never stays qualified.

There are no Negro firemen in the city of Wilmington. There has never been an issue raised as to Negro firemen, but if it were it would doubtless be dismissed with scant ceremony.

Yet there is no city in the country, no state in the Union where there is more complete amity between the races, more apparent respect for the Negro by the white man, where the one will help the other more quickly; nor where there is such easy intercourse, such dual familiarity. Main street stuff obtains from the highest to the lowest.

The above disabilities, inequalities, rather—no Negro policemen, firemen, jurymen, lawyers, and segregation in the only place where there is visible segregation, in the courts—make splendid campaign material when the Negro takes a notion to buck the Republican party and turn independent.

Of the 223,003 population, Negroes comprise 30,335, of which number nearly 11,000 are in Wilmington, where 110,000 of the total population lives. With a voting strength of approximately 13,000 in the state, it is easily seen that the Negro is the absolute political balance of power. The Republican party can never win an election without him, and the Democratic party can easily ride into power on his shoulders when he takes a notion to assert his independence.

An amusing instance of this was rubbed home in the elections of 1922, when because of the defection of the one congressman, Caleb Layton, on the Dyer Bill, the Negroes rose in their might and swept the Republican party out of power, returning a Democratic Senator, a Democratic Congressman to Washington, and electing a Democratic majority in the General Assembly. The original intention of the colored people was only to punish Layton by leaving him home, but the insistence of Republican leaders that the Negro did not know how to scratch the ticket so angered the Negroes that they did not scratch the ballot, but voted solidly Democratic—enough doing this to turn the state over to the Democratic party.

An amusing summing up of this situation was made by Mrs. Florence Bayard Hilles, national suffrage worker, daughter of Thomas F. Bayard and sister of the present Senator of that name. "The Democratic party," she said, "was afraid to give the colored woman the vote for fear of simply doubling the Republican vote, and the first time the party has been in power for a generation it was swept in by these same colored women, who rose in their righteous wrath against the traditions of their men."

As a recent writer in the *North American* said: "Delaware, as a state, is peculiar to itself. Because of its small area, and the population, the intimate knowledge the people of the state must have to those who aspire to high office, politics in Delaware are always intense, frequently dramatic and usually of nation-wide interest."

So the political situation lies in the hands of the Negro. Just now he is a sleeping giant, likely to awake, as he has awakened once or twice, and stretching his length, knock something over. He is a bit languorous—the climate is gentle, and the gardens and trees filled with luscious fruit, only for the plucking—so why work hard? Some interested colored newspaper man recently propounded the question, What is the trouble in Delaware? It amused the colored people who saw the query, for they were not aware that there was any trouble. Delaware believes in being conservative as long as there is no reason for being radical, but when an occasion arises and there is need for radicalism, house-cleaning, or what not, Delaware can rise and smite hard and effectively. Periodical political upheavals attest this in no uncertain manner.

Delawareans, colored as well as white, feel pride in the "first city of the first state," and delight in its history. They sing their state song, with its three stanzas, one for each county, with gusto and joy. They name their children after the famous statesmen, the Bancrofts and Bayards and duPonts and General Howard, and dare anyone to smile at the seeming incongruities. There are more colored churches in the city of Wilmington than in any other city its size in the country, and yet no one would accuse the city of being over-religious. It has a colored theatre, several large halls, two large colored club houses, occupying valuable property in the heart of the business section, and more fraternal organizations than churches. The social life divides itself into three distinct strata, which, however, mingle on the edges, until the sharpness of the dividing line is lost in a pleasant mist. The high school and the normal school—for there is also a colored normal school—graduate more children each year than are graduated from the Philadelphia schools, and the Negro Business League reports excellent advances in the marts of trade. There are no extremes of poverty and wealth among the colored people, but all are comfortable and moderately well-to-do. One of the largest real estate owners within the city limits is a colored man, Dr. Samuel G. Elbert. The Urban League, the Y.M.C.A., the Y.W.C.A. have never yet succeeded in making a headway in the state or city, perhaps because Delawareans are too conservative to welcome outside interference in what they deem family matters. Yet, the colored people, assisted by state appropriation, support a well-equipped and well-appointed Old Folks' Home, the Layton Home, and a splendid community center, the Thomas Garrett Settlement, which, founded by the City Federation of Colored Women, is being carried on a high plane by Mrs. J. B. Stubbs, with a fine building and an average annual ministration to about 8,000 persons. There is also a colored State Tuberculosis Sanitarium near the city of Wilmington, The N.A.A.C.P. has two live branches in Wilmington and in Dover, which are always on the alert, and see to it that "The

Birth of a Nation" and pictures of like ilk would always be banished from the state.

Another one of Delaware's anomalies was found in the fact that while a juvenile male delinquent was taken care of, when sentenced by the juvenile court, at the State Industrial School for Boys, where white and black alike were cared for, a juvenile female delinquent had to be sent out of the state, to Maryland or Pennsylvania, as the Industrial School for Girls, not being a state institution, would not admit a colored girl. When an alarming number of deaths from tuberculosis of these girls aroused the State Federation of Colored Women, they put on a drive, raised funds, bought a farm and buildings, opened up and conducted for two years a well-equipped institution for the wayward girls, to which the juvenile court promptly sent all offenders. In 1921, the farm, buildings, property, etc., amounting to about $10,000, were given to the state, it being the first time in the history of the state that the colored people had given it anything—on condition that the institution be supported by the state and the Board of Trustees appointed by the Governor be bi-racial, with the preponderance in favor of the colored people. At the last session of the legislature, that same Democratic majority, after whacking into bits every appropriation asked for by other state institutions, gave this Industrial School for Colored Girls not only all it asked for in maintenance and salaries, but an additional appropriation of $53,000 for new buildings and equipments. To this some philanthropist added an additional farm of 78 acres. Was that an evidence of gratitude on the part of that Democratic legislature for the political labors of the colored women who punished Caleb Layton?

Thus Delaware. A right little, tight little state of surprises, and inconsistencies, but like all inconsistencies, a jewel—and a jewel of a state she is, the veritable diamond center in the Atlantic seaboard circlet of states.

NEVAL H. THOMAS

The District of Columbia—
a Paradise of Paradoxes

VOL. 5, NO. 10, OCTOBER 1923

Neval H. Thomas spent twenty-nine years teaching high school history and also found time to conduct a considerable career in civic politics, to serve as a foreign correspondent to *The Washington American,* and to give public lectures based on his travels. He was born in Springfield, Ohio, on January 6, 1874, and he remained in the Midwest to attend Denison College in Granville, Ohio. Thomas later moved to Washington, D.C., and worked at the Library of Congress while he pursued his A.B. (1901) and his LL.B. (1904) at Howard University. An avid fan of *The Messenger,* he wrote a letter in 1921 (which the magazine printed) praising and endorsing the magazine and its enterprise.

Thomas was a major figure in the NAACP. He served as president of its Washington, D.C., branch and appeared before committees of the House of Representatives and Senate to speak on race issues and education. As the Washington, D.C., branch president, Thomas helped obtain a stadium for Dunbar High School, organize library training for all persons in the public library system, establish a new business high school "for colored boys and girls," and lobby for equal salaries for officers in both the black and the white segregated school system. While some of these may seem modest goals, they illustrate vividly the crucial day-to-day, local efforts of the NAACP—efforts that helped coalesce and define a communal identity and improve the economic and social opportunities of African Americans during the early years of the twentieth century. Thomas died at the age of fifty-six in 1930.

Since he is writing about the nation's capital, Thomas has more leeway to focus on national issues than the other contributors did. Presidents Washington, Jefferson, Adams, Madison, Jackson, Taft, Arthur, Garfield, Johnson, and Wilson all make an appearance in this essay, one mark of the breadth of reference and the economy with which Thomas covers ground. George Washington is Thomas's exhibit A of the paradoxes that define the capital city. Washington, so prescient in warning against future dangers to liberty and freedom in his farewell address, omitted any mention of slavery, considered by Thomas "the crowning infamy and most deadly social sin of the ages."

Skillful historical arguments run through this essay, as Thomas consistently draws upon historical documentation rather than facile polemics to make his points. In his analysis of how Washington City became the capital, he notes the convenient proximity of so many "land barons" and how, despite considerable expense, Virginia and Maryland were willing to transport officials from Philadelphia to D.C. To make this point Thomas invokes the actual travel expense accounts submitted by high government officials of the federal period. This sharp historical eye, coupled with a smooth prose style, ensures that documentation is fluently integrated into the piece, and that his vivid denunciations come across as fully supported, necessary responses to historical realities rather than as political posturings.

When Thomas rails against an unnamed African American who toadies to the reactionary white community, he is not simply griping. By refusing to call race traitors by name, he negates their value, their very being. As Henry Louis Gates, Jr., and others have shown, by "calling them out of their names," Thomas is turning the rhetoric of naming to his own ends, the opposite of the list of named achievement central to many of the other essays in the series. But Thomas, too, praises such achievement. He sketches a stirring portrait of Frederick Douglass, for instance, and praises Nicholas Franklin, Moses Liverpool, and George Bell, who bought themselves out of slavery and built a school. Thomas tries to fix the presence and names of these individuals in his readers' minds: "It is hard to estimate the influence of such a character," he writes, "upon the life of the people here, their racial pride, their sense of worthiness of the fullest citizenship, and the knowledge that the accident of color is too trivial to mention."

Here and elsewhere Thomas walks a fine line, spurning those "skin specialists who can determine every person's deserts, character and ability by the color of his skin" but insisting on a statistical entitlement based on race (the percentage of African American policemen and firemen should equal their percentage in the general population) and insisting on race pride at the same time that he asserts that "color is the least difference among men, in fact no difference at all." Thomas was too fine a rhetorician to have not noticed such paradoxes, and too fully a social tactician to have worried about them. Like some modern theorists, Thomas is much more interested in race as a rhetorical strategy than as a biological reality. Equality is clearly his goal, and race distinctions and the eliminations of racial difference are both valuable insofar as they might be deployed to advance that goal.

MR. THOMAS

"A paradise of paradoxes," is the description given to the District of Columbia by a New England traveler when visiting here some sixty-five years ago. This phrase would accurately describe it at any time of its history, from its very foundation in 1800 to this very hour, for the leading men who conceived the plan of locating the capital of the nation here and were the controlling forces for sixty years were slaveholders, and today with the Fourteenth and Fifteenth Amendments easily enforceable in this Federal territory, the great colored population with thousands of them among the most useful citizenry are only half free. The great leader after whom our beautiful city is named lived, grew rich and died a slaveholder. He could "wish for some means of abolishing slavery," yet he could become the lone millionaire of his day from slave labor, send the manly Negro Tom to a worse slavery in the West Indies in exchange for rum and "the residue in good spirits," and as the Father of his country could leave a Farewell Address warning the coming generation against "entangling alliances" and minor dangers without a word against slavery, the crowning infamy and most deadly social sin of the ages.

It was in the administration of Washington that the location of the capital was ordered here. The slave power was entrenched in the seats of power. The location of the capital near the estates of the great land barons would greatly enhance their holdings and help to keep the control of the central government in their hands. So valuable is the proximity of a capital to any community that there was the bitterest fight, and most important compromises made to secure the prize in Virginia and Maryland, and these two states gave from their public treasuries large sums of money for the erection of some of the public buildings, and the slave power had to agree to let Philadelphia have the capital there for nine years before removing it here in May and June, 1800. It is interesting to read the expense accounts of the *high* officials for their trips from Philadelphia here, a distance of 136 miles, ranging from $338 to $729. John Adams came with his slaveholding secretary of state, the learned John Marshall of Virginia. He could fill the judiciary with judges from the dying Federalists, naming Marshall for the Chief-Justiceship of the Supreme Court which he held ably for thirty-five years, and could even spend his last night in the White House signing commissions for his "midnight judges," and then leave the city the next day without even speaking to his successor, Thomas Jefferson.

Jefferson was the first president inaugurated here, and, in accordance with his preachments, with democratic simplicity. A champion of democracy and admirer of the black astronomer Benjamin Banneker, he could acquire his splendid culture and vast learning from the leisure that his slaves afforded him. He could pen the Declaration of Independence with its gospel of human freedom and equality, yet he could write when heavily in debt, "I am loath to part with any of my lands, but I *will* not part with any of my slaves, for out of their labor I can pay my debts." With his administration and with many succeeding ones the hated institution of slavery flourished. Within four years slaves made up one-fifth of the population. The White House, some members of the Supreme Court, many members of both houses of Congress, and many of the leading society people secured their menial service absolutely free from slave labor. The leading authority on the private life of President Madison is Paul Jennings, his Negro slave, who has left his *Reminiscences of Madison,* in which he draws a vivid picture of his master, and the story of the flight of the presidential family from the White House when it was burned by the British in the War of 1812. In several sections of the city there was an auction block where many a poor slave mother suffered the terrors of heart by seeing her beautiful daughter sold away to brutal slavers to be shipped to the far South. The District of Columbia is Federal territory, governed not by ballots of citizens, but by the national Congress, yet the cursed slave trade flourished for fifty years, and slavery for sixty-two, before Congress had the moral courage to assert its power to abolish them. No wonder our capital seemed "A Paradise of Paradoxes." The celebrated historian John Bach McMaster, in his "Political Depravity of the Fathers," says of the Revolutionary Fathers, "in stealing a governorship, gerrymandering a district, giving patronage to whom patronage was due, in all the tricks and *frauds* which go to make up the worst of our politics, they were easily our masters." Madison, like Washington and Jefferson, and others whose lofty preachments are directly opposed to their practices, "could wish" that slavery could be abolished, yet when he was in Philadelphia and his Negro slave boy Billy had run away, he could write to his father in Virginia telling him that "I am not going to whip Billy for seeking the same divine thing I have, yet I am not going to return him to you, as he will teach the other slaves to seek their liberty. Instead I shall hire him out here for seven years." The laws of Pennsylvania allowed no more. President Jackson was forced to give the Negro soldiers the credit for the victory of New Orleans in the War of 1812, yet as a slave-holding president years afterwards he welcomed the closing of the government mails to abolitionist literature which was seeking to give these poor blacks the liberty he said the war was fought for.

Save a few years of the Reconstruction, the national capital has been to the Negro a scene of sorrow. Even at this very hour the ghost of the slave power is stalking about seeking to perpetuate the aged master-and-slave scheme of society. The more cultured and ambitious the Negro, the greater is the delight in humiliating him, and in forestalling his progress, and since the World War for democracy the greater is that determination. There is not a theatre, restaurant, or other place of public accommodation where a colored man or woman can go, and even in the government restaurants segregation or exclusion is attempted while equality in the civil service, a reasonable number of Federal appointments, and a decent respect for manly complaint against social wrongs are unthinkable. We are excluded from public bathing beaches, the many recreational parks where the unworthiest white man is welcomed cheerfully, and a high governmental official, a pious North Carolina churchman, celebrated the glorious Resurrection Morn by placing segregation signs in the largest of our parks. Every one of us from the cradle to the grave is the victim of these American skin specialists who can determine every person's deserts, character and ability by the color of his skin. The glorious war for democracy, in which the draft boards took 43% of the conscripts from this District from the colored race when we were but 29% of the population, gave us a race riot and the Ku Klux Klan. Yet we must hear eloquent speeches on democracy in a capital where we are half a slave.

Prof. W. D. Nixon of the Dunbar High School, a constant contender for the rights of Negroes, has compiled statistics showing the shortages we suffer in every branch of our municipal service. His investigation discloses that we have but 36 colored policemen when our population entitles us to 320, entailing an annual loss of $440,000; that we have but 17 firemen out of a total of 663, or 2.6%, when our population is nearly one-third of the total for the city, a discrimination by which we lose over $350,000 per year. In our city library there is not a single colored employee, and the librarian, a native of Rochester, New York, told me plainly in reply to one of my protests that he would employ no colored person there save in the capacity of a charwoman, though every one of us is taxed 35 cents per year for the support of this institution. On the rent commission there is not a single colored representative, in spite of the fact that colored people are the chief victims of extortionate rents, while the Chamber of Commerce, Board of Trade, City Club, Board of Charities, and the so-called "white" universities would not even dream of admitting the best Negro who ever lived in this, our democratic capital.

Even Howard University, the great institution dedicated to the education of Negro youth, must have a white minister, instead of a great Negro educator, as its president; costing us $11,000 per year, when Charles W. Elliot, the Dean of American educators and the directive head of 500 professors and instructors, 10,000 students, and 50 millions of educational equipment received no more. This huge overhead expense is out of all harmony with the ridiculous under-pay of the teaching staff, who, with the alumni, containing many men and women of eminent achievement, and the student bodies struggling against huge handicaps to a place in the world, have given the University her high distinction among the great seats of learning in the land. Like several of his predecessors, he knows little of dealing with black men in high professional calling, and has little consideration for the ablest Negro members of the faculty who have done most to give Howard her fair reputation, but who dare to have a mind of their own.

He has even demanded the removal of his colored superiors from the trustee board, because, as an alumnus of 45 years, and an overseer for a decade, this man desires to discharge his trust. He has hired a convenient Negro at $4,000 per year and expenses to go over the country to offset the fight of the great body of the alumni for a place in the administration of their Alma Mater, and this Negro had the effrontery to rise in his church and say that Christ had called him to this princely salary, hence he must leave the ministry. More and more, the same opinion is growing that a black man or a black woman should head this, the finest experiment in education of its kind, for colored people know too well the marvelous success of Negro men and women in founding and administering important institutions of learning. On the board of education alone do we get a square deal, the judges of the Supreme Court of the District appointing three colored members out of a total of nine; but their estimates must pass through two other authorities before reaching congress; hence, in by far the majority of years, we fail to get our share of the school fund. During the entire Wilson administration the municipal fathers, young newspaper correspondents without executive experience, would recommend to congress that the colored schools have but 10 per cent of the appropriations for buildings and grounds when we were then 31 per cent of the school enrollment. It has reached as low as 7 per cent. We are supposed not to complain, and the white spirit of the community calls us "radical" and even "crazy" when we call attention to this fundamental injustice to the future citizens of the nation. The white academic high schools have spacious recreation grounds, equipped with magnificent stadiums, tennis courts, fountains and running tracks, while ours has a slum and a noisy stone yard within sixty feet of the building, allowing no play space at all. The whites have three such schools in different sections of the city within walking distance to the white population, while we have the one to which ALL pupils of color must come with considerable expense of street car fare. Thus, our colored parents suffer the double handicap of lower income and higher educational costs. Again, out of 56 superior salaries in the high schools, the whites have 54 and the colored 2. The colored teachers are restive under this discrepancy, as they claim that since so many economic opportunities are open to whites, not one whit better prepared than colored, that are closed to us, there would naturally follow a better selection among the colored teachers. The presence of more students in the colored normal school than the white, though the white normal school must feed more than twice the number of teacherships than the colored normal school must supply, is cited in support of their claim of finer selection.

In spite of a century of wrong and suffering here, though he has proved his capacity for the highest duties of a citizen by aspiration and achievement, the Negro is still determined to overcome his all but insurmountable obstacles. He glories in his history though the reward for useful living and contributions to the capital's greatness are denied him. He was here even before a stone was laid, for it was the great black mathematician Benjamin Banneker, who, with L'Enfant and Ellicot, surveyed the howling wilderness out of which this beautiful city was born. His labor created much of its wealth, in slavery and during our partial freedom. He has been identified with that fundamental thing in democracy, popular education, for 117 years. It was then that three colored men purchased their freedom and built a school house for the education of Negro children. The brilliant Jefferson was in the White House, but these three unlettered Negroes, George Bell, Nicholas Franklin, and Moses Liverpool, laid the only foundation upon which a nation must rest her greatness. In 1836 John F. Cook founded a church and school combined to do the work the state should have done, and in the long history of the Negro's heroic struggle for knowledge, and better things for his children, in this city there are many names of extraordinary personalities who must take high rank in the educational history of the nation. We have hundreds of men in the professions (many in the front rank), a growing number in large business enterprises, prosperous banks, insurance companies, newspaper and printing establishments, theatres, real estate, drug stores, etc., a large cultured and intellectual class, and a great mass of laboring people, the bone and sinew of any state, whose long hours of labor at meager wages are given gladly to prepare their children for fields of higher endeavor. It is from them that every uplifting movement must receive its chief support; they have but one ambition—the betterment of family, race, and state. We have over 150 churches, many of them pastored by ministers of piety and vision, who understand social problems and preach the gospel of practical human service. Our people are grouped in numbers of organizations and clubs, some for social service, others for self-improvement, like book-lovers' clubs; and in beneficial societies. We have many forward-looking men and women who study the world movements from such able and progressive magazines as THE MESSENGER, *The Nation, The New Republic,* and *The Liberator,* and at the Bethel Literary society we hear messages from every thinking group in the world. Washington's social life is the most cultured in the country. To attend any social function is to see a marvel in self-culture, for we see women of various colors, without social contact outside the race, the equal in physical beauty, refinement of conduct, grace in manner and dress, and exquisite social charm of the highest bred Anglo-Saxon woman anywhere in the world. The white man keeps the full weight of his superior numbers, oppressive spirit, and unjust monopoly of political power, hard pressed against this suffering, yet beautiful little world of striving, but we grow to fuller stature in spite of it all. Though he closes such splendid educational agencies as the opera, and such refining experiences as the exercise of civil privileges, to this struggling people, we acquire culture, not *through* segregation and oppression, but *in spite* of them.

We glory in the Reconstruction days, in their opportunity for the Negro to prove his capacity for statesmanship, and in the cultural equality he showed by the side of the ablest statesmanship and finest white culture the nation has known. The names of Revells, Bruce, Pinchback, Bassett, Langston, Elliot, Lynch, Garnet, and, greatest of all, Frederick Douglass. James G. Blaine, one of the ablest men the nation has produced, says in his authoritative work "Twenty Years in Congress" that "the colored men were students of public questions, able in debate, and, in fact, would have done honor to any race in any generation." They were men of the highest sense of responsibility to their constituency. They walked among men offering no apology for existence; with head erect but not with chest out; knowing that color is the least of difference among men, in fact no difference at all; entering public places at will, since such privileges should be as free as the sunshine; rose to forgiveness of the unmeasured sins of the Rebel South in supporting the Amnesty legislation; and stressing the enactment of human-rights laws whose enforcement redounds to the good of white and black alike. They knew that it was as fitting that black men hold office as it was for white, that the exclusion of one establishes the old ante-bellum master-and-slave relationship which brought on the war and which the war destroyed; hence, we have Hiram Revells taking the very seat in the Senate which Jefferson Davis abandoned when he put out to destroy the Union, and the black man filled it with greater honor; Blanche K. Bruce entering in 1875, with the Chesterfieldian Conkling offering his arm as escort to the bar of the Senate; P.E.S. Pinchback, fresh from the governorship of a sovereign state, with credentials for the Senatorship, with Bruce delivering an eloquent eulogy, in chaste speech for his admission; Elliot, Rainey, Menard, Lynch, and many others entering unchallenged their seats in the House. The men fought vigorously the first great set-back we have suffered in the "house of our friends," the withdrawal of the troops from the South whose presence was required there by the Constitution of the United States, the enlightened Force Bill, and the unreconstructed Rebels who make a mockery of democratic institutions. What a difference between representation by these able statesmen and misrepresentation by an ignorant political trickster who told Senators in the last congress not to pass the Dyer Anti-Lynching Bill, which was to protect his little children and his suffering race from burning at the stake. What a difference between them and the selfish patronage hunters who endorse such sentiments as, "The Southern white man is the Negroes' best friend," "Every Southern Constitution has placed a premium upon thrift and intelligence" (even the Grandfather Clause, which was so odious that a Southern Supreme Court ruled it unconstitutional). "It is not for the Negro to fight the Jim Crow car, but to see to it that it is a man and not a beast riding in the car." "Colored people can't have nervous prostration; hence, it is for the doctor to study, not nerves, but old hard chills and fevers" (a fine preparation for service to our wounded boys at the Jim Crow hospital at Tuskegee); reflections upon the higher education of Negro women which unfit them for their surroundings (Southern), and the ridiculing of the poor black boy, whose soul was fired like that of Lincoln and Douglass, for puzzling over a French book at his backwoods cabin door. The most reactionary element of whites stand unanimously behind a local Negro, and cite him to us at every protest we make as a model colored citizen, because he is ever ready in their service. He opposed the exodus, asked that a certain colored member of the board of education be not reappointed because that member kept raising the race issue on the board, fought the sending of colored men to the peace conference at Versailles, said that when colored servants and their white mistresses fall out the servant is in the wrong, and has refused to fight a single wrong during his long life here. He openly boasts that he gets his influence from white people and cares nothing about the opinion of Negroes. When he had his house wired with electricity he refused to let colored workmen even bid on the contract, though we have two of the best firms of electricians in the city, and gave it to an inferior white firm. When the Capital Savings Bank failed, with him as the responsible officer, carrying down the life savings of poor washerwomen, he hired an inferior white lawyer to defend him, while giving *cheers* to the colored profession. Whenever he is attacked in THE MESSENGER and other publications he buys copies and sends them to the white element who recognize him as our leader, telling them how much we are making him suffer in their service. He is solid with them, and no amount of protest can dislodge him from their consideration. The highest conception of leadership some of these *mis*representatives of our race have is dodging racial issues, getting along with our white enemies, manipulating delegates at national conventions, begging and dispensing insignificant patronage, paying the press to publish their pictures, and sitting on the platform at public meetings. President Taft said that he showed his inaugural address to three colored leaders before delivery, and they all endorsed it, yet that it is the message that removed all Negro officers from the South, and proclaimed to the world that the Negro is at the complete mercy of the white man, a second Dred Scott Decision pure and simple. We long for the return of the Negro to the halls of congress where he belongs, and we look to the great industrial centers of the North, increased in voting strength by this happy and historic exodus, to send him here. With this coming will mean the merit system in the civil service, West Point and Annapolis, and high offices from the White House. It has been said that "the destiny of nations is decided over the tea table." Nothing is truer, for over the official tea table and in the secret official chamber policies of government and parties are determined; so the Negro if he is to come into his own must work for his restoration to the high councils of the nation.

It would take pages to paint the whole picture of the Reconstruction days, the America of our dreams. Grant and his brilliant secretary of state, Hamilton Fish, sent Ebenezer Bassett as minister to Egypt, thus opening up the diplomatic service to the race. Mr. Bassett's delicate tact and discriminating consideration for the interests of his country and for his race in Hayti won for him the highest encomiums from no less an authority than Hamilton Fish, and lasting respect from the Haytians. They sent Milton

Turner to Liberia, and Negro consuls to both Spain and France. Black boys appeared on our streets in the uniforms of West Point and Annapolis, and Negro clerks in all of the departments of the government, where today they are of higher grade than their white co-workers. The leading hostelry of the city was the Wormley Hotel, which housed the most distinguished people in the country. The grandson of the founder and owner, Dr. C. Sumner Wormley, has many letters from such patrons as Charles Sumner expressing their high regard for the venerable James Wormley as a man of character and business ability. In the early seventies a prominent politician with his lieutenants paid his bill to Mr. Wormley with a cheque of $1,500, which afterwards was returned, "insufficient funds." Some big democratic politicians hearing of its existence offered to cash it in order to use it against the Republican party, then, *but not now,* the friend of the Negro. Mr. Wormley, ever loyal to his people, quickly replied, "That party has just freed my race and I would rather lose any amount of money than betray it." The cheque was never paid, and he secured the respect of both sides. On Lincoln's birthday, 1865, Henry Highland Garnet, orator, scholar and warrior of two continents for the slave, addressed the assembled House and Senate, and official and diplomatic society in the chamber of the House of Representatives, and they listened in deep admiration to his scholarly and eloquent sermon of the Thirteenth Amendment and the meaning of slavery and freedom. Compare this scene with 1922, when the time-serving Moton was chosen to speak at the dedication of the Lincoln Memorial, and rough marines were stationed in the audience to force colored people into the Jim Crow seats at the point of the bayonet.

Blanche K. Bruce came to the United States Senate a bachelor. Within two years he married Miss Josephine Wilson, a teacher in the public schools of Cleveland and noted for her beauty and culture. They toured the capitals of Europe on their honeymoon before the world was "made safe for democracy"; hence, our diplomatic representatives introduced them to the cultured circles of the continent. On one occasion they were passing through the Senators' dining room to a more private room when twenty-two stately Senators rose from their tables until Senator and Mrs. Blanche K. Bruce had passed. Senator James G. Blaine built a mansion at Twenty-second Street and Massachusetts Avenue, then the outskirts of the city. He wanted to make it a Senators' row to maintain the tone of the section and increase the values of property. He brought his carriage to the home of Senator and Mrs. Bruce, and conducted them to his section, where he urged them to build. Today when so many of our colored people are striving for better homes the powerful real estate ring presses upon courts, banks and brokers to throw obstacles in the way. The modern foolish psychology of the white man says that property values are destroyed by the advent of colored men. What a degeneracy! Let him think of Blaine and be cured! President Arthur invited Mrs. Bruce to stand in the receiving line at the White House on New Year's Day, 1882, with the ladies of the cabinet and other leaders of society, and Mrs. John A. Logan said years afterwards in the metropolitan press, "There was not a lady in line more beautiful in person, more elegantly gowned, more cultured in conduct, and more deserving of all of the social courtesies due the wife of a United States Senator than Mrs. Blanche K. Bruce." They named their only son, since distinguished in education, letters and racial service, after Roscoe Conkling, and this gallant knight ever ready to draw his fiery sword in defense of the downtrodden black man was proud to have a Negro boy named after him.

For forty years the Negro received inspiration by daily contact with one of the grandest figures of history, Frederick Douglass. The story of his rise, his conquest over incredible obstacles, and his immortal service during the most stirring periods of our national history has no parallel in the Arabian Nights Stories. He came among us after a miraculous escape from slavery, roaming over continents, appealing to the sympathies of the world, a self-taught giant who matched his intellectual powers and golden eloquence against the best the world held. From an ignorant slave he had become the associate of Garrison, Sumner, Phillips, Stowe, Tubman, and John Brown, while in the old world he was the intimate of Clarkson, Buxton, Cobden, and Ireland's peerless son, Daniel O'Connell. Governors of states had placed a price upon his devoted head, and presidents were asked to throw the entire weight of the government to silence his mighty voice that was destined to shake the continent. He labored at the White House with Lincoln for the admission of the Negro to the army, and then for his equal treatment with his white comrades. He waged a long war against the benighted reconstruction policy of President Johnson, and once checkmated him after an interesting interview by getting the front page of the American press for the speech the President refused him the opportunity to make in this interview the day before. He was in the thickest of the fight for the Thirteenth, Fourteenth, and Fifteenth Amendments, and on April 14, 1876, delivered the Negro's message to the world at the dedication of Lincoln's statue before President Grant, Congress, Supreme Court, and the rest of the highest officials and social circles in an oration that has passed into the oratorical classics of history. For four years he was United States Marshal with the duty of introducing all guests at the social gatherings at the White House, and at the inauguration of President Garfield he led the procession, beside the President, from the Senate Chamber to the east front of the capitol. It is hard to estimate of the influence of such a character upon the life of the people here, their racial pride, their sense of the worthiness of the fullest citizenship, and the knowledge that the accident of color is too trivial to mention. He was ever our unfailing champion. He gave President Johnson lessons in the fundamentals of statesmanship by such unanswerable arguments as "Peace between races is not to be secured by degrading one and exalting the other, but by maintaining a state of equal justice to all classes." "How can you deprive the Negro of all means of defense, and clothe his enemies in the full panoply of political power?"

Although an appointee under President Hayes, he criticized the withdrawal of the federal troops from the South. When the Supreme Court read away Sumner's Civil Rights Bill, for which he, too, had fought, he spoke in fearless criticism of the powerful tribunal before a large gathering, white and black, and the last day he spent on earth, though nearly eighty years of age, was with Susan B. Anthony in the interest of this great people to whom he had given his long life and his great heart. The National Association of Colored Women has raised a large fund to purchase his estate, and now Cedar Hill, once a slave master's estate, then the home of "the grandest slave ever born," is now a sacred shrine, the property of Negroes of the nation to which our children make pilgrimages for deepening faith in the glory of their people.

But we are not discouraged by our mighty fall from our high estate. Rather, we have girded on our armor to "regain that blissful seat." The descent from deserved equality to the abyss of disfranchisement, denial of civil rights, the exclusion from all participation in government, and the Ku Klux Klan is loud and dismal, but hope and determination are with us yet. Our local branch of the National Association for the Advancement of Colored People demands full equality of citizenship, which, of course, is against the prevailing white opinion here, yet 95 per cent of our colored officers and teachers, and the majority of the employees of the national and local government, dare to support it. Its leader and president, Archibald H. Grimke, has brought to us the splendid idealism of these better days, and through its vigorous protests against hostile legislation, both national and municipal in scope, we are able to save some of the wreck of our fortunes. There are other organizations working for the same end which are evidence of healthful racial growth that will some day realize more and more that though we won the war, unless we consider all the Amendments equally sacred; and spend as much money and national energy upon the enforcement of the Thirteenth, Fourteenth, and Fifteenth, as we spend upon the Eighteenth, we shall lose the Peace.

NATHAN B. YOUNG

Florida:
Our Contiguous Foreign State

VOL. 5, No. 11, NOVEMBER 1923

For biographical information, see the headnote to Young's essay on Alabama.

DR. YOUNG

Non-residents are too apt to think of Florida as a *foreign* country like Canada and Mexico, as sustaining only a sort of detached relationship with the United States. As a matter of fact, it is a state of vast, undeveloped resources, and is destined eventually to rank among the wealthiest of this country. It is also thoroughly American in its moods and tenses. Jackson accomplished an exceptional day's work when he *snatched* it from Spain, thereby winning a place alongside of Thomas Jefferson, who found it necessary to make the Constitution "show its teeth" in the purchase of Louisiana.

Like Texas, Florida is a state of "magnificent distances." One can entrain at Pensacola and detrain at Key West, having traveled well nigh *one thousand miles,* and that too, with but one change at Jacksonville. Nearly *two hundred* miles of this journey are across seas on a *literally* seagoing railroad, a marvelous engineering feat. On this trip one passes through *three Floridas:* West Florida, Middle Florida and South Florida, each a potential state.

The first state of this journey, from Pensacola to Jacksonville, leads through the naval stores section—the pine barrens and cattle ranges that are being transformed into cultivated fields of cane, cotton and tobacco. This is West, or *near,* Florida, an extension of Alabama and Georgia, and very much like these states in manners and customs.

The *real Florida* begins at Jacksonville, and extends south to Sand Key Light, the southernmost extremity of the United States.

From Jacksonville there are two routes to Key West, our most southern (geographically speaking) city, literally founded upon a rock in the Gulf of Mexico, defiant alike of hurricanes and tidal waves: The East Coast via

Miami, the city of phenomenal growth, and the West Coast via Tampa. These routes reveal Florida at its best, just as the Pensacola-Jacksonville route reveals it at its worst.

The East Coast is the route of jaded millionaires and their plutocratic attaches, whose social terminus is Palm Beach, where wealth disports and, ofttimes, debauches itself, and whose commercial terminus is Miami, where fortunates are made and (mayhaps) lost over-night in a real estate way.

This route leads through the potato belt, touches the citrus fruit country, and finally skirts the Everglades, about to become the "actual garden spot" of America. All along this route, one sees a wonderful admixture of pleasure and of thrift, of playgrounds and business marts. The merchant prince and the "gay brummel" are everywhere apparent.

The West Coast is the route of the "tin-can tourist" and the tired business man who, while resting, speculates in real estate and climate around St. Petersburg. The rapid growth of that town and of Tampa across the bay is an excellent exhibit of *climate exploitation*. Upon the completion of the Gandy bridge, one of these competitive little cities will necessarily become the suburb of the other, with the odds in favor of Tampa. This route leads through an agricultural section well nigh Western in its development. It also touches the mining (phosphate) and celery sections, passing through the heart of the citrus country.

The scenic glory of the East Coast is the Indian River, which in one form or another travels with one practically the entire journey. The lakes are the beauty spots of the West Coast whose silvery sheen constantly flashes through the car windows, and pleases the eye of the traveler.

By this same sign, Florida will never be a "dry State." It is too well watered by nature and by the Bahamas. In this connection it might be remarked that, while *sunshine* centering upon St Petersburg advertised as "the Sunshine City" may characterize the West Coast, "moonshine" streaming from Bimini into Palm Beach and Miami may with equal propriety characterize the East Coast, each becoming respectively, the *sunshine* and the *"moonshine"* coast.

And so it comes to pass that Florida's leading natural resources are climate and water. It is both a summer and a winter resort, because it is not as *hot* in the summer nor as *warm* in the winter as it is "cracked up to be." Those who go there for the winter ofttimes find it awaiting them. Florida's climate is almost as variable as Mark Twain's New England's Winter-Day. And yet men are growing rich selling Florida's climate to those who would escape pneumonia and coal bills. A glance at the map of the state will explain its climatic temperament. It is as water-bound as it is anti-Volstead, no part of which being a hundred miles from the sea, and "aquardiente."

But, what about the people of Florida? especially the Negroes? That is the uppermost question in the serial of which this paper is to be a chapter. What part does the Florida Negro play in these *Colored* United States?

Taken by and large, the Negroes of Florida are very like the Negroes elsewhere in these United States. They are as progressive as the progressive elsewhere, especially in Yankee (South) Florida; and as backward as the backward elsewhere, especially in "Cracker" (West) Florida. In the central and southern parts of the State they are a shade more commercial minded than elsewhere in the Lower South. They are rapidly winning economic independence in that section.

Just here it is interesting to note that the migratory movement of Negroes from the Lower South expresses itself in a drift from West Florida to South Florida, where industrial opportunities are well nigh as attractive as in the North and West.

Of course, everywhere in the state the Negro is a political non-entity, and an educational negligible, sustaining in all matters of citizenship a sort of *ward* relationship to his white fellow-citizens, who are his self-appointed guardians. The astuteness of the Southern white man (aided and abetted by white men elsewhere) in no instance has expressed itself more emphatically than it has in his maneuvering himself into the position of guardianship of the emancipated Negro—a control well-nigh as complete as that of the old master over his slave. And he has accomplished this *coup d'etat* so shrewdly and blandly that the *unthinking* Negro has not yet discerned that he is the white man's ward, but little removed from that of slave.

From Jacksonville south, here and there, serious gestures are made towards educating him in a public school way. In West Florida with a few *poor* exceptions practically nothing is being done, especially in the rural district, towards his public education. In this regard, the white Floridian's policy toward his black fellow-citizen is as tragic as it is short-sighted. Florida is excelled in this niggardly educational policy only by Georgia, the most sinning of all the Southern States in its educational neglect of its Negroes.

Florida unwittingly was led, however, into making a real effort at the *higher* education of the Negro. But when this fact was ferreted out by federal vocational agents, there was a sharp reaction against such an educational program. Frantic efforts were made to put the A. & M. College for Negroes into reverse gear, to "soft-pedal" *cultural* education as being undesirable for Negroes. They are busy even now trying to make that school function in a way that shall be pleasing to those who have a low-browed conception of the mission of education to the Negro.

This suggests the remark that there seems to be a well-defined movement, quickened by federal vocational agents, throughout the South to *sub-standardize* the few State-supported Colleges for *Negroes* by devoting them solely or mainly to vocational training with the evident purpose of making the Negro a permanent economic asset to the white South, with but small regard to his own group welfare—to educate him narrowly as a Negro, not *broadly* as a man and a citizen.

It appears also that the Federal Board of Vocational Education is in full cooperation with this propaganda. The real friends of Negro education ought to look into this phase of the federal educational activities and see to it that the federal vocational agents do not work *overtime* in industrializing the State Institutions for Negroes.

And finally, Florida is making strenuous efforts to win the pennant in the lynching league for 1923. It came to the end of the first half with a *terrible* lead that Georgia and Texas may not be able to overcome. This is an additional exhibit of its full Americanization.

In a word, Florida has lost the racial catholicity of Spain, and has found the racial prejudice of these United States. Nothing is now foreign to it that is common to Anglo-America, and hostile to Afro-America. The Florida Negro is in fact part and parcel of these Colored United States, maltreated and cheated, cajoled and paroled with occasional justice even as his fellows of the other States.

E. FRANKLIN FRAZIER

Georgia, or The Struggle against Impudent Inferiority

VOL. 6, NO. 6, JUNE 1924

E. Franklin Frazier, born in Baltimore, Maryland, on September 24, 1894, graduated with honors from Howard University in 1916. He taught a variety of subjects first at Tuskegee Institute and then at several private high schools. He began his study of sociology at Clark University at Worcester, Massachusetts, where he received an M.A. in 1920. He then studied under a succession of fellowships at the New York School of Social Work (now the Columbia University School of Social Work) and then in Denmark. He moved to Atlanta in 1922 to accept a joint position as director of the Atlanta University School of Social Work and instructor of sociology at Morehouse College.

Frazier was one of the most prominent sociologists and educators of the twentieth century. A prolific writer, his many studies of race and social structure often came under sharp attack. One of his early articles, "The Pathology of Race Prejudice," caused such a furor among the white community in Atlanta that Frazier had to flee the city, quite literally, for his life. His first major book, *The Negro Family in Chicago* (1932), came out of his work with Robert Parks at the University of Chicago and has often been compared to Du Bois's *Philadelphia Negro* in terms of its import and significance to the fields of both sociology and African American studies. Frazier taught at Fisk University, where he was a close colleague of Charles S. Johnson, from 1931 to 1934, and then became head of the Department of Sociology at Howard University. *The Black Bourgeoisie* (1955) caused enormous controversy at its publication and is the book with which Frazier is most often identified. Frazier also taught at the University of California at Berkeley, Carleton College, the New School for Social Research, New York University, Sarah Lawrence College, and the New York School of Social Work. His election to the presidency of the American Sociological Society marked the first time an African American led a major national professional organization. He died in 1962 at the age of sixty-eight.

The "Impudent Inferiority" referred to in the title of this essay is a complex image: Frazier coins the term in reference to the "poor whites" he sees as desperately trying to oppress African Americans as a way to bolster their own sense of self, but Frazier further uses the phrase to mimic the supposedly "inferior" position of African Americans. In a state where the great crime for an African American is to appear "uppish," Frazier subverts the idea of impudence and inferiority and applies it to those who would look to skin color for human merit. This essay, showing its sociological underpinnings throughout (such as when he concisely delineates the five levels of tenant farmers at the base of the social structure), steadily makes a case for increased social activism and implicitly recommends the use of sociology in an applied form.

His argument that separation causes ignorance, which in turn fuels racism, has a contemporary ring, as does his claim that African Americans are commonly thought of by whites as criminals or servants. White Atlanta does not know black Atlanta, and the greatest horror is that "it may even be said that White Atlanta does not want to know any more."

In 1925 W.E.B. Du Bois wrote an essay on the state of Georgia for *The Nation*. Du Bois, not surprisingly, uses the forum to indict racism, poverty, and most of all the Ku Klux Klan. Du Bois was the only African American who contributed to *The Nation* series on the states, and his portrait of Georgia as the "Invisible Empire State" was one of the few essays to consider race as an important issue. Du Bois's essay would perhaps have been more congenial to the remnants of radicalism in *The Messenger*'s editorial department, since he tells the history of Georgia as the history of labor. Although he was also a sociologist, Du Bois uses little of the sociological perspective in his essay, however much more poetically and powerfully he makes his case at a literary level. Frazier's essay of 1924 was doubtless known to Du Bois, whose decision to ignore the small African American middle class in Georgia may have been a reaction to what he saw as Frazier's overemphasis on this group and its importance. Frazier and Du Bois both contributed pieces to Alain Locke's *New Negro* in 1925, and their differences of approach are even more striking there. Du Bois analyzed the contemporary state of the "color line" by surveying world imperialism and international economics, while Frazier wrote of the growing middle class of Durham, North Carolina.

For Du Bois, finally, white Georgia is an enemy of civilization. Frazier agrees with him here, decrying "supposed representatives of civilization" who have oppressed, cheated and murdered their fellow citizens. Du Bois calls on a national audience to redress the wrongs, while Frazier argues for the support of the nascent middle-class African Americans in their attempts to capitalize and build businesses. Frazier's middle-class allegiances can also be seen in his rejection of popular culture: "On week days," he writes disapprovingly, workers "seek as stimulus for their drab lives the puerile movies,"

In Frazier's endorsement of middle-class initiative we see the intellectual justification for such probusiness essays as those by William Twine on Oklahoma and Noah Thompson's on California. Frazier was the most important intellectual in the decade supporting the entrepreneurial and corporate activities of African Americans. However, his attitudes toward the middle class would change by the time he wrote *The Black Bourgeoisie*, in which he claimed that the class "lived in a world of make-believe." But in 1924, he saw this class as the hope for improving the African American reality.

PROF. FRAZIER

Come, make a circle around me, and mark my tale with care,
A tale of what Rome once hath borne, of what Rome may yet bear.
This is no Grecian fable, of fountains running wine,
Of maids with snaky tresses, or sailors turned to swine.
Here, in this very Forum, under the noonday sun,
In sight of all the people, the bloody deed was done.

Rising from the Atlantic Ocean, Georgia stretches across the Atlantic lowland to the Appalachian Mountains. This slope comprises the Atlantic Coastal Plain, the Piedmont Plateau, and the Appalachian Highland. The Coastal Plain, which occupies more than half the total area of the State, extends from the ragged coastline with its small bays and sandy islands to the Fall Line Hills. Once this plain was the bottom of the sea and after emerging from the ocean became covered with dense forests. The Okefenokee Swamp, consisting of dense masses of moss, peat, lakes and islands, supporting valuable forests, lies north of the Florida line. North of the Coastal Plain lies the Piedmont Plateau, rising from three hundred to one thousand feet above sea level. The rivers flowing from this plateau to the coastal plain form many rapids and waterfalls which could furnish abundant water power for manufacturing.

The Appalachian Highland in Georgia consists of the Appalachian Mountains, Appalachian Valley and the Cumberland Plateau in the extreme northwest of the State. The State is traversed by many rivers and drained by nine streams. Because of its wide latitude, different altitudes and sea coast, Georgia has a varied climate. Its altitude ranges from sea level to four thousand feet in the North. The mean annual temperature varies from 57 degrees in the north to 67 degrees in the southern counties; while the growing season usually lasts from eight to ten months. The rainfall which comes chiefly during February and March is heaviest in the mountain region, where it reaches seventy inches during the year. During the summer months the usual thunder-showers of the Gulf states are frequent.

In such a varied climate we find Magnolias, Palmettos and Live Oak with trailing Spanish Moss on the coast; and the Cypress in the southern counties. The Pine, the most important tree in the State, grows mostly in the southern half. Opossums, squirrels and rabbits are still plentiful in the less densely settled districts. Game birds still attract the hunter. Song birds serenade the forests while fish abound in the streams and oysters lie in the mud along the river mouths. Richer still is Georgia in clay and stone deposits. Marble, granite, limestone and coal line the hills; while manganese and asbestos are sequestered in the bowels of the earth. The soils of the Piedmont and low-land districts are capable of producing any crop grown in the temperate zone. From such soils have sprung King Cotton, potatoes, rice, sugar cane, peanuts, peaches and melons to feed the sons of men.

Such is Georgia as the gift of Nature and the habitation of bird and beast. Let us see what Georgia has been and is as the habitation of men—especially black men.

Georgia, the last of the English colonies to be planted in America, was founded by James Oglethorpe. His purpose was to transplant the miserable inmates of the debtor's prisons of England to America where they could begin life anew. The colony was named after George II, who granted the charter. Oglethorpe as governor sailed from England with thirty-five fami-lies and reached the mouth of the Savannah in 1733. A shipload of Salz-burgers, Protestant refugees, joined the colony the following year. During this same year John Wesley, the founder of Methodism, and his brother Charles came to Georgia. Although the Wesleys and the benevolent protec-tors of the colony forbade the importation of intoxicating liquors and the holding of slaves, they were finally overruled in 1749 by the planters. George Whitfield, the eminent evangelist, who maintained a slave planta-tion in South Carolina to support his orphanage in Savannah, defended the introduction of slavery on the ground that it would save the slaves from heathenism. So Georgia, because of greed with priestly sanction—which has always been invoked to sanctify the lust of men—began her career of exploiting men. This career she has pursued to this day.

After Georgia became a royal colony in 1752, the settlement progressed rapidly and at the time of the Revolution the population was about 50,000, a half of whom were slaves. Georgia remained, however, to the end of the Colonial era the southern frontier of South Carolina.

During the Revolution, Georgia was overrun by British troops. As there was a strong loyalist sentiment among the people, only a feeble resistance was offered the invaders. It was the Black Legion, organized in San Domingo by Count D'Estaing, that saved the French and American armies from annihila-tion when they were defeated at Savannah by the British in 1779.

Georgia, once launched upon her career of greed, outstripped the other colonies in opposing humanitarian movements to limit slavery. It was Geor-gia alone that offered opposition to the declaration of the Continental Congress in 1774 against the further importation of slaves. It was Georgia again, this time in league with South Carolina, that caused the denuncia-tion of the slave trade to be struck out of the original draft of the Declara-tion of Independence. Again, we find Georgia and South Carolina in their mad lust for blacks to supply their rice swamps threatening to stay out of the Union if the majority sentiment of the Constitutional Convention for prohibiting the foreign slave trade prevailed. Such then has been Georgia's early history as the abode of men.

Georgia, before the Civil War, was ruled by a slave-holding oligarchy. In 1786 experiments were made in the growing of West India cotton on the sea islands, off the coast of Georgia and South Carolina. It was the invention of the cotton-gin, however, that caused the rice and indigo plantations and even the "back country" to be turned to the growing of cotton. Since cotton was most economically cultivated by the employment of unskilled labor over large areas, the advantage was on the side of the owners of large estates. Consequently, the man without capital was forced into the clay hills. Thus arose the aristocratic order of planters with their large plantations cultivated by hundreds of black slaves. Cotton was king.

According to the census of 1790 there were about 2,400 slave-holding families in Georgia owning on the average of 12.1 slaves. There were only 398 free Negroes at the time this census was made. In a region where the economic order rested on slave labor it was natural that any attempt to enlighten the slaves was severely suppressed. Following South Carolina, Georgia enacted a law in 1770 against the teaching of Negroes. In 1831 the slave-holders had a new law passed imposing a fine and whipping on any Negro teaching another. But in spite of these efforts to prevent the Negro from receiving intellectual improvement, his employments gave him an opportunity to get the rudiments of education. The State then made it criminal to employ a slave or free colored person in a position requiring a knowledge of reading and writing. Even the activities of religious bodies were restricted because they enlightened the slave. Therefore, in 1834, Georgia passed a law providing that neither slaves nor free Negroes might preach to a group of more than seven without a license from "a justice on the certificate of three ordained ministers." Religious organizations, especially the Baptists, succeeded in spite of these handicaps in spreading their teachings among the Negroes.

In 1860, the number of free Negroes had grown to 3,500. They had always been subject to harsh regulations; for Georgia was one of the two states that had at no time given the free Negro civil recognition. The slaves, it can be said to their honor, had made two attempts to liberate themselves before freedom was bestowed upon them. As early as 1768 an insurrection was planned in Savannah, but failed because of disagreement as to procedure. The second, attempted in Augusta in 1819, came to a similar end. It was the Civil War that destroyed the structure of society in Georgia and initiated the struggle of the freedom against a new class. In September, 1864, Sherman captured Atlanta and began his famous march to the sea. Sherman's march through Georgia not only broke the backbone of slavery in one of its most insolent strongholds, but brought the hope of freedom to Negroes in the lowest depths of servitude.

TOP ROW, LEFT TO RIGHT: Dr. John Hope, Pres. Morehouse College; Dr. John H. Lewis, Pres. of Morris Brown University; Dr. M. W. Adams, Pres. Atlanta University; Dr. W. J. King, Prof. at Gammon Seminary. MIDDLE ROW, LEFT TO RIGHT: Miss W. Louise Harden, popular Atlanta beauty; (TOP) Main building, Morris Brown University, Atlanta, Ga.; (BOTTOM) Morehouse College Campus; Miss Louise Heard, popular Atlanta school teacher. BOTTOM ROW, LEFT TO RIGHT: Mrs. Geo. S. Williams of Savannah, former Pres. of the Georgia Federation Women's Clubs, Rep. Nat'l. Committeewoman; Prof. H. A. Hunt, Principal of the Fort Valley High & Industrial School, one of the leading Negro educators in Georgia; Atlanta U. teachers having taught from 20 to 35 years: women l. to r., Miss Swift, Miss Pingree, Miss Hancock; men l. to r., Prof. Webster, Dr. Adams, Prof. Towns; Mrs. Rebecca S. Taylor, teacher of English Auyler Junior High, Savannah, Ga.

The Civil War was a real social revolution in Georgia. In destroying slavery it destroyed the political supremacy of the slave-holding oligarchy. Even the temporary return to power of such men as Hill and Gordon did not change this fact. Georgia met the attempt to educate the freedman and fit him for citizenship with the Black Code. The Fourteenth Amendment was rejected in 1866. When the Federal Government enforced recognition of the Negro as a citizen, some were elected to the Legislature and served with credit. As soon, however, as the Federal forces were withdrawn the real significance of the social revolution was apparent. The poor white, with hatred for slave and aristocrat and resentful of his former degradation, came into power. Through violence, fraud and murder, he opposed the education of the Negro; prevented him from voting and reduced him to economic slavery. To justify this barbarism he has invented lies concerning the Negro, and has thrown a veil of legality about it with Jim Crow and Disfranchisement laws.

Without either blood or cultural relationship to the vanished aristocracy, the poor white sentimentalizes about his aristocratic lineage. Without tradition and sensitive of his lowly origin, he glorifies his white skin. Ignorant, cultureless and crude, he boasts of his superiority to the Negro. He lynches in the name of Chivalry and steals in the name of Law. Whether we meet him on the street car, on trains, in court, in office or in the Legislature, he is the same. It is against this Impudent Inferiority that the Negro, especially if cultured and thrifty, is struggling.

According to the 1920 census Negroes in Georgia numbered 1,206,365, or 41.7 per cent of the total population. They were most numerous in those middle counties running diagonally across the state from northeast to southwest. In two of these counties they form over 80 per cent of the population. They are least numerous in the Northern counties, being absent in Dawson County. Over three-fourths of the Negro population is rural; so that any account of the Negro in Georgia must portray the condition of the rural Negro.

Rural life in Georgia revolves principally about cotton; it suffers, therefore, all the narrowing and debasing effects of single crop communities. The Negro is at the base of the social structure. In 1920 colored farmers owned 1,331,828 acres of farm land, about a half of which was improved, valued at 45,486,236, including buildings. They managed about 29,000 acres, valued at nearly two million dollars. It is the tenant with whom we are chiefly concerned, for 87.5 per cent of Negro farmers in Georgia are tenants. The tenants are divided into five classes: the share tenants, who pay a certain share of their products for the use of the farm, but furnish the equipment and work animals; the croppers, share tenants who do not furnish work animals; the share-cash tenants, who pay part of the rent in cash and part in products; the cash tenants, who pay a cash rental; and the standing renters, who pay a stated amount of products, as four bales of cotton. The most alarming aspect of the tenant situation is that while the number of colored owners has increased only 2.2 per cent, the number of share tenants and croppers, who form two-thirds of the tenant class, has increased 38.4 per cent. The other classes, who represent a more or less approach to independence in bargaining, have decreased. The position of the Negro cropper in many cases is very little improvement over slavery. He is dependent upon the white landlord for everything. He must get his household supplies as well as his seed from the landlord. At the annual settlement the landlord, who has kept the books, determines whether the cropper has produced as much as he has consumed. It generally happens that the landlord's account shows the Negro in debt, and the latter must be "advanced" supplies to begin another year's work. Under such circumstances the Negro can be arrested if he attempts to escape from the vicious circle of debt. To demand an open verified account would brand a Negro as "uppish" and "unruly." This is why the new white master in Georgia obstructs the education of Negroes. The position of the Negro farm laborer is somewhat different. He can get away at times. Yet the writer has been informed by Negro farm laborers in Central Georgia that they suffer brutal floggings and are warned not to run away.

To this picture of how the Negro lives in rural Georgia must be added the Negro peon, who is turned over to the white landlord to work out his fine which the latter has paid. To repay a few dollars, Negroes have been compelled to work months. Williams' murder farm is the classic example of this system of peonage and barbarism. As long as the present system of tenancy continues there can be neither freedom nor rural community life for the Negro. With the flow of Northern capital into Southern cotton mills the Negro has found his place to some extent in these mills. Here he is coming under a narrowing, yet beneficent in some respects, form of industrial paternalism.

With rural society resting upon such an economic foundation as described above, it will not be surprising to find what little progress education has made among Negroes in Georgia. In Georgia 29.1 per cent of the Negroes are illiterate. In rural Georgia 31.9 per cent are in this class. While the Negroes form 41.7 per cent of the population, they receive 12 per cent of the State appropriation for education. This amounts to $2.83 for each Negro child of school age. A Negro child attends on an average of 88 days a year. Another view of the situation shows only 47.4 per cent of the colored children in school. The presence of the Rosenwald schools in the State is doing much to lift the Negro out of his ignorance. This patent discrimination against Negro children represents theft and the determination of white people to keep the Negro ignorant and exploitable. So determined is this effort on the part of the poor white to keep Negroes ignorant that Negro students in the colleges of Atlanta are insulted and threatened when they return home during vacation. Because of this situation some students do not return home, but are visited by their parents.

What is the relation of the Negro to the Law? In Georgia the law is made by white men, administered by white men, in the interest of white men. No

Negro's word is of equal value to any white man's word. If a Negro is the favorite of an influential white man, he is treated leniently for crimes against other Negroes. This privilege does not extend to crimes against white people. White people are inviolate. Self-defense is no plea when a white person is concerned. Georgia, with 414 victims to her shame, led the country in lynching and burning Negroes from 1889 to 1921. Men, women and children have been the victims of the savage lust of white mobs. Even as I write I read that a fifteen-year-old colored boy was lynched on the third of April for shooting an officer. Under pretense of protecting white womanhood, Georgia has even lynched and burned colored women. While declaring in her laws that marriage between the races is forever prohibited, null and void, white men have continued to violate Negro womanhood and bastardize their offspring. No colored woman in Georgia could invoke the protection of the law against white men. In her filthy jails are herded together colored men, women and children. Her black chain gangs build her roads by day. At night they are caged. The writer has seen colored women wearing stripes, working under an armed white guard. Brutalized and nurtured in ignorance, the Negro of Georgia is the scapegoat *par excellence* for the self-righteous whites.

The Negro in Georgia is practically eliminated from politics. Through the white primary candidates are practically elected when chosen in the primary. Even where Negroes, in spite of the ostensibly impartial voting requirements, are eligible to vote, they are disqualified by fraud and intimidated by threats. The demagogues are always present with the battle cry of white supremacy. The Republican organization, which is split at present, has no force in political issues. Colonel Henry L. Johnson is still the leader on one faction. Georgia is as Democratically solid as she is politically stolid.

An excellent example of the working of race prejudice in Georgia is found in the relationship between white and colored boys in a reformatory near Macon. These boys work, play and attend entertainments together, but on Sundays they worship separately! Perhaps the gods of Work and Play are less discriminating than the God of Love.

Let us consider some of the social forces that are uniting Negroes for their cultural development. The Order of Oddfellows loomed for years as the most comprehensive attempt at social organization. It attracted Negroes of every station through its various appeals. Besides the fellowship it built up, it helped the accumulation and concentration of Negro wealth into the hands of Negroes. But because of internal strife the Order has been torn to pieces. Today one factor has the Order and the other, headed by Ben Davis, the property. Through litigations and mortgages even the wealth has been dissipated. In the field of religion we find the different branches of the Methodist and Baptist churches not only controlling the spiritual life of the people, but providing educational opportunities. Yet it is a sad and disheartening spectacle, in spite of the culpability of the State, to see a Negro rural community swarming with well-built churches of every denomination, raising their spires above the solitary ramshackled schoolhouse without floor or benches. Such a sight makes one feel that the Negro perishes because of a vision—of heaven. Another very potent social force is the State Federation of Colored Women's Clubs. At present the Federation is planning the establishment of a home for delinquent colored girls, which they hope the State will take over when a more enlightened public opinion prevails. Another proposal illustrative of the social vision of this organization is the plan to furnish a scholarship for a young woman in the Atlanta School of Social Work. The Negroes of Georgia have made some worth-while and promising progress in economic enterprises. This is represented on a small scale in the more than two thousand retail stores and seventeen newspapers, of which four are religious and fraternal. Economic co-operation on a large scale is found in the eleven insurance companies and nine banks in the different sections of the State.

We come now to the city of Atlanta. Years ago Dr. Du Bois bade Atlanta not to stoop as Atlanta in the race with Hippomenes to pick golden apples; but Atlanta was deaf to his plea as she is today to the cries of black men, and has gone her way in her mad pursuit of wealth. It was in Atlanta that Booker Washington made the famous "separate as the five fingers" speech, and thereby not only became the accepted leader of the Negroes, but gave the moral justification to Jim-Crowism.

At the time of the Civil War, Atlanta was a city of a little over 2,000. At the last decennial census her population had grown to 200,616, of which 62,796 were Negroes. Of these, 37,891 were gainfully employed. Nearly 8,000 of the men were in manufacturing and mechanical industries, a half of whom were laborers. There were hundreds, however, in skilled occupations as carpenters, brick and stone masons, bakers, machinists and plasterers. Domestic service still claimed about a half of those employed. The women numbered nearly 15,000. There were nearly 300 teachers, nearly all women. The doctors numbered 41; dentists, 14; and clergymen, 224. There were three hundred and one retail dealers. The foregoing occupational statistics, together with the fact that 17.8 per cent of the Negroes were illiterate, will form a basis of our story of colored Atlanta.

What is the relation of Black Atlanta to White Atlanta? When this question is asked most people recall the Atlanta Riot of September, 1906. Many people outside of Atlanta are still ignorant of the fact that this riot was fomented by the publication in the now defunct but ever infamous *Atlanta Evening News* of fictitious accounts of assaults upon white women by Negroes. As is always the case, Negroes were disarmed and clubbed and murdered by those who were supposed to represent white civilization. Negroes did try to protect their homes and persons against white thugs and bloodthirsty ruffians. When Atlanta found that lawlessness was economically disadvantageous, she re-established law and order. Today, when some think of Atlanta, they think of her as the home of the present Ku Klux

Klan. Although this organization, which is primarily engaged in duping ignorant and gullible white men out of their money by transporting them from their eventless lives into a world of mock heroism and by making them believe that a white skin can make a somebody out of a nobody, is a menace to civilization wherever it is found, it is not as active in Atlanta as in places where Negroes enjoy a greater share of freedom.

White Atlanta knows nothing of Black Atlanta, except through Negro servants and criminals. It may even be said that White Atlanta does not want to know any more. The Atlanta *Constitution* that speaks out against lynching occasionally and poses as a friend of the Negro, has no real appreciation of Negro manhood. It has openly declared that the South wants the Negro servant who will stay in his place and that other Negroes can go. The *Constitution* continues to insult Negroes by refusing to print Mr. and Mrs. or Miss before their names. It further insults Negroes in its Sunday pictorial section by picturing Negroes as "contented darkies," criminals and clowns. Such is the type of "friendship" of which the Southern white man boasts. When the Negro enters the courts he is presumed to be guilty. Every Negro who enters a court in Atlanta is treated as if he were a dangerous criminal. Not only are they insulted and threatened in the court room and at times not permitted to give testimony, but they are clubbed and tortured until they give testimony to their guilt. A civilized man cast among cannibals would have a better chance of justice than a Negro in an Atlanta court where a white man is involved. Even when a Negro gets on a street car he may be insulted or have a pistol pointed in his face by a barbarous conductor for no provocation whatever. White Atlanta is determined to segregate Black Atlanta in spite of the Supreme Court. So to be sure to know as little as possible of Black Atlanta, while judging and writing about Black Atlanta, White Atlanta has passed zoning laws, which are nothing but a flagrant violation of the Supreme court decision. But it is the custom to violate the law where the Negro is concerned. To complete this picture of repression we must add the fact that Negro doctors are not permitted to work on Negro patients in the city's clinics.

Black Atlanta did bestir itself and hold back the tide of repression when White Atlanta tried to fasten ignorance on it forever. This was done, contrary to Booker Washington's advice that the Negro should not insist upon his right to vote, through the ballot. At two successive elections the Negroes defeated the bond issue, because it carried no provision for their schools. When it was stipulated that they should receive their share of the bond issue, they voted for the issue and it was carried.

Not all of white opinion is represented by the spirit that caused the riot in 1906 and continues to repress and libel the Negro. In Atlanta we have the headquarters of the Committee on Inter-racial Co-Operation. This committee is headed by Dr. Alexander and Mr. Woofter. This committee is endeavoring, first, to get the South to provide the same educational and health facilities and protection of the law for Negroes as for other citizens. In order to evaluate the work of the committees which have been organized in about eight hundred counties, one must recall that such a sense of social responsibility is not prevalent in the South. Moreover, the reactionary opinions held concerning the relation of Negro to the rest of the community have been part of the mores of the South beyond discussion. This committee is putting questions as to the status of Negro upon the discussion level. Besides its present achievements this committee holds great promise for the future.

Another promising feature of the inter-racial situation is the attitude of those engaged in social welfare work. The Department of Public Welfare is entrusted to a woman of broad sympathies and social vision. Her program includes both white and colored people; but the carrying out of the program must, of course, wait upon public sentiment. This attitude was also shown in the recent State conference of Social Workers. Negroes participated as other human beings, without being segregated as cattle or microbes, as is the orthodox way of dealing with bootlicking Negroes who submit to such humilities. President Hope of Morehouse College presided over one of the general sessions. This gave added encouragement to those who believe that social work has a definite contribution to make to race relations.

On the side of Black Atlanta we are able to see marked social progress. We note, first, among the landmarks of economic progress the Standard Life Insurance Company, with over twenty-eight millions of dollars of insurance in force; and of more recent development the Atlanta Life Insurance Company, with over a million of dollars of insurance in force. The Citizens' Trust Company, which has been doing business for about two years, represents the latest adventure in banking. Besides these large undertakings the Negro is operating drug stores, various retail stores, and the always profitable undertaking establishments and barber shops.

Atlanta is the colored educational center of the South. As one surveys the hills of Atlanta from North to South, one beholds Morris Brown University, Atlanta University, Morehouse College and Spelman Seminary on the West and Clark University and Gammon Seminary in the South. Morris Brown University, which is presided over by Dr. John H. Lewis, is one of the largest schools conducted by the African Methodist Episcopal Church. Atlanta University, of which Dr. Adams is the president, and whose white teachers, like Professor Webster, have identified themselves with Black Atlanta, has "kept the faith" through all its years of struggle for Negro manhood. Morehouse College has made rapid strides under the presidency of Dr. John Hope. Spelman Seminary is devoted to the education of women. Under the presidency of Miss Lucy Hale Tapley, the school will open with a college department next year. Morehouse and Spelman are both conducted by the American Baptist Home Mission Society. Clark University, which is under the Northern Methodist Church, was the scene of the Professor Crogman's years of teaching. Gammon Seminary, which is also conducted by the same church, is devoted to the training of colored ministers. As Dr. John Bowen has labored there in the past and is still active, Dr. Willis King brings to his work Biblical scholarship, and stands as an exponent of a social gospel among colored people. Naturally in such an environment as Atlanta, Negroes have reached a high cultural development, but this does not mean that White Atlanta has shown any more respect for Black Atlanta. In the first place, White Atlanta feels that such schools are unfitting Negroes for their proper place in this world. So whenever the *Constitution* pays its respects to Negro educational institutions, it is not to these well-managed schools, but to the Atlanta Normal and Industrial Institute, a grossly mismanaged elementary school with sewing and unworthy of aid, according to the 1917 report of the United States Bureau of Education. This school is held up as the criterion of Negro education, because its kow-towing Negro principal flatters white people by pretending to give Negroes industrial education and tells Atlanta periodically that Negroes are children and should stay in their place.

Although the Negro colleges of Atlanta have had something to do with determining the culture of Black Atlanta, they have not done what they should. To many colored people of Atlanta the colleges are merely organizations for athletic contests. Black Atlanta has failed to build up a community of scholars who, through contact and mutual criticism, would be productive as other scholars. Social life in Atlanta revolves about the churches. Most of the people go to church all day Sundays. On week days they seek as a stimulus for their drab lives the puerile movies. The colleges should give to Atlanta a richer and deeper community life. Although Atlanta has its Decatur Street, its Auburn Avenue and its Hobo Bottom, it has one of the large Y.M.C.A.'s, a Y.W.C.A., the Southern Headquarters of the National Urban League and the Atlanta School of Social Work. The Atlanta Branch of the National Association for the Advancement of Colored People, which almost disappeared during the past two years, is attempting to regain its former place of honor. Such then is the story of Black Atlanta, with college-crowned hills looking down upon White Atlanta scrambling in the market places for gold.

From Atlanta let us go to Augusta. Here we find Haines Normal and Industrial School, founded by Miss Lucy Laney in 1886. Under Miss Laney's wise administration this school has served the community and won the confidence of white and colored people. Here also is the Paine College, conducted by the Southern Methodist Church. It represents active cooperation between the Southern Methodist and the Colored Methodist Episcopal churches. Augusta has its antagonism between the rising generation of educated Negroes and the poor whites in the mills. Augusta was also where the late Rev. C. T. Walker, the eloquent preacher and founder of Walker Baptist Institute, attracted white and colored hearers. Without lingering longer in Augusta, except to note the presence of a bank as an indication of Negro enterprise, we shall pass on to Savannah beside the sea.

Savannah has a very enterprising colored population. There are four banks operated by members of the race. The State has located the colored branch of the State University here. This school shows up clearly the Southern method of cheating Negroes out of their right to education offered the citizens by the State. To this poorly equipped school doing mostly secondary work the State of Georgia gives $10,000 annually for 41.7 per cent of its citizens. At the same time, the State provides a well-equipped university for the white youths of the State. In Savannah the Negro is not only making himself more efficient socially, but is endeavoring to use the ballot effectively.

For a longer story of Georgia there is not space. In Rome, Georgia, Albany and Columbus, the Negro has his schools and is struggling to know. In Americus we have Professor Reddick and in Fort Valley, Professor Hunt engaged in the work of acquainting the Negro with the world he lives in. Before leaving Georgia we must pause at Andersonville, the location of a Confederate Prison, where Union soldiers were tortured, to pay respect to those "who died to make men free."

Through Georgia, whose story I have just told, Major Moton led his Good Will Tour. Why the oppressed, the cheated, and the murdered should apologize for existing to the supposed representatives of civilization, we are unable to learn. But as long as white Georgia commemorates the insensate dead upon Stone Mountain and turn stonier hearts to the cry of children in her mills, and shuts her ears alike to the groans of her black peons and to the golden voice of Roland Hayes, one of her sons, because he is black, Georgia might as well be at the bottom of the sea from which she rose.

CHARLES S. JOHNSON

Illinois: Mecca of the Migrant Mob

VOL. 5, NO. 12, DECEMBER 1923

The first black president of Fisk University and editor of *Opportunity: A Journal of Negro Life,* Charles S. Johnson was one of the most important African American intellectuals of the mid twentieth century. As editor of *Opportunity,* Johnson published and promoted many Harlem Renaissance writers, including Claude McKay, Countee Cullen, Aaron Douglas, Arna Bontemps, Alain Locke, and Langston Hughes. He has been called one of the three "midwives" of the Harlem Renaissance, along with Locke and Jessie Redmon Fauset. He was the primary or coauthor of major works such as *The Negro in American Civilization: A Study of Negro Life and Race Relations in the Light of Social Research* (1930). Other major publications include *Shadow of the Plantation* (1934), a consideration of the economic organization and construction of black social patterns; *Growing Up in the Black Belt* (1941), a study of youth and the caste system in the South; and *Patterns of Negro Segregation* (1943), an examination of different behavioral patterns in different classes.

Johnson was born in 1893 in Bristol, Virginia. He received a B.A. in 1916 from Virginia Union University and went on to graduate studies at the University of Chicago. While studying there for a Ph.B., he concurrently served as the director of research and records at the Chicago Urban League from 1917 to 1919. Johnson served a short stint fighting in France as a regimental sergeant major but in 1919, returned to Chicago, where he was appointed associate executive director of the Chicago Commission on Race Relations, an organization created to examine the race riots of 1919. He moved to New York in 1921 and that year was named director of the Department of Research and Investigations for the National Urban League. Johnson took over the editorship of the league's magazine, *Opportunity,* in 1923.

Fisk University offered him the chair of the social science department in 1928, and Johnson's career as an eminent educator began. He published prolifically and from 1943 to 1948 edited *A Monthly Summary of Events and Trends in Race Relations,* a publication that apparently grew out of a personal request from President Franklin D. Roosevelt. Johnson's association with the executive branch continued; he served as a consultant to every president from Hoover to Eisenhower. He was part of the delegation to the first UNESCO conference in 1946–47 and was an advisor to the Ford Foundation, the Carnegie Foundation, the Rosenwald Fund, and numerous other philanthropic organizations. Fisk University appointed him president in 1946, and he held that position until his sudden death on October 27, 1956.

The Chicago race riots of 1919, some of the deadliest and most destructive of that year of many such disturbances, is both text and subtext of Johnson's essay on Illinois. He uses sophisticated sociologic and economic analysis to track the racism he sees as fueling the riots. He traces the impact of the relationship among different immigrant groups, labor unrest, the preponderance of African Americans in domestic service, and the changing nature of capitalist exploitation to account for the violence of everyday oppression and the more obvious violence of the uprisings. Economic tensions exacerbate sociologic tensions and can only result in, in Johnson's words, "smoldering resentment!"

Johnson's scrutiny falls short at times, and the essay sometimes seems hastily put together. He cavalierly remarks, for example, that Illinois was "shallow from the first in indigenous culture." He inserts what can only be construed as an advertisement for his own work *The Negro in Chicago:* "Six Negroes and seven white men, financed by a hundred citizens, worked together two years on the causes of the Chicago riot and produced a volume of findings whose merit is equalled only by its daring." He laments the lack of literary or artistic work being produced by the African Americans in Chicago but claims that there is little to write about.

These criticisms aside, Johnson more than any other writer in the series recognized the Great Migration for what it was: the largest demographic shift ever seen in the United States, and one that necessarily completely transformed the northern cities. Johnson sees Chicago rejuvenated and redefined by the infusion of African American blood. He is sensitive to the promise Chicago holds for the "bruised, crushed, and thwarted manhood of the south," and his essay suggests that such radical transformations of social relations cannot come without struggle and, occasionally, violence.

I.

MR. JOHNSON

One end lapped by the waters of Lake Michigan, another dipping like an inclined shovel into the Mississippi Embayment, fifty-eight thousand square miles of rich black flatness—this is Illinois, the Prairie State, "spreading with incalculable leisure to the sudden climax of the Rocky Mountains." An ideal agricultural country delivered up to the iron gods of industry. It holds the central position in the Great Mississippi Valley, with a climate that blends all the virtues of the Middle West; well watered, alluvial, and a larger cultivable area than any other state in the Union save Iowa. Its crops are valued at eight hundred million and its manufacturing at three and a half billion. The state ranks twenty-third in area and third in population, has a per capita wealth $3.45 higher than the average for the nation, stacks more wheat, slaughters more cattle, handles more freight, made more whiskey, and has had more bloody clashes between races and classes than any other state in the Union.

It is one of these perplexing border countries which only by the most reckless interpretation of statehood can be referred to as a sovereign unit. The northern end is a polyglot of races, characters and cultures, that might reasonably be a separate state. Herein lies Chicago, with more than half the population of the state and two-thirds of all the wealth. Second largest city in the United States and third largest in the world, the largest young city and the youngest large city, "stormy, husky, brawling, City of the Big Shoulders . . . a tall, bold slugger set vivid against the little soft cities," with a Negro population as large as Nashville and twice as large as Savannah, a Polish population larger than Warsaw—the second largest German city in the world.

The southern end is more homogeneous. Its first strata of population come from the contiguous south, cherishing the traditions of a system whose blind and brutal operation had driven them out. The first six governors of the state, six of eight senators and all representatives save one during its formative period (between 1818 and 1838) were men of southern birth. They left their stamp. It is no accident that the most momentous questions of its history centered about slavery.

From its very founding these dissimilar strains have forced every important issue into a ridiculously impracticable compromise. The first important act of this commonwealth was to try to get into the Union demanding a special concession granting *complete* state sovereignty. The state motto that still stands is a paradox: "State Sovereignty, National Unity." In one of the first constitutions drawn a rider clause was inserted preventing Negroes and mulattoes from immigrating, voting, or holding office. Illinois rejected the constitution and passed the rider. She sent 70,000 troops to defend the Union and on the same gesture drew up resolutions asking Lincoln to withdraw his proclamation emancipating the slaves. In 1864 there were no less than 50,000 members of the Sons of Liberty and Nights of the Golden Circle in the State working secretly for the Confederacy. The number has since grown to 165,000 and the name has been changed to Realm of Illinois, Knights of the Ku Klux Klan.

This conglomeration of vagrant and dissimilar strains and this lack of a common background no doubt account for the absurd contradictions in the life of the state: for Springfield, from whose soil both Lincoln and a bloody race riot sprang; for Chicago, where Negroes may hold responsible office, and Granite City, where they by ordinance may not live within the city limits; for Brooklyn and Robbins, in which only Negroes live, and 200 other towns where they may not live at all; for a clause in the constitution vouchsafing equal rights without respect to color and separate schools in practically every town south of Chicago; for the wanton bloodshed of East St. Louis, Springfield, Chicago and Herrin, in spite of God, and civilization.

II.

The East was in the first deliriums of ancestor worship and the South swaying above the rotten foundations of an impossible economic system before Illinois began to function as a state. Had it been nearer in point of geography to the beginning of things the slow processes of time might have permitted it a more orderly growth and perhaps an indigenous culture. Through these years it slumbered quietly, a remote but fertile virgin, at one time a part of Louisiana, at another a part of Virginia, of Canada and of Indiana. Like most belated frontiers this state was built on borrowed cultures—cultures so diverse both in type and character that assimilation has been impossible. Its greatest figures migrated from other sections: Lincoln from Kentucky, James G. Blaine from Maine, Harrison from Virginia. The Mormons were here before they were driven out and went to Utah. Not until 1901 was a native born Illinoisan allowed to be governor.

Its destiny was fixed when the railroads discovered that tracks could be laid across its flat, rich back without cutting through mountains. In 1850 Congress granted a concession of land to the Illinois Central railroad to help the state. Twenty years later a state board had to be created to protect the state from the railroad. Since it became accessible (to borrow an expression that fits) its progress has far outstripped its civilization. It has drawn in excess every nature that combines with the spirit of adventure: the sturdy frontiersman and the aimless hobo; the brawny youth seeking his fortune and the sleek confidence man seeking the fortune of the youth; Spartan mothers and scarlet women, and a torrent of aliens. The Irish political malcontents, Germans, problems of overpopulation in the fatherland, and in order, Swedes, Poles, Canadians, Norwegians, Danes, Scotch, Swiss,

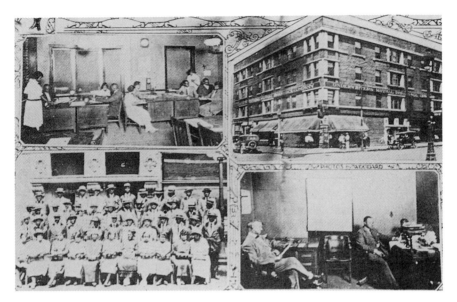

The Underwriters Insurance Company: A Big Negro Business in Chicago. UPPER
LEFT: Office. LOWER LEFT: Employees. UPPER RIGHT: Exterior of the building.
LOWER RIGHT: President Bowser (left), Treasurer Wright (right).

Welsh, Belgians, and after 1900 an avalanche of Slavs and Italians. Together these made the state. Stephen Douglas descended from the Irish
who settled in the southern part of the state. The Catholic Encyclopedia
claims the first sixteen governors were also of Irish descent. No other state
in the union, so shallow from the first in indigenous culture, has been
exposed to such an exotic and contradictory mixture of strains.

The spirit of the frontier still survives with its characteristic philosophy of
"individual aggrandizement and collective irresponsibility," its blustering
contempt for culture, its childlike indifference to law, and its swift appeal to
violence. Massachusetts disagreed with Garrison's program for the slaves
and dragged him through the streets of Boston. Illinois disagreed with the
philosophy of Elijah P. Lovejoy on the same subject and murdered him,
just as it murdered Joseph Smith, the founder of the Mormons. The tradition of violence hangs on like a witch's curse. In a very normal year, 1916,
Chicago with one-third the population of London had twelve times as many
murders and twenty more than all England and Wales with a population
almost fifteen times as large. Nor is this far fetched. With almost two
million less people than New York City it has more murders. Three times
the militia has been called in to put down strikes. It rid itself of anarchists
by a wholesale hanging feast. Four of the seven cities of the state: Chicago,
East St. Louis, Springfield, and the mining town of Herrin have provided
the world with the most atrocious riots in the history of the country.

III.

A ribald history indeed. But this is what results when the process of evolution is hastened. Here there is not so much the deep set, innumerable layers of carefully cultivated hatred as the raw nature of the savage. The East St. Louis massacre was an abominable affair between races. The Herrin massacre was just as abominable without the Negroes. These raw phases of the life of this country are outstanding because they are flagrant and dramatic. But they balance the throbbing animation of youth—the spirit that has fought its way to power and consequences in spite of its cultural backwardness. Carl Sandburg knew the country and he knew Chicago, which, so far as we are concerned, is the significant half of the state:

> Fierce as a dog with tongue lapping for action, cunning as a savage pitted
> against the wilderness,
> Bareheaded,
> Shoveling,
> Wrecking,
> Planning,
> Building, breaking, rebuilding,
> Under the smoke, dust all over his mouth, laughing with white teeth,
> Under the terrible burden of destiny laughing as a young man laughs,
> Laughing even as an ignorant fighter laughs who has never lost a battle,
> Bragging and laughing that under his wrist is the pulse, and under his ribs is
> the heart of the people,
> Laughing!
> Laughing the stormy, husky, brawling laughter of
> Youth, half-naked, sweating, proud to be Hog Butcher,
> Tool Maker, Staker of Wheat, Player with Railroads, and Freight Handler to
> the Nation.

There were 182,274 Negroes in Illinois in 1920, of whom 109,594 lived in Chicago and all but 20,000 of the rest in six other of the State's 930 municipalities. And of these, 182,274 or 76 per cent are migrants. That is why one hears so little of family trees and ancestry. For the State, and even more Chicago, is a composite picture of the Negro population of every southern state in the Mississippi Valley. Twenty-three thousand from Tennessee, 13,000 from Alabama, 19,000 from Mississippi—this is colored Chicago— the dream city—city of the dreadful night! Chameleon-like these expatriates reflect the color of their surroundings. They too are adventurous, daring, spirited and—raw.

Chicago is in more than one sense the colored capital and in every sense the top of the world for the bruised, crushed, and thwarted manhood of the south. In ten years its colored population jumped from 44,000 to 109,000, an increase of 148 per cent. Here they are in open country and on their metal. In a slice of the city between nineteen blocks live 92,000 of them, nauseated by the stench of the stockyards on the west and revived again by the refreshing breezes of Lake Michigan on the east. Forward and effective in politics, they boast of three aldermen at various times, one the floor leader for the administration, a half-dozen state representatives, assistant state's attorneys, a traction attorney for the city drawing a salary of $25,000 a year and a standing army of smaller political appointees. Their combined strength elected one mayor and now threatens to send a representative to Congress. It is indeed nearer to that body than any other section having achieved, through their enforced concentration, one congressional district in which they out-number their white neighbors four to one. Although Republicans by birth, they have shown, as in a recent election, that they could break ranks when their interests were threatened.

Here also is the home of the world's greatest weekly with a circulation of more than a hundred thousand and a plant valued at as many dollars; the Liberty Life Insurance Company with $3,500,000 worth of insurance in force after two years' work, the only such institution in the north; 2 banks; 2 hospitals; 200 churches ranging from the air-tight store fronts of illiterate cults, dissenters and transplanted southern churches to the imposing structure of the Olivet Baptist Church, with a membership of ten thousand; and 1,800 business establishments, varying in size and characteristics from nondescript fly-traps called restaurants to the dignified Overton Building.

These are its boasts. Besides, it points with pride to the physician who made the first successful operation on the human heart, indeed, to Jean De Baptiste, Pointe de Saible, San Domingo—a Negro, the very first settled in Chicago, to the largest number of successful young Negroes of any city in the country. Other things make it the capital. It is the headquarters of the peripatetic Knights of the Whisk-broom—the generic George; of the largest independent Negro labor union in the country; and of the fighting Eighth Illinois Regiment with a colonel who went further into service than the gentlemen in Washington intended.

The story of the rise of Negroes in Chicago has its high lights and deep shadows. Fifteen years ago over 60 per cent of all those working were engaged in domestic and personal service. There was nothing else to do. Then the fashion changed in servants as Irish and Swedish and German tides came on. An unfortunate experience with the unions lost for them the best positions in their traditional strongholds as waiters and poisoned their minds against organized labor. Racial exclusiveness, tradition and inexperience kept them out of industry. Then a strike at the stockyards and the employers miraculously and suddenly discovered their untried genius, while the unions elected to regard them as deliberate miscreants lowering wage standards by design and taking white men's jobs. Smoldering resentment!

When the war brought another shortage they came in again, this time in a torrent. The migration to Chicago has continued to this day, and industry has absorbed fully 80 per cent of the working members. They have overrun the confines of the old area and spread south in spite of the organized opposition of Hyde Park and Kenwood, where objection was registered with sixty bombs in a period of two years. They have bought homes and put money in the bank. Three banks alone have $3,150,000 of Negro money on deposit. One bank has 4,000 depositors. One can make money in Chicago. This is its most respectable attraction.

The second ward is both a political unit and an expression used to characterize an exclusive residential area. it is an institution in itself. On one corner once lived the wealthy first residents, now departed for the north shore; at another, the city's protected red light district, dispersed by a wave of reform and driven into the neighborhoods of the Negroes to be enumerated by the reform papers and purity leagues in their convincing statistics on the "frightful immorality of the Black Belt."

No one escapes Chicago without an impression of State Street, in the second ward. Tawdry stretches of brick and frame decrepitude, leaning in rather discordant obliquity, here and there snapped into order by the rigidly erect lines of a new building. Crowds—almost static crowds—a rich but impossible mixture. Each strain of this enforced homogeneity must set up its own antitoxin of indifference, for "the stroll" appeals in motley indiscriminateness to the Negro in Chicago.

The social set is still a bit promiscuous—vague and uncertain, lacking in definite standards of ancestry and culture and even wealth—a sort of one big union as contrasted with New York City's confederacy of small groups and Charleston's rigid color-caste lines. New countries are always democratic.

The intellectual life has numerous excuses for not existing. The frontier mind is too suspiciously sentimental about the virtues of mother wit and too brutally contemptuous of culture. The new Chicago School of Writers are post-impressionists who take their inspiration from the decay of life. Colored Chicago has enough decay but no one to write about it or about anything else for that matter. Who can write of lilies and sunsets in the pungent shadows of the stockyards? It is no dark secret why literary societies fail, why there are no art exhibits or libraries about, why periodicals presuming upon an I.Q. above the age of 12 are not read, why so little literature comes out of the city. No, the kingdom of the second ward has no self-sustaining intelligentsia, and a miserably poor acquaintance with that of the world surrounding it. But it leads these colored United States in its musical aspirations with, perhaps, the best musical school in the race, as these go. The City has developed many accomplished artists who incidentally have been forced to seek recognition in the "Loop."

The race question is a big issue in Chicago as well as the state. That is because relations are not fixed, and they are not fixed because Chicago is the open ground for myriad transplanted traditions. Sentiment shifts with majorities and recently the migration of whites from the south has almost equalled that of the Negroes.

These authorities on the character and methods of handling of the Negro race are most advantageously distributed from the point of view of peaceful

Chicago is a great musical center for blacks as well as whites. Here is the popular orchestra of Robert Rugland.

penetration. One stronghold is the press. The Chicago *Tribune* is a scourge, though perhaps no worse than some of the others who with the brave hundred percenters and the Nordics by fiat and the propaganda of protective associations are quite capable of lashing the low-browed graduates of the stockyards, the moron population, job-scared aliens, the innumerable gangs organized as athletic clubs and the city's massive criminal fringe to a state of murder lust, and lulling the respectable into blind complacency.

Economic competition is severe. It is severe because the groups in contact are so nearly equal. Combine this with the tricks of employers to get the cheapest labor, the tricks of labor to keep Negroes out of white men's jobs, talk mysteriously about sex and black and tan cabarets, and the deed is done.

But if Chicago boasts of bad strains—murderers who can kill without hating and their less violent brothers who can hate without killing—it is also has in its mixture a more tolerant—a radially just strain, whatever its present proportion in the population. Six Negroes and seven white men, financed by a hundred citizens, worked together two years on the causes of the Chicago riot and produced a volume of findings whose merit is equalled only by its daring.

IV.

One need not wonder why with all its wealth and conflict, its feverish activity and its contempt for refinement, its smoke and blood, and frank vulgarity, that this country grips and holds and fits like a snug garment. It is because beneath these surface irritations there is a young and hopeful spirit "bareheaded, shoveling, rebuilding . . . laughing the stormy, husky, brawling laughter of Youth."

Go West, young man, and grow up with the country.

LIONEL F. ARTIS

The Negro in Indiana, or The Struggle against Dixie Come North

VOL. 6, NO. 3, MARCH 1924

One of the many young contributors to this series, Lionel F. Artis was only twenty-seven years old when his essay on Indiana was published. Born in Paris, Illinois, on December 3, 1895, Artis seems to have created a new career for himself by returning to school as an adult. He received a Ph.B from the University of Chicago in 1933 and an M.A. from Indiana University in 1941. He remained in Indiana for at least nine more years, as *Who's Who of Colored America* lists him as still living in Indianapolis in 1950.

A housing management policy expert, Artis served on various federal housing committees; he was also on the board of directors of the American Association of Social Workers, the YMCA, and the NAACP. Artis served in World War I and worked with the War Housing Project during World War II. He was also a frequent contributor to *Opportunity* and numerous other journals.

Indiana has always played a special role in typifying or epitomizing American society of the 1920s because of Robert and Helen Merrill Lynd's *Middletown* (1929), a landmark sociological study of Muncie, Indiana—a supposedly average American town—as it teetered through the changes of the twenties. Like the Lynds, Artis sees Indiana literally and figuratively as a state in the midst of everything. Like many of the other articles in this series that extol or condemn their states' paradoxical or contradictory natures, Artis argues that Indiana's middling stance is far from neutral in its effects on African Americans.

As his subtitle indicates, the story of the Negro in Indiana is "the struggle against Dixie come North." Artis paints a vibrant picture of the often corrupt racial politics of the state. Despite Indiana's becoming a free commonwealth in 1816, Artis dryly notes that slaves were held as late as 1840. Although in theory Indiana law at the time of this essay protected African Americans against discrimination, he notes that " 'Jim Crow' runs wild." According to Artis, the political clout of the African American community was less than it should be, and as with other states this was at least partly the result of rampant buying and selling of "the Negro vote." Again pinpointing a typical contradiction, Artis explains that most African American voters stick to the G.O.P ticket even though "almost every prominent Republican has been unearthed as a member of the Ku Klux Klan." That the community finds reason to vote at all is encouraging, and Artis observes, with some bemusement, that "the morale of the Negro voter has been raised considerably by the advent of women at the polls."

"The Negro in Indiana, or The Struggle against Dixie Come North" is another one of the essays framed with portrait photographs of well-dressed and -coiffed African American women, including Mrs. Sue V. Artis, "Wife of Lionel F. Artis." Labeled with impressive accomplishments or pedigrees ("President Educational Society for Colored Orphans") or simply as a "member of the younger set," these photographs proudly display the bourgeois attainments of the African American women of Indiana. They also make visible the intractable and indelible presence of the population that so many of these essays ignore: professional and accomplished African American women.

Artis inveighs against the widespread resurgence of the Klan in Indiana and the hypocrisy practiced by upstanding white slumlords, but saves some of his most damning remarks for the passivity he sees in the African American population. Artis locates legitimate historical reasons for this "lack of racial solidarity and aggressiveness," but nonetheless, like so many of our other contributors, Artis calls for change and action within the community and within the very character of African American men and women in Indiana.

The project of this essay is to relate the conditions of life in Indiana for African Americans, a minority population that by its very definition is "atypical" or not part of the majority. Yet ironically, Indiana—the *Middletown* of white America—is not so far from also serving as the *Middletown* of "These 'Colored' United States." The double-barreled critique of white racism and black ineffectiveness may be the most common theme in the collection. At times, Artis makes this critique with great force: "Justice runs crying in the street while the Negro remains divided by envy and jealousy and petty allegiance to white masters." The answer, Artis suggests, is solidarity.

MR. ARTIS

From the earliest record the Negro has been inextricably bound up with the history of the development of Indiana. In fact, so intimate has been the connection that so meticulous a historian as J. P. Dunn in writing the history of Indiana has given his book the sub-title "A Redemption from Slavery." The history of the state is marked by a series of sharp, bitter, and prolonged struggles between the antagonists and protagonists of Negro freedom and rights.

With seemingly good cause one would suppose that the status of the Negro so far as chattel slavery was concerned had been definitely settled by the

Ordinance of 1787, which forbade the extension of slavery in the Territory of the Northwest, which included Indiana, Ohio, Illinois, Michigan and Wisconsin. The Ordinance was specific in that it prohibited the *extension* of slavery, but long legal battles ensued over the meaning of the Ordinance in regard to those Negroes who were already held as chattels. The French, who had first settled the section which later became known as Indiana, had held slaves and the elimination of these was only loosely followed up.

The census of 1800 gives the number of free Negroes in the Indiana Territory as 163 and the number of slaves is listed at 135. Of these slaves 107 were in Randolph County and 28 were in Knox County. The total population of the entire Territory was only 4,875. In 1810 there were 393 free Negroes and 237 slaves, and in 1820 there were 1,230 free Negroes and 190 slaves. However, in 1830 the census lists three Negroes as still being held in slavery. The significance of this we shall see later.

The Territory of Indiana began its formal existence July 4th, 1800, with William H. Harrison as the first Territorial Governor, assisted by three judges. In his history of Indiana J. P. Dunn gives the population of the territory as 6,550, but the census figures as reported to President Thomas Jefferson list the inhabitants as 4,875. Most of the population were of Anglo-Saxon descent, having migrated into the territory from South Carolina and the Virginias and Kentucky. Alongside these settlers came some Negro freemen, among whom was the father of my own great-grandfather, who was born in Charleston, Indiana, in 1822.

Personally, Governor Harrison was in sympathy with the slaveholders, and in December, 1802, elections were held in the counties to select delegates to a convention to be held in Vincennes to decide whether Congress should be petitioned to suspend the anti-slavery proviso in the 1787 Ordinance. On December 20th, 1802, these delegates passed such a memorial and sent it to Congress, but the congressional committee into whose hands it was turned never reported it to the floor of the Congress; hence, no action was ever taken by the national body. During all this time the anti-slavery element, although a minority, was by no means idle, and a sharp

political battle raged in Clark County and after a vigorous campaign Jonathan Jennings, a young Presbyterian, was elected first Governor of the newly-formed state of Indiana in 1816. In the same year a clause was inserted in the new state constitution which made Indiana theoretically a free commonwealth. I say theoretically because actually as late as 1840 slaves were reported as being held in the state.

Mrs. J. H. Ward, Indianapolis, Ind. Wife of Dr. James H. Ward, recently appointed Surgeon-in-Chief at Veteran Hospital 91, Tuskegee, Alabama.

   Despite the prolonged show of hostility and in spite of the restrictive legislation, Negroes continued to settle in the state and in 1829 in a public document Governor Ray deplores the excessive influx of Negroes into Indiana,
saying, "they represented an uneducated and immoralized element, most of
whom were paupers on society." As a remedy he advocated the colonization
scheme. This plan seems to have won some support, for the Constitution of
1851 expressly provides that "no Negro or mulatto shall come into or settle in
the state after the adoption of the Constitution." All contracts made with a
Negro were declared void and the person making the contract was subject to
a fine of from $10 to $500, the money to be used to colonize the Negroes
already in the state who might be willing to emigrate. This same act also specifically denies to Negroes the right to vote and it was not until sixteen years
after the close of the Civil War that these restrictions were removed.

   So intense was the feeling at the beginning of the Civil War that it was an
open question as to which side Indiana would throw its support. "Copper-
heads" were to be found everywhere, and though they resorted to every
measure to embarrass Governor Morton in his stand for the Union, he
stood adamant. When the legislature refused to appropriate money with
which to run the state, he borrowed money privately and carried on affairs
for two years until a new legislature could be elected. Acts of sedition were
common and United States Senator Bright was unseated for treasonable
commerce with the Confederacy.

   Among the organizations that launched strong opposition to the Unionist
policy of the administration was that known as the "Sons of Liberty." In
reality this was but the northern branch of that rebel organization, the
"Knights of the Golden Circle," whose chief object was the propagation of
slavery. So pronounced was this opposition that acts of violence were en
gaged in but Governor Morton enforced drastic measures against the order. In spite of the attempts of some historians to sugar-coat the purposes
of these men it is evident that treason was in their hearts, and in 1862 the
Federal Grand Jury unearthed 15,000 names on the roster in Indiana.

What was the Negro doing all this time? What
was his reaction to his situation? Did he have no
friends among the whites and how did he justify
the hopes of these friends?

   Staunch friends of the Negro were to be found
among the whites and the "Underground Railroad" did a flourishing business through the
state. The Quakers of Whitewater and Clark
Counties were thorough Abolitionists and encouraged many Negroes both to settle in the

*Mrs. Eulalia Proctor, Indianapolis, Ind. On the staff
of the Indianapolis "Freeman."*

state and to pass farther into Canada. As late as 1857 a man named Purdum in Hamilton County left $1,000 in his will to assist fugitive slaves to freedom. Most of the Negroes in Indiana were men who had been freed and who had come across the mountains from Virginia. Others had escaped from Kentucky and the story of Uncle Tom's Cabin vividly portrays the flight across the Ohio. These pioneer souls represented good, sturdy stock—the best that could be produced under slavery regime.

Indiana was one of the northern states that did not permit the Negro to join in the fight for his own freedom during the Civil War, but some of them took advantage of the opportunity to serve as mule-drivers and cooks and thus had some share in the liberation of their people, a thing which was destined to send more Negroes northward and into Indiana.

THE NEGRO OF FREEDOM
PART 2

This rapid glance into the political history of the Negro in Indiana serves to throw a light upon the peculiar psychosis that makes many of the existing conditions possible. It may justify us in the point of view that Indiana has never been a "northern" state in the full sense of what that term implies but its tendencies when they have not been openly southern have always exhibited a marked strain of "Dixie." Conditions which have been unremittingly fought in Illinois and Michigan and New York have been accepted as more or less inherent in the fibre of Indiana.

The Civil War found the Negro engaged almost solely in work of a personal character—occupations such as those of porter, barber, cook, household servant or the like. It is true that a few worked as farmers but in practically every case none of these owned their own farms but were hired or indentured to white landowners. Sixty years have brought a considerable addition in the number engaged in work of a professional nature, but still the vast number are menials. It may be cited that there is a large and growing class of physicians, lawyers, school teachers, dentists, pharmacists, clerical workers of various sorts. It cannot be denied that many Negroes have found places in skilled industry as molders, or pattern-makers, while others are employed in the packing industry as meat cutters, meat trimmers, and the like. However, at the same time one is astonished at the large percentage employed at unskilled or common labor—construction gangs, street cleaners, hod carriers, janitors, and other laborious and otherwise undesirable work.

Usually it is the lowest sort of work that falls to the colored man, his choice oftentimes coming after that of the foreigner. The field for Negro labor in Indiana is decidedly limited. Take the automobile industry as an example. Indiana ranks high in the manufacture of motor cars. Negroes are allowed to drive them—in some instances they may repair them—but after they leave the molding floor as castings no Negro does anything in the manufacture of them. The outlook for colored women is even worse be-

Mrs. Sue V. Artis, Indianapolis, Ind. Head of the Visitation Dept., Flanner House Social Settlement. Wife of Lionel F. Artis.

Miss Cordia Jones. Office Secretary, Y.M.C.A., Indianapolis, Ind. Member of the younger set.

Mrs. Myrtle Summers De Frantz, Indianapolis, Ind. Wife of F. E. De Frantz, Sec'y Y.M.C.A. Teacher and social worker.

Mrs. Frances B. Coston. Principal in Indianapolis Public Schools. President, Educational Society for Colored Orphans.

cause except for domestic service in private families there is relatively little else for them to do.

With the door to economic progress so tightly closed it would seem that the Negro in Indiana would organize for his own economic advancement. But this appears to be a wild dream for there are no successful co-operative business enterprises. The nearest approach to anything like co-operation is found in lodge and church and this is interspersed with the pyrotechnic of factionalism and quarrels. The lodges build rival halls to be rented for dances and the churches build an increasing number of "meeting houses," but nothing is done to improve the status of the people economically. Trinity Masonic Lodge in Indianapolis is a notable exception, for with an eye to relieving the acute housing situation these men under the able leadership of Worshipful Master Frank Alexander built twelve living apartments and five storerooms in connection with their lodge hall proper. This investment is a sample of what could be done by co-operative effort.

It may be argued that Sanders Lamp Shade Co. and Martin Bros. and H. L. Sanders Co. and the Mme. C. J. Walker Co. have factories in Indianapolis and employ a large number of colored people. But the answer is that these are strictly private enterprises.

Whatever success they have attained is due to the sacrifice and genius of their proprietors and the loyalty they have been able to engender in the employees.

Indianapolis can boast of no bank, although it has a population of forty thousand Negroes. This, too, in face of the fact that a white bank has a branch in the Negro business district and is collecting Negro dollars by the thousands.

There is, however, a Colored Business League which is launching an experiment that might well recommend itself to other cities. John Bankett has been engaged as Propaganda Secretary, and his whole time is devoted to offering suggestions to the merchants as to how to improve their businesses and to stirring up an interest in and loyalty to Negro business on the part of the citizens. So far the endeavor has proven successful and both efficiency and patronage of business establishments operated by Negroes have increased. Although there is an absence of large scale co-operative business among Indianapolis Negroes, there is a horde of small shops and businesses which afford a comfortable living for their keepers. Martin Morgan can boast of one of the few and perhaps the best hardware store owned by a Negro in the country. One other Negro, John Jones, dug a hole in the bed of the river and has dredged hundreds of thousands of dollars worth of sand. He furnishes perhaps one-quarter of the sand which goes into the building construction work in the city. The Gibralter Life Insurance Co. was organized a comparatively short time ago and under the direction of Chas. M. Hayes bids fair to achieve some of the success which has come to those great organizations in the South. Williams and Walker operate a first class up-to-date drug store and a large percentage of their patronage is white. Fleming has one of the finest equipped cafeterias in the Middle West. Several progressive undertaking establishments are run by people of color and Hill Brothers own and operate a chain of moving picture theatres. Dr. E. N. Perkins operates one of the finest chiropody and beauty parlors in the Middle West, surpassed by none outside of Chicago and New York. An up-to-date shoe store maintained by the pluck of Samuel Grizzle, a young man; several small groceries, some small restaurants, dozens of barber shops (otherwise forum centers), a galaxy of hairdressing parlors, automobile repair shops, gambling shops, soft(?) drink parlors, pool halls,

Mrs. Maud Hoag Milton, Prominent club woman and instructor in Domestic Science, Kokomo, Ind.

Mrs. Geo. L. Riffe, Social leader, Muncie, Ind.

Miss Edna Perkins, Daughter of Dr. E. M. Perkins, of Indianapolis, Ind. Popular member of the younger social set.

and a host of pressing and cleaning establishments are other manifestations of the attempt to enter the commercial field. A few Negroes own farms and are working on them; some others are share tenants but the number of both is negligible. The Unions are solidly against Negro participation and although "open" shops flourish the colored man finds himself barred from most of them.

One does not stay satisfied with merely feeding himself. The life is more than meat or raiment and one is quite as eager to express himself as he is to keep body and soul together. After economic standing is gained perhaps the most vital thing is political status. What the political status of the Negro in Indiana was prior to 1881 has already been hinted at. He simply had no status, being regarded as a chattel at law. The wording of the law was changed to meet the demands of the Federal Constitution but one has a right to doubt if the fundamental spirit behind the law of Indiana has

changed very much. Theoretically the Indiana law provides against discrimination against any person on account of race or color or religious belief,
but in actual practice "Jim Crow" runs wild. The framers of the State
Constitution must have had the idea that white women would flock into the
arms of Negro men as wives and to prevent this they inserted a prohibitive
clause against inter-marriage—a clause which stands to this very day.
Doubtless the present law-makers have the same opinion because every
effort to have the clause stricken out has failed.

Negroes are forbidden to bear arms in the State National Guard and in
1921 the attempt to amend the Constitution to permit colored men to be
sworn in to protect the state failed to pass a referendum vote. The state law
empowers local school commissioners at their option to establish separate
colored schools (and rare is the locality where this option has not been
exercised).

Hoosier Negroes do not seem to have learned the lesson that power comes
sometimes through sheer force of numbers and at other times through strategy of position. Numerically the dominant political parties—Republican
and Democratic—are about evenly divided in Indiana and it is a toss to
decide who will win in any election. The Negro vote is reputed to carry the
balance of power. For instance in Marion County, of which Indianapolis is
the seat, the Negro could command most any concession for his ballot. I say
could for this is as yet only potential. The time is not far past when election
time meant "red lantern suppers," free beer, torch light parades, watermelon and ice cream feasts, the hearty handshake of some white politician
and the free flow of "persuader"—this persuader usually taking the form of a
two-or five-dollar note. These were the days when the "Black Cabinet"—a
group of unabashed money-seeking Negro politicians—held sway. So near
has the regime been that even yet whenever a delegation seeks an audience
with a public official the first reaction on his part is that they desire an
opportunity to "bum" some money.

Fortunately a new element is gaining control; partially because younger
and better trained men both colored and white are becoming interested in
politics—partly because death is cutting into the ranks of these former
Negro political sages. As a sop colored men are appointed to minor
clerkships in county and municipal offices but no Negroes win elective
offices. Six years ago, after a break of almost twenty years, a Negro, Dr.
Sumner A. Furniss, was elected to the City Council of Indianapolis and
served with distinction. However, the jealousy and bigotry of Negro quasi-
leaders have kept another from succeeding him. It has been years since a
Negro sat in the State Legislature and although Negroes could elect any
man upon whom they would unitedly decide, there seems to be little pros-
pect of a Negro representative for some years.

In spite of the fact that there is no real recognition given the Negro voter,
one finds little tendency to vote anything other than the straight "G.O.P."
ticket—and this in face of the fact that almost every prominent Republican

has been unearthed as a member of the Ku Klux Klan. Scattering ones have dared support the Democratic ticket amidst the curses of their neighbors and a few have been prominently identified with the Socialist Party. That party ran a Negro for Auditor of the State at the last state election. One bright side is that the morale of the Negro voter has been raised considerably by the advent of women at the polls.

For several years Negroes have served on the police and fire departments of Indianapolis and have reflected credit on the race. Both of these appointments are nominally by Civil Service but political preference is not without influence.

Speaking of schools—it is only a question of time when Indianapolis, the capital city, will have a "Jim Crow" high school. Already the bond issue has been approved for the project and except for loud talk the Negroes are sitting idly by. This year colored children have been ejected from several white schools which they have attended for years unmolested. Slowly but steadily the ground is being harrowed for the growth of suspicion and racial misunderstanding. Be it said, on the other hand, that all this segregation has not been due to the meanness or prejudice of white people alone, for it is a fact that in the early days certain Negro leaders made a bid for separate schools. The only creditable aspect is that in most instances the standards for teachers and equipment for the buildings and the course of study have been kept on a par with those for the whites. Evil is seldom unmixed and it is a question whether what the children lose in the way of contact with the whites may not be compensated for by the gain derived from racial self-government and the resultant qualities of self-reliance, initiative, and pride engendered. These public schools are preparing an increasing number of Negro children for college and this year finds 139 colored boys and girls in colleges within the state. This takes no cognizance of a large number who attend institutions in adjoining states.

Particular mention should be made of the high calibre of work done in Booker T. Washington Junior High School under George L. Hayes. The teaching staff of this school is exceptionally well trained, almost every member being a university graduate. School No. 26, which John Dewey praised so highly in his book "Schools of Tomorrow," is the central influence for good in the East-side community. Under William R. Valentine and Arthur T. Long it touched the community life, and under its present head, Matthias Nolcox, it gives promise of even greater power.

Often one has heard the phrase "Negro Heaven" used to describe Indianapolis—and the situation there can be taken as typical of the whole state. If people mean by that that there have been no lynchings and hangings (the cruder forms of murder), we agree that the situation is good, but if they mean that here Negroes enjoy the full measure of their rights as citizens and men, Indianapolis must be accounted as far from the celestial regions.

In the "social" life of the community there is a separation of the races as distinct as anywhere in Mississippi. It is true that Negroes may ride on street cars but these are re-routed, adding several miles to the trip to obviate passing through Negro residential districts. There are many theaters in which a Negro has never looked except to mop and polish; and he might pass a hundred restaurants, no matter how famished he might be, and starve in the street. One or two might hand him a sandwich in a paper sack.

The housing situation is acute and little sign of relief appears. Deacons and elders of the fashionable white churches of the city own rows of shacks in the undesirable sections of the city for which they exact high rentals from widows and hard working Negroes. The death rate among Negroes remains high but real estate men refuse to provide sanitary and desirable dwelling places due to what seems to be a covert understanding that conditions must not be made too attractive or more Negroes would immigrate here, and as added one prominent member at a Chamber of Commerce dinner, "That would never do."

A small measure of civic recognition is accorded the Negro, but on important civic committees for important visitors no Negro is ever named. Wherever the "social" aspect obtrudes itself the Negro finds participation restricted.

Among the younger business men and among a liberal element of the older men there is a tendency to face this issue squarely and to treat colored men of intelligence and culture on terms of cordiality and equity. There is an enlarging group of white people who really want to be just and fair and who speak boldly for the Negro in any group. Outstanding among this number are men like Dr. F.S.C. Wickes, pastor of the Unitarian Church; Dr. Howard E. Jensen of Butler College, and Dr. C. H. Winders, secretary of the Church Federation, and Rabbi M. Fuerlicht. On the other hand, among many of the older generation there is an air of patronage—the "Good mawnin, George," attitude which is the survival (vestigial, we hope)—of the "Copperhead" Civil War feeling here. One can get so far with them and then he meets an immediate "impasse." They are inclined to be friendly after a fashion but they view the Negro through 1860 glasses and stubbornly refuse to have their opinion changed. One feels like repeating with him of old, "Would that they were either hot or cold." Then would one know how to handle them. Too, one will run into a large section of the lower middle class of whites who are as "red-necked" as in Dixie, who hate every Negro. Why? No matter; no reason—they just hate a "coon" cause they can!

This last class forms the bulk of that vast army of "Koo Koos" in Indiana. Reliable figures place the membership of the Klan in Indiana as second or at best third in the country. A comparatively small number of established business men belong; a large group of demagogues and hosts of narrow-brained, ignorant "poor whites." One jocularly remarked the other day, "Well, you can count a thousand '100 per cent American' Fords but no Packards," and he spoke truly. Indiana still raises as gullible a lot as ever and many of these poor "Koo Koos," like their forerunners, the "Sons of Liberty," in 1860, are fools who join for the notoriety and the mystery

connected with the order and have no appreciation of the deeper significance of the movement. The fight thus far seems to be political and the
program in the state has been confined to that aspect.

Firmly have I come to believe that no people rises higher politically than
its economic status and the history of the Negro in Indiana confirms this. It
is significant that where Negroes have no economic status and where their
living has depended largely upon personal service jobs that there is a lack
of positive, aggressive leadership. Indianapolis and Indiana as a whole are
no exceptions. In few places does there seem to be such an utter lack of
fearless, unselfish leadership (and nowhere is it more needed). Justice runs
crying in the street while the Negro remains divided by envy and jealousy
and petty allegiance to white masters. Only with the increase of external
social pressure due to a more marked manifestation of prejudice and discrimination is the Indiana Negro being *driven* together. How be it, the
forces are external rather than cohesive.

This absolute lack of racial solidarity and of aggressiveness makes for the
increase of discrimination, segregation, and other marks of inferiority status. "The half-loaf-is-better-than-none" attitude is apparently the heritage
of the historical development of the state. Now and then a Negro raises his
head to fight for justice and civil rights but he has to fight not only against
the whites but against his self-styled Negro "leaders" who are content to
"let well enough alone." The case of Dr. Lucian Meriwether, a young
colored man, and his plucky lawyer, R. L. Bailey, who fought for two years
through every branch of the courts to uphold the right of Negroes to
purchase and live in property in any section of the city, illustrates the point.
Singlehanded, he bore the brunt of the fight (later assisted in the Supreme
Court by the N.A.A.C.P.), and not withstanding the disapproval of many
colored people won a favorable decision in the Supreme Court. Now the
Negroes who opposed him at the start are loudest in the praise of his
stamina. The point I am driving at is that no one seems willing to fight these
issues when the outcome is uncertain.

Perhaps it would be more charitable to class the Indiana Negro as a
stand-patter rather than as being cowardly. He will sputter and spew; he
will "resolute" and protest and hold indignation meetings; but when it
comes to a prolonged fight he would rather "let George do it." White
people have found this out and discrimination grows apace.

The biggest co-operative endeavor accomplished by Negroes in Indiana
is the Colored Branch of the Y.M.C.A. in Indianapolis. This organization
has just celebrated its tenth anniversary in its modern building and with a
membership of 2,500 leads all the other "Y's" in the country in the amount
and character of work done among the population. For years it has served
more of the population than any other Y.M.C.A., but perhaps its greatest
contribution is the manner in which the best idealism and life of the Negro
is interpreted to the thinking white people.

One word ought to be written about the Indiana Negro press, which is represented at its best by the *Indianapolis Freeman*. This paper, which has run for almost half a century, has always stood out for its able editorial department. The change in personnel in recent years has helped the organization and its editorials are powerful forces in striking at things which affect the welfare of Negroes throughout the country. It is absolutely unfettered by political allegiance and is one paper which realizes the constructive force of the press in raising the standard of Negro citizenship and conduct.

I have not spoken of the church and fraternal life of the Indiana Negro because this is of the character common to the people of other states. Neither have I spoken of the amount of property owned by Negroes. Material assets are by no means an index of progress and happiness, for along with the possession of money must go the freedom to spend it for one's cultural and recreational and living needs.

In conclusion, the Indiana Negro may be described in the words of the Hebrew prophet of old as "a peculiar people." He has cast off the slothfulness of the Delta Negro; lost the backwardness of the Alabama Negro; thrown away the the submissive demeanor of the Louisiana plantation— yet he lacks the pioneer spirit of the Kansan. He possesses none of the breeziness of the Chicagoan nor the sophistication of the Easterner, nor the hauteur of the Virginian. The Hoosier—white and black—is "just folks"— plain, solid, unvarnished, home-loving, law-abiding, maybe with too much complacency with life "as is," but withal true at heart.

The Negro in Indiana is like a mighty lion asleep. Infinite power and opportunity lie with him but he knows it not. He has been asleep so long except for sporadic fitful stretches—that one begins to wonder if he will ever awaken. Not only is he asleep but he is sick as well, his body aching with the injustices and discriminations heaped upon him; but like one drugged he moves on.

The time has come when the Negro here must either wake up or be *blown up*. The rising tide of Kluxism, of "Jim Crowism" in school and state, of base segregation and rankling race hatred sends out a challenge that must not fall on deaf ears. Whether the Negro shall attain his full stature of manhood rights depends upon two factors: the Negro's awareness of his own powers and a desire intense enough to constrain him to work together for the achievement of his political and economic emancipation. Rest assured that with the peculiar psychosis of the native Hoosier in mind, this achievement must be won by hard fighting and united efforts. It will not come from out the clouds nor by prayer.

J. EVERETT HARRIS

Kentucky: (Janus Bifrons)

VOL. 6, NO. 10, OCTOBER 1924

Little is known about J. Everett Harris. Chilling and compelling, Harris's story of Kentucky moves with an impelling argument toward a disturbing end. One of the most rhetorically complex of the series, "Kentucky: (Janus Bifrons)" is an essay featuring considerations of class and contradictions of race and of geography, providing an outline of a history that is seemingly out of control.

The single-bodied, two-faced Janus Bifrons of Roman mythology (although Harris mistakenly says Greek) is invoked by Harris for metaphorical purposes not simply because it suggests the fundamental connection between the northward-gazing and southward-gazing "faces" of Kentucky. Janus the Roman deity was the god of thresholds, of doorways, of beginnings. Janus was never two men, or even one man with two opinions. He was a god with divided loyalties, and as invoked by Harris, the Janus of history becomes the Judas of history. The division of loyalties is only a facade. The mythological figure from the state seal "is represented as having two faces on one body, but the body, hands and feet are turned in one direction." Harris paints the Kentucky Janus as lumbering threateningly toward the South.

The southern "love of leisure" was never fully developed in Kentucky thanks to its tradition of small farming and, as Harris further argues, thanks to its lack of laws of primogeniture. Since with every successive generation land was divided up into increasingly smaller parts, slavery—at least the kind of large plantation slavery that fueled the more southern economies—was never quite the same in Kentucky as it was in other states. Nevertheless, Harris argues that an African American culture developed within a system almost as insidiously oppressive as that of the southern plantation system. Because of their heritage as only moderately oppressed (Harris describes their bonds as "not very irksome"), African Americans in Kentucky led a life which was "bifrontal." Harris claims that the thousands of slaves who were relatively content with their lot (as illustrated by the numbers who remained with their masters when they might easily have escaped across the Ohio river) successfully laid the groundwork for a society in which voting is desultory, and in which African American business enterprise is only beginning to escape from the stagnation that had characterized it for so long.

Despite opening with the story of a child disowned by its mother because of its sullied blood, Harris refuses, point by point, to provide any easy closure. Whatever happened to the baby? Will his father come and claim him? Will he stay in the orphanage? And how shall he claim this biracial heritage? Harris leaves the story unresolved, using the child as a metaphor for the contradictions he saw underlying any sense of Kentuckian identity. If the child had been born further south, Harris suggests, a far less civilized and perhaps bloodier chain of events would have ensued. And yet it is the unresolved quality of the story that is most telling: we never find out what actually happened to the principals in the story.

Harris's conclusion tends toward the negative. However much Kentucky maintains a "northern" belief in freedom and justice, it is the southern face of racism and hopelessness that determines African Americans' true options. Harris suggests, especially in his last, pessimistic sentence, that this negative fate is inescapable, though his description of the new growth of African American businesses and his belief in the fighting spirit of Kentucky's citizens tempers that pessimism. "Kentucky's compromise between justice and prejudice," as Harris shows, remain an unfinished story.

MR. HARRIS

A peculiar letter came to the President of the Board of the Colored Orphans' Home of Louisville, Kentucky, in his morning's mail some few months ago from the leading merchant in the little town of G———, Kentucky. It ran:

Dear Sir:

I have been advised to write to you in order to get a little colored child into your Orphanage. The child is not exactly what you might call an orphan because both his mother and father are living here in G———. But his mother is a white woman and his father is a colored. The mother is married and living with her husband and four other children.

The child which I am writing about is about two years old and all of us thought that he was white until recently when the colored blood began to show in his color, features, and hair. The mother admitted that he is not her husband's child but that of a well-known and popular colored man around here. The woman and her husband asked me what to do about it as I have been a friend and adviser to them for years. That is the reason I am writing to you. I am not connected with the matter except as an adviser.

It is impossible for the child to continue growing in the family although all are fond of him and the mother especially hates to give him up. You know how mothers are. But if you could find a way to take him, a lot of unpleasantness for the child, the family he is in, his father, and all concerned would be avoided.

Hoping to hear from you soon and that you will take him, I am

Very truly yours,

————

We wrote back to this guardian of his township's peace expressing our interest and asking how the child would be delivered to us in the event that we could take him. We asked what would be the community's attitude toward the child's father and what the woman's husband intended doing. By return mail the answer came, jubilant in its hopefulness, saying that the mother would bring the child, that her husband would come with her if necessary, that the child's father would be unmolested and might continue in the even tenor of his way to live in G————and to pursue happiness. With these assurances we arranged a date for the mother's coming.

We met her at the train,—a rather robust, red-necked country type, shabbily dressed, holding her big bundle closely to an ample bosom and looking around for her child's future protectors with wide watery-blue eyes in whose tragic wistfulness a world-sorrow smouldered. We took her to the home where, incoherent with sobbing, she told us that she loved the child's father and loved the child best of all her babies. She begged us not to give the baby away, assuring us that the father would come to take him to care for him as soon as he was able. Then she went back to G————and to her family pathetically dabbing at eyes that had looked upon sorrow and tightly compressing lips that had tasted of pain.

This was in Kentucky, and exemplifies the fundamental dichotomy which characterizes that state,—Kentucky on the border of Mason and Dixon's line,—Kentucky which may be appositely represented by the Greek god *Janus* of two faces. In fact, the seal of the Commonwealth of Kentucky presents two men facing each other and clasping hands. One face gazes across its northern boundary, the Ohio River, the widest river in the world, when on one shore was slavery and oppression and on the other comparative justice of the northern states. The other face is set steadfastly toward "Dixie," toward the land of cotton whose old times there, it seems, will never be forgotten. Under the aspect of the northward-gazing face this white mother unreservedly gave her love to a brown man, her neighbor; under the aspect of the southward-gazing face she unwillingly gave the child of their union to the uncertain guidance of an institution. Under the aspect of the northern face her husband spared the countryside a possibly bloody show of Anglo-Saxon heroics; under the aspect of the southern face he spared his four little blond Americans the inconceivable ignominy of eating bread with their half brother whose face is golden and whose hair curls.

How, now, may we account for the contradictory temper of this state, this bifrontal aspect? Its history largely determined, as in all other states, by its geography gives a deal of light. Kentucky's earliest settlers were not the religious enthusiasts of the northeastern states, nor yet the poverty-ridden nondescripts of some of the southern states, nor yet the mock-heroic, impecunious gentry of the mother state, but the hard-headed, industrious, adventurous pioneers recruited from England's pride and strength, its yeomanry. This early pioneer was a land-thirsty individual willing to pay the price of life for the free lands of this beautiful hunting ground of the aborigines. He was characterized by a certain dauntlessness and a habit of asserting the independence of all control except that of the written law. To this day the habit of lawlessness as expressed in mob-violence has never taken root in Kentucky's soil, and the Ku Klux Klan is not regarded sympathetically in the larger centers. Kentucky was never burdened by the weak incompetent men who led other societies into political debasement. The criminals, weaklings, and other *rejects* of society had no place in this furiously embattled colony; rather, the solid land-seekers were bred in a frontier life to habits of independence and self-control. Every inch of their ground was disputed with the Indians with a result that for two centuries their blood was stimulated by contests and rising generations caught from their forbears the love of conquest which the subsequent commercial life, tending toward the ways of peace, has never quite succeeded in eradicating. There is not a time in Kentucky's history in which we do not find some evidence of the hunger for adventure, until the war of the Rebellion with its hard fighting wore out the old humor,—at least for a time.

The nature of the inhabitants and of the land determined the state's interesting attitude toward slavery. Along with some of the earliest pioneers came the Negro slave. Daniel Boone in one of his letters mentions the fact that a certain one of his men and his slave were killed in an encounter with the Indians. The slave, however, made a not very dauntless pioneer. His forte was tilling not winning the soil. Consequently, it is long after Kentucky was settled, long after the ever-menacing danger of Indian invasion, then a bloody memory, that Negro slaves appear in any great numbers. Slaves did not begin to be a considerable element in the population until about the time of the separation from Virginia, when, the Revolutionary War having ended, there was a richer class among the immigrants. The earlier settlers, then, men and women alike, did their own work. They planted their own small crops, harvested them, and were content with comparative poverty and the thrill of adventure just around the corner. Inured to toil and hardship, and depending for a living upon his good right arm, the first Kentuckian had no opportunity to develop the love of leisure which prompted the development of the slave holding system among his more southern brothers. He preferred the zest of dangerous living to the ease of leisurely loafing.

Then, the land played its part. Only a small part of the Commonwealth is

LEFT TO RIGHT: Miss Kathryn Wise, Louisville, Ky.; Mrs. Wilson Lovett, Louisville, Ky.; Mrs. Fanny B. Postille, Hopkinsville, Ky.

fit for anything like plantation life. The greater part of the area requires the thrift and care of the owner to make its cultivation remunerative. Even that part of the land of Kentucky that may be used for tillage in a large way is decidedly more profitable in the hands of farmers who cultivate small areas. Further, the principle of primogeniture which lasted so long in Virginia never gained a place in Kentucky. The result was that each generation saw the lands more completely divided, and the area fit for slave labor became constantly less occupied by large farmers.

But slaves there were in abundance, and the large slave holders formed a powerful element in the new state. The result is Kentucky's north-south, Janus-faced attitude toward slavery. From the earliest of times through the Rebellion, the Negro slave was a bone of contention. The first constitution formed in 1792 contained an article which shows a decided prejudice against the commerce in slaves. They are not to be brought into the state as merchandise, and none are to be brought that were imported into America since 1789. It also recommends to the legislature to pass laws permitting the emancipation of slaves under the limitation that they shall not become a charge on the community. Again, about 1798, when Henry Clay began to be a power in the nation, his plan of emancipation became an article of faith with his party and was approved by the larger part of the conservative whites. The Federal Census of 1800 shows a population in Kentucky of 221,955. Of these, 179,873 were whites, 40,343 slaves, and 737 free Negroes. In 1810 out of a population of 406,511 there were 324,237 whites, 80,561 slaves, and 1,713 free Negroes,—more than two per cent of the total Negro population. Through the succeeding years, what with the anti-slavery sentiment fostered by Henry Clay and the frank abolitionist, his relative, Cassius M. Clay, the percentage of free Negroes grew faster than the percentage of additional slaves. The majority of these slaves were of the domestic sort who bore not very irksome bonds and who, for the most part, were, as Stephen Foster claims, "gay." This is shown by the fact that thousands quietly remained with their masters in the counties along the Ohio River, when on any night they might have escaped across the border.

The dichotomy in the state's attitude toward slavery is elaborately illustrated in its action during the War of the Rebellion. The inhabitants moved to the Stars and Bars and to the Stars and Stripes in equal numbers while the state remained neutral as long as possible. When, finally, it joined the ranks of the Union, it was merely a gesture under the aspect of the northward-gazing face, while half its sons cast their lots with Lee under the influence of the southward-gazing face.

The war over, the freedman in Kentucky found his situation not so difficult. He continued to farm, raising chiefly tobacco, on ground he was permitted to purchase on comparatively fair and easy terms. In the cities he continued in domestic service, and as an employee in the rapidly growing industries. On the boats which plied the Ohio River he continued in various capacities from stevedore to steward. There was no marked upheaval in his life and he quickly adapted himself to the ways of peace and profitable labor. Since then the years have slipped by and the Negro in Kentucky has adapted himself now to the state's northern proclivities, now to the southern,—more often to both.

Trusting in the justice of the northern face, the Negro has developed no strong institutions of instruction like those in other southern states which take the place of high and normal schools. The public school facilities, although inadequate, have yet been respectable. The state supports two Normal Schools, poor, but not the poorest. Louisville boasts a high school which ranks just a little below the best Negro high schools in the country. There are thirteen high schools in the state with four year courses and ranked by the state 1A, as well as a large number with three-year courses. The American Missionary Association has only one school in the state, Chandler Normal at Lexington, and it is now dead because it could not compete successfully with the local public schools. Simmons University, a Baptist institution in Louisville, has dragged along ineffectively through the years but is now improving and bids fair to become a decent college in the not too distant future.

The most interesting case, however, in the history of Negro education in Kentucky is that of Berea College. Founded in 1874 by a group of abolitionists for the joint education of whites and blacks, it continued until 1904 to admit Negroes and whites with little or no discrimination or show of prejudice. At the opening there were 181 colored and 106 white students, and in 1903, the colored students comprised one third of the attendance. Under the smile of Kentucky's northern face Berea was founded and flourished, turning out Negroes, the majority of whom have figured prominently in Kentucky's life. Under the frown of our southern face, Berea closed its doors on Negroes after the legislature had made it unlawful for whites and blacks to attend the same schools. To take the place of Berea, a separate school named Lincoln Institute was established in 1909. It has a good plant, a faculty of white and colored teachers, and offers normal and industrial training of the kind and extent so popular in southern states. Only yesterday I heard someone say that Lincoln Institute had everything it needed with the exception of some students.

Fortunately there has been no law aiming at the disfranchisement of the Negro in Kentucky. Instead, he is the mainstay of a Republican party which shares about equal honors with the Democratic party. The Negro voter, therefore, can be the deciding factor in all state elections when he learns to think instead of merely remembering. In spite, however, of his political strength he has never succeeded in electing a member of his race to a public office although he several times attempted it. Rather, he has been content with the meager crumbs from his party's table in the form of inconsequential jobs, petty grafts, and privileges for exploiting his own people. There are, of course, a few desultory Democrats who mean, as yet, little or nothing in Kentucky's political life. But there are hopeful signs of discontent,—menacing signs which made the last city election in Louisville a bitter affair—which encourages one to believe that before long the Negro will use his ballot as it easily can be used,—as a mighty weapon of offense or defense.

In industry the same north-south temper is apparent. Negroes furnish the majority of labor in the tobacco factories. Incidentally, the work in these tobacco factories has done more to degrade Negro women than any other agency in the state. But many Negroes make high wages and colored foremen and forewomen are not uncommon. In most of the factories, tobacco and other, these workers are provided with recreational facilities, company insurance, health-protecting devices and the like. On the other hand, they are not admitted to the labor unions. Colored carpenters, concrete workers, bricklayers, stone masons and other artisans are seen working on almost every building under construction. Invariably, however, they are paid just a little less than the price which white union workers demand for the same work—a wage which represents Kentucky's compromise between justice and prejudice.

Stagnation which customarily accompanies compromise was until recent years the characteristic of Negro business in Kentucky. Of course, there were the usual successful drug stores, undertaking establishments, pressing shops, saloons, groceries, fish and bread joints which styled themselves cafés, and other such little enterprises administering to personal capital needs, but the great majority of these represented individual capital invested on a small scale. Negroes had free access to white businesses and were for the most part courteously treated. They, therefore, evinced the commercial backwardness common in northern communities. Further, the failure of some Negro commercial experiments shook the Kentuckian's faith in all colored business enterprises. In the last few years, however, the

Kentucky Negro with his face toward the south has caught the vision of corporate endeavor with the result that a number of substantial Negro corporations have grown and flourished almost overnight.

The pioneer in big Negro business in Kentucky is W. H. Wright of Louisville. In 1915 he was the moving spirit in the establishment of the Mammoth Life and Accident Insurance Company. This company became a legal reserve life insurance company in 1924 with an authorized capital of $200,000 and a reserve and surplus of $123,000. It has over $5,000,000 worth of insurance in force and its income in 1923 was over $320,000.

In 1919 he organized the Mammoth Realty Company, which is now capitalized at $250,000 with resources over a half million dollars. It is now erecting a six-story building which will contain apartments, offices, stores, and a theatre.

In 1922, Mr. Wright organized the American Mutual Savings Bank (of which he is President) with an authorized capital of $150,000 and with resources at present close to a half million dollars. In the following year he organized the Mammoth Building and Loan Association with a capital stock of $250,000, which has been recently increased to $750,000. This remarkable organization paid a seven per cent dividend in 1924.

Mr. Wright has also been instrumental in establishing the Fayette Realty Co. of Lexington, the Davidson Mutual Savings Association of Paducah, the McCracken Mutual Savings Association of Paducah, and the Home Mutual Savings Association of Bowling Green.

The first bank owned and operated by Negroes in Kentucky was the result of the enterprise of Wilson Lovett, who, in May, 1920, interested leading colored men and women of Kentucky in the establishment of a banking institution. Using a selling organization which he formed, he succeeded in selling stock which represented a capital of $100,000 and a surplus of $10,000. Early in 1921 the First Standard Bank opened for business. its capital stock and surplus have recently been increased to $220,000. Since its organization, this bank has handled over five million dollars worth of business, has assisted more than fifteen hundred separate Negro businesses and corporations, and loaned more than half a million dollars to colored men and women. At the present time, the resources of the bank are more than $500,000, with deposits of more than $400,000.

Mr. Lovett has, further, established the James T. Taylor Real Estate Company, which now has assets of close to $50,000, and the Standard Building and Loan Association, with a capital of $100,000.

The Domestic Life Insurance Company, of which G. P. Hughes is president, began business in 1921 as a legal reserve life insurance company with a $100,000 capital. Its articles of incorporation have been recently amended, increasing its capital to $200,000. They have issued over fifty thousand policies for nearly $6,000,000 worth of insurance. The total income since its organization is over a half million dollars and it has paid to policy holders $130,000.

Mr. W. W. Wright, President of The American Mutual Savings Bank, Louisville, Ky.

Mr. Wilson Lovett, President of The First Standard Bank, Louisville, Ky.

This mushroom growth of business in Kentucky may be a part of the development of corporate activity among Negroes which seems to be sweeping the country just now. Again, it may mean that colored Kentuckians have stopped wasting thought and energy trying to decide which of Kentucky's faces to believe, and have started to build a solid economic foundation for their bifrontal life. Probably both are indicated. We are hoping that

Kentuckians are learning to use effectively the money which previously they squandered on our fleet-footed horses and the choice Bourbon whiskey which, in the distant halcyon days, flowed from our stills. The thoroughbreds for which Kentucky is so justly famous and which Negroes have bred and nursed now find themselves running against firmly established commercial institutions, and our money is on the institutions.

The god Janus is represented as having two faces on one body, but the body, hands and feet are turned in one direction. Kentucky, the Janus Bifrons of the United States, in spite of his northern face, yet reaches out with open arms to the South and his feet move in that direction. Its Negro citizens trust in its northern face but notice the southern steps. Ever and anon with the fighting spirit inherited from their adventurous masters, they wake up to effectively protest against proscription. In Louisville they have fought to a successful issue the Segregation Ordinance, and have defeated at the polls candidates and bond issues inimical to their best interests. But Janus is a god who moves relentlessly and ruthlessly, if slowly, on, as gods have a habit of doing. The Negro may halt him for a time, but his southward march is, it seems, an Olympic decree.

THEOPHILUS LEWIS

Maryland:
The Seventh Heaven of Rotarians

VOL. 5, No. 8, AUGUST 1923

A native of Baltimore, Maryland, Theophilus Lewis was born on March 4, 1891. After serving in World War I and spending several years in Detroit, he moved to New York City in 1922. He appears to have had little formal schooling, which makes him a bit of an anomaly among the many contributors boasting several postgraduate degrees. But Lewis, who supported himself for many years by working in the New York Post Office, developed a reputation as a formidable literary and theater critic. He wrote a number of short stories for *The Messenger* as well, and was, in the words of Arna Bontemps, "the literary brain" of *The Messenger* staff. According to Theodore Kornweibel, Jr., the scholar who knows *The Messenger* best, Lewis's contributions to cultural criticism were the most significant the magazine made.

Lewis's regular drama column in *The Messenger* from 1923 to 1927 was perhaps the most reliably lively and provocative feature, rivaled only by George Schuyler's Menckenesque *Shafts and Darts* column (which Lewis occasionally collaborated on). The first African American drama critic of note, Lewis reviewed serious plays from time to time, but spent most of his energy on the musical revues then all the rage in Harlem. The main concern of his criticism was the development of an independent African American theatrical tradition, one that would employ African American playwrights, directors, and actors and be produced by African American businesses. To forward such a project, Lewis promoted even the goofiest of musical revues as potential vehicles for racial pride; he deplored the preponderance of light-skinned African American women in the chorus lines and sarcastically remarked that one cast featured women who were almost all "biological whites." Eschewing white racial standards for beauty was only part of the new Negro ethos that Lewis promoted in his drama criticism. He complained bitterly that the current African American theater was merely imitating theatrical traditions of white America; "What we call the Negro Theater is an anemic sort of thing that does not reflect Negro life, Negro fancies, or Negro ideas. It reflects 100 per cent American Theater at its middling and cheapest." Lewis's most common proposal for improvising African American theater was that there should be more of it, the more theater the better. Lewis's concern for what role the Negro theater was going to take in the drama of the twentieth century, and how the New Negro Movement could best be articulated on and from the stage, was shared by many of the thinkers and artists of the Harlem Renaissance. After *The Messenger* folded in 1928, Lewis continued to write about the theater in the Jesuit magazine *America* for over twenty years after the end of the renaissance.

How many states outclass Maryland? Well, "You can count them on the thumbs of one foot." For Lewis, appropriating such a slangy, folksy style to convey the conditions of life in Maryland was a calculated attempt to amuse and to make a serious comment about the shortcomings of boosterist rhetoric. But unlike H. L. Mencken, who wrote the essay on Maryland for *The Nation* the previous year, and whose sarcastic antibourgeois spirit hovers over this essay, Lewis acknowledges the power of the ideology of property and prosperity. Mencken truly pines for the days of aristocracy and "civilization" that existed before the industrial revolution, and so he sees bourgeois sentiment as degraded. Lewis sees the revolution instead as incomplete, its advances unevenly distributed. As Lewis knows, the eighteenth-century that Mencken reveres was not a great time for people of color in Maryland either, and for African Americans in the 1920s, "owning a little property or being sure of a good job" were nothing to scoff at.

Lewis's essay "Maryland: The Seventh Heaven of Rotarians" is relentlessly funny ("If there is another such rococo record of devotion to liberty in the annals of these States I have yet to hear of it"), and his pose on the subject of the "Nordic" handling of the "race question" ("The fine old pastime of lynching has fallen somewhat in decline") is scathing. Lewis writes with the voice of a white Marylander to illustrate how a "white" definition of African American identity is inherently misleading. The cheery booster voice he is both using and mocking is so thoroughly "white," Lewis's essay suggests, that even when invoked seriously by African Americans (as in Noah Thompson's reverent essay on California) it will fail in its mission.

In fact, Lewis challenges the entire premise of "These 'Colored' United States." By mocking the obvious limitations of the white voice with reflections such as "when a black man sets a white man up for a pattern he can't help admiring him in his heart, and a white man can't help being flattered by seeing himself exalted to the rank of an exemplar," Lewis questions whether *The Messenger* series—which was modeled after *The Nations*'s series—could ever adequately convey the African American experience. Yet, by disassembling the pretense of such a mission, he makes known the terms in which modern racism could be couched, terms that are necessarily ironic and multivalent: "We've sold the American idea with so much success that even Black Marylanders are on the side of normalcy." Lewis's essay was the fourth of the series, and although distrustful of the mission and its tools, he succeeded in setting a literary standard for all the essays to come.

Mr. Lewis

You don't have to go far to run across wealthier and more populous states than Maryland, and here and there you can point to one with a more dazzling history behind it; but when it comes to locating a commonwealth richer in the high ideals, fine spirit, and pep and go that make America the greatest and grandest country on earth you will find precious few states that outclass the old Panhandle. In fact, you can count them on the thumbs of one foot. I mean they don't exist. As I see it, the Marylanders deserve a lot of credit too; they started off with a bigger handicap than any other state and they've had to overcome greater obstacles all along the way.

In the first place, the soil and climate were against the Maryland men. Up in New England, for example, the Pilgrim Fathers started out with the country on their side. The land is poor and stony, the summers are short and cool and the winters long and severe. The settlers up there, in the words of a funny fellow, had to hoe corn all summer in order to have strength enough to dig clams the next winter, and dig clams all winter in order to have strength enough to hoe corn the following summer. A country like that could not fail to harden the muscles and bring out the stamina of a people.

But the country of the Chesapeake basin seems to have been especially designed to discourage the development of the good American spirit of progressiveness. There is a great diversity of good, well watered soils down here, and the summers are sufficiently long to ripen even the slowest crops. Besides that, when the founders landed here the streams were teeming with fish and the marshes and forests were fairly alive with game. It was the kind of country that tempts people to work a little and loaf a lot, while it assures them of plenty to live on. Mr. James Wright, in his book called "The Free Negro in Maryland," says it was so easy for laborers to become proprietors that pretty soon there was hardly anybody in the colony willing to work for wages; and slavery, black and white, was the only way out. Then there's something in the air that makes a man lazy and dreamy, enchants you like, so you haven't any heart for useful work, but just want to lie out in the grass and gaze at the multi-colored landscape while the humming-birds flash in the sun and the orioles and bluebirds deluge the world with song.

Thank God! the pioneers had the right kind of stuff in them. Otherwise they would have succumbed to the blandishments of the country right off, like they did over in Virginia before the right men got in power. But they had the good old Anglo-Saxon grit in them, and didn't give in to the country one bit. No, sir. They pitched right in and thinned out the forests and killed off the game and scared most of the birds away and started things moving in the right direction.

Unfavorable natural conditions presented only a few of the difficulties the settlers had to struggle with. The big problem they had to solve was how to put down the radicalism that cropped out almost as soon as the colony was founded. You see the Calverts wanted the colony to be the home of religious liberty. That idea had never before been proclaimed in Christendom. It was something new and it went big. But a new idea must be managed in the right way; otherwise it will work more harm than good and never amount to anything. Well, there were a lot of bolsheviki here, wolves in sheep's clothing, right among the founders, who could not understand the difference between liberty and license, and it seems that they almost persuaded Leonard Calvert to their way of thinking. The Calverts were Catholics, you know, and Catholics are always rather romantic and inclined toward mysticism and hardly ever able to get the simon-pure American spirit. Or maybe Leonard Calvert succumbed to the spell of the climate. Anyway, he lost his control, and for a while things were in a pretty bad way. But eventually good solid men came over from Virginia and joined with the right thinking people here and put things in order. We've been plugging along onward and upward ever since, and the result of it is we've developed the finest bang-up American State in the Union.

Take our metropolis, for instance. Baltimore is bigger than any city in Europe, except half a dozen capitals, and when it comes to being wide awake and enterprising, I'll bet there's not a town over there that can class with it. We've got a fine big harbor that's crowded with shipping from all over the world, and we've got some of the biggest steel mills in the country down at Sparrows Point; and at Nobles Point we've got great fertilizer warehouses that stink something grand. Our manufacturing district is a beehive of the busiest sweatshops you can imagine, and we have miles on miles of factories containing marvelous machinery that can crush a child's finger off just beautiful. I won't bother to describe the big way we carry on banking and insurance and mining; you might think I'm just bragging. If you're interested in those things, read the reports of the Department of Commerce, or write to our Board of Trade or ask the secretary of the local Kiwanis Club.

The big thing about all this is that we've achieved our prosperity without sacrificing our freedom and upstanding manhood. After all, the main thing that distinguishes us Americans from other nations is our love of liberty. And we Marylanders are the most liberty loving Americans in these States. Our history proves it. We fought and died for the old flag in the Revolutionary

War, and in the War of 1812 we gave the country a great victory and the National Anthem. In the Civil War, when Massachusetts soldiers closed in on us
before we could get a chance to line up with Jeff Davis and fight for the
South's liberty to hold slaves, one of our citizens named Randall wrote another national anthem especially for us, so we could express our martial ar-
dor vicariously, in a Freudian fashion. If there is another such rococo record
of devotion to liberty in the annals of these States I have yet to hear of it.

There are captious people, I suppose, who will argue that the success the
State has achieved in other lines is compromised by its failure to handle
the Negro problem in a proper way. In answer to that I can only say that the
Nordic go-getters who run the State are only human, and you can't expect
them to be perfect in every respect. Besides, when you take a broad view of
it, the way they're handling the race question isn't bad at all.

It is true that there are no nigger-read-and-run signs on the public high-
ways, as there are in other places in the South; and in Baltimore City there
are no dogs-and-niggers-not-allowed placards gracing the public parks. It is
also true that the fine old pastime of lynching has fallen somewhat in
decline; that is, compared with former standards. A disfranchising act, with
a nifty grandfather clause and a property qualification clause and other up-
to-date appurtenances, failed to go over; a ghetto law was passed once, but
it wouldn't work; and the jim crow law is so imperfect that a Negro can ride
in a white coach from one end of the State to the other if he wants to take
the time and trouble. So far this looks like a flat failure to uphold the
tradition of blond truculence in the presence of an "inferior" race, but read
on and see how education and example have won the results coercion failed
to obtain.

A Maryland Negro named Fred Douglass made quite a stir in the world
once. He was born a slave but before he died he made himself one of the
foremost figures of his time, a renowned publicist, associate of diplomats
and statesmen, and envoy of his government to a foreign country. One
Northern city has named a public square after him and another has erected a
monument in his honor. Do the histories we buy for our colored schools tell
all about him, so little black Marylanders can be inspired by his example and
emulate him? I'll tell the world they do not. And when we look beyond our
borders for a hero to canonize we never forget to make sure his complexion
was right. The reward of our constant vigilance is this: for every fifty Marylanders who know that Freedom shrieked when Kosciusko fell, you'll have a
hard time finding one who knows that Toussaint L'Overture ever lived. So
much for what is being achieved through education.

The results we're getting by making ourselves an example of sound
Americanism are still more gratifying. If you observe Maryland's sepia
Society of doctors, lawyers, ministers and school teachers, you will find
that it differs very little from Maryland's blond Society of bankers and
merchants and their female satellites, except that the latter are richer and
more accustomed to circumstance. And the denizens of Druid Hill Avenue

are working three shifts and overtime to eliminate the remaining differences. It's really inspiring to see the enthusiastic way they're going in for Elks Lodges and Y.M.C.A. drives, sensational journalism and political crusades. They're branching out in business in a small way, too, being engaged in operating various enterprises ranging from drugstores to a steamboat line. The expansion of Johns Hopkins University has been matched by their enlargement of Morgan College. The black wards vote as wise as you can expect, and usually elect a sound colored man, sometimes two to represent them in the Baltimore City Council. I could go on for hours describing how the black Marylanders are advancing along the main lines of progress where white Marylanders have led the way, but I guess I've pointed to enough instances already. There are still points of friction between the races, I admit, but their number is constantly diminishing; for when a black man sets a white man up for a pattern he can't help admiring him in his heart, and a white man can't help being flattered by seeing himself exalted to the rank of an exemplar. I don't think I'm stretching it a bit when I say that an era of good feeling exists among us, and I'll shout it loud that our way of handling the color question has the old system of antagonism and oppression beat a mile.

I'm glad I branched off on this color question now; it helps to illustrate what a sane and solid State we've developed. When I tell you that every year Negroes own more farms than they owned the year before it gives you an idea of how deep rooted our prosperity is. Keeping the whole population of a community saturated with prosperity like that is the best guarantee of stability you can have. Nothing makes a man a satisfied plugger and booster like owning a little property or being sure of a good job. Well, we've sold the American idea with so much success that even black Marylanders are on the side of normalcy.

EUGENE F. GORDON

Massachusetts: Land of the Free and Home of the Brave Colored Man

VOL. 7, NO. 6, JUNE 1925

Eugene F. Gordon was born in Oviedo, Florida, on November 23, 1890, and went to school in Hawkinsville, Georgia. He attended Howard University Academy and College from 1910 to 1917 and the prestigious Negro Officers Training Camp in Des Moines, Iowa. He also took classes at Boston University from 1921 to 1923. Gordon founded and edited *The Bayonet,* a publication of the Massachusetts National Guard, before becoming an editor and writer for the largely white *Boston Daily Post.* At one point he was the editor of all the women's pages in that newspaper, a largely unprecedented position for an African American male journalist. Author of editorials as well as satirical essays, Gordon also published regularly in *American Mercury, Fourth Estate, Scribner's,* and *Plain Talk. Opportunity* published many of his short stories throughout the 1920s and 1930s. He was an active member of the Communist party and lived in the Soviet Union for three years, where he worked for the *Moscow Daily News.* When he returned he wrote for the *Daily Worker.* His books include *The Position of the Negro Woman* (1935), jointly authored with Cyril Briggs; *Pancakes and Caviar: The Food Industry in the U.S.S.R.* (1936); *You're Not Alone* (1940), for the International Workers Order; and *An Essay on Race Amalgamation* (1951), which was published in Brazil with an introduction by Gilberto Freyre. He announced in 1935 that he was leaving journalism to write a novel, but it apparently never appeared.

Gordon is an excellent writer, and this lively and rhetorically adventurous essay manages to address the issues of race, ethnicity, and history with great complexity and sophistication. He has a journalist's flair for compressed narrative and characterization and a good journalist's eye for the value of multiple perspectives. Massachusetts is a state with an unparalleled history of freedom and liberalism, especially as the center of abolitionism, but it also, as Gordon reminds us, had its share of slave traders. Crispus Attucks and Peter Salem may have been early African Americans fighting for the Revolutionary cause, but they "were fighting not as Negroes, but as Americans." This is an important point for Gordon, since he sees abolitionism's legacy as worthy of honor. Nevertheless, he sees that "an almost reasonless abolitionist-ancestor worship" has turned some in the African American community into "spoiled children when they discovered that the world no longer made them the heroes of its imagination." That legacy of heroism has been important for some, like the famous radical preacher Monroe Trotter, who, inspired by a Massachusetts-bred sense of his constitutional rights, went to Washington and called the president "a ding-dong liar." But for others it has meant a sense of entitlement, leading to "more freedom than material possessions, more rights than initiative, more mouth than a desire to work."

He waxes on about the "glory that was ours" to remind readers that the state "has given something of value to the country and to the world, although at present she may appear to be indifferent and incompetent." The contrast between the inclusive Reconstruction governments and the repressive post-Reconstruction governments of the South is discussed in a number of the southern essays, and Gordon uses the same technique to hammer home his disquietude about the state of Massachusetts in the 1920s. Gordon also notes that while there were many elected officials of color in Massachusetts before the turn of the century, there were none in 1925, and only one African American in any office of importance in the state government.

So while Gordon pays due attention to the cultural, political, and economic accomplishments of African Americans in Massachusetts, he notes a decline of such accomplishments since the turn of the century. Most of the essayists in this collection attribute such decline to increasing racism, but Gordon blames "the typical Massachusetts citizen of color" for these problems. "He talks when he should act; he spends when he should save; he thinks in terms of 'race' when he should think in terms of nationality; more often than not his 'culture' is a mere fancy, his worth a conceit, and his accomplishments just ideas." In such language Gordon presages later black conservatives, sounding much closer to Clarence Thomas than to the communism Gordon espoused elsewhere. In a statement that could have come out of the very recent debates about the end of affirmative action, Gordon agrees with those who have decided that "the white folk of Massachusetts have done their share for the colored folk, and now it is time the colored folk helped themselves."

Massachusetts, one of the thirteen original States, ranks forty-fourth in area, sixth in population, and first in the practise of those humanitarian principles upon which the foundation of these United States allegedly stands. To say, however, that Massachusetts is the Utopia of the other forty-seven varieties of oppressed is to tamper with the sacred truth, for— but I am running ahead of myself. Let us begin again, and continue more circumspectly. So . . .

Generally considered to be the original stronghold of the Abolitionists, Massachusetts to this day is looked upon as the land of the free and the home of the brave colored man. How the impression grew into conviction that Massachusetts originated the Every-Slave-a-Free-Man slogan is somewhat veiled in mystery; but such an impression there is, fairly widespread, and generally concentrated in the minds of native sons—and daughters—themselves.

Not only do the older residents of the state believe that Massachusetts is the guardian of all their rights, but they believe that Boston, the capital, is the seat of human justice. Faneuil Hall in Boston is the cradle of liberty, it is said; our colored citizen is sincere in the belief that this designation was made with him alone in mind.

Passing by this very natural mistake, we must concede, nevertheless, that most of the agitation to free the slaves was centered in Boston. We may justly give to New York the honor of being the first to establish an abolition society, but we shall not forget that "the town of Boston as early as 1701 (eighty-four years before the New York City movement) had instructed its representatives in the general assembly to propose putting an end to Negroes being slaves." Boston, therefore, is entitled to considerable praise for its early efforts in behalf of Negro freedom.

There did not exist, however, even at the most enthusiastic agitation for freeing the slaves, a universal sympathy throughout Massachusetts. Many men opposed the radical movement, just as many today oppose the institution of prohibition against liquors; it interfered with their business and threatened their "personal liberty." While some of the organized societies made speeches and published tracts against slavery, others worked with desperate energy to offset anti-slavery influences. There were men and women whose incomes depended almost wholly on the perpetuation of that inhuman institution; there are, today, men and women whose millions had their beginning in that very institution.

It was under the constitution of the United States that Massachusetts began to attract attention to herself as a haven for freed men. Having herself abolished slavery, she furnished to the anti-slavery cause some of its most brilliant minds. Against discouraging odds these men and women preached, plotted and wrote against slavery in the South. They were such persons as Harriet Beecher Stowe, whose "Uncle Tom's Cabin" began running as a serial in *"The National Era,"* Boston, in March of 1852; Wendell Phillips, that eloquent Bostonian who, because of a speech in Faneuil Hall in 1807, became the principal orator of the anti-slavery party, and who, from then until Lincoln's proclamation, was Garrison's loyal and valued ally; William Lloyd Garrison himself, whose fiery denunciations of the slave traders in his paper the *"Genius of Universal Emancipation"* led to his imprisonment for libel, who published in Boston the *"Liberator,"* and who became the head of the American Anti-Slavery Society, and who, finally, barely escaped with his life from a pro-slavery mob in Boston in 1835.

Even though there was much strenuous opposition to the friends of freedom in those days, yet, because of Massachusetts' lead in fighting the evil institution, she won the reputation far and near for whole-hearted benevolence, for unanimous indignation at slave holders, and for universal acceptance of the code involving the brotherhood of man. As most students of history know, and as has already been intimated, that was an erroneously bestowed reputation.

The sentiment of a majority of the people of this state, from the inception of slavery until its abolishment by proclamation throughout the nation, inclined more toward a desire to render the Negro contented with his degraded lot than toward an effort counter to slavery. In other words, the attitude of most citizens was passive, with strong sympathies for the slave trader and his business, rather than actively for or against it. Those who most directly opposed interference with the traffic and the institution were those whose interests were more or less involved in a financial way. Trading in slaves paid big dividends.

Not wholly a story of his inactivity while others fought to free him is the history of the colored man in Massachusetts. The story of Crispus Attucks, while often nowadays too evidently embellished with fictitious trimmings, is one of the attractive legends of the Revolutionary period, and outshines in popular imagination even the story of Peter Salem's spectacular killing of the British Major Pitcairn at Bunker Hill. These men, however, were fighting not as Negroes, but as Americans, a fact that we of today often overlook. Nevertheless, they fought, and in doing so established their right to freedom. Scattered over the Commonwealth of Massachusetts today are many direct descendants of colored men who fought at Bunker Hill and previous to the Battle of Bunker Hill, whose forebears themselves fought in the French and Indian wars just as did other Americans. Descendants of these men are today due as much and as exalted regard as is paid those white men who fought to establish American independence and, later, to preserve the American Union. The ancestry of such Negroes is traceable for a farther distance than that of many a person hereabouts who boasts his pure "Nordic" strain.

Justification in a measure has been found for the belief that Massachusetts is the land of the free and the home of the brave colored men, when it is remembered that this Commonwealth afforded asylum and encouragement to a long list of illustrious Negroes. Everyone knows of Frederick Douglass, who lived for a time at New Bedford; not so many are acquainted with the activities of Lewis Hayden, who fled from Kentucky to Boston and who was an influence in the underground railroad, or with William C. Nell, who taught the first Negro school in Boston, or with Lunsford Lane, who was arrested in his native state of North Carolina on the charge of having delivered abolition lectures in Massachusetts; or Charles L. Redmond, the first Negro to take the lecture platform as an anti-slavery speaker, or David Walker, who came to Boston as a young man and entered business, later publishing an anti-slavery pamphlet called "Walker's Appeal," which pamphlet the governor of Virginia referred to in a note to his legislature as "a seditious appeal sent from Boston." These men were not only free to say what they wished, but they manifested bravery in that they always ran the risk of being most severely dealt with if caught beyond an uncertain, imaginary line.

We have arrived now at a point where we may with safety draw a conclusion: It is a fact that the early activity on the part of a few white citizens of Massachusetts, coupled with activity on the part of a few colored men, for the cause of human liberty, established this Commonwealth as the land of the free and the home of the brave colored man.

II.

Without doubt Massachusetts remains until now the most liberally disposed state toward Negroes. Like New York, this commonwealth is strongly tinged with a foreign element, and where these people occur in large numbers prejudice against the Negro is not strongly developed. In addition, Massachusetts is supposed to nurture in its descendants of the abolitionists all of the abolitionists' fervid hatred of race discrimination and injustice. Of course this supposition is not altogether true, and it is doubtful that few, except the descendants of abolitionists themselves, take it seriously.

As a matter of fact the descendants of abolitionists are an aloof and sacred lot—all except a very few. Most of the original denouncers of the slave traffic and slavery have departed, only a sprinkling of bent old white haired men and women tottering here and there; but the sons and grandsons, the daughters and grand daughters of these fine old citizens, are almost as unknown as some rare New England fauna, and almost as sacred in their exclusiveness as the grasshoppers on Faneuil Hall. Their decision was made long ago, presumably, and it was, in effect, that the white folk of Massachusetts have done their share for the colored folk, and that now it is time the colored folk helped themselves. With which decision the recorder of these events has no quarrel.

It has been a matter of course that Negroes everywhere would look to Massachusetts as the bestower of prerogatives, and the colored section of this State's population, even today, demand certain mythical privileges. The average colored citizen of Massachusetts, especially if he be able to name a relative that was born here, is far more interested in boasting of his black lineage than of his American nationality. His religion is a passionate, an almost reasonless, abolitionist-ancestor worship, and he parades the fact of his Negro antecedents not so much because of pride of race as a desire to continue as the "man of sorrow," the object in earlier years of impassioned oratory and underground machinations, the hero of one of the greatest episodes in American history, the War of the Rebellion. His reaction is similar to that of the soldiers who returned from the trenches and the late World War. Not being content merely with occupying a conspicuous place as men who had been the center of a great event, they were like spoiled children when they discovered that the world no longer made them the heroes of its imagination.

For a long time our amiable citizens of color in Massachusetts occupied the spotlight along. He was the object of many benevolences. He was often (and sometimes is now) welcomed in a social way. He contributed generously to the commercial prosperity of the Commonwealth. Often he was sent to the common councils, made a member of boards of aldermen, sent to the State Legislature, and with hardly more than white support behind him. He did thoroughly and well what was given him to do, but he did it with the consciousness of a man who is being accorded honors not because he deserves them but because of what he once was—the hero of a great cause—or what he is now—the descendant of that hero.

This interesting state of affairs continued uninterrupted for years. But after a while there came another seeker of publicity—an arrogant, domineering, boasting fellow. He desired a little petting too. He couldn't see why "the niggers" should have it all. This newcomer was the Irishman.

Note these figures. Today, with a population (quoting the 1920 census) of nearly four millions. Massachusetts has fewer Irishmen than Canadians, and fewer Negroes than either Irishmen or Canadians; yet, the Irish today in this Commonwealth are the most dominant group in politics, religion and blatant mouthing. The Negro is slightly in excess of 45,000, and, next to the Irish, makes more noise with the mouth than all other racial groups combined.

The quietest, least obtrusive, more self-effacing, most indifferent to clamor and agitations; the butt of whatever jokes everybody else wishes to make him—this is the hardworking native Yankee, often a descendant of abolitionists, often of slave traders, often of Mayflower immigrants and now and then just of plain everyday common Yankees. In Boston the Irish have driven the Yankee from South and East Boston, the Italians have banished him from the North End and the vicinity of the Old North Church, the Jews have crowded him from the West End and the larger portion of Beacon Hill, and the colored folk long ago saw to it that if the Yankee did not mind too much he might get out of the South End. Today the genuine Yankee, the kind with the twang like Coolidge's and who eats baked beans for Saturday night's supper and apple pie for breakfast (others try to do it, but it looks so much like gross imitation that they can't get away with it)—this Yankee hangs on along Beacon street and Commonwealth avenue and certain sections of the West End, while, in recent years, considerable numbers have migrated to these suburbs which surround Boston on the north and west. This Yankee does not know the Negro and the Negro does not know him—except as a white man; and this Yankee does not care to know the Negro. He is all sufficient unto himself taking all the glory that is given him for an apocryphal love for all black skins. He tolerates the colored intruder because to do so is easier than fighting him; because, chiefly, makers of history with scant regard for facts, and fools who believe everything, and human lolly-pops who take everything for granted that appears on the printed pages of a book, have built behind him a background of glamorous romance, which makes him a hero and a humanitarian. He has a role to fill, a part to play, a little piece to speak. He does all capitally.

Even though the Irishmen have eclipsed most of the glory that once blazed around our colored citizens, leaving them often very much in the shade when matters of importance are brewing, yet the colored citizen is undoubtedly bolder here than in any other State of the Union. He is never afraid to speak, be the issue what it may, and he does not falter in saying what he has to say in the manner that best appeals to his sense of the dramatic. Being the land of the free and the home of the brave colored man, is it any wonder that Massachusetts has produced the only citizen, white or colored, who has dared walk into the White House and call a President a ding-dong liar? A sense of his freedom to speak, a right he recognizes as his under the constitution probably imbued him with a feeling of safety, even though he stood on a plot of ground between Maryland and Virginia. That man, of course, was William Monroe Trotter.

Most colored folks in Massachusetts are either black or brown, and there is no middle ground—or so little of it that it is not worthy of mention. Those few who might be mistaken, in a gathering, for "Nordics," either have not yet discovered that they could "pass for white" if they wished, or they find it difficult, after years of associating with "blacks," to cross the line. The majority of light-colored persons who come from the South, where, traditionally, the colored man is detected even unto the sixteenth generation, are mistaken for foreigners here, and if they move into the North End or the West End they may forever after become lost to their darker brothers from "down home." This is no idle statement facetiously made; a number of instances might be cited were it necessary. Suffice it to say that there are hundreds of "Portuguese" who were once just plain Jack Johnsons and Mary Browns. They may be found in Boston, New Bedford, Lynn, Worcester and Springfield. There are scores of "Armenians" and "Greeks" and a few "Italians" who came to this great center of culture and liberty from Shoe Button, Mississippi; Hop Toad, Georgia; and Corn Pone, Arkansas. It is a simple matter to become "white" where so many whites, were they in Georgia, for example, would without question be classed as colored.

So those who came with the sole thought in mind of seeking larger freedom found it much larger than they had suspected even in their most rhapsodic dreams. They took advantage of it. And that was natural; not only was it natural, but it was human. Perhaps ninety-nine men out of a hundred, faced with the same situation, would have done similarly. Most of the colored folk who settle here, with every intention of remaining loyal to their smaller percentage of black blood, later, after being constantly mistaken for "whites," come finally to resent the imputation that they are anything else. And now a case to illustrate:

A short distance from where lives the recorder of these facts there resides a family of as handsome colored persons one could hope to meet. The straight hair of the father, the crinkly hair of the mother, and the varying degrees of texture in the hair of the children; their brown complexion, shading from light to dark; their evident Negro characteristics of facial contour—these are signs which long since established them in our neighborhood as one of the "good looking" Negro families hereabouts.

There came a time when the National Association for the Advancement of Colored People began collecting funds for backing the Dyer anti-lynch bill. The handsome daughter answered the agent's ring, and she seemed puzzled when told what she was expected to do. She stepped back into the hallway, half closing the door in the agent's face, and called for Mama. Mama came.

"Yes? What can we do for you?" Mama asked, eyeing the young woman agent suspiciously.

"Well, you see," explained the agent, "I represent the N A A C P—the National Association for the Advancement of Colored People, you know, and we have a campaign on to raise money to stamp out lynching in the South . . . "

She detailed at length.

"Yes?" said Mama again. "And what do you want us to do, please?"

"Why, to help—if you will. Being colored—"

Mama put up a deprecating palm, signalling silence.

"I'm very sorry, but we're not interested, not being Negroes . . . Oh, that's all right; others have made the same mistake. We're Portygeese . . ."

That is a true story. A friend to whom it was repeated took pains to explain the aversion of most Portuguese to the designation Negro; but, most interesting of all, he happened to know this family intimately, and remembered the time when they trailed through South Station on the morning train from Washington, at which place, some hours earlier, they had come in from "points south."

III.

Other factors beside that one of greater freedom have entered into the general attraction to draw colored people to Massachusetts; these same factors have served to hold fast those who are native to the soil. Chief of these are the educational advantages.

For its total population, all racial groups combined, Massachusetts has proportionately the largest enrollment in institutions of learning than any other state. Negroes have honored with their scholastic attainments Harvard, the Institute of Technology, the State Agricultural, Tufts, Williams, Clark, Worcester Polytechnic, Boston University, Radcliffe, Mount

Holyoke, Simmons, Lasell and Auburndale. In addition to these well established institutions there are the University and State Extension courses that run the full college length term.

Negroes have been students at all of these, but there have not been nearly so many as there should have been. The criticism for ignoring unequaled opportunities like these is laid at the doors of natives of this state more often than elsewhere. A majority of all college and university students come from other sections of the country, particularly from the South. For some reason, these men and women seem more appreciative of the store houses of priceless gems that only await claimants. Later, when the visitors from the South "make good", they will be pointed at as representative of the type of men Massachusetts produces! Most of Massachusetts' so-called native sons, who have accomplished anything worthy of note, came here from the South.

IV.

Massachusetts occupies the leading place among the States in industry, the 1920 census indicating the value of all industrial products to be considerably more than four million of dollars. This state is the most prominent textile manufacturing center in the Union; it dominates in the manufacture of boots and shoes. According to an authoritative statistician practically everything manufactured in modern industry is included in the manufactories of this state, "excepting in those basic industries in which the cruder materials, such as ores, are needed." Agriculture, once the dominant industry of the commonwealth, has been reduced amazingly by the cityward movement of the once large rural population. This desertion has left several scores of farms without tenants. Hay, tobacco, wheat, corn, oats, rye, buckwheat, maple syrup, apples, and various small fruits, such as cranberries, are the chief commodities awaiting both producer and consumer. Besides all this, Massachusetts is the leading fishing state of New England.

And now we come to the kernel of this most attractive nut. This is it: Of all the rich, flavored and wholesome meat here shown—the shoe factories, the mills, farms and fisheries, the slaughtering and meat packing concerns, the department stores and the bakeries—of all of these industries and businesses and enterprises, how many are owned, in whole or in part, by the free and brave colored man? And this is the answer: Not one tenth of one percent!

The typical Massachusetts citizen of color and of money is seldom interested in much more than maintaining a "front." There is not much behind the front, as a rule, but only those initiated into the intimacies of certain social circles ever see back of the scenes. Too much "freedom" has made him indolent; why should a free man work like a slave? Too much adulation—often, true enough, as hollow as his head, has caused him to place an exaggerated value upon his importance. He talks when he should act; he spends when he should save; he thinks in terms of "race" when he should think in terms of nationality; more often than not his "culture" is a mere fancy, his worth a conceit, and his accomplishments just ideas . . .

V.

Once upon a time Massachusetts stood gloriously forth as the exemplar for people all over these Colored United States. In those days she had something to offer her sister states in both precept and example as regarded her attitude toward her colored sons. With which introduction we bring ourselves to the crucial question: What did the Negro of the past in Massachusetts have that the Negro of the present has not? Moreover, what has this State given the world?

Well, let us see. The Negro of the past had members of his family in the State Legislature, in city councils, on boards of aldermen; he had a member of his group as headmaster in one of the most important graded schools of Massachusetts; he had business men, and statesmen—and politicians, who knew the game of politics as well as their opponents knew it.

Massachusetts gave Phillis Wheatley, the first Negro poet in America, to the world. It gave to America the beginning of Negro masonry when, on March 6, 1775, an army lodge of one of the regiments of Britishers stationed under General Gage, in or near Boston, initiated Prince Hall and fourteen other colored men into the mysteries of Freemasonry. "From that beginning," says an authority, "with small additions from foreign countries, sprang the masonry among Negroes of America."

Massachusetts gave to America Lieutenant James T. Trotter, who wrote brilliantly on music and musical people, as well as served the people of the District of Columbia as Recorder of Deeds during the administration of Grover Cleveland. In those dear dead days there were office holders aplenty, both under the national government and under the Commonwealth.

Archibald Grimké, if I am not in error, went from this Commonwealth to serve as consul at Port au Prince, Hayti. George Lewis Ruffin, seeking freedom in Massachusetts after tiring of the increasingly oppressive atmosphere of Virginia, came to Boston, went to Chapman Hall school and Harvard University Law school, got married, and was elected to the State Legislature. He even went to New Orleans as a delegate to the National Republican Convention in 1872, where he presided as chairman! Later he was appointed by Governor Ben Butler police court judge in the city of Charleston!

Then there were Oscar Armstrong, Andrew B. Lattimore, Julius C. Chappell, Charles Harris, Robert Teamroah, William L. Reed and William H. Lewis, all members of the State Legislature. Lewis was the last to hold that office, the last Negro office seeker to be so completely supported by the wealthiest and most influential white residents of the vicinity of Harvard

Square and Brattle street, Cambridge. Later, Lewis became Assistant United States Attorney, then Assistant Attorney General under Taft.

Colored Boston boasts—yes, boasts—of the only Negro who ever had as an office boy a youth who later became mayor of Boston. That man was Robert Morris, a famous Catholic in his day, attorney for Catholic interests, and a lawyer of ability. The office boy who became mayor was "Mike" Collins.

So far as history goes, the last man to hold elective office in Massachusetts was William P. Williams, later, Captain Williams, of Company L. He was for years a member of the board of aldermen of Chelsea, serving for some time as chairman.

Besides these men, Massachusetts has given to America some of its romantic figures of actual life. Take, for example, the case of Mrs. Arianna Sparrow, of Boston. Does the mention of her name kindle no flame in the imagination, set the heart to beating a little faster? If not, it is because you do not really know. If you could imagine seeing in the flesh, for example, say—well, the daughter of Eliza, who, in "Uncle Tom's Cabin," fled with her child across the ice to escape the ferocious "Siberian bloodhounds" and the cruel brute with the murderous whip, would you not wish to see her? Would you not think that the State who claimed her as a citizen was one to be envied?

Massachusetts has that honor, in the person of venerable Mrs. Arianna C. Sparrow, who was born in Virginia, in 1841, but who has lived in Boston since long before slavery was abolished by Lincoln's proclamation. So those persons who have experienced sorrow at poor Eliza's plight might cheer themselves now with the knowledge that Eliza reached Boston after successfully eluding the bloodthirsty bloodhounds, and settled down here, where she sent her little daughter to the first school ever established in Massachusetts for colored persons. No historian who wishes to embellish his dry material with some living matter can afford to miss a chat of an hour or so with Eliza's little daughter. She holds a key to the gateway of a past that few even know.

The purpose of the foregoing paragraphs, under the Fifth section, was for reminding the reader that Massachusetts has given something of value to the country and to the world, although at present she may appear to be indifferent and incompetent. The foregoing represents somewhat the glory that was ours; we shall now compare that past glory with the present possessions. Lend attentive ear.

VI.

In politics there is only one office under the State government, and that is Mr. Reed's. He is the newly appointed executive secretary.

Mr. Reed has been in a mediocre job at the State House so long that it is a pleasure to all of his friends to see his deserved promotion. There has always been something just a bit pathetic in the sight of that dignified, scholarly gentleman of the older school running errands for some of his inferiors who have sat in the Governor's seat.

But that is all that the colored man in Massachusetts may claim in the way of political office under the Commonwealth. The estimate John W. Schenks holds a second rate assistant attorney's job to the United States District Attorney. He is worthy of something bigger, but whether or not he will get it is a matter for speculation. However, prospects do not seem very promising, in view of Mrs. Willebrant's recent ousting from office of the man Harris, from whom Schenks received his appointment.

William C. Matthews is not holding public office, but, like our old friend Barkis, is willin'. He holds, though, what many Negroes throughout the United States think to be a strategic position in the White House anteroom. He is looked upon as the man who has Coolidge's ear—as though it would mean anything to the office seekers at large if he did have it. In the meantime, Mr. Matthews sits in his law office in the Old South building, while a million dusky politicians sigh, "Ain't the Bay State lucky!"

There is one colored assistant corporation counsel in Mr. Lucius Hicks, an ardent little Democrat. That is under the city government, of course. Mr. Curley was responsible for that assignment, as he was also for the designation of Joshua H. Jones as editor of the Boston City Record.

In Pittsfield there is Mr. Stevens, one of the State's bright legal minds. He is a good Republican and has represented his town in more than one Republican convention. Others here and there make noises, but neither they nor the noises count very much. Let us pass them by.

Massachusetts, as the whole world knows, has given to the world of literature an important figure in William Stanley Braithwaite. More interesting than the announcement that he has added another anthology of magazine verse to the long list already published is the fact that he is president of the B. J. Brimmer Company, publishers, of Boston, a situation that recalls pleasantly the days when colored men were important figures in the business and industrial life of the Commonwealth. One recalls in this connection Gilbert, the nationally known wig-maker, and J. H. Lewis, who owned one of the largest tailoring establishments in Boston. Both these men are gone, and both their businesses with them.

So Mr. Braithwaite is one of those landmarks to which we, of Massachusetts, point with pride. Another is Mrs. Meta Warwick Fuller, the sculptress, of Framingham, Rodin's brilliant pupil, who would add lustre to the fame of any state and country. Still another is that remarkable real estate man of Brockton, whose name is Terry, and who owns properties in other states than this.

Joshua Jones, who was mentioned as Mayor Curley's appointee to editorship of the City Record, is remembered as the author of "By Sanction of Law," that novel which should have been a greater success than it was. He is now writing numerous short stories, all of which he intends to launch at the same time, soon. In addition, the public may expect soon to read his "Fairlee of Methuen," which, thank the Muses, is not a "race" novel. Josh is a credit to his adopted State.

Probably one of the best known women in New England lives in Boston. She is a member of the colored citizenry, born of free parents at Oberlin and educated in Washington, D.C., and Boston. This woman is Mrs. Mary Evans Wilson, who, in 1899, organized a great forenoon mass meeting in old Chickering Hall, Boston, to protest against the lynching of Sam House and others in Georgia. Julia Ward Howe was there, and spoke, and so were Alice Freeman Palmer, Edna D. Cheney, Anna D. Hallowell (granddaughter of Lucretia Mott), Florida Ridley and Maria Baldwin.

Since that time Mrs. Wilson has organized various movements seeking the welfare of colored people.

It was she who introduced Coleridge-Taylor to Boston; it was she who was instrumental in raising the greater portion of the money which paid for the Buffalo auditorium at Camp Upton during the war; and it was she who started the movement for the Women's Service Club in Boston, one of the most successful social service bodies in the State.

Incidentally, Mr. Butler R. Wilson is Mrs. Wilson's husband.

Just as actively engaged in welfare work is Mrs. Florida Ridley, daughter of the late Judge Ruffin, and one of the few persons hereabouts, of any consequence, who was born in Massachusetts. She is imbued with this State's holy traditions—and with more. She is the friendly rival of Mrs. Wilson's in performing for sweet charity's sake those benevolences which were begun during the war and which were continued afterwards as being wholly essential to the welfare of the community life.

Georgia has rendered one good service to the Negro and to the world of art. She gave to Massachusetts Roland Hayes, and Massachusetts polished him off and sent him to Europe. Everybody knows the rest. A similar statement might be made with respect to Maud Cuney Hare, who has given the big, blustering, countrified, ignorant State of Texas about the only just claim she has ever had to aesthetic culture.

Now to sum up: Massachusetts is the land of the free and the home of the brave colored man by virtue of her humanitarianism and justice wherever and whenever he has been concerned. The colored man of Massachusetts has more freedom than material possessions, more rights than initiative, more mouth than a desire to work. He is ever ready to damn his State to his friend, but he is immediately on the defensive when an outsider presumes to damn.

And perhaps the first part of this last sentence will make clear to the reader why the recorder of these facts removed his kid gloves before he began the task of handling his home State.

ROBERT W. BAGNALL

Michigan— the Land of Many Waters

VOL. 8, No. 4, APRIL 1926

Born in 1883 or 1884 in Norfolk, Virginia, Robert W. Bagnall attended Bishop Payne Divinity School and was ordained as an Episcopal priest in 1903. He worked for churches in Pennsylvania, Ohio, and Maryland before moving to Michigan, where he became affiliated with St. Matthew's Church in Detroit. At St. Matthew's he was recognized for his success in raising money and for his work on social issues; and his career forever after, until his death in 1943, combined social activism and religious leadership.

Bagnall moved within both NAACP circles and the more radical *Messenger* crowd. Known in the black community for his forceful oratory and skillful organizing (he was credited with founding twenty-five new NAACP chapters), he gained national attention for his crusading work against Jim Crow schools and police brutality, as well as for his work in defeating an anti-intermarriage bill in Michigan in 1913. Bagnall understood his roles as civil rights activist and church leader as complementary, and his example helped lead to a new prominence of the clergy in the national civil rights movement.

Bagnall published, in *The Messenger,* a famous 1923 attack on Marcus Garvey, whose flamboyant rhetoric and style was criticized by many intellectuals. Bagnall mocked Garvey personally: Garvey was either "insane" or a "demagogic charlatan"; he was "boastful, egotistic, tyrannical, intolerant, cunning, shifty, smooth and suave." But more important, Bagnall decried Garvey's association with the Klan— Garvey agreed with the Klan that blacks and whites should remain separate and accepted from the KKK money for his United Negro Improvement Association. Although as "adroit as a cuttle-fish in beclouding an issue he cannot meet," Bagnall hoped that Garvey's association with the Klan was enough to convince his followers of how dangerous the man was, and called for his deportation. The kind of polemical skill that made Bagnall's essay on Garvey such a cause célèbre in the African American press is in strong evidence in this essay on Michigan as well.

Although much of the essay focuses on Detroit because "Negro Michigan" *is* Detroit, Bagnall employs playful phrasing to promote the rest of his state. "Grand Rapids suggests the idea of furniture; Battle Creek that of breakfast food and sanatoria; Kalamazoo, succulent celery." Alongside such tossed-off thumbnail sketches as these, Bagnall offers harrowing accounts of mob action in Detroit. These detailed scenes make Bagnall's essay on Michigan one of the most memorable of the series. He has an exceptional economy of language ("The older residents who remained aloof from the new-comers," he writes, "found their crudities obnoxious—as was inevitable") and an admirable narrative skill, with an eye to the telling detail ("Reeking alleys with six foot piles of manure can be found in the heart of the city").

Notable too in this essay are the troubled reflections he shares when talking about Henry Ford. Cognizant of Ford's "genius for mass production" and social progressivism, he nonetheless remarks on Ford's "disorganized organized mind" and his anti-Semitic campaign. Bagnall's identification of Henry Ford with the city of Detroit leads him to employ the paradoxical metaphors so common in these essays: "Everywhere there seems to be a struggle between the small town and the great industrial city—a physical body politic in internal dissension." Ultimately Bagnall's portrait of Detroit, and of Michigan, is a significant marker of what the Great Migration and northern industrialization promised for African American communities during the 1920s. With its vast demographic shifts of the early part of the century ("Negro Detroit jumped from 8,000 in 1914 to 85,000 in 1926"), Detroit is a city Bagnall recognizes as having an ability, both supple and baffling, to adjust to such changes. Unlike later views that reduced the city's dynamic sociology to a black-and-white dichotomy, Bagnall shows how important it is to understand the "polyglot" nature of Michigan, a place where civil rights bills were resisted by citizens unwilling to share their restaurants with Indians. He notes the agonizing but predictable troubles of racial antagonism and urban hardship, but also calls to our attention the historical tension between the recent migrants from the South and older African American residents.

Bagnall is cautious in his predictions about African American life in Michigan, saying simply that "the Negro is destined to play a large part in the life of Michigan. . . . Just how big that part shall be, no man can say." Bagnall's cautious optimism seems uncannily prescient. As Detroit gradually struggles back from its infamous postwar urban decay, Bagnall's recognition that it can serve as a touchstone for diagnosing the ills and the promise of modern America (not just for African Americans) is especially compelling. Detroit as both city and symbol has long been identified with its African Americans, and Bagnall's essay helps us understand an important chapter in the history of that identification.

Michigan—"The land of the great waters" as the Chippewas aptly named it, is the 22nd state in size and the 7th in population. It is really two states in one, for the Upper and Lower Peninsula are so different one from the other that they have little in common.

It is a state whose shores are lapped by all the great inland seas—the uncertain and treacherous Lake Erie; the wide reaches of Lake Michigan; the rolling waves of Superior; and the blue waters of St. Clair and Huron.

In addition that straight known as the Detroit River and many other streams and lakes are found within the 58,000 square miles which comprise her territory. In the north there are many resorts and medicinal springs. There you find the famous Macinaw Islands.

Its mean temperature is just over 46 degrees and the summers, which are short, hover around a mean of 68 degrees and the winters around 23 degrees. However, zero is frequent and 15 below is by no means uncommon as the wind races over hundreds of miles of ice hummocks and the frigid waters of the Great Lakes.

The Upper Peninsula is rough and rugged, wild and barren, but rich in mineral deposits. Copper and iron are there in rich quantities as well as deposits of coal and statuary marble. Gold, silver and lead are also found in small quantities. There, yesterday, the great lumber industry flourished and the name of Michigan pine became famous. Even yet in some sections of the state the lumber industry is very important, and like Maine, each year sees the forest fires jeopardize millions in property as well as human life.

In some parts of the Upper Peninsula the frontier yet remains, and Indians in considerable numbers earn their living as trappers while others are found in the settlements. Deer, bear, and the wolverine, together with the great timber wolf, are by no means scarce. In fact, a few winters ago packs of timber wolves invaded villages and towns in the Upper Peninsula attacking the live stock. It is here that we find the only mountains in the state—the Pocupine, which are about 2,000 feet above the sea. Here is the great Sault Ste. Marie Canal, which accommodates more tonnage than the Suez, Panama or any other canal in the world.

It is interesting to note that when the writer some years ago had the present Civil Rights Bill introduced in the Michigan Legislature, and organized a lobby for its passage, the principal objection in the Legislature to its passage was offered by members from the Upper Peninsula, where there are few Negroes. They objected to the bill *because they did not want Indians to eat in the restaurants with them.*

It is the Upper Peninsula in which old Father Marquette worked and even today it suggests hardship and heroism. It is the Lower Peninsula however where Cadillac and his soldiers played their part, and it is this section of the state which makes Michigan today famous as the great capital of motordom.

Here we find the great agricultural region of the state with its crops of waving corn, wheat, oats, rye, barley, buckwheat and hay; with its potato and sugar beet fields; its beans, peas, and famous celery; and along Lake

Michigan, its vineyards and fruit orchards. Quite a number of these farms are owned by colored people,—old residents of the state. It is in this region too that we find stock and dairy farms and sheep herds.

In the Lower Peninsula we find the principal cities of the state and consequently most of its educational institutions, among which is the famous State University. Here abound foundries, iron and steel mills, grist and salt mills, machine shops, furniture factories; the manufacturing of wagons and farm implements, and a great multitude of automobile factories and plants for automobiles' accessories.

Grand Rapids suggests the idea of furniture; Battle Creek that of breakfast food and sanatoria; Kalamazoo, succulent celery; Port Huron, steel mills and shipping; Saginaw, salt and lumber; and Jackson, Lansing, Pontiac, Flint and Detroit, the great automobile industry, for in these places more cars are made than anywhere else in the country.

Detroit is the dynamic city of Michigan and it dominates the whole state. It is a name to conjure with; the largest growing great city in the Union, bursting out of its clothing, with a polyglot population of over a million souls. It has been so busy making money that it has never had time to stop to find itself.

Just as Detroit dominates the state, so is it dominated in the mind of the world by the remarkable figure of Henry Ford, whose genius for mass production of a cheap car has enabled him to build up the biggest motor factory in the world, covering miles of ground.

In his Detroit plant are employed around 8,000 Negroes, mostly doing heavy work. A considerable group however do skilled and semi-skilled work, and there is a Negro foreman, several Negro clerks, and one Negro, Glenn Cochran, a young graduate of the University of Michigan, who is employed in the experimental department as an electrical engineer. Detroit in 1919 has 2,176 manufacturing establishments with about 176,000 workers. Ford employes over 50,000, or nearly one-third, of all the city's factory workers.

Detroit has developed other notable figures—the Dodge brothers, the Lelands—father and son; Chalmers, Chrysler, Willys, Couzins, Lee, Norval Hawkins, among others.

But Ford's name dominates all others like Pike's Peak the surrounding mountain tops. His personality has caught the imagination of the world, as it is a peculiar combination of the naive and sophisticated, the efficient and the erratic.

His stunts have been so extraordinary that they have startled the world, nor were they advertising schemes, but sincere efforts. His peace ship, his notion that every criminal could be reformed merely by giving him a job, his anti-semitic campaign—all reveal a peculiar type of mind. S. S. Marquis, who for years was head of his social service department, says that he has the most disorganized organized mind in America.

Detroit—the city reminds one of Ford—the man. It has the same disorganized organized characteristic. Skyscrapers and unsanitary hovels that few modern cities would permit are in stone throw of one another. Reeking alleys with six foot piles of manure can be found in the heart of the city along with dirty, miserably paved streets. On the other hand, not many minutes ride away, one finds wonderfully paved broad streets with beautiful homes and even magnificent show places.

Everywhere there seems to be a struggle between the small town and the great industrial city—a physical body politic in internal dissension. And this too is true of its government, which certainly cannot be said to be noteworthy for economy, efficiency or freedom from corruption. When one remembers that Detroit in 1910 and only around 376,000 people and now numbers over a million you have the explanation for much of this.

Some one has said Detroit is Michigan and Michigan is Detroit. While this is hardly true of the state as a whole, it is true of Negro Michigan. The bulk of the Negro population in Michigan is found in Detroit and in cities near by.

Michigan has always had its Negro contingent and many of them have been noteworthy characters. William Lambert, a successful tailor in the old days, together with Charles Webb and Elder Munroe conducted there the underground railway on a large scale, safely piloting, it is said, thousands of slaves to Canada.

Lambert is reputed to have been the author of the code of the underground railway and he and Munroe were friends and advisors of John Brown. Lambert was the founder of St. Matthews Episcopal Church and Munroe its first minister. It was this church which gave Bishop Holly to the ministry and where he was ordained, although he was living in the East when he lead a colony to Hayti.

Dr. Levi Johnson in the early days enjoyed a lucrative practice as a physician among the whites of the city, these forming a majority of his patients. His son, Dr. Albert H. Johnson, yet is called into the families who were served by his father and until recently he and his brother continued the drug store his father founded. William Cole had one of the principal moving and trucking firms for many years in Detroit and for a long while his sons carried on the business. Pelham, a colored man from Virginia, whose sons and daughters are well known, led the fight which removed the "black laws" from the statute books of Michigan and ended compulsory separate schools and the prohibition of intermarriage. He was the father of Robert Pelham of the Census Bureau in Washington.

Negroes had won some place in the arts and inventions in Detroit at this time. Shoecroft had gained a number of important commissions as a portrait painter, Mollie Lambert had won a local literary reputation, and Elijah McCoy had invented the automatic lubricator from which developed the whole principle of automatic lubrication of moving machinery, and on which the great Michigan Lubrication Works were built up. McCoy of course, got little as the result of his work.

In Detroit at this time there had been a few Negro private secretaries to important officials like Charles Webb, a number of clerks and carriers, a number of teachers in the mixed schools, a few clerks in political jobs, a county accountant, some seven or eight physicians, and a few prominent lawyers like Judge D. Augustus Straker, who was elected a magistrate. Samuel Thompson, Francis Warren, Robert Barnes, Walter Stowers. To these could be added the names of a few younger men, some of whom now have considerable practice. There was very little in the way of Negro business, and most of the 8,000 Negroes were settled around the Antoine district, within walking distance of one another, and were served by four churches, whose ministers worked together in civil matters in perfect accord.

Among the names mentioned above several are worthy of notice. D. Augustus Straker was not only a good lawyer but a man of considerable literary attainment and the author of several volumes of interest. Francis Warren was a most unselfish champion of his peoples' rights, but never received the honors he deserved because himself a mulatto, he chose to take a white woman as a second wife,—a woman who at all times proved an excellent helpmate. Warren—stocky, with a leonine head crowned with a thatch of white hair and big voice, was absolutely fearless and utterly militant, and was always on the battle line when the rights of his race were challenged. He was a single-taxer, a democrat, a radical in many ways, and a generation in advance of the provincial group about him. His death robbed Detroit of one of her most valuable Negro citizens.

Around this time the Rev. Robert L. Bradly began his rise to prominence in Detroit. He is perhaps today the largest Negro figure in Detroit and a force to be recognized. Bradly is a born leader, an excellent organizer, a good business man, and an unusually able orator who makes full use of his nearly 3,000 devoted parishioners and while keen for an opportunity to make money, he is ever ready to champion a race cause.

W. C. Osby should be mentioned in this connection—for he, too, did much to help Detroit to give Negroes justice. The Reverend Doctor Gomez, a young West Indian clergyman of the A.M.E. church, should also be mentioned as one of the outstanding leaders in the life of Detroit—a dynamic personality with a very large following. He too, has been interested in most public matters concerning the Negro. When the migration came, Negroes poured forth into Detroit at the rate of 100 a day from all parts of the South. Jobs begged for men. Wages were sky-high. Labor was King. Night and day the factories were kept at full speed. Money was plentiful, and the Negro got his full share. He saved money so that later when unemployment came, it was found that his group was the last to ask for charity. He made good; established bank accounts and bought homes. He broke into semi-skilled and skilled work. The masses of him were followed by doctors, lawyers, business men, and a great company of preachers. Negro Detroit jumped from 8,000 in 1914 to 85,000 in 1926, for Detroit became the mecca of the Negro.

But along with him came the whites from the South until now they say these number between 200,000 and 300,000. A surprising number of these joined the police force and stupid commissioners have permitted many of these to be assigned to Negro districts with resultant bad relations between the police and Negroes.

Just this last year police shot nearly seventy Negroes in Detroit, and evidence indicates that most of these shootings were unwarranted. No police officer, however, has been punished as the result of such shootings.

With the coming of great numbers of southern whites and Negroes, with the necessity of whole districts being taken over to house the Negroes, prejudice grew apace. Discriminations became frequent, and the prejudice terminated in the succession of riots to prevent Negroes from occupying homes in districts which previously had none of them, riots which culminated in the now famous affair of Dr. Sweet.

The Sweet case was not an isolated instance. As far back as 1919, there had been threats and slight overt acts when colored people moved into so-called white districts. But with the coming of southern whites and the rise of the Ku Klux Klan, these demonstrations against colored people living in white neighborhoods took organized and determined form.

A colored blacksmith who fired into a mob who stoned his home was arrested but released when he agreed to move; a colored woman, the mother of a young baby, was arrested and kept in jail over night when she fired on an attacking mob that stoned her house; and Dr. Bristol, a young Negro, moving with companions into his house on American Avenue, had to open fire before an attacking mob retired.

The most important of the cases prior to that of Dr. Sweet's was the case of Dr. A. L. Turner. Dr. Turner was a successful surgeon who was on the staff of Grace Hospital and had been most instrumental in founding the Negro hospital in Detroit. He was a graduate in arts and medicine from the University of Michigan, and had studied elsewhere as well.

His wife and mother-in-law had inherited a considerable fortune from A. L. Loudin of the Jubilee singer fame, and their means and his earnings permitted the Turner family to live in a comfortable manner.

Dr. Turner was regarded as one of the Negro leaders in Detroit in business and in his profession, and had been long known as a public-minded citizen. He bought a home in the district wholly peopled by whites—a community where the Klan was very strong.

A mob of 6,000 gathered in front of his home, and when the police came, they stood idly by as onlookers. The mob stoned the house, breaking windows, but the police did nothing.

Within the house were Negro men with an ample supply of ammunition, who wished to fire into the mob when they stoned the house—but this Turner would not permit. Finally Turner opened his front door to let in the police, and these were followed by a group of the mob, who destroyed the furniture, tore down hangings, and threatening Dr. Turner with a gun, compelled him to sign an agreement to sell—the police meanwhile looking on.

The mob then loaded Turner's furniture on a van, the police hurried him to his car, which was stoned, and he was moved back to his old house. Dr. Turner's wife refused to sign the agreement to sell, but Turner did not return to the new house, in spite of offers of help from many colored citizens and promises of protection from the police.

The Turner incident encouraged the mob in Detroit to believe that they could easily segregate Negroes by force and intimidation. It aroused much indignation on the part of the colored people, who felt that Dr. Turner should have returned and protected his home. These determined not to be intimidated.

Dr. Ossian H. Sweet, a young Negro physician who had studied in America and Europe, bought a home in a district largely peopled by artisans and factory people. On his coming to the neighborhood the white people of the community organized the Water Works Association, whose raison d' etré was to force the Sweets to move. There the steps to be taken were planned.

On the night the Sweets moved in, a demonstration in front of his home was held. On the second night, his home was assaulted with stones and shots were fired from within and without. The inmates of the Sweet home opened fire above the heads of the mob, but one of the mob was killed, and a second wounded. The Sweets and the nine other inmates of the house were arrested and indicted for murder in the first degree. The N.A.A.C.P. employed Clarence Darrow, A. Garfield Hayes, Walter F. Nelson, and three local colored attorneys—Cecil W. Rowlette, Charles Mahoney and Julian Perry, to defend them.

The first trial ended in a hung jury and the second will shortly be held.

Weeks before the Turner and Sweet incident, Detroit papers insisted that Negroes must surrender their rights to live wherever they please and accept segregated districts—ghettoes—or else be held responsible for race riots. The police in all these cases were notoriously lax in protecting the Negro homes, and in some instances, aided the mob.

The Sweet trial resulted in many Detroiters gaining a new viewpoint and today many whites of that city acknowledge the rights of any racial group to live wherever it can buy.

In spite of the increased prejudice, Detroit gives promise of being one of the most prosperous cities in the country for the Negro. Its business opportunities are many and are rapidly developing. The city as yet lacks a crystallized Negro leadership, but one will, of a certainty, shortly emerge.

The overflow population of Negro Detroit is rapidly building up other cities in Michigan such as Flint, Saginaw, Alpena, Pontiac, and Jackson.

In these places there are a few outstanding figures like Oscar Baker, prominent lawyer and leading citizen of Bay City, who is highly esteemed by both races. A number of such individuals will steadily increase as the

Negro population grows and the smaller cities will play a large part in the future of the Negro in Michigan.

The coming of the large number of migrants not only precipitated many problems but set in array against one another many of the older Negro residents and the newcomers. On the other hand, a number of the older residents realize that their strength lay in combining with the newcomers and systematically assisting them to adjust themselves to their new environment. The older residents who remained aloof from the newcomers regarded them as a menace to their numbers, and found their crudities obnoxious—as was inevitable. The smallness of the numbers of these older citizens caused them to be overwhelmed by the great horde of newcomers, so that their influence lessened until it has now become almost nil in Detroit.

In looking over the names of candidates for the Legislature and the common council among the Negroes, it is to be noted that the names of those who lived in Detroit before the migration are conspicuously absent. The great mass of Negro migrants for the first time are beginning to pause to consider their cultural life. Heretofore they have been too busy making money and seeking to adjust themselves to their new world.

They have now in Detroit a well-furnished clubhouse; and a well-organized social life is rapidly crystallizing such established social life as we find in the major cities of the South.

The Negro is destined to play a large part in the life of Michigan. He is yet in a period of storm and stress. Just how big that part shall be, no man can say.

ROY WILKINS

Minnesota: Seat of Satisfaction

VOL. 6, NO. 5, MAY 1924

Roy Wilkins, one of the most important civil rights leaders of the twentieth century, was born in 1901 in St. Louis, Missouri. Raised by his uncle and aunt in St. Paul, Minnesota, he remained to attend the University of Minnesota, and worked as a night editor for the school's *Minnesota Daily* and as an editor for the *St. Paul Appeal,* an African American weekly. He graduated in 1923 and began a career as a journalist with the Kansas City *Call,* another African American weekly. In 1931 he left his newspaper work to begin what was to be a very important career with the NAACP.

Executive secretary of the NAACP for twenty-two years, (1955–77) Wilkins was also the chairman of the Leadership Conference on Civil Rights, and numerous other civil rights and peace organizations, crusading against lynching, segregation, and other forms of discrimination and injustice. Editor of *The Crisis* for fourteen years, he was a contributor to dozens of other journals throughout his lifetime. He died in 1981.

This essay on Minnesota was published when Wilkins was only twenty-two years old, but it already demonstrates his formidable gifts as a writer and polemicist. In this often caustic, sometimes obviously youthful essay, Wilkins rails against what he sees as the apathy of African Americans in the state. Because of the relatively slow growth of the African American population and their relative prosperity, Wilkins proclaims that "satisfaction and its handmaiden, stagnation, have been the inevitable results." These successful Minnesotans seem unaware of the "vanguard of proscription marching down upon them," of the new restrictions on access to services, opportunities, and neighborhoods that attended the spread northward of Jim Crow. Wilkins's ire at the self-satisfaction of Minnesotans in the face of the increasing racism of the twenties and its institutionalization—there is "scarcely a whimper of protest"—made sense from the national perspective and for rhetorical purposes, but one also senses that for the young Wilkins, stagnation was an almost unforgivable sin. He wanted "new blood, new birth, . . . young men who will think and dare to do," where he found instead bourgeois complacency.

The essay is consonant with Wilkins's life work in the civil rights movement, as the impassioned fury he directs toward the African

American population of Minnesota is a fury calculated to arouse, not merely irritate. He makes sweeping generalizations to hammer his points home: "Negro parents sit back in complacency and content themselves with the mediocre scholastic achievements of their children." His deliberately provocative style leaves no doubt that the impetus behind such criticism is to ignite a response. Later criticisms directed at Wilkins during his tenure as the executive secretary of the NAACP frequently painted him as too conciliatory, or accused him of placing too much blame on the African American community rather than on the white individuals and institutions that contributed to the oppression of African Americans. This early essay on Minnesota certainly hints at that tendency, but it nevertheless attacks with vehemence and passion what Wilkins views as the most dangerous result of prejudice and discrimination, the creation of a population that in adopting the mainstream American goals of individual determination and satisfaction had become blind to the necessity of organized responses to racial discrimination.

"Minnesota: Seat of Satisfaction" theorizes regionalism, identity, and race very differently than those essays that celebrate diversity. Most obviously, Wilkins finds fault with the complacency regional comparisons can breed. "While the forces of discrimination make inroads upon his freedom the Negro in the North Star state rests in satisfaction, contenting himself with the thought that Georgia is so many and so many miles away." For Wilkins, recent lynchings in Duluth dispelled the myth that Georgia was far away or that the tragedies incurred by racism were of concern only to the South. When he wrote this essay, Wilkins was living in Kansas City, Missouri, and as his autobiography *Standing Fast* recounts, the young journalist was appalled at the racism and discrimination he encountered there. Rather than lead him to appreciate the relative comfort he had enjoyed in Minnesota, after his experience Wilkins may well have caused assess his experiences in Minnesota with even more bitterness. Regional pride, including pride in the race's accomplishments in the state, many of which Wilkins dutifully notes, can create its own blindness. Wilkins complains of the "individualism that so far has successfully resisted group organization. The Negro feels no necessity for co-operative groups. . . . He is a contented isolationist." The problem of increasing racism will soon overwhelm Minnesota's African Americans, Wilkins warns, and they will be unorganized and therefore unprepared to meet the challenge. Their local complacency will result in local disaster. But more important, the individualism of African Americans in the state carries with it a larger problem: it serves to undermine the project of creating a national racial identity, one that could be mobilized to combat racism both inside and outside the borders of any particular state.

Following the standard regionalist essay form, Wilkins begins with general descriptive information about the geography, economics, and population of the state before moving on to cultural description. His boosterish recounting of accomplishments, while it follows the standard essay form, is somewhat at odds with his critique of complacency, but at all times his rhetorical skill and power are evident.

MR. WILKINS

Minnesota, state of ten thousand lakes; Minnesota, bread basket of North America; Minnesota, mineral depositary extraordinary; Minnesota, fountainhead of the mighty Father of Waters; Minnesota, home of the blond Northmen and the apathetic Negro—all these are the state whose Indian name means "sky-tinted water."

The state is the very central spot of North America and has an area of fifty-three millions of acres, one-fifteenth of which is under water. Its rich lands and huge mineral deposits coupled with its water power have aided in its development and prosperity. From the little town of St. Anthony on the banks of the Mississippi has grown Minneapolis, milling center of the world; from the shabby mining shack communities on the great Mesaba iron range has grown Hibbing, the richest village in the world, the splendor of whose civic development is the envy of many a metropolis; from the fertile lands has grown the second largest butter production in the country.

Nearly fifty per cent of the 2,300,000 people in the state live in urban communities, and the majority of these urban dwellers is found in the three large cities: Minneapolis, with a population of 400,000; St. Paul, with 300,000; and Duluth, with 110,000. Of this number the 1920 census describes 8,809 as Negroes and places 8,250 of these in cities. Allowing for the errors in classification invariably made by census takers, and considering the influx since 1920, it is safe to conclude that there are now in the state approximately 15,000 Negroes, 13,000 of whom are in the Twin Cities.

Increase in the Negro population has been slow. When the Emancipation Proclamation became effective there were already 500 free Negroes in the state. It was 1880 before the number went over 1,000, and the census of 1910 gave only 7,000. The decreasing severity of the winters and the wave of migration are responsible for the influx of recent years.

To this slow growth of population may be attributed the development of the outstanding characteristics of Minnesota Negroes: apathy and self-satisfaction. The infusion of new blood and new initiative has been so meager and so slow that natives have not benefited by the process. The hundreds of visitors that come annually to the lakes and homes of colored Minnesotans are either too polite or too busy seeking relaxation to offer criticism or suggestion. Satisfaction and its handmaiden, stagnation, have been the inevitable results of this condition.

No more prominent example of the apathy of the brownskin dweller in the North Star state can be found than his neglect of the educational opportunities at his doorstep. A public school system that ranks among the best is maintained by the various communities in the state. In the Twin Cities alone there are six colleges and universities; music, art and night schools there are without number. In Minneapolis is located the state university ranking as the fifth largest university in the world and not far below that in point of excellence. Its last biennial budget was the huge sum of $13,000,000.

Notwithstanding these advantages at their doors, colored students and parents more often than not take instant advantage of the law which permits the withdrawal of students after they have finished the eighth grade or reached the age of sixteen. Hundreds drop out at the conclusion of the grade school curriculum, dozens more have a high school diploma as their ultimate goal. All too few press on and through college. In the University of Minnesota today there are approximately 8,000 students enrolled. Of that number fifty are colored, and of this fifty not more than fifteen could reasonably be classified as native sons and daughters.

Girls are scarce at Minnesota's institutions of higher learning. The fall of 1922 was the first season when as many as six young women were enrolled at the university. In the other colleges and in the excellent normal schools of the state there are altogether not more than four. Fathers and mothers would rather have their daughters stay home and keep house, or get a position as maid or elevator operator in a downtown building, or putter with music than continue beyond the high school. Were these same people in a community which discriminated in tendering educational opportunities to its citizens they would be fretting because their children could not secure the same education as the child of their pale neighbor. Here where there are absolutely no restrictions in the public schools, Negro parents sit back in complacency and content themselves with the mediocre scholastic achievements of their children.

One of the most telling evidences of apathy in the far northern state is found in the activities of the church. Here, strange to say, the church business is not so good. Negroes go to church, and have managed to split often enough so that there are plenty of churches; but the churches do not do anything. They do not even build themselves suitable houses of worship. Two of the largest churches in the Twin Cities worship still in frame structures erected before 1900. Two attitudes may partly account for this state of affairs. First, the Negro here is an individualist, unwilling to work in groups. His churches, therefore, are split in factions, no one of which is large enough to advance a comprehensive program. Secondly, no amount of "soul-stirring" preaching has succeeded in making congregations forget that coal is eighteen dollars a ton and winter is seven months long. If a church program hurdles the first great barrier of utter indifference which the Negro is sure to erect, it is certain to trip on one of the two attitudes mentioned.

Further evidence of the indifference of the colored Minnesotan is shown in his lack of resistance to restrictions that are creeping in upon him. He offers little or no resistance to the dangerous and often vicious propaganda of the press of the large cities. In Duluth there is little need to protest, for the Duluth dailies are fairer and more generous than most papers in the country. Two Minneapolis papers are fair and friendly, but in St. Paul, the capital, one powerful daily speaks always the bad word and seldom ever the good. Against this destructive agency at the seat of the state's government the Negroes of the city have made practically no move. Some protest has been made by individuals and some little agitation begun by a local paper, but never have organized groups functioned.

Slowly, but surely and without appreciable resistance, discrimination is making its way into public service. Many restaurants are open. Some are "just known" not to want colored trade. Virtually every drug store in the state will serve Negroes soda fountain orders. A glaring exception to this is a large drug store in the heart of St. Paul *whose advertising is accepted by the leading colored paper in the state.* Department store cafeterias are open to all, but few of these same stores will serve Negroes in their exclusive tea rooms. The largest vaudeville house in St. Paul attempts to sell colored people seats in the same row and is successful most of the time. To these encroachments on his civil liberties the St. Paul Negro (and he is nearly one-half the Minnesota Negro) offers scarcely a whimper of protest. Minneapolis has been apathetic enough, but in that city a few able lawyers took advantage of the civil rights bill on the state statutes and by just a few prosecutions made Minneapolis a much better place in which to live and enjoy the living.

In politics the story is the same. The bronze Northmen are content, always content. They look first for the sign of the elephant; that found, they look no further. Despite the fact that they were laboring under many of the adverse conditions agitating the farmer-laborites, they swallowed the "red" talk of the newspapers, stood pat and watched Henrik Shipstead go to the Senate. A few months later they repeated the performance and had the satisfaction of seeing Magnus Johnson roll a majority of 100,000 over their stand pat heads. Intelligent voting, unfortunately, requires thought, and the Minnesota Negro, not unlike voters everywhere, does not care to think.

Notwithstanding all this, the Negro in Minnesota has accomplished some notable tasks when his environment and competition are considered. Here he has matched wits and brawn with the pure Nordic-Scandinavians and Germans. A few Negroes in nearly every line of endeavor have met the competition offered by these so-called supermen and found the task not too difficult. In the professions he has had lawyers who rank with the best. The fame of a colored lawyer in Bemidji, who is a member of the chamber of commerce of that city has spread to all the state.

In the classroom and on the athletic field, which are the scenes of the preliminary struggles to the battle of life, he had punctured the myth of Nordic superiority again and again.

At the state university he has had at one time a lecturer in the medical school, assistants in pharmacy and chemistry laboratories, an editor on the student daily paper, and a Phi Beta Kappa. On the athletic field he has made similar triumphs.

His success in the business world is doubly to be commended when it is remembered that here he must build businesses to compete with that backed by the brains and capital of the whites, for there are not enough Negroes in any one city, or in any one part of one city to support Negro business men. They must compete with the white business, therefore, for white trade. This condition is undoubtedly unique, for even in the large Northern cities there are enough Negroes to support dozens of businesses.

When this is considered, the fact that five brothers have built in Minneapolis a family wash laundry with a capital value of $90,000 becomes remarkable. One of the brothers finds time to serve as secretary for the Minneapolis laundrymen's association. Some idea of the scale of the company's business can be got from the fact that in addition to its daily paper advertising, it leases billboards in various sections of the city. Its trade, needless to say, is nearly 100 per cent white.

At Northfield, Minn., a college town located on the paved Jefferson highway, a Negro-owned grill room and restaurant serves students in the winter and tourists in the summer, doing a tremendous business.

In St. Paul, a shoe repairing and tailor shop, owned and operated by a colored man, employs fifteen persons, white and colored, and is conceded to be the finest shop of its kind in the northwest. Ninety-five out of every one hundred patrons of the place are white. In St. Paul, too, three brothers own three barber shops for whites, jointly, and make enough money to have automobiles and summer cottages at a suburban lake. In Minneapolis, two brothers own a drug store in an exclusive residence section where all customers are white. Other smaller businesses are operating, but these are the outstanding ones—all the more prominent because of the competition they meet.

To match this initiative of the very few in successful business is the initiative of the masses in acquiring homes. In this one respect the rank and file is free from the charge of apathy. Negroes in Minnesota, as a whole, own and keep beautiful a larger percentage of homes than anywhere else in America. Restrictions on the locations of their homes are few and of recent origin, applying for the most part to expensive additions where the Negro cannot yet afford to live, even though he had the desire to do so. This has resulted in Negroes locating in fine middle class neighborhoods, and to his credit it may be said that his sidewalk is cleaned of snow as soon as his neighbors', and his lawn and shrubbery are as neatly kept.

The regrettable and almost tragic feature of life in Minnesota is that Negroes are so satisfied with their condition that they are blind to the signs of a new time. While the forces of discrimination make inroads upon his freedom the Negro in the North Star state rests in satisfaction, contenting himself with the thought that Georgia is so many and so many miles away. His civil rights organizations are dead. The so-called leaders do not see the vanguard of proscription marching down upon them, or if they see it, they choose to ignore it. There is another side to this indifference of leaders, however. In this north country the business and professional men who happen to be in the places of leadership are not dependent wholly upon Negroes for a livelihood. These men do not care to jeopardize (as they think) their career by a too outspoken criticism of the treatment of their fellows. They juggle issues, and ignore what they consider insignificant discrimination rather than cut off their revenue from whites by standing too closely, and too volubly, perhaps, for principle. Thus we have indifference complicated by a state of mind induced by the necessity of earning the dollar—and the dollar wins, as it usually does.

Partly from this type of leadership and thinking, and partly from the comparative freedom which the colored Minnesotan enjoys as a citizen has resulted an individualism that so far has successfully resisted group organization. The Negro feels no necessity for co-operative groups. Had he builded well in the individual temples he has erected, the necessity for group organization would have been farther distant than it is; but he has not builded well. He has been asleep in mediocrity. As problems appear that demand thought, initiative and group action, he is helpless because he is a contented isolationist.

The Negro in Minnesota needs new blood, new birth. A jolt like the Duluth lynchings will not be sufficient to accomplish the purpose, for with the exception of the Duluth Negroes, who form a small minority of the population, others in the state have learned little from the occurrence. Young men who will think and dare to do, assisted by older heads who will work together, will be the agents through which Minnesotans will conserve that which they possess, and guarantee to their children the full enjoyment of those advantages which they themselves have lightly passed by.

J. EGERT ALLEN

Mississippi—Home of "Sun-Kissed" Folks

VOL. 5, NO. 9, SEPTEMBER 1923

Born in South Carolina in 1896, James Egert Allen moved to North Carolina to earn an A.B. degree from Biddle University, now Johnson C. Smith University, in Charlotte. He did graduate work at Columbia University, Syracuse University, and New York University, and eventually received an M.A. from City College of New York and a Ph.D. in education from New York University.

Allen was active as a lecturer, community activist, and writer throughout the South and, later, in Harlem. He worked as a public school teacher in Arkansas, South Carolina, Mississippi, and New York City and served as the New York State president of the NAACP from 1937 to 1950. Many journals carried his book reviews and articles, among them the *Negro History Bulletin* and *Kappa Alpha Psi Journal*. His dedication to the promotion and study of African American history resulted in two books, *The Negro in New York* and *Black History: Past and Present*. Allen received numerous awards, including the 1937 NAACP Peace Prize and the Silver Beaver for "distinguished service to boyhood" awarded by the Boy Scouts of America in 1949. He lived until the age of eighty-four.

Although most of his later career was centered in and around New York, he justifies his authority to comment on life in Mississippi (a justification no other contributors bother to make) by stating that "these are the observations of three years spent as a teacher, field representative and research worker in the state." Charged with saying in "plain language just what conditions" African Americans in Mississippi face, Allen's essay nonetheless teases all the irony possible from his material, and his tone modulates from anger to amusement to amazement.

The most obvious example of Allen's rhetorical playfulness is his use of the phrase "sun-kissed folks," which he manages to say twenty-two times in twenty-three paragraphs. Allen's skill and sophistication in relentlessly evoking the term for dramatic effect renders this essay one of the most memorable, if uneven, in the series. This comic repetition is a deliberate play upon the elaborate names assigned to African Americans in so many of these essays ("Sons of Ham," "the darker brother," etc.). At first, the repetition has the effect of emptying the euphemism of significance, but with each use new meanings accrete. By the end of the essay, the entire process of racial designation has gone through an important transformation, however subtle and unnamable.

Allen also mocks the gravity and the inherent duplicity of flowery language: "Her [Mississippi's] citizens have applied the cognomen 'Magnolia State' to their earthly paradise and solemnly declare that you can be lulled into the arms of Morpheus by the sweet-scented evening breezes and awakened in the morning by the silver-toned mockingbird." In this same paradise, of course, "families of ten live in two rooms," and breaking Jim Crow laws is "an unpardonable sin." The language of southern gentility, however much it might describe a particular experience of the South, denies the realities of those barred from the paradise.

Allen was writing about a state that had a notoriously bad reputation for its treatment of African Americans. Although according to a study by the NAACP, Georgia actually led Mississippi in the number of lynchings between 1889 and 1918, the margin was narrow. Allen catalogues some of the horrors he sees in the poverty and exploitation of sharecroppers in the Delta region, including some less obvious deprivations, such as when he points out that there are still many people who attain "the age of seventy-five, without ever riding on a train or visiting a town." But he knows his largely northern, urban audience is aware of the "rottenness" in the state, and his critique is somewhat muted. When he pays attention to more positive aspects of Mississippi life, too, he does so without sounding cloying or filled with false bravado. He writes glowingly, for example, about the town of Mound Bayou, as an "oasis in the desert" in which African Americans run the local government and businesses, but even here he is far from the boosterism we find in other essays in the series. This is not "plain language" at work, but a considerably astute and complex rhetoric.

Nonetheless, his rhetorical sophistication never leads Allen into the trap of noncommittal relativism. Allen points out that the "great mass" of white men are still "goose-stepping" in the old familiar way, a phenomenon he feels may have led to the mass exodus of African Americans from that state. This exodus also leads Allen to conclude with the somewhat enigmatic sentence: "I sit on my stoop on Seventh Avenue and gaze at the 'sun-kissed' folks strolling up and down and think that surely Mississippi is here in New York, in Harlem, yes, right on Seventh Avenue." As in several of the essays, such an observation suggests that African Americans in the United States have a commonality, a shared identity, whether in Harlem or the Mississippi Delta. But unlike those essays that find such an observation an occasion for celebrating a growing sense of identity, Allen's essay remains somewhat ambiguous. The shared identity of "sun-kissed folks," like the appellation itself, may be, Allen suggests, the dubious gift of white racists. Allen's curious essay does not resolve such issues. But it certainly makes clear the nature of the problems and the lack of piety Allen believes his readers should bring to understanding them.

MR. ALLEN

To those who have been fortunate enough to read Shand's "Black and White," a description of conditions in Texas, Stribling's "Birthright," portraying the acute situation in Tennessee, and Clement Wood's "Nigger," openly denouncing the rottenness in Alabama, Mississippi may be described as the embodiment of all.

This home of "sun-kissed" folks can be found in the southwestern section of our group of Southern states. Its area consists of over 46,000 square miles and a population of approximately 1,800,000. Her citizens have applied the cognomen "Magnolia State" to their earthly paradise and solemnly declare that you can be lulled into the arms of Morpheus by the sweet-scented evening breezes and awakened in the morning by the silver-toned mocking-bird.

The climate is rather constant. Summer extends until October oftentimes. In late September many flowers are in full bloom. Last Thanksgiving Day a year ago, a party was motoring through the country from one village to another and all were in shirt and waist sleeves. It was so strange to a New Yorker in the group that she had to wire this bit of information home.

Very little snow falls during the Winter but a tremendous amount of rain falls throughout the year and causes rivers and creeks to swell and oftentimes overflow the surrounding country.

There are two principal geographical divisions of the state; the Prairie or higher level and the famous "Delta" or lower section. The great majority of "sun-kissed" folks live in the lower regions. A decided contrast can be seen in the people of each division. They differ *inter se* in language, customs and institutions.

The Delta region is truly one of the wonders of the age. The majestic "Father of Waters" sweeps along a wide area in his final dash to the Gulf and has deposited rich layers of sediment that have meant millions of dollars to the Cotton Kings of the State. The huge concrete line of levees extends the length of the State to assist in keeping the waters in the proper channel, and just the word "levee" has been the source of many songs, plantation melodies and tunes dedicated to the "sun-kissed" laborer.

The oceans of cotton fields, bedecked here and there with cabins, are the daily scenes of our "sun-kissed" folks. The White House of the master with its barns, out-houses and commissariat, is the nearest thing to a village that some of these toilers have ever known. Many instances of people attaining the age of seventy-five, without ever riding on a train or visiting a town, can be shown.

One oasis in the desert can be found in the little "sun-kissed" town of Mound Bayou. Situated in the heart of the Delta, it stands as a monument of inspiration and hope for the Negro youth of that "weary land."

The "sun-kissed" Mayor will invite you into his court; the "sun-kissed" banker will discuss finance with you; the "sun-kissed" postmaster, ticket agent, telephone operator, merchant, and druggist will all welcome you, and the "sun-kissed" marshal will march you off to the "sun-kissed" caboose if you do not wish to receive the welcome!

The chief product of the State is cotton. It grows up to the doorstep. The "sun-kissed" folks are trained against diversification in farming. An amusing incident is always seen in this fertile country when one beholds carloads of corn from Ohio and Iowa standing at the station. Then a wagon drawn by two husky mules draws near and fills up, then stops at the store for a "side" of meat and finally wends its way homeward. In spots, potatoes, peas, tomatoes and alfalfa are grown, but all are limited. All worship cotton and buy food out of the store instead of raising it.

In the Delta region, six of the seven coaches attached to the regular trains are used by "sun-kissed" folks. One for whites. That has been the ratio of white and black. But to-day, the situation is changing. Mississippi no longer has a larger "sun-kissed" population. In two decades the percentage has decreased from 58.2 per cent to 48.8 per cent. Other races catered to this race and even forgot some of their jealously guarded Jim-Crow laws. In many drug stores all races drank at the same soda fount! But in the Prairie region, such an act would be considered an unpardonable sin.

The social and religious life is inseparable in Mississippi. The church is the social center. Poor housing conditions often prevent much home social life. Families of ten live in two rooms. Such congestion barely leaves space for anything else than eating and sleeping and many will wonder how that is done. Many ignorant preachers are found there as well as in New Jersey and North Carolina, and many of the services degenerate into vaudeville before they are over.

The church is the great show-place for clothes and finery. A buxom maid with turban of loud yellow and orange, scarf of sforzanda red and imperial purple, dress of wild Irish green, rich maroon and romantic blue, trimmed in ultra-violet and infra-red is just from Paris, and as Mencken uses the phrase, "all the vibrations from the impalpable to the unendurable" are felt.

The problem of Education is still in the acute stage. The church schools have been the salvation of those who were saved from the clutches of illiteracy and superstition. There is not an A-1 High School in the state, publicly supported. A knowledge of the educational status, so far as the "sun-kissed" folks are concerned, was given to the world recently by one of the state's leading citizens.

The private schools are entirely too dogmatic. Jealousy shows its green fangs and poisons much of the good that might be done. Teachers from the North can never assimilate with the teachers of the South in their common work, and thus a constant stream of teachers going and coming, pours into and out of Mississippi, as in the other Southern States.

"Half done is good enough" seems to be an inherited motto with them. A young lady from New York upon her arrival at one of the schools was shown to her room. It happened to have been on the top floor of a four-story building and was without ceiling or plaster. "Why," she exclaimed in amazement, "this room is not finished!"

She received the calm reply: "Very few of them are, Miss."

However, in spite of all these handicaps and adverse conditions, we have our share of "sun-kissed" eminent men from this state. A glance at the list will bring forth: Hiram Revels and B. K. Bruce, the only two "sun-kissed" senators to grace the Chamber in Washington. John R. Lynch, who represented the state in the National Legislature; S. D. Redmond, an eminent lawyer, doctor and business man. In Washington, D.C., to-day P. W. Howard, Special Assistant to the Attorney General, hails from the Magnolia State. A Civil Service Commissioner in New York City and an Assemblyman from New Jersey also proclaim the Magnolia State as the place where they first saw day.

In conclusion allow me to say to the sympathizers of Mississippi that these are the observations of three years spent as a teacher, field representative and research worker in the state.

Of course there are fine homes, automobiles, intelligent people, wealth, aristocratic churches and cultured society in the state among the "sun-kissed" folks as well as in Philadelphia and New York. A friend from the state is visiting my wife in New York at this writing and by her dress, carriage and culture, I cannot distinguish her from any other New Yorker.

The historical spots are dear to the "sun-kissed" folks in the state. They know Grant at Vicksburg and Corinth better than you or I. The famous resorts along the Gulf coast are familiar to many outsiders because of the leavening effect upon all races residing in that section.

My prophetic powers will not permit me to fathom the racial problem and the attitude of the white man towards it. Yet, I have found white men there as fine as white men I know in New York and Illinois; but that is not the great mass who are "goose-stepping" in the old familiar way. Sometimes the Klan terrorizes and sometimes it soothes "sun-kissed" folks. At a Klan meeting in th Delta, some "sun-kissed" folks were so foolish as to endorse the movement.

Perhaps the day will come when I can picture Mississippi, the home of the sun-kissed folks, in a different way—yet it is not so different after all. I sit on my stoop on Seventh Avenue and gaze at the "sun-kissed" folks strolling up and down and think that surely Mississippi is here in New York, in Harlem, yes, right on Seventh Avenue.

ROBERT P. WATTS

Missouri: A Literal Paradox

VOL. 7, NO. 5, MAY 1925

Little is known of Robert P. Watts other than that he was an English teacher at Sumner High School in St. Louis. By May 1925, when his essay on Missouri was published, *The Messenger* had already published twenty of these essays, and *The Nation* had published all forty-eight of theirs. One of the common rhetorical ploys that emerged in both series was that of the state as an oxymoronic site. A large, small space. A freely oppressive society. Watts's essay on Missouri gives the oxymoronic trope another outing. Written with an English teacher's attention to details of style and form (and occasionally an English teacher's overestimate of such devices as alliteration—"Negroes had played a moving part in the pageant of progress"), the essay begins and ends with the assertion of the "literal paradox" of African American life in Missouri, illustrated with examples throughout.

In discussing the "paradoxical" history of slavery in the state, for instance, Watts recounts a proposal by a "liberal minded" Missourian to illustrate some of the early compromises imagined by Missourians "looking to the abolition of slavery." Slavery was to remain legal, under this plan, but all slaves would be freed upon reaching the age of twenty-five. The failure of this proposal notwithstanding, Watts's curious valorization of such an obviously problematic suggestion is one of several indications in this essay that the dangerous paradoxes he sees in Missouri culture are not as predictable as one might imagine. His inclusion of this odd proposition as part of the good side of Missouri's double sensibility illustrates the way his rhetoric moves away from the Manichean divisions that so infused the racialism of the 1920s.

Sometimes Watts's paradoxes seem like contradictions. The 124,000 black voters in the state are a "conjecturable force," but the 58 Indians in the state probably have more clout. The African American population has to solve its own problems by "continued, consistent, persistent effort," but at the same time "the Negro requires as sympathetic treatment as is accorded to the foreigner." But when the essay works well, it helps break down strictly racial and geographic boundaries. As he explores the "literal paradoxes" of Missouri and the great diversity of its black and white communities, Watts continually demonstrates not paradox but a dense matrix of conflict and compromise.

The photographs that accompany the article follow the practice of such uplift publications as the Washingtonian *Colored American Magazine,* with its pages of portraits of society matrons and maidens. The women in the first photograph are not mentioned in the article, and neither is the dancing school of the second. The women in the photograph and the girls in the dancing class are very modern—the fashionable hats and dresses are almost flapperesque in their modernity, and the dancers are in modern rather than classical ballet costumes. Nevertheless they affect none of the Africanisms promoted by some in the Harlem Renaissance group of artists and writers, remaining thoroughly middle class in appearance and implied aspiration.

In a very literal sense, Missouri is a region of paradoxes. At one time, it was both slave and free. It is both plains and mountains. The bowels of its land contain incalculable mineral wealth, yet the fame of its waters is widespread. Discussion concerning Missouri precipitated the Civil War, yet Missourians were among the first to take active steps looking to the abolition of slavery.

Such is the State whose 69,415 square miles of land was the seat of a vast population with a fixed habitation which tilled the soil, and canoed the streams, centuries before the Nordic invasion. In fertile places near the sites of its ancient cities are found the famous mounds which served for the cremation of bodies, burial, and defense during the successive periods of Missouri as province, district, territory and state. From a wild waste of forest and prairie these same mounds peered at De Soto, who in 1541 came in search of gold and silver, but found the Mississippi river.

While the Spaniards were the first discoverers, the French made the first permanent settlement in the region divided by the Father of Waters; and thus nearly two centuries after, Napoleon, with coffers depleted and harrassed by the exploits of the black Toussant L'Ouverture in Hayti, sold Louisiana and adjacent territory to the United States. Along with the Indians, Spanish and French, through all these years, Negroes had played a moving part in the pageant of progress in Missouri. They blazed trails, bridged streams, harvested crops, and helped defend white settlers against the Black Hawks, the Sioux, and the Pottowatomies. When in 1723 Francois Renault worked five hundred Santo Domingo Negroes in a Madison County mine, he introduced large scale production in Missouri. Thence forward came such an immigration of freemen and manumitted slaves that fifteen years after the close of the Revolutionary War 197 free Negroes and 883 slaves helped to make up the population. Not only did these people till the soil and work in mines, they followed in the wake of explorers; for, when Lewis and Clarke crossed Missouri a century and a quarter ago, they had with them Negro servants who bore with fortitude all the hardships of pioneering. Thus when the State applied for admission to the Union, there were those who feared that life at outposts had made of the erstwhile slave

Some Ladies of Kansas City, Mo. Top Row, Left to Right: Miss Margaret Browning, Miss Effie Penniston, and Mrs. Roy Barker. Bottom Row, Left to Right: Mrs. Corinne S. Wilson and Miss Margaret Lane.

too independent a man. They opposed any measures that would make of the Missouri Negro a freeman. So, when on February 15, 1819, Mr. Tallmadge moved to amend the bill for admission of this commonwealth to the sisterhood of states, so as to prohibit slavery in this region, he precipitated a discussion which became the storm center of politics for four decades. Yet, a century later, a Negro, J. Gerald Tyler, then Supervisor of Music in the Chas. Sumner High School of St. Louis, was chosen as the composer of the music to the Centennial Pageant which was held in honor of the admission of Missouri to the Union.

Though the slavery agitation in Missouri kept the nation in a ferment for forty years, in 1828 Col. Thomas Benton, Judge Barton, and other residents of the state made some of the first concentrated efforts against slavery. These men purposed to urge upon all candidates at the coming election the necessity of considering means to rid themselves of the curse of human bondage. They planned for the future emancipation of bondsmen in Missouri, and set about influencing other states in the same direction. The plans of these early abolitionists were frustrated, however, by reports that Arthur Tappon of New York had entertained Negroes at his table, and after dinner had taken them driving in his carriage with his daughters. Though the untimely hospitality of this early 19th century New Yorker gave a temporary setback to the plans of the liberal minded Missourians, the spirit of freedom was abroad in the land. Mr. Breckenridge proposed that after January 1, 1865, Negroes and mullatoes be in servitude until the age of 25 only; and that then owners be compensated for their manumission. In 1863, Mr. Gamble and Mr. Bush of St. Louis proposed similar measures. Yet none of these measures was designed to give suffrage to freedmen. They were emancipated by law in Missouri on January 11, 1865, while disqualifications were abolished by constitutional amendment voted on November 8, 1870. Such was pre-abolition Missouri that furnished to the forces of freedom during the Civil War approximately 8,344 black soldiers and sailors.

During all these years, however, the economic horizon of Negroes was small. They were restricted to a few trades. Farm owners were few. The black population was small. Now, though the Mississippi rolls on the east coast of the state for 500 miles and though the muddy Missouri stretches 250 miles up its western boundary, at every bend of these mighty streams farms of black men grace the landscapes in smiling verdure. They own $16,000,000 in farm land and equipment, and share in the incalculable wealth of its coal, iron, lead, zinc, and silver mines. And now, the rural black population varies from 1 person in Schuyler, and Texas Counties, to 4,729 in St. Louis County. The urban population varies from 3 in Chaffee to 102,000 in St. Louis.

Kansas, Iowa, Arkansas and Oklahoma border Missouri. It is separated from Kentucky, Illinois, and Tennessee by the Mississippi river, while the Missouri comes between it and Nebraska. Each of these states has a different attitude toward the Negro, and the sentiments of all of them are reflected in the attitude of Missouri toward its citizens of color. No Negro may attend any school supported by public funds, where whites are educated; yet St. Louis was probably the first city with a distinctly biracial system of schools whose white and colored teachers are on the same pay schedule. Jim Crow cars are not legal; but such conveyances run into the Union station, St. Louis, and the races are separated in waiting rooms in the southern part of the State. There are Negro detectives, constables and uniformed policemen in St. Louis, Kansas City, and other places. A Negro magistrate holds forth in St. Louis. An ebony face graces the halls of legislation. But notwithstanding the proven ability of Negroes to make and execute the laws, 53 men of color have had their lives taken without due course of law in 33 years. Then, too, there are Negroes on the Central Republican Committees in Kansas City, and St. Louis. A Negro inspects rural schools of color. Lincoln University has a Negro as one of its curators. The Negro Industrial Commission is the most important body of its kind in the State. In St. Louis is the Chas. Sumner High School, one of the largest secondary schools in the country for the training of Negro children. In the same city is a hospital operated by the city, but managed by Negroes. Here, internes receive clinical experience, and nurses are trained.

In business, the Missouri Negro has covered virtually every field from a "hole in the wall" grocery to a life insurance company which covers the State. By far the largest and most successful cooperative financial enterprise is that of the Peoples Finance Corporation of St. Louis, which in three years has handled sums which approximate a million dollars, and which promises to become the first Negro bank west of the Mississippi. The St. Louis Negro Business League has a paid field secretary who devotes his time to surveying business conditions. In Kansas City, an outstanding business is the Roberts Motor Mart, which is as well equipped as any other like enterprise. Then, too, Negro newspapers perform yeoman service as gatherers of news and moulders of public sentiment. It is not possible to calculate the good done by such papers as the St. Louis Argus, and the Kansas City Call.

Much of the progress indicated by these achievements, however, has been made not because of State help, but in spite of a lack of it. The legislature has just appropriated $187,000.00, a king's ransom, for the operation of Lincoln University in Missouri at Jefferson City. For the University of Missouri at Columbia was set aside the miserable pittance of $3,000,000.00. For the more than 3,000 Negro farmers in the state there is no agricultural experiment station. Such an institution is an immediate necessity. If black farmers are to be kept interested in their farms, if the depletion of farm laborers is to be arrested, if constant migration to cities is to be stopped, the two Smith-Lever workers must have a vast array of assistants. First class high schools must be established in other cities than St. Louis, Kansas City, St. Joseph, Sedalia, Cape Giradeau, Hannibal, Columbia, Springfield, and Jefferson City. The twenty-eight Negro high schools of the third class do not at all meet the demands for secondary education. Of the state institutions for charitable relief, three only admit Negroes. Their health is not properly safeguarded, and as a natural consequence 1/15 die annually, and of these 1/5 die from tuberculosis. There is a direct relation between crime, and physical and mental deficiencies; so it is not surprising that 1/3 of the penitentiary inmates are colored; and as long as the unsocial Negro is not properly cared for, crime, disease, and death will continue to mar the effectiveness of the Negro as a citizen.

The Negro requires as sympathetic treatment as is accorded to the foreigner who comes into the gates of liberty, and sits down at the hearthside of democracy. He needs more care for the girls at Tipton, and the boys at Boonville. He needs to be called in from the outer pockets of industry, to sit down in the central councils of labor, cheek by jowl, with others who are striving to make this the greatest of states. More than anything else, he needs a larger consciousness of his own powers, a growing pride in his own race, more knowledge of his own achievements, a keener appreciation of

Dancing pupils of Miss Margaret Lane, Kansas City, Mo.

the advantages of racial solidarity. In St. Louis alone there are enough Negroes to accomplish what has been done in all the state. Yet, there is no bank, no department store, no theater of the first class, no hotel of the first class owned, controlled and operated by Negroes. These institutions the Negroes must build for themselves, slowly, carefully, through various kinds of corporations, and through welfare organizations. The appearance of colored real estate companies always means the relaxing of a tight money market. In Missouri, particularly in the large cities where influx of southern migrants has caused housing crises, colored real estate companies have rendered valuable aid. At times when a Negro householder finds himself *persona non grata* in a white neighborhood, and realtors refuse to renew loans, the colored real estate operator comes to the rescue of his brother. This is particularly true in St. Louis and Kansas City.

The Y.M.C.A. and the Y.W.C.A. furnish lodgings, meals, wholesome recreation, and spiritual guidance to thousands, while churches of various denominations, in large numbers, flourish in every city, town and hamlet. These institutions are enthusiastically supported, and some people have made really noteworthy contributions. No record of philanthropy is complete which fails to note the gift of $25,000.00 made in 1924 to the Pine St. Y.M.C.A. of St. Louis by Mrs. A. E. Malone of Poro College.

Politically, the Missouri Negro is a conjecturable force. Approximately, there are 124,000 voters of Negro blood in the State, and most of these are in cities where problems of organization are comparatively small. Yet, the question arises whether the 58 Indians in the State, acting as a unit, could not get more recognition than all the Negroes in their present chaos. They enjoy every school facility, stop in any hotel, purchase any seat in any theatre, and in general are accorded all the privileges of the average American citizen. The Negro has yet to enjoy these privileges, most of which he can in a measure acquire, if he but manifests normal interest in his own affairs—an interest more of deeds than of words,—an interest exhibiting itself in continued, consistent, persistent effort, and not in spasmodic demagoguey. Such is the Missouri Negro, a real problem in a region of literal paradox.

MAMIE ELAINE FRANCIS

New Jersey;
Those Inimitable Individualists

Vol. 7, No. 8, August 1925

Mamie Elaine Francis, which may have been a pseudonym, remains the most elusive of all the authors in this series. Two stories were published in *The Messenger* under this name, "Souls for Gasoline" and "Raum-Sheba (The Ruby Girl)," as well as this essay on New Jersey. Beyond these works, this fascinating writer seems to have left no other traces.

The stories, which appeared at the height of the debate over the defining characteristics of "true" African American art, explore competing theories of African American aesthetics and folk culture. They are written with a sure hand and easy economy of expression. When the narrator in "Souls for Gasoline" worries about being in a high-toned nightclub, she describes her embarrassment in an offhand, complexly expressive displacement: "My evening dress laughed sadly at itself." The second story, "Raum-Sheba (The Ruby Girl)" is a highly condensed tale within a tale that takes us from Harlem to the southern swamps and from the folk tales of "Aunt Chloe" to the fashionable metaphysics of reincarnation in a few short pages. Both stories invoke the modernist desire to cast off the traditional shackles of religion and experience the new, while exploring the various routes to mystically "primitive" experience lauded by the writers of the Harlem Renaissance.

Her essay "New Jersey; Those Inimitable Individualists" shows little interest in the mysticism apparent in her fiction, but her concern about modern contradictions manifests itself in her oxymoronic title, which calls immediate attention to the foolishness of generalization. "Those" African Americans in New Jersey are less individual than they may think. And just in case the irony of her title gets by her readers, her opening paragraph firmly instructs the reader not to expect the usual stately introduction. Likewise, in calling New Jersey "the wettest state in the Union" she not only winks at rampant violations of Prohibition but also satirizes the kind of geographical information provided by the other essays. She makes light of the attempt to sum up the attitudes of an entire state even while doing so, as when she writes that political apathy is central to "the psychology of the New Jersey Negro," for while the rest of the country may have a "view toward the Negro Problem," New Jersey simply does not.

Organizing for more political clout was the prescription for many of the series' authors, whatever their political positions. Labor unions, the NAACP, or community consensus are all held up as tools by other contributors to demand the justice so obviously eluding African Americans during the 1920s. Francis, however, sees organization differently. For her, organization is predicated upon "social adjustment," and she argues that it is the "individualist" nature of the African Americans in New Jersey that hinders them from progress. She calls instead for a "unified social life." To illustrate her point she discusses the exclusivity of African American high society, not as a point of pride as in some of the other essays, but instead to pronounce it a failure as a tool for cultural and political development. Furthermore, she theorizes that increasing social contact between the professional and the working-class African Americans of New Jersey will result in "the binding of common interests that is so essential to true progress." As she reworks the idea of "segregation" in her delineation of class relationships, Francis centers her discussion around an understanding of women as central to creating the community solidarity requisite for racial solidarity.

Francis's voice in this piece is personal and playful—"I gained an excellent bottle of Chianti for voting a split ticket"—and her courage in employing the first person voice is notable. No other essay in the series has the inclusive engagement evident in statements such as "I wonder if the native has not an inherent selfishness of spirit," "All other sects he [the New Jersey Negro] takes experimentally, even as you and I," or "We are happy to have Mrs. Randolph, a very charming and talented young woman, become one of us." This intimate involvement in the subject at hand gives "New Jersey; Those Inimitable Individualists" more than just a genuine and convincing authority. The narrative presence enhances her thesis; indeed, a thesis that infuses the entire series: the United States is made up of individuals, many of whom are African American, and only by acknowledging individuals can you move on to acknowledging how to redefine "states." At the same time she recognizes that rampant individualism can work against the kind of communal organization necessary to make changes in the social order.

Francis offers a similar analysis of notions of "social equality," although she avoids that dread phrase. First she establishes the actual equality of the races: "The average Negro in New Jersey differs not a bit from his white neighbor." She then suggests that the blinkered individualism that keeps African Americans from seeing their common interests also keeps them from seeing the way their rights are infringed. This is compounded by the "inferiority complex" shared by the professional and working classes alike. "Those who would most vigorously deny this complex are those who most calmly submit to infringements of personal freedom," she writes. The lack of a "point of view" means a lack of community, and ultimately a lack of progress.

Although not couched in traditional leftist rhetoric, Francis's article is among those most closely aligned with *The Messenger*'s original radical ethos.

New Jersey was one of the original thirteen states. It remains one of the most original. Aside from being the wettest state in the Union, it maintains a rather unique point of view toward the Negro Problem. The country as a whole, may have one, but never New Jersey! And why? Let us examine a comparative analysis of the psychology of the New Jersey Negro.

There is no segregation in the educational programme of the state. Negro students in the elementary and secondary public schools are given the same opportunity for individual advancement as is given to students of any other race. Negro teachers are appointed to teach from the various normal schools in the state. Of course there is the case of Miss Laura Smith, a graduate of the Newark Normal School. Miss Smith passed her examination to teach and was refused a license by the Hon. Mr. Lowenstein of the Department of Education in Newark, because she happened to be colored. A most unfortunate case—but one case could never constitute a Negro Problem. And who could persuade the twenty thousand Negroes in Newark to worry about it? They are individualists—these Negroes. Now and then a little matter of this sort pops up. It is generally very decently permitted to die of inaction. Of New Jersey's two famous colleges, Rutgers will always thrill to the name of Paul Robeson, even as all Negroes thrill to his name. But will Princeton care to remember that Dr. L. Z. Johnson of Howard University graduated from its theological seminary? Do Howardites, who so deeply respect and admire Dr. Johnson, care to recall that Princeton regards the admission of a Negro to its classic portals as a social error of the gravest nature? The fact remains that Princeton does not desire Negro students. But even that cannot be considered a "Negro Problem." Not by the state as a whole, and yet it does present a serious problem to every Negro who is sensitive to the stigma of segregation. It is easier to forget Princeton, and think of the splendid work being done at Bordentown. We are proud of Bordentown, and justly so. It is progressive—this institution for the training of Negro boys.

In an analysis of the religious life of the New Jersey Negro, we find that he takes his religion seriously, if he be a Methodist; piously if he be a Presbyterian; emotionally if he be a Baptist; and intellectually if he be an Episcopalian. All other sects he takes experimentally, even as you and I. The religious life of the Negro is the same throughout the country. The extra collections for coal and palm-leaf fans, the picnics and socials! Environment never deeply affects religion. A carefully applied intelligence does—radically. The Reverend Louis Berry, pastor of St. Phillip's Episcopal church in Newark, has dared to apply his own brilliant intelligence to his church work, with a most gratifying result. He has revived a church that was amiably approaching a tradition. He has had leaders of the race address his congregation, and they are being stirred to an intellectual activity that must necessarily precede any spiritual uplift. And there are the old conservatives, the "pillars of the church," who dare to dampen his fine enthusiasm with the usual murmur of "But we never did that before." Perhaps here we have a real problem; not necessarily a Negro Problem. It is a universal ill—this stupid clinging on to worn-out traditions. The younger people of the church feel his enthusiasm. They work with him, and it is to the younger spirit everywhere that we must look for the finer things of to-morrow.

The outstanding figure in political life is that of the late Dr. George Cannon. A splendid man, whose loss is mourned by the entire state, regardless of creed or color! He was recognized as a leader, and who is there quite ready to forge ahead in the path of his blazing? As head of the Negro Republican party in New Jersey, he was responsible for the appointment of many Negroes to political positions. As a man he was loved and respected by all who knew him. With New Jersey politics torn by the conflict of wets and drys, with the Ku Klux Klan as a side show, what can become of the Negro Republican party? We look to Oliver Randolph, former Assistant United States Attorney, as a political leader. Mr. Randolph has had much valuable experience as an attorney, and as an associate of Dr. Cannon. We cannot forget his splendid record in the State Assembly. Little can be done, however, until New Jersey decides whether it wants its liquor with, or without legal interference. Mr. Randolph has done another generous thing for New Jersey, by bringing his wife, the former Bertha Bowman of Boston, to Newark. We are happy to have Mrs. Randolph, a very charming and talented young woman, become one of us.

Dr. William Alexander has also been a member of the State Assembly, and Attorney William Brandon is destined to become a member soon, we hope. As for the mass of colored citizens of New Jersey—they are Republicans because their fathers, back in Alabama, were; or they are Democrats because they were told that Republicans weren't doing anything for (or for that matter, against) them. And then there are nonchalant individuals who do not vote at all, because they cannot make up their dwarfed minds as to how to vote, and there are capricious souls who vote for purely inspirational reasons. (I gained an excellent bottle of Chianti for voting a split ticket.) Again, there must be a reason. Taxes go up, the installment man calls, and bootleggers continue to prosper, no matter how one votes, therefore the average New Jersey Negro turns his attention to the winter's coal supply at election time.

In the social life of the New Jersey Negro, we can place a thoughtful finger on the pulse of the composite "problem." There is no unified social life. Nowhere in New Jersey do we find the closely woven social fabric that characterizes Negro life in Washington, Philadelphia, New York, Chicago or any Southern city. Atlantic City, during the last few weeks of August, has an artificial replica of this social life, merely because people from all parts of the country are there to play. Arctic Avenue takes on the aspect of Seventh Avenue in New York, or of U Street in Washington. During these two or three weeks one can get everything from the thrill of cosmopolitan contact to a new fiance. But it is too fleeting, too obviously a vacation, to be classed as part of the social life of the state. At the Hotel Dale, at Cape May, or in Asbury Park and smaller coast resorts, there is the same amalgamation of interests on a smaller scale, but the Negroes one finds at these resorts are rarely from New Jersey. At times I wonder if the native has not an inherent selfishness of spirit. The average person of the northern part of New Jersey goes to Harlem when he feels the social urge. The lonely soul from southern Jersey goes to Philadelphia. And it is so very pleasant to come back to New Jersey to rest. The golf club at Westfield should have afforded stimulating week ends to Jerseysites, but it would have passed out of existence long ago, had not New Yorkers taken an interest in it.

The average Negro in New Jersey differs not a bit from his white neighbor. He has probably come up from the South, worked hard and bought a home in the suburbs, has the usual difficulties with his radio and his Ford, grumbles about his wife's bills, and still prefers poker to bridge. His philosophy centers about his home. If he can afford it he wants his children to have the advantages of higher education. His wife does practically no entertaining as it was done back home. Colored people do not colonize to any great extent in this state. One must go too far to visit friends, and it is easier to stay at home. He grapples with the selfishness of the elder settlers, and drops the problem in perplexity. He learns to approach the level of contentment, but he asks more for his children. He dreams of a professional career for his boy. But when his boy has been graduated from college he seeks a home elsewhere, where he can find the social life so strangely absent in his youth.

The professional men of New Jersey, as a group, do practically nothing toward the creation of a solid social life at home. Their wives are far better known in the society of New York, Philadelphia and Washington, than in Newark, Jersey City or Trenton. Yet professional men realize fully the excellent possibilities of New Jersey as a field. There are the thousands of Negroes who came here during the World War, who work hard and pay promptly for services. There are foreigners to whom a doctor is a doctor, regardless of color. In an organized society it is difficult to collect money from one's friends. It is the poorer class that supports the professions, but these people are given no tangible social contact in return. When the professional classes entertain their friends, it is done in a senseless imitation of Park Avenue precedents, to create a paralyzing effect of boundless wealth. The mass of colored people are fortunately spared this "striving neurosis."

When economic conditions force a closer union of these two classes, there will be a new social life, caused by the binding of common interests that is so essential to true progress. So long as the Negroes of New Jersey remain merely scattered individuals, there can be no class problem. Individuals are segregated in the theatres and restaurants. The group is apparently unaware of this. When Negroes are segregated in New York, every one knows about it, and something is done about it. When Negroes are segregated in New Jersey, no one is particularly interested, so long as he was not concerned, and segregation continues. When social contact has brought about a group interest, there will be protests against segregation, and against the anti-miscegenation law, and perhaps then New Jersey will recognize its own race problem. There is a law in New Jersey forbidding segregation, but even if a Negro could recite it verbatim, he would have to wade through a pretty expensive law suit before he could eat a dinner at the Robert Treat Hotel in Newark. There are probably not more than a thousand people in New Jersey who are aware that they are legally entitled to dine at the Robert Treat.

Here we have earnest, law-abiding people, working toward social efficiency and economic progress, seeking fulfullment of life, hampered only by lack of social harmony and an inferiority complex. Those who would most vigorously deny this complex are those who most calmly submit to infringements of personal freedom. When these social adjustments have been brought about, we will find the entire group working harmoniously for the advancement of the race.

GEORGE S. SCHUYLER

New York:
Utopia Deferred

VOL. 6, NO. 10, OCTOBER/NOVEMBER 1925

As an editor at *The Messenger,* George Schuyler not only wrote for but also oversaw much of "These 'Colored' United States." Schuyler, who by all accounts functioned as the unacknowledged managing editor of *The Messenger* for many years, was a fitting choice for writing what was arguably the most important essay in the series. Schuyler's New York City credentials were much the same as other African Americans in New York City at the time, most of whom, in 1926, were neither born nor raised there. Schuyler was himself born in Providence, Rhode Island, on February 25, 1895, and attended public schools in Syracuse, New York. After serving in the U.S. Army from 1912 to 1920, he began a career as a journalist in New York City.

Schuyler's career moved into high gear when "The Negro Art Hokum," an article he wrote in 1924 for *The Nation,* caused a huge stir in literary circles. In it, he mocked the craze of white America for anything black, but his views did not preclude him from later cashing in on the popularity of African American writing with his own satirical novel *Black No More* (1931). A futuristic novel about a scientifically developed formula that would turn black people white, *Black No More* received a considerable amount of attention for its self-reflexive, biting humor and topicality. But while his novel was well received, it was his career as an investigative journalist and popular columnist that made Schuyler one of the best-known African American writers of the twentieth century. He investigated charges of modern slavery in Liberia and used his findings to write a novel, *Slaves Today: A Story of Liberia* (1931). He wrote continuously on the issue of interracial marriage and interracial cooperation, and his regularly syndicated features ran in over thirty weekly Negro newspapers. H. L. Mencken, who published Schuyler's work in the *American Mercury,* called Schuyler "the best columnist of any race, now in practice in the United States."

Much of Schuyler's work examines the interaction of regional identities and ethnic diversity. He published a group of vignettes titled "Southern Snapshots" in the journal *The New Masses* in 1926. His series "Racial Democracy inside Latin America" ran in the *Pittsburgh Courier* in 1948 and gained national attention, as did a later series, "What's Good about the South." A regular contributor to the *Pittsburgh Courier, American Mercury, Reader's Digest, The Nation, Negro*

Digest, and *American Spectator,* Schuyler moved from an earlier career as a left-wing socialist writer to an enthusiast for the Radical Right and a member of the ultra-conservative John Birch Society in the 1960s. His autobiography, *Black and Conservative* (1966), chronicles this quixotic odyssey. He died in 1977.

Schuyler's immensely popular column "Shafts and Darts" had already run in *The Messenger* for two years when his essay on New York appeared. This column had earned Schuyler the dubious honor of being called "The Black Mencken," and although much of his column was consistent with *The Messenger's* editorial policies (as in the case of his attacks on Marcus Garvey), Schuyler's columns became famous for sparing no one. Thus, the sharp and idiosyncratic nature of his New York essay would have come as no surprise to his regular readers.

He begins: "Here are the greatest contrasts of extreme wealth and dire poverty to be found in our (?) country." His parenthetical query is one of the many ways he gestures with a rhetorical raised eyebrow during the essay. Schuyler continually lets us know that he will participate in this project, this inquiry, into "colored" America, but he will not embrace it unless he can at the same time attack its very precepts.

The assumption that American identity is somehow uniquely tied to essentially arbitrary political boundaries, for instance, meets with his easy dismissal. He seems very little concerned with New York State as a whole. "New York: Utopia Deferred" is an essay about New York City—not New York State. Schuyler's treatment of upstate New York is cursory at best, and one suspects that Schuyler would have preferred to follow the model of *The Nation* and split New York into two articles, one for the city, another for the state. The state did indeed have a substantial population of African Americans, and so its omission is significant. Yet written as it was during the boom in Harlem, it is hard to imagine how Schuyler might have done otherwise, especially as the essay was already one of the longest in the series. Still, never content to take a single stand when another is available for discussion, he attacks those who claim that Harlem is the capital of the Negro race. To this he offers the enigmatic retreat of "I won't touch that."

Epigrams are sprinkled throughout this essay with mixed success. "Every State has the Negroes it deserves" is a memorable quip, but provides little information. He lauds the inclusion of both schoolteachers and "druggists (ecclesiastical and pharmaceutical)" in New York's African American high society, both an insult to clerics and to the pretensions of high society. The overall feel of this essay might be characterized as equal opportunity cynicism.

His writing here, much like the writing in his "Shafts and Darts" column, is more cynical about hypocrisy in general than it is about any particular practitioners. His treatment of the labor movement in New York and its relationship to African American workers deserves comment; its placement in a magazine expressly devoted to forwarding the unionization of Pullman Porters is ironic, to say the least. He claims that Marcus Garvey's "Universal Negro Improvement (sic) Association" has done nothing for workers, "even less than the N.A.A.C.P., if that is possible." Since the black bourgeoisie, according to Schuyler, is in the same business of exploiting black workers as the white bourgeoisie is, any talk of racial "advancement" is hypocrisy.

The glorious and the mundane exist side by side in this essay. Grand statements about freedom of speech appear in one section of the essay, while a serious discussion about how rarely dead cats and dogs are found on the streets of Harlem appears in another. Conservative and radical opinions exist side by side as well, although at this time the radical still had the upper hand. By the 1950s and 1960s, Schuyler's archconservatism led such papers as the *Philadelphia Courier,* which still ran his columns, to disavow any endorsement of his views. These views became more and more extreme over the course of these decades, and he developed a reputation as a somewhat wacky crank, claiming, for instance, that the NAACP and civil rights agitators, mostly communists, were to blame for racial tension, not the Ku Klux Klan. In 1951 his daughter, the pianist Phillipa Schuyler, wrote a piece for *Our World* titled "Meet the George Schuylers, America's Strangest Family." There is some reason to think that ability to entertain paradox and contradiction, however much it may have been difficult for his critics to accept or his acquaintances to live with, helped make Schuyler a good editor, and, thereby, helped make for the great diversity of opinion and approach in this collection of essays.

MR. SCHUYLER

A SUPERLATIVE STATE

Here are the greatest contrasts of extreme wealth and dire poverty to be found in our (?) country; the largest and most heterogeneous population to be found anywhere in the republic; the tallest buildings, the most populous jails, insane asylums, hospitals, orphan asylums, universities, and the world's greatest seaport. Here are the greatest aggregation of uplift and philanthropic organizations in these astonishing states, the richest and best organized bootleggers, and the most powerful labor unions. Here is the greatest art and dramatic center in the commonwealth, the longest canal in the world; the biggest, the best and the worst newspapers. Here cheek by jowl, are the scum and dregs—the upper and lower crusts—of society in large numbers. Here we find every philosophy and foolosophy—religious, economic and social—vociferously expounded from platform and soapbox. Here also is the greatest number of automobiles, criminals, intellectuals, illiterati, politicians and parasites. The state can also claim the largest and most efficient rapid transit system in the world, the greatest congested area ever seen or heard of (Manhattan), with 103,000 people to the square mile—one square mile in this borough is said to contain over a half million folk.

GREATER SCENIC BEAUTY

There is a pleasing diversity of scenic beauty as one travels up and down and across the Empire State; the picturesque Catskills and Adirondacks, the lordly Hudson, the dainty Thousand Islands, the beautiful Finger Lakes, Ausable Chasm, Niagra Falls, the Palisades, the Ramapo Hills, the vast apple country, grape growing sections of West New York, the dairy farms and rolling meadows. On the west are those expansive sheets of fresh water, Erie and Ontario; on the east, the charming Lake Champlain. Here the winding Susquehanna and Delaware begin their journey to the sea and the Mohawk flows through its narrow valley to join the Hudson, while the Genesee and Oswego replenish the waters of Ontario. In the Adirondacks are those two jewels, Lakes Saranac and George; in the southwest is Lake Chautauqua upon whose delightful shores yokel charming was first organized on the chain store principle and dispensed the length and breadth of the land. Here, in short, is scenic beauty rivaling any in the world and places of historic interest too numerous to mention here. Few if any areas of similar extent can surpass it. A boyhood spent in its woods and dells, rowing and fishing in its many streams, exploring its verdure-clad hills, swimming in the tree-banked pools and skating, snowballing and coasting in the winter, is unforgettable.

RICHER THAN INDIA

In this area slightly smaller than Roumania we have more people than inhabit either Abysinnia, Argentine Republic, Canada or Siberia, and more than any other of the forty-eight states: over eleven millions; one-tenth of the population of the United States. Its wealth is twenty billions of dollars, or about one-sixteenth of the national wealth, while it pays into the coffers of Uncle Sam nearly five hundred million dollars annually in income taxes, or one-thirteenth of the national income—this is aside from other revenues. It is richer than India or Belgium, three times as rich as Australia, seven times as rich as South Africa or Hungary, and as rich as either Japan or Canada.

SETTLED BY DUTCH

The first Hudson River Day Line was established by Hendrick Hudson. It was in 1609 that he piloted his *Half Moon* up that wide stream of water now bearing his name. He claimed the territory for the Dutch. From that time on the Indians were in Dutch. Caught between the French on the north, the

English on the east and the Dutch on the south, the Confederacy of Six Nations was soon shown its place. After some bitter struggles, this first and last New York democracy went out of existence. Now you have to read Morgan's *Ancient Society* to know much about it. Today the state is ruled—like the other states are ruled—by the politicians for the plutocracy. The Dutch West India Company got the usual charter to colonize and exploit the land. Tradesmen of a half dozen nationalities were soon bartering whiskey and woolens, guns and gin for valuable furs and real estate. Later came wealthy men and courtiers. They bought, stole or were granted large tracts of land on both sides of the Hudson, which they worked with serfs cajoled from Europe by lurid tales of streets paved with gold and diamonds, trees growing ham and bacon and rivers flowing with lager and Rhine wine. New York of that time was about like any European country of that time—ruled by lords and worked by serfs—the same as today. The freedom-loving English succeeded the Dutch but slavery and serfdom went on as openly as it does today. New York City rapidly grew into a great commercial center where slaves ships to Africa and rum ships to the West Indies were fitted out by the deeply religious bourgeoisie. This early ruling class never lost an opportunity to make a penny, honest or dishonest—whatever the difference may be. They enslaved blacks and whites and aped the decadent nobility across the pond almost as assiduously as their descendants in 1925. When the Revolution broke out, the yokels burned King George in effigy and tore down his statue, but the ruling class was a bulwark of loyalty to the British Raj—until the American Army got the upper hand.

MECCA OF IMMIGRANTS

Since the early days the practice of recruiting wage slaves abroad to extract profits from the virgin American soil has extended the length and breadth of the land. New York has been the port of entry—only the recent restriction legislative enactments stopped the rush. A large number of these people never got farther than the Harlem River or to upper New York cities. So New York has always had a diverse population: about one-fourth are Catholics, one-fifth Jews, and there are huge colonies of Greeks, Russians, Finns, Spanish, and a profusion of other nationalities. There are even small groups of Chinese and Hindus. Of Americans of old colonial stock there is a minority, and a large number of them are migrants from the south (the number of crackers one meets in New York is amazing—carrying on their propaganda, too)—and many of them are flocking to the Ku Klux Klan. Burning of crosses is not uncommon in the Empire State but in the face of so much racial and religious opposition, the hooded order is rather impotent. There have been no tarring and feathering or castrations; King Kleagles wield little influence, as yet. There is considerable tolerance on the part of this diverse population. In fact, New York has always been noted for its tolerant spirit. One is allowed freedom of speech and assembly and press to an extent not obtaining elsewhere—which isn't saying much. Soapboxers can, and do, attack God, Gary or Garvey under the protection of "harness bulls." For "subversive" elements with plans for substituting crooked Commissars for crooked Congressmen, there is an exceptionally teethy criminal anarchy law and convenient disorderly conduct and traffic ordinances.

DIVIDED LIKE GAUL

All New York is divided into three parts: Upstate, meaning that portion above Westchester County; Downstate, which takes in Westchester County and Greater New York; and Long Island. The first is a vast section of farms, orchards, game preserves, vacation resorts, and big manufacturing cities which are a delight to the non-union, open shop employer. The second is a vast beehive of humanity, steel and concrete. The third is the bedroom of the bourgeoisie and playground of all classes. Over half the people in the state live in Greater New York; yet the state is controlled politically by the Upstate section because of the antiquated system of districting that everywhere in this country gives the rural sections the control. It would be as hard to get the farmers to consent to a re-districting as it would be to force Tammany Hall to install voting machines in Greater New York.

FLOWER OF CAPITALISM

Over three-quarters of the inhabitants are tenants, and half of the remainder are humpbacked with mortgages. There are usually about a quarter-million people out of work—not counting the parasites at each end of the social ladder who don't and won't work. Rents are high and houses inadequate in number, which makes the state a landlord's paradise. The wealth of most of the "old families" is based on land, which the great congestion of population has made fabulously productive of dollars. In short, New York is the perfect flower of capitalism in these United States: at one end a mass of propertyless proletarians; at the other end a small group of *haute bourgeoisie* owning the means of production, distribution and exchange; while in between is a vanishing group of *petite bourgeoisie*—independent storekeepers and small merchants fighting a losing battle against the great grocery, drug, tobacco and meat combines.

NATIVE VERSUS ALIEN

Beginning with the Dutch and English, successive waves of Germans, Irish, Italians and Jews came rolling in. The early Colonial stock was swamped. Many of them fled to the West. It is interesting to note that Mormonism was born in this state (at Palmyra) and recruited the largest part of its members here. The finding of gold in 1849 took even more of these people, but with the closing of the West, the descendants of the 49'ers are turning their steps again toward the Great Babel. Many of the people, of course, never left. They just receded into surburban towns and villages before the rush of outlanders with a lower standard of living and a lower wage demand.

Between the thirties and the fifties of the last century there grew up quite a powerful labor movement. They fought hard and gained the right to strike, agitated for public schools and sent representatives to Albany. They drew up resolutions and manifestos that stated the militant working-class point of view as ably as European thinkers years afterwards. There have always been a sprinkling of Socialists and Anarchists here, with the former quite strong. With all the conditions present for the foundation of a strong labor party or even the taking over of the socially necessary means of production, distribution and exchange for all the people, one rather marvels that the working class is not better organized and more powerful politically. It might have been had the social problem not been so complicated. But race, nationality and religion enters where only economic considerations should tread. Immigration has probably retarded more than it has assisted labor. It might well be discontinued for a hundred years or more, and the European countries decrease their populations by contraceptive methods.

A QUARTER MILLION NEGROES

Every state has the Negroes it deserves. The generality of whites in a given community are not much different from the generality of Negroes. According to the latest figures available (1925) there are about 250,000 Negroes in New York state; in 1910 there were 135,000. Today there are 196,199 in Greater New York alone. The others are scattered throughout the suburban cities surrounding New York City, and the upstate communities.

RESTRICTED ECONOMIC OPPORTUNITY

The Negro in New York has been what the white man let him be—like the Negroes in the other states. No comparison will be made between the Negro here and elsewhere in the Republic because the Negroid percentage of the population differs in each state, economic conditions differ, and consequently the thought and action of the people differ. Even in pigment, the Negroes of the country range all the way from pink to black. The New York Negro constitutes only about one-fiftieth of the state population, and he suffers from economic discrimination. He functions best on the labor market as an individual rather than a group. He is not in large enough numbers anywhere to control an industry or a single factory. The competition between the white proletarians is very great and Negroes are often faced with the alternative of not being hired at all or accepting the worst positions. The unions control many industries and it is next to impossible for the dark brother to get admitted to many of them. The union workers do not hire Negro apprentices and thus enable them to learn certain trades, or they practice the old dodge of telling him he must get a job before he can become a member while the employer tells him he can't have a job unless and until he joins the union. This is true of some unions of skilled workers, notably the machinists. Still others, as in the clothing industry, will accept Negroes in the semi-skilled branches, but Negroes seldom or never reach the higher paid positions. The clothing industry is controlled by Jews and Italians who are prone to be clannish, no matter how capable the Negro may be. So-called radical unions who yelp about the co-operative common-wealth, howl the "Internationale" and bleat about "workers of the world unite," will not even hire a Negro stenographer in their well-appointed offices. Nor will any of the unions hire a Negro to organize members of his group. In the foundation workers', brick-layers', plasterers', building labor-ers' and carpenters' unions Negroes are accepted. The bricklayers and plasterers are still a little reluctant to see the black brothers hold a union card and draw union wages. They also play, sometimes, the old see-saw game with employers. Fact is, the Negro of New York state is very largely restricted to working as porter, cook, elevator operator, messenger, la-borer, musician, chauffeur, laundress, maid, cook, dishwasher, stevedore, waiter and janitor. Negroes doing other kinds of work are the exception. Nor has the Negro the above field exclusively to himself. He did to a great extent in former years, but—"Them days has gone forever." There are not enough Negroes to go around on this sort of work and the serf classes from Europe, who are quite docile and servile—hence better slaves—have en-tered the field and threaten to preempt it. Today the majority of the big hotels and clubs and the richest families are using white help. With the growing proletarianization of the white population there are and will be more and more of them competing with the sons of Ham for these jobs.

FEW FARMERS

There are very few Negro farmers in the state—probably no more than a thousand. In Colonial times Negroes were worked on the large estates up the Hudson as chattels and indentured serfs but mainly as domestics. It was so in New York City. Gerrit Smith started a movement to get the Negroes on the farm before the Civil War—he donated a deal of territory—but the plan fell through. The Negroes who come here—like the whites—are gen-erally fleeing from the farm and they make a bee line for the cities. There is much abandoned farmland all through the state.

NEGRO BOURGEOISIE

In the upstate cities there are always to be found a half dozen or more Negroes, who, to use Dr. Du Bois's phrase, have lifted themselves "above the mired mass." In the suburban towns around Gotham this group is a little larger. Greater New York, of course, contains the majority, since four-fifths of the Negroes in the state live there. This black bourgeoisie consists of doctors, lawyers, dentists, undertakers, school teachers, kink removers, editors, barbers and the proprietors of some small businesses. Many of these people have considerable means, but in the main, they are really black coated workers—white collar slaves—catering to the needs, desires and whims of the Negro population. The Negroes of the Empire State are precariously hanging on to the fringes of the economic life of the communities in which they live. The whole Negro population could be dispensed with and not be missed except for a few Jewish pawnbrokers, delicatessan proprietors and number bankers, Greek shoe repairers, restauraters and bootleggers, and Italian icemen, fruit dealers and dope peddlers. The Negro knows it and the whites know it.

ORGANIZING NEGRO WORKERS

Where the Negroes are organized, they are just dues payers because they never get elected or appointed to any of the many offices in a trade union which pay a fat salary. He is subject too to all kinds of petty practices on the part of white brethren, especially when work is scarce. There are thousands of Negroes in the clothing trades unions, the foundation workers' union and the stevedores, yet there is not a single Negro in a paid position. All the unions in the city have had these evils pointed out to them time and time again by Negro radicals and labor agitators. But heretofore the Negro has been numerically weak and the unions have turned a deaf ear. Negro unions are not at all feasible in New York because of the paucity of Negroes in comparison to whites and the further fact that they are a small minority in any industry. With increasing numbers due to the migration, however, the unions became more attentive. It was only recently that after years of agitation and propaganda several unions and organizations sympathetic to the cause of labor advancement have been persuaded to form a committee for organization. Much credit is due Mrs. Gertrude E. McDougald—a native daughter—Assistant Principal of Public School No. 89, for the untiring energy with which she pursued this ideal. A. Philip Randolph and Chandler Owen first gave voice to the necessity of the Negro workers joining the trades unions and the trades unions admitting them. Others who have given of their time and energy to alter the Negroes' economic outlook and position are Frank Crosswaith, Executive Secretary of the Trade Union Committee for Organizing Negro workers; Wilfred Domingo, Richard E. Moore, William Butler, George Frazier Miller, Otto E. Huiswoud, Cyril V. Briggs, Miss Grace Campbell and Miss Helen Holman. These Negroes have spoken to tens of thousands of white and black trades unionists and unorganized workers in New York City and upstate. This phase of their activities is beginning to show results. Along with organizing the Negroes in industry, however, must come the breaking down of the present color line in the trades unions. Negroes laborites are raising the cry "No Taxation without Representation." The first Negro organizer of labor to be hired by a union in New York City was Miss Nora Newsome, who was employed a short time by the Amalgamated Clothing Workers of America. Later Mr. Crosswaith was employed for several months as organizer for the Elevator Operators' Union, from which job he was ousted as a result of internal intrigue. While the foundation workers are 90 per cent Negroes, all of the officials are white. This is one of the mysteries of the labor movement in New York City. There are hardly more than 10,000 organized Negro workers in the entire state, and most of them are in the Big City. With the coming of more black workers from the South, the unions will probably (and probably not) become more hospitable to Negro applicants. That, or the Negro must scab his way in—a difficult and hazardous undertaking where unions are so strong and Negroes numerically so weak.

BIG RACE ORGANIZATIONS IMPOTENT

The war is over now and it is safe and popular to espouse many things that four or five years ago might have cast a cloud of suspicion over one's good bourgeois character. Then too, in the face of a vanishing *raison d'etre*—what with the sudden slump in lynching and the growing willingness of employers to try Negro labor without being beseiged with data and conferences—one is forced often to the familiar alternative of any port in a storm. The National Urban League and the National Association for the Advancement of Colored People have, with surprising suddenness, gotten interested in the cause of the Negro worker. To be more exact, the former has collected data and the latter has sent out releases on the subject. This is commendable zeal, but bold fellows state that neither organization is in touch with the masses of workers and not very much in sympathy. Both are bourgeois organizations supported by the dilettante of both races and "good" white people, who get a thrill by chasing around the country holding conferences and "viewing with alarm" the condition of the "deah workers." Neither organization has a single union worker in its offices nor has any real effort been made to organize them and thus get a group of intelligent young Negroes into the labor movement via the stenographer's union. Neither organization has ever held a meeting to organize any workers although Dr. Du Bois swore in a recent number of *The Crisis* that the next three years were to be devoted to the Negro workers. True, the Urban League has established an Industrial Department and feigned great interest—probably intent on rousing the interest of certain sources interested in such work. But sophisticated students of the subject are anxious to see something concrete achieved. They too, are more interested in enlarging the Negro's opportunities than seeing him accept alms. The Universal Negro Improvement (sic) Association has done nothing in this basic work. They have done even less than the N.A.A.C.P., if that is possible. They have wasted the hard earned dollars of their dupes in all sorts of clowning and knavery but never bent a finger to lead them toward more wages, shorter hours and better working conditions. Instead of sending some of their orators into trade union circles and among the black and white proletariat generally, spreading the message of education and organization, they routed them around the country, deluding the Negro masses and raking in coin which went to shrewd owners of floating scrap iron. None of these organizations has spread any information about consumers' co-operation. In fact their chief benefit has been to supply jobs to a group of white collar slaves. To a smaller extent the Negro churches, fraternal orders and various benevolent societies have been guilty of the same negligence. The very thing upon which all Negro organizations in the state should lay greatest stress, they pay little attention to at all.

FEW NEGRO BUSINESSES

With this hard economic battle to wage, it is not strange that there are few Negroes of wealth in the state. There are not even the proportion of well-to-do people one will find among the whites. So there is little Negro business (and what there is, is little) and few Negroes in general business. Business is wound up with social intercourse, with family and friends, and the Negro's social life here is apart from the whites. So most of the Negro business men are in lines depending almost exclusively on the Negro proletariat: real estate, sickness and death. Years ago they were largely in the catering, saloon and dive business. Even in the districts—like Harlem— where white residents are as scarce as robed Klansmen in a Catholic cathedral, the Negro business man has to fight the competition of the efficient chain stores, and the Jews, Italians and Greeks, with their larger and wider credit and banking facilities. Because there is no insulting of or discriminating against Negro buyers on the part of white tradesmen, he hasn't got the advantages enjoyed by Negro business men catering to Negroes in the South. Negroes in New York can trade anywhere providing they have the money, and, like most poor people, they trade where commodities are the most reasonable in price. Then there is the matter of place utility. When the white residents move out of a district and Negroes move in, the storekeepers stay right there and cater to the new trade. There are whole blocks where not a single store or market has moved. They are right there close at hand and people are not going to walk five or six blocks out of their way to get a loaf of bread or a pound of sugar, often at a higher price, from a Negro.

Many of the fraternal and benevolent societies, of which there are a legion, have millions of dollars in the banks of the city (they don't employ Negro clerks in them), but they have not yet seen the necessity of investing it in anything except meeting rooms and conventions. One or two of them have bought real estate other than buildings to meet in. St. Luke's and the Odd Fellows own apartment houses in Harlem. Some of the churches own considerable property, but their economic vision seems also to become obscured when it comes to shoe stores, meat markets and grocery stores. There is not a single theatre owned and controlled by Negroes in the state and only one moving picture house is alleged to be owned by a Negro. There are Negro cabarets (or white-owned cabarets with Negro shirt fronts), restaurants, news stands and laundries, and three or four grocery stores, but generally speaking the New York Negro has no business worth mentioning. Of course, to the Negro masses it wouldn't make much material difference if there was a flourishing Negro bourgeoisie. It will be recalled that the existence of a powerful white bourgeoisie doesn't make any difference to the $20-a-week white wage slave. It does however furnish delusions about climbing the ladder of success which probably have some psychological and sociological value. A flourishing Negro bourgeoisie would admit *some* Negroes to work they couldn't get otherwise, even though the aggregate wouldn't be sufficiently large to effect the mass materially. The fact that the Negro is virtually barred here from promotion to high place in industry has undoubtedly taken away much of the incentive to study and prepare for these higher positions. Why spend time and energy in acquiring knowledge you cannot put to use? Very few whites take up astronomy, archeology or Sanskrit as a life work, and for the same reason—there is little call for it. This economic blank wall has evidently had much to do with the large number of pimps, gamblers, "sweet back" men and sports. Although it must be said that New York generally seems to be a sort of Happy Hunting Ground for these gentlemen, no matter of what color.

Such is the economic background of the Negro in New York State. I have dwelt on it at length because the way people make their living and the kind of living they make largely determines their psychology, morals and ethics. Now let's go on with the story.

HIGH LIFE COMPLEX

There is so much wealth and ostentatious display in the Great City that it is not strange that much attention is given by everyone to personal appearance. The poor are always aping the rich at any price. The tradition of the well dressed New York has its effect on white and black alike. This is less true of the rest of the state. Large numbers of the Negroes go to the extreme in following the fashions. A stroll on Seventh Avenue on Sunday afternoon or any evening is unforgettable. In the parade one sees the handsomest girls and women to be found anywhere, and there are no better dressed people in the city. Many of these Negroes will go without proper nourishment in order to present a "front" to the promenaders, the members of her club, or the sisters of the church. To dress shabbily here is to lose caste—and the peculiar economic situation facing the Negro here makes him lay more stress on social prestige. Everybody seems to be "striving." Life here is one continual round of dances, socials, picnics, excursions, parties and liaisons. All this is a great economic drain but under the circumstances nothing different could reasonably be expected.

GAMBLING GENERAL

New York's chief Negro district—Harlem—is a mecca of fakirs of all kinds: Garvey officials, "African" witch doctors, magicians, medicine men and jack-leg preachers. The chief pastime of Harlem seems to be playing the numbers, a gambling game based on the balances of the New York Stock Exchange. Now and then a player wins. Then there is frenzied paying of back rent, redeeming pawned articles, buying new clothes and touring the cabarets. Few win, and seldom. The people who win the most consistently are the bankers. They have become the newly rich of Negro Harlem— those who are Negroes. The toll these bankers extract from Harlem every week would certainly buy an up-to-date apartment house.

NEGROES FROM EVERYWHERE

The majority of the Negroes in New York state were not born or raised here—they are not a homogeneous group by any means. The majority come from the Southern states along the Atlantic seaboard, and, I suspect, came chasing that will-o'-the-wisp, Freedom. Like the majority of the white proletariat in the hinterland, they look upon New York city as an earthly Valhalla: a place of perpetual pleasure, boundless gaiety, pagan pastimes and eternal plenty. That this is an illusory Valhalla it is useless to tell them. Have they not seen Gloria Goo-Goo in her latest picture "Love on the Great White Way"? Do they not read the Sunday supplements of the yellow journals? Enough! They come, they see and they are conquered by the amazing complexity that is Gotham. Soon they get on the treadmill of New York: a vicious circle of employer, landlord, delicatessan and pawn-broker. Most of them can't get away if they would; many of them wouldn't get away if they could—there is something fascinating about this modern Babylon (one thinks of the spider's web and the fly). In 1920 only 40,000 of the Negro inhabitants were natives; the rest were born elsewhere. 35,000 were foreigners. These diverse groups develop problems not present in many other Negro communities. It is this massing of Negroes from every-where that has caused many writers to refer to Harlem as the capital of the Negro race. . . . I won't touch that. The native sons—it's hard to find one—are typical New Yorkers rather than Negroes. They are intelligent people with a background of a hundred years of freedom—in fact there were free Negroes in the state as far back as the middle of the 17th century. There are very few of them, however. Most of the 40,000 native sons are themselves the offspring of migrants from the South or the West Indies. Then there are the huge mass of Southern migrants who, like the mass of white yokels, flock to the American Valhalla in search of freedom and a good time. Last, are the West Indian, Central and South American Negroes: British, French, Spanish and Dutch. To weld this heterogeneous group into a homogeneous one is a difficult problem.

INTRA-RACIAL FRICTION

It's bad enough to have a quarter-million of our folks massed close together when they are all from the same place, but imagine them from all over the world! The task of leavening this mass has fallen to the lot of the native. He must set the standard of refinement. So, since long before the Civil War New York's Negroes have been faced with the problem of civilizing this mob. No sooner was one wave assimilated and refined than another rolled in. In later years came thousands of bombastic, litigious foreign Negroes with a lower standard of living whose penchant for underbidding and undermining the native Negro workers (this happens among the whites, too) has engendered much bad feeling. Then there is a difference in the psychology of the two groups which is best expressed by stating the obvious fact that the American Negro is an American, the British Negro an Englishman, the Spanish Negro a Spaniard, the French Negro a Frenchman, etc. This difference in thinking and feeling is reflected in the churches, the fraternal societies, at the social gatherings and on the job. Time, and the restriction of immigration, will probably remedy that. In later years differences in skin coloration have been stressed as a mark of social cleavage by newcomers: West Indians and Southerners. This was previously unknown here. White people are now helping this along by advertising for "light colored" help, and I learn from good authority that black maids are offered less money than high-brown ones. One merely mentions these things as part of the picture—they are not general or predominant.

SOCIAL EQUALITY

The New York Negro has all the rights of an American citizen—and darn few they are. He has a vote and he is not jim-crowed. Hardly a place in the state will refuse point-blank to serve him if he persists. When he is refused, he can readily invoke the law protecting him from discrimination. In New York (Manhattan) he suffers from what is practically residential segregation. One piece of legislation for which the Negroes should agitate is a law compelling a landlord to rent an apartment or a house to anyone willing to pay the price. There are ample precedents. Outside of New York City the Negro suffers very little from the various subtle forms of residential segregation which the superior mind of the dominant Nordic thinks up. He can buy property wherever he has the money to buy and live in peace. The southern white migration and the consequent growth of the Klan has somewhat altered that situation, but not much. White and black families living side by side in the same apartment house is not unheard of, while living in alternate houses in the smaller cities is very common, in fact, the rule.

INTER-MARRIAGE AND INTER-MIXTURE

White and colored children attend the same schools, sit side by side in the same classrooms, go to and from school and play together; Negro school teachers teach white children; blacks and whites sit side by side in the theatres and eat side by side in the restaurants, and yet—despite the theories of the Southern crackers and their demagogues—there is very little open social intermingling and almost no inter-marriage. Yet there is considerable racial inter-mixture under cover—or should one use the plural? I doubt if there are one hundred mixed couples who have gone the city hall-preacher route, and I know of only two or three that have turned out in accordance with the formulas of Vera Simonton, Eugene O'Neill, Sarah Millen and Leonard Merrick. Racial inter-mixture differs here in New York from most places in the country, in that there are as many white women parties to it as colored. With the white women it is usually a case of love; with the Negro women it is money. The number of white women who shower their favors on Negro men would be surprising if statistics were compiled. As a result of this the New York Negro man has largely become disillusioned about the alleged superior value and charm of white women. Needless to say this is not true of those sable folk who migrate from elsewhere. The people who do inter-marry here suffer less from social ostracism than in most parts of the country where there are a quarter million blacks. Especially in the great metropolis are the people more tolerant and sophisticated.

Employers, white storekeepers and icemen hold out considerable temptation to Negro women. Negroes with the features of Jews and Chinese are not entirely unknown. Since inter-marriage is so rare one grows thoughtful upon seeing so many young white Negroes on the streets.

HIGH SOCIETY

High society in New York is more democratic than in centers of snobbery like Washington, D.C. In a social gathering of the "best" people one may see hairdressers, seamstresses, doctors, dentists, undertakers, discreet demi mondes, journalists, writers, musicians, social workers, insurance agents, nurses, school teachers, druggists (ecclesiastical and pharmaceutical), college students, Pullman porters and housemaids. I think it can be fairly said that society here is not based on money, but on culture, refinement and sophistication. Some of the wealthiest people in Harlem do not move in the highest social circles and some of those who move in the highest social circles are trembling every time they hear the landlord's footsteps. There are of course no rigid lines of demarcation. This high society consists of little cliques. The more intellectual group have the advantage of social intercourse with whites of a similar status. Prominent artists, novelists, journalists, musicians and writers visit the homes of these Negroes and invite them to theirs. These affairs are very brilliant. Here the prominent white and black intelligentzia—pseudo and genuine—of America may be seen. Of course there is a deal of less open social intercourse between the white and black theatrical-gambling-sporting-bootlegging set. But there is snobbery: I have heard numbers of women boast that "they never go on Lenox Avenue." That thoroughfare is supposed to be the habitat of the rough proletariat.

WELL HOUSED

While suffering much from high rents and the necessity of taking in roomers (to say nothing of other methods of getting the rent), the New York Negro is probably better housed in the mass than any other group of Negroes in the country. Steam heat, hot and cold water, bath tubs, gas and electricity, hard wood and parquet floors are the rule. Elevator apartments with marble and tile entrances are common. A word must be said here for the much-maligned real estate agent: He was an effective agency for carrying the needed Negro expansion into the so-called white sections. Still the Negroes paid dearly for his services, and still do. The Negro population in the suburban towns is largely recruited from disillusioned New Yorkers who managed to escape from the Gotham treadmill after a fierce struggle. The New Yorker enjoys clean streets and prompt garbage and ash removal. True, one can occasionally see a dead dog or cat on the streets of Harlem, but that is as much the Negroes' fault as the city's. In the first place the city is no place for an unleashed dog or cat, and when an animal is killed the Health Department should be pestered until it is removed. The Negro here is vouchsafed about as much police protection as anyone enjoys in these hectic post-war years. I estimate the Negroes own about one hundred million dollars worth of property in the state. Of course that property is only owned by a few and much of it is mortgaged. As for the masses, they have nothing but hopes.

POLITICAL ACTIVITIES

Your New York Negro is a hard proposition to figure on politically. In the upstate section he is, like most of the people up there, a Republican; although small groups of Democrats have sprung up since the late war for democracy. In Greater New York, however, it is difficult to say just how an election will go in the sections largely populated by Negroes. Harlem has sent both Republicans and Democrats to the State Legislature and the Board of Aldermen. While there are over a hundred thousand Negroes in Harlem, they are not in a position to elect a Congressman (and it wouldn't make any material difference to the masses if they did). Probably there are seventy-five thousand or more Negroes living in the 21st Congressional District, while the total population of that district is close to a half million (415,000 in 1920). Too, there are a large number of foreign Negroes who cannot vote. Many Negroes (and whites) are disfranchised each year by moving in October, which seems to be a custom in the city—the law requires three months residence in the district. Then too, there is a deal of political cynicism, probably justifiable. Still the Negroes have gained a little by their political independence. They have a large number of policemen and other city workers, probation and truant officers, and one Negro is on the Civil Service Commission. Since the chief value of voting seems to lie in getting jobs for somebody you like, it cannot by said that the New York Negro is politically a failure. Harlem is unique in having a branch of the Socialist Party in its midst. The Socialists once polled 5,000 or more votes in that section, but, sad to relate, the vote has since declined, as it has declined everywhere in the country. There are also a few black Communists, more vocal than virile, and largely of foreign extraction, like the white Communists. These people don't seem to understand that Homo Americanus is more anarchistic than communistic. Still, they add to the gaiety of the passing show. An interesting sidelight on the political thinking of the New York Negro is the fact that thousands voted for the white, Democratic Congressional candidate in the last election and against the Negro, Republican candidate. This is independence with a vengeance. In New York State the Socialist Party polls around 200,000 votes each election, so nomination by them means something. Often the Republicans and Democrats have to combine against the Arm and Torch. Well, the Socialists led the way in nominating Negroes for office. They have nominated A. Philip Randolph and Lucille E. Randolph for Congress and Frank Crosswaith for Secretary of State of N. Y. State. Each year for years they have nominated Negroes in various districts for the Assembly and the Board of Aldermen. They have nominated Negroes in districts where very few or no Negroes lived. The Republicans and Democrats (the too-old parties) have never nominated Negroes for any but minor offices, except in the last Congressional election when the G.O.P. nominated Dr. Roberts in a district where they knew he couldn't win.

N.Y. NEGRO MILITANT

The New York Negro has always been outspoken and militant. Much of the agitation for freedom, equal rights and opportunity has had its source here. It is never difficult to organize a big mass meeting against any real or fancied evil. Today, I believe it is fair to say, Negro America looks to New York City for advanced leadership and opinion. These Negroes are cosmopolitan and sophisticated. They know of the history and achievement of black men and women. A white man here will think several times before hanging the hated epithet "Nigger" on one of the sons of Ham.

HISTORICAL NOTE

As early as 1643 there were Negroes in New York as land patentees under the administration of the Dutch. Slavery began in 1650. At the time of the making of the Constitution all free Negroes in the state could vote. Around the time of the Civil War, however, there were restrictions placed on that right. One slave insurrection was attempted in 1712 and another on 1741. Both were ruthlessly suppressed with many hangings and burnings. In 1782 the introduction of slaves was prohibited and gradual emancipation began in 1799 and ended in 1827. In 1704, Dean's school, the second school for Negroes in the country, was established. Mother A.M.E. Zion Church came into being in 1796. The Abysinnia Baptist Church was founded in 1803 and became the fountain head of that faith among Negroes in America. Beriah Green's Institute at Oneida in the second quarter of the last century was the mecca for Negro youths in search of an education free of molestation. Such New Yorkers as Alexander Crummel, Thomas B. Downing, Henry Highland Garnett, George T. Downing, Isabella Sojourner Truth, James Varick, William Howard Day, Garnett D. Baltimore, Ira Aldridge, Edmonia Lewis, Harry T. Burleigh and F. J. Ferrell have brightened the record of Negro achievement in the United States. Numerous others have reached great prominence after coming to the liberal and cultured atmosphere of the great metropolis. Space will not permit mentioning them, but they are well known and numerous.

Detachments of New York Negroes have fought in every war (except the Mexican) waged by the United States. During the Draft Riots the New York Negroes fortified themselves in Weeksville, a part of Brooklyn, with plenty of ammunition, rifles and cannon, waiting patiently for the white mob. New York Negroes took a very prominent and leading part in the various conferences held in Pennsylvania and New York beginning about 1830, and the later movements for African, Haitian and Central American colonization of free Negroes. James M. Whitfield, a Negro poet of Buffalo, took a leading part in the colonization schemes. There was a much more powerful group, headed by Frederick Douglas, whose activities after returning from England were centered in New York State—he lived in Rochester—which was opposed to colonization and fought for equal rights and opportunities right here. The same arguments and charges bandied nowadays back and forth between the pro-Garvey and anti-Garvey Negroes were made much more ably nearly a hundred years ago. The National Colored Convention was formed here (Troy) and made rapid strides in formulating programs and plans of action for the guidance and betterment of the free Negro. They brought out at the time (1847) in reply to charges by the governor that Negroes in New York had $839,100 invested in business and $1,160,000 in real estate exclusive of incumbrance.

The first college-bred New York Negro in the United States was John W. Russwurm, of West Indian extraction, who graduated from Bowdoin and later edited in New York City the first Negro newspaper in America, *Freedom's Journal*. There were many notable Negro caterers in New York City from 1780 on. They did business with all of the prominent families of their time. The most noted were Cornelia Gomez, "Aunt" Katie Ferguson, Peter Van Dyke, Boston Crummel (father of Alexander Crummel), Thomas Downing and David Roselle.

The N.A.A.C.P., the U.N.I.A., the A.B.B. and the F.N.F. were all founded here. So today the U.N.I.A. and the N.A.A.C.P. are carrying on the agitation of the two schools of opinion that have been at loggerheads in Aframerica for over 100 years. Needless to say, the majority of intelligent Negroes, here as elsewhere, recognize that the United States with all its faults is heaven compared to most any other place on the planet. The Negro Socialist have caused the Negro masses to think as never before but your average Negro like your average white man, shies at the Flaming Torch and the Red Flag. The Negro Communists (about six in number) have made no headway at all—except vocally—despite the rumored funds from Moscow. A. Philip Randolph and Chandler Owen of New York City are unquestionably responsible for founding the economic radical movement among Negroes.

ECONOMIC ORGANIZATION ONLY SALVATION

As to the future of the Negro in New York, it is hard to say. One no sooner waxes optimistic than new developments make him pessimistic, and vice versa. Most of the New York Negro's energy should be concentrated on his economic advancement. The various fraternal, benevolent and church organizations should learn how to use their money to better advantage than erecting architectural monstrosities. They could break the chains of economic bondage tomorrow if they invested their large funds now reclining in white banks (that do not even employ Negro janitors) to open grocery stores, meat markets, shoe stores, and other business now largely dominated by Greeks, Jews and Italians who don't live in the Negro districts, don't contribute to Negro welfare and don't inter-marry with Negroes. Such development should be by these organizations rather than by individual Negro capitalists, in order that the profits realized may benefit the people who spend the money. There is plenty of farm land within a few miles of every big city in the state where the Negro community could raise much of the produce they use every day. In the field of labor they must lay more stress on efficiency, capability and organization. Most of the big chances still come from the capitalists rather than organized labor, yet the Negro must leave no economic weapon unused. The membership of the various Negro organizations and churches need to be more inquisitive about the disposal of funds and more aggressive in forcing mentally lazy officials into constructive economic activity. In fine, the Negro fraternal, benevolent and religious organizations of New York need to become institutions of, by and for the proletariat rather than economic and social bulwarks of the black bourgeoisie, who, from a broad point of view, are but agents and guardians of the system that exploits the urban Negro. Otherwise, despite the pious lallygagging of sleek and well-paid professional uplifters, the future will, like the writer's complexion, be very dark.

JAMES E. SHEPARD

North Carolina— Its Educational Progress

VOL. 8, NO. 3, MARCH 1926

James E. Shepard was born in Raleigh, North Carolina, on November 3, 1875, the son of a minister and the eldest of twelve children. He studied pharmacy at Shaw University, receiving a graduate pharmacist degree in 1894. A man of varied interests and talents, he worked as a pharmacist; a clerk in the Washington, D.C., recorder of deeds office; and as the deputy collector of U.S. revenue in Raleigh, North Carolina. He helped found the North Carolina Mutual Insurance Company and the Mechanics and Farmers Bank of Durham. He was appointed field superintendent for the International Sunday School Association in 1899, on whose behalf he traveled a great deal organizing Sunday schools in the South. In 1910 he was the only African American speaker at the World Sunday School Convention in Rome. Concerned that the potential of Sunday schools for racial leadership was going unrecognized, he created an institution in 1910 to train ministers and teachers. This institution went through several identities but eventually became the North Carolina Central University at Durham, "the first state-supported liberal arts college for Negroes in the United States." By 1941 it was a four-year liberal arts college with graduate and undergraduate degrees. Shepard served as its president until his death in 1947.

Controversial in his politics and renowned for his contributions to education, Shepard's career represents the breadth and difference that *The Messenger* was trying to present in its view of African American life in the 1920s. Shepard came under fire from many progressive groups for his conservatism and accommodationist positions and was embroiled in controversies throughout his career. Observations such as "the Negro begs little for himself as an individual, but he does beg for his schools and his churches, so that the masses may be lifted up" were not always popularly received, and his support of the purportedly racist and antilabor Supreme Court nominee John J. Parker drew fire from many camps. At one point a communist paper, *The People's Voice*, dubbed him "Minister of Apology in the Department of Propaganda for the Southern States and Their Sympathizers Who Believe in Racial Discrimination Predicated on the Legal and Systematic Repression of Negroes." Yet prominent voices like those of W.E.B. Du Bois and Benjamin E. Mays defended him staunchly as "a supreme strategist." He was a leader within the Republican party in North Carolina and was an advisor to Theodore Roosevelt. The *Dictionary of American Biography* curiously notes that "if he belonged to the NAACP, he did not publicize the fact."

His dry, well-documented article on North Carolina demonstrates one reason Shepard raised the hackles of many an activist. Scads of statistics attest to educational progress in the state, as represented by salaries, enrollment figures, and the growing number of credentialed African American teachers in the segregated school system. Yet Shepard completely avoids any comparisons with the white half of the system. His facts are carefully couched in hopeful terminology, and all the information he delivers can lead only to the conclusion that the white government of North Carolina is fully committed to the education of all of its citizens. Whether this was a genuine opinion or a strategic rhetorical move is not clear, but Shepard's conciliatory and cheerful essay is in staggering contrast to an open letter by A. Philip Randolph to the Brotherhood of Pullman workers, which ran in an adjacent column on the same page in *The Messenger* as Shepard's essay. In his letter, Randolph harnesses apocalyptic bombast ("Let us not retreat from the field of Armaggedon a single step") to enlist Pullman porters into the union. This juxtaposition of empassioned rhetoric with Shepard's sprightly litany of educational statistics was doubtless a coincidence, but its irony calls attention to the significance of Shepard's studied dullness. There were extreme differences of opinion about what strategies to adopt to advance the idea that, in Shepard's words, "Negroes are not wards of the nations, but citizens entitled to all the rights and privileges as others." Shepard's choice was to announce, at all times, the self-sufficiency and achievements of the moment.

A note at the beginning of the article claimed that this essay was to be the first of two parts, with the second essay to be titled North Carolina—Its business and political progress. Despite its promise, *The Messenger* ran no such sequel, perhaps because Shepard was too Pollyannalike for the radicals on *The Messenger* staff. Although at times his writing is powerful—the early part of the century, he writes, was "the period of racial rancor, of disfranchisement, dehumanization, depersonalization"—this piece is more a compilation of numbers than an essay and is therefore of more historical than literary or cultural interest. The last sentence quotes St. Paul, advising us to " 'Thank God and take Courage,' " an admonition that adequately sums up Shepard's mix of congratulation and cautious demands for more progress.

We make no pretense of thinking that all has been done for the White or the Colored Schools in North Carolina that could have been, and should have been done. But it has become a commonplace observation that North Carolina never goes backward. It does not always go forward at the rate that we might wish; but it goes in the direction of progress. Having invested in the Negro Schools and found its capital well spent, we have an abundant hope that the next school year will mark the greatest advance in education for the colored people of the State.

The chief problems in North Carolina along educational lines:

First—Is to improve the condition of those teachers who are already in harness.

Second—Is to secure a larger number of well-trained efficient teachers to supply the growing demands of an improved school system.

What have the teachers done by way of increasing their number? What about their certification, what of their scholastic training? What is the number taught by each teacher, what is the average salary paid these guardians who hold the future of the Negro race in their patient and faithful hands?

I have been able recently to read and study the progress of the school teaching profession in this State for 25 years. This quarter-century has been epic among our people. Beginning in 1870 there were 490 Negro teachers in North Carolina. Not one taught in the city schools. By 1880 there were 17 in a profession of 2,117. In 1890 there were 2,225 rural school teachers and 70 city school teachers. In 1900, just 25 years ago, there were 2,400 rural teachers and 167 teachers in the cities. These were revolutionary years for our people, the period of racial rancor, of disfranchisement, dehumanization, depersonalization. It is not an accident that 1901 saw just 1 teacher added to the rural force, in 1902 only 4, in 1903 only 7, 2 more in 1904, 4 more in 1905. There was a drop in the number of rural school teachers in 1906 to 2,367, but all this while the city schools were improving. There were 167 teachers in 1900; in 1901, 212 teachers; 220 in 1902; in 1903, 225 teachers; 250 in 1904. At the close of 1909 there were 384 city school teachers. The growth was slow, but it always gave promise. Occasionally there was an actual falling off of teachers, but only three times in 45 years did this occur. Two of these years naturally fell together during the world war. The influenza epidemic took its toll also.

There are now 4,070 rural school teachers and 1,240 city instructors among our people. That makes a total of 5,310. This represents a gain of 190 over the preceding year, when 3,942 rural and 1,178 city teachers made up the Negro teaching profession in the state. For the year 1923 there were 3,820 rural and 1,051 city teachers, making a total of 4,871. After 1923 there had not been less than 5,000 teachers.

For 1925 there was a percentage of 76.6 rural teachers and 23.4 city. The greatest percentage increase has been in the cities. The teaching profession was doubled in the 25 years from 1900 to 1925. In the city schools the percentage of increase has multiplied itself seven times.

The improvement in teaching has been one of the outstanding accomplishments of our people. The third grade county certificates have almost disappeared in the state—there were only 5 for the present year. The second grade county has dropped in two years from 1,237 to 998. Increases in high school "C" certificates went from 59 two years ago to 121; from high school "B," 48 two years ago to 100 this year; and from 25 high school "A" two years ago to 99 today. In 1923 about 51 per cent of all the colored teachers held standard certificates. In 1925 the percentage increased to 57. This is helpful for it carries with it corresponding decrease in non-standard certificates. In the five-year period just passed, the number of nonstandard certificates held by colored teachers has decreased from 2,834 to 2,298, a total of 536 or 19 per cent during that period. In other words, 106 standard teachers each year displace non-standard teachers in our schools.

In our city schools our teachers have something more than a year's advantage over the rural instructors on the score of training. The city schools furnish teachers with an average of a year and third in college. For the whole profession among our race, there is a training equivalent of 3.96 years above the elementary schools, not quite equal to graduation from a standard high school.

THE ENROLLMENT

There were 24,991 pupils enrolled in the colored schools for this year. Of this number 190,968 were in the rural schools. This gives 59,983 or 23.6 in the city schools.

They did not attend specially well. Of every 100 colored pupils enrolled, an average of only 67 attended school every day. The rural schools averaged 65 daily attendance and the city 74. The big cities furnished the best attendance, an average of 80.4.

The average number of pupils to each teacher was 47 enrolled, but on attendance basis there were only 35 for the cities and 32 for the county.

SALARIES

In no realm has there been such manifest satisfaction as there has been in the compensation of the teachers. Just eleven years ago, for the year 1913–1914, the 3,173 colored teachers received $484,114.83. Five years later 3,388 teachers were paid $667,697.47, and five years after that, at the close of 1924, there were 5,120 teachers drawing $2,233,983.29.

The average monthly salary paid teachers eleven years ago was $26.75. In the next five years this has increased to $37.18 and at the close of 1924 this figure has been increased to $64.83. We have not reached any sublime heights, to be sure, and we have far to go; but there is some satisfaction in knowing that the mountain peak differences which separate the intellectual guardian and the hod carrier, the light bearer and the brick-layer, the leader of the community and the driver of the scavenger cart, are passing. The signs are salutary. The intellectual Negro is being recognized by his own and by the white people.

It is a truism hoary with age but always with the dew of morning on it, that men will esteem the causes into which they put their money. How could North Carolina think highly of a Negro school teacher or a white teacher, so long as the state had in its heart the power to think of that teacher in terms of $26.00 a month? In these days of rigorous economy in state and national governments we must not confound intelligent business methods with parsimoniousness. If we skimp on schools we shall have to write ourselves among the myriads of forgotten statesmen who thought to save money by knocking the brains out of their communities. That is the poorest political economy yet devised by intelligent man. It costs much to educate a child, but it costs vastly more to keep one illiterate.

And herein, I think is the soundness of North Carolina's school work. When that great-hearted man, Thomas W. Bickett, was governor, he conceived a great spiritual duty for himself and his administration and he demanded that the property owners of North Carolina lay their hands on the Bible and swear to what they owned. They did and the result was a marvelous triumph for righteousness. The dashing Governor Morrison coming after him perceived that North Carolina is a rich state and to all its citizens, he said, it owed the obligation to educate. And during Mr. Morrison's administration more money was spent on the Negro schools than was spent during the Aycock administration on the entire system. And glorious Governor Aycock had fightfully won the name of "Educational Governor of the South."

The day that North Carolina began to think of Negro schools in terms of longer sessions and better paid teachers, that day North Carolina registered a great moral advance. It decided that ignorance is a cure for nothing and that any other philosophy is monstrous. If in the present period we do not see all the hope that we saw a year or two ago, let us not forget that sentimentally, at least, the white people of the state never were in quite so thoughtful or generous a mood toward us as they are now. Let us remember that a larger number than ever wish to carry on. Let us remember that $26.75 monthly salary of eleven years ago and the $64.35 of today is a long stride. Let us not forget that our term has lengthened from 114.8 days in 1914 to 134.4. Let us recall that our average number of days in school has gone in these eleven years from 72.3 to 89.1.

We have a school population of 293,185 as against 253,276 eleven years ago. The 40,000 gain is not so impressive; but when we reflect that the school enrollment then was only 189,919 and that it is now 248,904, we do have something for which to be happy. And against the 119,630 school attendance of 1914, we now have 164,698.

In 1914 we spent $74,405.65 for new school buildings and sites and in 1924 we spent $772,992.25. In 1914 the total value of our school property in the state was $1,021,736.93. In 1924 the total value of our school property had gone to $6,580,770. In 1914 the average value of our school houses was $396.60 and in 1924 it was $2,705.91. Moreover, our one-teacher rural schools in these eleven years have dropped from 1,972 to 1,356; our log houses from 125 to 53; our percentage of illiteracy from 31.9 to 24.5.

Our maintenance appropriation for normals has gone from $14,000 in 1914 to $148,000 in 1924 and for colleges it has increased from $12,500 to $62,500. And best of all our investment in instruction, the cost of teaching to each pupil, has mounted from $5.38 in 1914 to $26.44 in 1924.

Perhaps the greatest tribute to the breadth and depth of the desire of the white people of the State to do justice to the educational progress of the Negro was shown by the action of the Legislature of 1924, which passed an act with but one dissenting vote to establish an "A" College for Negroes leading to degrees in Liberal Arts and Sciences.

North Carolina thus paves the way for the other Southern States and registers its belief that more than a common education should be provided for all classes. North Carolina is the first State in the South to provide such a college, separate and apart from A. & M. Colleges.

One very hopeful situation in the educational condition of North Carolina is the attitude of the present State Superintendent of Public Instruction, who is advocating an eight-month school term for all people. He is a man who is absolutely fair and just in his conclusions and desires that the Negro population of North Carolina have the things to which they are entitled, as citizens.

Another encouraging condition is that the affairs of the Negro schools are under a very efficient department devoted exclusively to the development of Negro education. The director is white, but his assistants are equally divided between the two races. People everywhere are recognizing the fact that Negroes are not wards of the nations, but citizens entitled to all the rights and privileges as others.

In the foregoing article, I have not mentioned the private schools and colleges of North Carolina which have aided in every way possible the State of North Carolina to develop this high educational system.

Wherefore, may we not follow the example of the Apostle Paul as he sighted the three taverns—"Thank God and take Courage"?

WENDELL P. DABNEY

Ohio— Past and Present

VOL. 7, No. 4, APRIL 1925

Wendell P. Dabney was known as a musician and composer of some significance before he ever moved into politics and journalism. Born in Richmond, Virginia, on November 4, 1865, he attended school there until he moved to Ohio to attend Oberlin's conservatory. He remained there for only one year before he had to return to Virginia to help support his parents by waiting on tables. In 1890 he founded a music school in Boston and soon afterward began to make a name for himself in politics, serving for many years as the city paymaster for Cincinnati. He and several associates founded a political league named for Frederick Douglass (with whom he worked on the Emancipation Exhibition at the 1893 Chicago World's Fair), and his career thereafter became intrinsically associated with the African American political situation in Ohio. Dabney's major book, *Cincinnati's Colored Citizens* (1926), which originated from his *Messenger* article, is an authoritative source for assessments of African American life of the 1920s. For over forty-five years, Dabney edited and published *The Union,* an Ohio newspaper. He died in 1952 at the age of eighty-seven.

Dabney was a prolific poet who was regularly featured in the *Amsterdam News* throughout the 1930s and 1940s, but his *Messenger* essay eschews poetic writing for a matter-of-fact style that befits his role as journalist. The prose is serviceable, but he opts for sentence fragments and frequent subheads rather than sustained argument or exposition. Rayford W. Logan, a long time acquaintance, remembered Dabney as "a man of pungent wit" who "could keep several stories going at the same time," but little of that kind of narrative felicity is evident here. Several aspects of Dabney's analysis of Ohio merit note, nonetheless, not the least of which is his accounting of the backlash aimed specifically at the partly integrated school system. Dabney's version of Ohio's educational history, in which the "mixed schools" of earlier years were replaced with more-segregated schools, illustrates the conviction felt in so many of these essays that the progressive spirit that characterized the prewar era was replaced in the twenties by a less tolerant atmosphere.

The irony of naming the newer segregated schools after Frederick Douglass and Harriet Beecher Stowe is not lost on Dabney, and he implicitly highlights the ironies of white backlash in the 1920s by opening his essay with a section devoted to "distinguished white friends," while ending with an embittered account of the abandonment of the African American population by the Republican party and the concomitant "gang" control and corruption he sees at the polls. Although Dabney ends with a tacit nod to the hopeful future ("The future looms before us brighter by far than the past, with its sad story of our slavish servility to an ungrateful party"), his overarching assessment of what life in Ohio has to offer to African Americans is cautious at best.

Garveyite politics provide one subtext for this essay. Dabney's history of Ohio in Africa, although it never mentions Garvey by name, is directed against Garvey's Back to Africa program. Ninety percent of the participants in the Ohio of Africa venture did not survive the settlement, Dabney notes. The rejecting of American identity by emigrating to Africa is precisely what so much of the "These 'Colored' United States" series, with its inclusive nationalism, was working against. As part of the series, Dabney's essay on Ohio, however ambiguous its thesis may be, integrates African Americans into the very history and identity of the state.

Before assuming the form with which we are familiar, Ohio was a part of that vast territory claimed by the French and known as Louisiana. Conquest by Great Britain resulted in the Treaty of Paris, April, 1763, which transferred that immense body of land to the English, and under the name of Northwest Territory, it was in 1783 subdivided. The state's name, Ohio, was derived from the river Ohio, which meant, in the Indian vernacular, "River of Blood." The Massachusetts Land Company began colonization of the territory, and under Ordinance of 1787, enacted by the Continental Congress, slavery was prohibited. Five states were made from this territory, and Ohio was the first to get the 60,000 inhabitants requisite for her admission into Statehood, which occurred February 19, 1803. Now in 1925, her population stands at 6,321,539, of which about 300,000 are colored.

Early in the history of the State colored people came. They settled everywhere. In the northern part, then as now, less prejudice prevailed. Those who settled there remained. They were successful in farming, industries and general business. Many intermarried with the whites and their descendants are conspicuous in the affairs of State and Nation. A number of slave owners freed their slaves and established for them a residence in Ohio. Bethel was founded in 1797 by Dedham of Virginia, an ex–slave holder.

After the Indian Wars, abolition sentiment was fanned into flame by the tales of Southern cruelty, the capture and return of runaway slaves, and the rapid growth of the Underground Railroad System. In defense and advocacy of Negroes and their rights, both before and after the Civil War, the names of hundreds of whites are written in letters of gold upon the glorious pages of history. A few only can we mention but the young of our race will do well to treasure their memory.

DISTINGUISHED WHITE FRIENDS

Senator J. B. Foraker, Civil War hero, Statesman, Governor. While United States Senator, made the fight of his life for the company of colored soldiers, so ignominiously dismissed during the reign of Roosevelt.

Lyman Beecher, President of Lane Seminary, famous institution of learning in Cincinnati. Strong in abolitionistic sentiments. He was a wonderful orator, father of Henry Ward Beecher and Harriet Beecher Stowe, who wrote "Uncle Tom's Cabin." Forty years ago it was a common saying, "The United States has two great things; the Flag and the Beechers."

Judge Albion W. Tourgee, abolitionist, author of "A Fool's Errand," "Bricks Without Straw," and "An Appeal to Caesar"; wonderful works for moulding pro negro sentiment.

Salmon P. Chase, however, Governor of Ohio, U.S. Secretary of Treasury. Born in the East, located in Ohio, famous as an abolitionist. He defended so many fugitive slaves that he became known as "Attorney General for Negroes."

Thomas Morris, United States Senator for six years and a wonderful orator. Answered most effectively John C. Calhoun and in his reply to Henry Clay, February 9, 1839, he ended with these prophetic words: "I conclude that, the Negro will yet be free."

John Brown, from five to twenty years of age, lived in Ohio and there his determination to free the Negro was formed.

Levi Coffin, head of the Underground Railroad in Ohio. Thousands of slaves were assisted to Canada. His book tells the tragic story of Margaret Garner, who when captured, cut her little daughter's throat, rather than have her a slave.

General Grant and hundreds of other great men dwelt in Ohio and with their mothers' milk absorbed the spirit of liberty and love of justice.

EDUCATION

Ohio was always strong for education. Even when it became a territory, resolutions making provisions for schools were adopted. The educational history of Ohio's colored inhabitants practically began in Cincinnati, which was the second oldest settlement in this State. In the minutes of its school board, April 5, 1830, is the following: "The people of Colour in the First Ward pray that a school may be opened in it for the benefit of their children." According to John I. Gaines, the first school organized for colored people in Cincinnati was in 1825, in an old Pork House by Henry Collins, a colored man. It lasted a year. The colored population of Cincinnati at that time was about two hundred and fifty. In 1834 Owen

Nickens, a colored man from Virginia, opened a school which was successful. In "Schools of Cincinnati," page 448, we note: "Mr. Nickens was
succeeded by John McMicken, a natural son of Charles McMicken,
founder of the University of Cincinnati!" Being importuned to do something for the education of colored youth (Old McMicken) bought 10,000
acres of land north of Liberia, called it "Ohio in Africa" and told them to
go there and settle. About 119 started. In the Gulf of Mexico, smallpox
attacked them. The Captain sailed to Charleston, S.C., for medical assistance. Those who were well were jailed for coming into the State in
contravention of law. They go out in three months. On to Africa again. In
six months, 90 per cent were dead! McMicken felt that he had done his
duty and therefore inserted a clause in his will prohibiting colored youth
from sharing in the benefits of any educational facilities he might provide
for the youth of Cincinnati!

An association was formed which helped in the establishment of schools
in Columbus, Chillicothe, Circleville, Zanesville, Dayton and other cities.
Notwithstanding the rowdiness of the whites, who by mob violence sought
to drive away colored pupils, notwithstanding intimidation, ostracism and
cruelty to white teachers, the schools grew in numbers and excellence, for
the colored people of those days fully realized and appreciated the value of
education. A law was passed for the establishment of schools providing
free admission for all white children. We are informed that light colored
children were often barred from, or subjected to, much discrimination in
the white schools.

In 1849 there was a tie in the Ohio Legislature between Whigs and
Democrats. A handful of Free Soilers held the balance of power. They
made a proposition as a requisite for their vote:

(a) Repeal the Black Laws.
(b) Establish free schools for colored children.

The Democrats agreed. The law was enacted. But Cincinnati School and
Civic authorities declared it unconstitutional and refused to maintain such
schools. The colored people got busy, elected trustees, appointed teachers,
sued for the money and in a year won! Thus colored schools were legiti-
mized. Peter H. Clark, still living in St. Louis, made a glorious record in
this fight and afterwards in struggles for political freedom.

In 1886–87, Bishop Benjamin W. Arnett was largely instrumental in the
repeal of the laws establishing separate schools. Thanks to our colored
people of "Jim Crowistic" inclinations, there have been re-established in
several cities separate schools for colored pupils. Leading in that regard is
Cincinnati, which has lost the valiant, fighting progressive spirit of its early
days. It has two large Negro schools. Strange to say, they were named in
honor (?) of Frederick Douglass and Harriet Beecher Stowe. A Negro
High School is looming in the distance. And yet, not many years ago, Prof.

Chas. Bell was teacher of penmanship and other colored teachers, taught in our mixed schools!

Columbus also has Negro schools and Dayton has its annex and segregated rooms for colored children. Colored citizens of Springfield, about a year ago, made a wonderfully successful fight against segregated schools. Of all large cities in this State, Cleveland stands well out in front for its victorious battles against segregation in schools and other public institutions. It has a large number of colored teachers in its "mixed schools."

COLLEGES

Oberlin College, founded in 1834, almost from its inception became famous or infamous for its advocacy of freedom and acceptance of colored students, many of whom attained national distinction. When the discussion of slavery was forbidden about 1834, at Lane Seminary, in Cincinnati, the students rebelled and many of them went to Oberlin.

The Western Reserve or Adelbert College, Ohio State University, Cincinnati University and practically all of the big colleges now receive colored students.

In 1856 the M.E. Church laid the foundation of Wilberforce University. In 1863, the University passed into the possession of colored men. It is now an institution of the great A.M.E. Church but since the passage of an act in 1887 by the Legislature of Ohio, the State contributes to the maintenance of its mechanical and industrial departments. Many notable men have been associated with the school as students, instructors or trustees. Its reputation is world wide.

LITERATURE AND ART

Many of our men have enjoyed exceptional prominence in every field of human endeavor. Those who were pioneers in attainment of educational opportunities, racial rights and political recognition are too numerous to mention. In literature and art we may name:

Charles W. Chestnutt of Cleveland, author, novelist. Paul Lawrence Dunbar, poet. Justin Holland, famous musician and composer.

Duncanson, Cincinnati's wonderful artist of the early days, whose paintings are now beginning to arouse great interest. Thomas and Ball, leading photographers of Cincinnati in its early days, were famous for artistic ability.

ATHLETICS

DeHart Hubbard, all-round athlete and winner of the World's Broad Jump Championship at the Olympic Games, leads for this State a brilliant galaxy of young college men famous in the field of sports.

BUSINESS

In the realm of business, Gaines of Cincinnati, who died in 1859 at the age of 38, had a big provision store, famous for steamboat supplies, located on the river front. He was known to the trade from Pittsburgh to New Orleans. Because of his fight for, and interest in, education. Gaines High School was named for him. There was Gant of Zanesville, very successful farmer, wealthy real estate owner and proprietor of Gant's Park, probably the first of its kind in this State. "Bob" Mallory of Dayton, whose hotel, a famous colored resort years ago, is still catering to the public.

Gordon of Cincinnati, who came originally from Richmond, Virginia, and with a laborer's start, developed into a controller of the local coal market, amassed vast property interests and became our richest citizen. He was grandfather of Dr. Gordon Jackson of Chicago.

In the land of the living there still dwells Giles of Piqua, who also from a shoe string has run his wealth into thousands. Anderson and Son, contractors of the same town, are making good.

Moore of Dayton, one of our greatest capitalists, owned the San Marco Hotel of Dayton, several cafes, cabarets and on the turf had and sold horses of international reputation. He still has great property interests.

Around Wilberforce there are Bishop "Josh" Jones and many other owners of immensely valuable property and farms.

In the upper part of the State dwells Mr. Mushaw, the famous "Onion King," who is identified with the largest white business enterprises in that section. There are others scattered here and there in regions where the color line is so little recognized that they have almost lost their identity as members of our race. Berry of Athens, Ohio, whose hotel was, for many years, known throughout the United States as the greatest hostelry within many miles of that city. It was ever crowded with the most select of the white race. In fact, Elbert Hubbard devoted much space to it in his magazine and besides eulogizing the proprietor, characterized Berry's Hotel as "The Best Family Hotel in America."

Parker, of Ripley, owner of a big iron foundry and in his day one of the biggest business men in his town and rated as one of the wealthiest men of our race in the State. Meyers of Cleveland, confidant of Mark Hanna, said to be very wealthy, owns a magnificent tonsorial establishment, one of the finest in America. Senator John P. Green, of Cleveland, wealthy, one of our richest lawyers and formerly State Senator.

SOME OHIO CITIES

Springfield has four doctors, two dentists, five undertakers, two lawyers, two drug stores, one hotel with over forty rooms, two movie theaters, seven grocery stores, three buildings, the Odd Fellows Temple, Pythian Temple and the "Gray Office Building," three automobile garages, two newspapers, a number of contractors, business men and hundreds of mechanics and laborers.

Dayton has nine doctors, four pharmacists, six dentists, four lawyers, two drug stores, one office building, four hotels, two fraternal buildings, one Building and Loan Association, one realty company, two newspapers. Thousands of colored laborers and mechanics find ready employment in hundreds of big manufactories. The Duiron Company employs one electrical chemist with three assistants, two of them college graduates, and the other a high school graduate.

In one of the grade schools, colored children are taught in an Annex of frame portables by colored teachers, while the white children are taught in the main brick building by white teachers. In another district four rooms are set aside in the basement for retarded colored children and their colored teachers. Parents protested, "went to law" and a settlement in court is still pending. The other schools are mixed.

Columbus has twenty-four doctors, twelve dentists, fifteen lawyers, twenty-nine teachers, one principal, eight undertakers. Long Street is the principal business street and a number of its business blocks have colored owners. It boasts the only colored picture house west of Philadelphia built, owned and managed by colored people. A medical arts building, also built and owned by colored people, thoroughly modern and architecturally perfect. It has a Building and Loan Association, several Insurance companies, two oiling stations and business enterprises of all kinds, including one of the largest house movers and wreckers in this State. About forty thousand colored people are in the city and they find employment in every capacity.

Toledo has five doctors, five lawyers, two dentists, two undertakers, two newspapers and one draughtsman, several creditable church buildings, and thousands of mechanics and laborers.

Cincinnati has a colored population of 50,000 with seven dentists, seventeen doctors, twelve undertakers, two fine cemeteries in which our people take great pride and to which they give illimitable patronage. Fourteen lawyers, one of whom, Mr. A. Lee Beaty, is a United States Assistant District Attorney, six drug stores, one large printing establishment, one haberdashery, a large amount of real estate owned by Masons and Odd Fellows, two Building and Loan Associations, and Creative Realty Co., several real estate dealers, the foremost in holdings and age being Mr. Horace Sudduth. One of the largest furniture moving and storage plants in the State, a white company whose president, Mr. M. L. Ziegler, is a colored man. Two principals and about 130 teachers in our separate schools.

Cleveland has a colored population of approximately 50,000 people. There are thirty lawyers, one of whom, Alexander Martin, is a United States Special Agent. There are thirty-seven physicians, of whom three are on the staff of leading hospitals of the city, twenty-four dentists, the Empire Savings and Loan Company, the Peoples Collateral Company, two architects and six realty companies, four jewelers and ten garages. Cleveland has several office buildings and apartments, a Welfare Federation, Cedar Avenue Boys "Y," which is a mixed institution. Two strictly first-class drug stores, three moving picture theaters, six undertakers, two large coal yards and four hotels, three newspapers. There is a Caterers' Club with a membership of four hundred. One hundred and fifty school teachers, who teach in mixed school; twenty social workers, several truant officers and Juvenile Court Officers. Some of the churches are beautiful edifices, costing around $100,000. There is one State Representative, Harry E. Davis, and a City Councilman, Thomas Fleming.

Cleveland claims a full quota of lodges, nearly all of which own their own buildings, and a great institution in the Phillis Wheatley, a home for colored girls, which now has on a campaign to raise $600,000 for a new home.

HOMES, ETC.

All of the cities of this State have splendid residences and there are thousands of moderately wealthy people. There are churches galore and much of our capital has gone and is still going in building or renovation of such properties. The brevity of the article prevents enumeration of the many "Y's," male and female, the hundreds of Associations for general or specific betterment and hundreds of fraternal organizations for philanthropic purposes. The thousands of small stores and shops, the hundreds of beauty parlors, etc., bespeak the vast onward movement towards financial independence, the desire to speedily reach that prosperity so long enjoyed by the people whose energies and ambitions caused our arrival in this country.

NEWSPAPERS

Hundreds of newspapers have died aborning; others have lingered a few months or years and gone to join the great majority. The oldest are:

The *Gazette* of Cleveland, nearly forty-five years of age, edited by Hon. Harry C. Smith, several times a member of the legislature and well known as a staunch advocate of race rights.

The *Dayton Forum*, Dayton, Ohio, has been in existence several years and its editor, John H. Rives, is a well known public spirited citizen of Dayton.

The *Union, Cincinnati*, Ohio, is nearly twenty years old, edited by W. P. Dabney, for many years City Paymaster of Cincinnati.

There are many little bulletins owned by various churches.

POLITICS

As the strength of the Republican Party has grown greater, the prominence of the Negro has grown smaller. The passage of the 15th Amendment in 1870 gave him the right to vote in Ohio. "In the good old days," he served on campaign and executive committees, held many positions in our municipal governments, went to the Legislature, and even to the State Senate. No conference or convention could go on without him. But alas, today he stands dishonored, stripped by the very party he has so blindly worshipped, so loyally served.

Few, if any, colored men hold executive positions in our cities. There is one Assistant U.S. District Attorney, several deputies or clerks in municipal offices and one councilman. Few serve on committees. Few are ever consulted and fewer get into conference or convention. Not a delegate at large in a National Convention for many years. The Legislature in late years has rarely had over the number it has now, namely, one. In Cincinnati, for years, not a single Negro has been on any campaign or political committee!

Our women take little interest in voting and our men with few exceptions are "gang" controlled. Fortunately, judging from the independent sentiment and vote in the last campaign, the colored brother has seen a great light. By voting for people rather than party, the future looms before us brighter by far than the past, with its sad story of our slavish servility to an ungrateful party.

Phyllis Wheatley Home for Girls in Cleveland.

W. H. TWINE

Oklahoma—the Land of the Fair God

VOL. 8, No. 5, MAY 1926

Little is known about the early life of William Henry Twine. Born during the Civil War in Richmond, Kentucky, on December 10, 1862, he married in 1888 and fathered six children. He taught school in Texas and read law there. The Texas bar admitted Twine in 1888, making him one of the earliest African American lawyers to be so recognized. He moved to Oklahoma in 1891, settling in what was officially Indian Territory in 1897. His career included arguing a capital case before the U.S. Supreme Court and serving as the editor of the *Muskogee Cimeter,* the first African American paper in the Indian Territory. The booster agenda promulgated by the *Cimeter* is evident from its assessment in *Who's Who of the Colored Race* (1915): "Its activity induced great numbers of colored people to locate in the vicinity of Muskogee" and it "may be partially credited with conditions in that section; no person was ever lynched in Muskogee," a fact Twine proudly reiterated in his *Messenger* essay. Rather more mysteriously, the same source describes Twine as "a leader of 'the boys in the trenches' who 'fought with knives and revolvers for the stand 'patter's'' against the 'lillie white' faction of the Republican party of Oklahoma, in the 'Battle of Lannings Hall,' " one of the historical events connected with the selection of delegates to the Constitutional Convention, related to the time Oklahoma was admitted as a state, November 16, 1907.

During the early part of the twentieth century, lawlessness and lynchings were rampant in Oklahoma. And yet what Twine always calls "our group" in Muskogee stood fast against mob violence. Twine's understanding of the African American population of Oklahoma as a cohesive group is no simplistic generalization about racial identity. As much of his essay elaborates, the racial makeup of the Oklahoma population is the product of the unique political history of the state and its intermingling of Native American, European American, and African American populations. Twine tells this history with anecdotes, such as that of Reverend Harry Island, or "Coonskin Harry," a former slave who lived in a Native American community and served as a translator. He worked for the commissioners appointed by the U.S. government to form a new treaty with the Indian tribes that had rebelled and aligned themselves with the southern

Confederacy. According to Twine, "Coonskin Harry" single-handedly ensured that any African American who had been held as a slave by Native Americans in Oklahoma was not only freed but was given the same rights and political status as "a full blooded Indian," including a land grant of 160 acres per individual before the opening of the territory to new settlement in 1889. Since over eight thousand African American slaves were held by Native Americans in Oklahoma according to the 1860 census, this land grant was substantial. Although, like many Reconstruction promises, the land grant was never fully realized, some land was distributed to tribal freedmen in Oklahoma. Regardless of the historical accuracy of Twine's story about Coonskin, the essay compellingly demonstrates that the African American population of Oklahoma is deeply enmeshed in social and political traditions unlike those in the rest of the United States.

Twine's fascination with the state's earlier status as Indian Territory sometimes overwhelms his concern for other aspects of African American life, including the fact that the African American population by mid decade was larger than the Native American population, in part due to considerable African American immigration after World War I. Twine does not even mention one of the worst race riots in American history, which occurred in Tulsa, Oklahoma, in 1921 and in which approximately eighty people died and fifteen thousand African American homes were burned.

Twine does recount the brave stance of Oklahomans against other mobs, with a tacit admission that he was himself involved in a standoff with a lynch mob. And when his essay takes such a turn it begins to take on a tone that, despite some bravado, is genuinely moving and persuasive. Unlike the many essays that end with guarded optimism or unsupported boosterism, Twine's almost Babbittlike invocations of "the best town on earth" are accompanied by hard-won and heartfelt understanding of the necessity for courage, conviction, and unity. The violence faced in the young western state of Oklahoma was not abstract or historical; it was faced by group effort, by "our group." There is little doubt that Twine meant it literally and figuratively when he wrote: "In spite of the many obstacles in our way, we are determined to stand by *our guns and stay in Oklahoma,* and continue to battle for our rights." Since his essay has already represented African American Oklahomans as hardy pioneers and frontier homesteaders, this rhetoric remains free of the aura of radical, revolutionary threat, and instead becomes a simple application of the western ethos, invoking not an ideology of revolution but one of grit and self-determination.

"Oklahoma, the Land of the Fair God," is the forty-sixth state to be admitted into the Union, and is the forty-sixth star in the "American Constellation."

It is really two states in one, having been formed by the Union of Oklahoma Territory and the beautiful Indian Territory, and became a state November 16th, 1907. The western part of the state is the old Oklahoma Territory and the eastern part is the beautiful Indian Territory in which was, and is located great Muskogee, the Indian Capitol of the world, and the very best city in the United States for our group.

Oklahoma Territory was thrown open to settlement by proclamation of President Harrison, March 23rd, 1889, which set the time for opening at noon, April 22nd, 1889, and all persons were warned about the penalty of the law regarding those who went into the promised land ahead of time. Afterwards, the Iowa, Sac and Fox, Kickapoo, Cheyenne and Arapahoe Indian reservations, and the Cherokee strip were made a part of the territory, and after the Indians were given their allottments of one hundred and sixty acres each, the remaining land was thrown open for settlement by citizens of the United States. (Later, the Osage Nation, composed of the Osage tribe of Indians, was made a part of Oklahoma.)

The throwing open to settlement of the lands of Oklahoma was the first time in the history of our country that the American Negro was given the opportunity to become a pioneer as a free man and show the mettle that he was made of, and he proved equal to the occasion. On the day of the opening, the race was made for FREE HOMES and the first one to locate on a quarter section of land claimed it as his homestead.

"As the time drew near for the race, the people grew anxious and excited. There was every conceivable vehicle of conveyance. There were men, women and children waiting for the signal to go; they were on foot, horseback, wagons, ox-carts and buggies, ready to run as noon approached. Just before noon, there was a lull, and eager faces turned toward a new land of virgin soil and watched the officers with watches and guns in their hands. Suddenly there came the puff of smoke from the carbines of the soldiers and at the reports of the guns the mighty rush of thousands for *free homes* was on and the first to stake a claim was the owner of the farm staked."

This was all new to the Negro, but soon caught the spirit of the game and in many instances beat his white neighbor to a valuable claim. He had the nerve, grit and manhood to stick to it through all the hardships incidental to pioneer life, and made the prairie and forest blossom as the rose. He proved to the world that he could pioneer as well as the best of them. As a result of the noble fight made by these Negro pioneers, many of the best farms in Oklahoma (old Oklahoma Territory), are owned by Negroes. This is true in Logan, Lincoln, Payne, Pottawatomie, Oklahoma, Kingfisher, Blaine and Garfield Counties.

In the cities of Guthrie, Perry, Chandler, Oklahoma City, Enid and others, our group is represented in the business world and is making good. Politically, they have made a good record, having held many positions of honor and trust. Hon. R. Emeett Stewart, one of the leading attorneys in Oklahoma, was the first of our group to be elected County Clerk of Logan County, which position he held for several years with honor to himself and to our group. He made such a splendid record that his successors for several terms were of our group. As I recall it now, Prof. N.J.C. Johnson of Guthrie was one of his successors. Hon. Roscoe Dungee, editor of the *Black Dispatch* at Oklahoma City, is a descendant of one of the pioneers of Oklahoma and is keeping the record clear, as is shown by his work as editor and owner of one of the greatest newspapers in the southwest. There are many bright and shinning lights in the legal and medical profession and among them are E. T. Barbour, attorney at El Reno, Doctor Horace Conrad, Guthrie, Dr. A. Baxter Whitby, Grand Master of Masons, and Dr. Charles B. Wickham, Grand Chancellor of the K. of P., both of Oklahoma City.

In this part of Oklahoma, our group has made greater strides from a political standpoint, for the reason that they have never been denied the right to vote, as has been the case in the eastern part of the state. Even the Democrats are making inroads in our ranks, and they go the limit to see that their black followers have the right to vote. The population of Oklahoma at State-hood was about one million five hundred thousand. Our group numbered about a hundred and fifty thousand and the greater part of these had come from the Southland.

The eastern part of the state was formerly known as the Beautiful Indian Territory, and was composed of the Five Civilized Tribes, to wit; the Creek, Cherokee, Seminole, Choctaw and Chickasaw Indian tribes. Living among these tribes were twenty-five thousand Negroes, about five thousand in each tribe, who were former slaves of the Indians. When President Lincoln issued his proclamation giving freedom to the slaves, these slaves of the Indians were included.

The Indians had violated their treaty with the government of the United States when they rebelled and went with the Southern Confederacy and it was necessary for a new treaty to be made in order that they again could have their tribal government restored. A Commission was appointed by the United States government to meet with a like Commission appointed by the Indian tribes, and these Commissions were to meet to form a new treaty.

The Commissioners appointed by the United States government could not speak the Indian language and the Commission appointed by the Indian tribes could not speak English; hence, they were compelled to have an interpreter. Providence provided one, for there was an old Negro preacher who had been a slave and had lived with the Indians many years and learned to speak their language. He could also speak English, and being the only man who could fill the position, he was made official interpreter. He was known as Coonskin Harry (Rev. Harry Island). The Commission submitted their proposals to the Indians and Coonskin would inform the Indians what the Commissioner desired and the Indians in turn would tell their desires. All went well and all were satisfied until they got down to the question, "What was to be the status of the Negro or freedmen," and it was that Coonskin got in his fine work. He told the Commission that the Indians desired that their slaves be given the same rights that were given to the Indian and that he should be allowed the right to vote and take part in the political affairs of the tribe, also that he should share in the land and annuities as though he were a full blooded Indian. It was so written in the treaty, and the Commissioners for the United States government and the Commissioners for the Indians signed the treaty. It was approved and stands today on record. The Negroes of the Creek Nation especially owe a debt of gratitude to Coonskin Harry that they can never repay. THEY SHOULD BUILD A MONUMENT TO REV. HARRY ISLAND.

When the Indians were allotted their land, the Negroes, ex-slaves and their children were each allotted a quarter section of land just the same as the Indian and it is from this land that so many Negroes have grown wealthy in the eastern part of Oklahoma. Providentially, the allotment of the Negroes has been in localities where there were great reservoirs of gas and oil and great mountains of coal, lead and zinc and other minerals. Oklahoma is the treasure house of these United States. What is true of the Negro of the Creek Nation is true in all of the Five Civilized Tribes. They are the most fortunate Negroes of our country, having been born with "A Golden Spoon" close at hand.

These Negroes, while the tribal government existed, took active part in the affairs of the nation. Some of them were members of the Supreme Court, and we recall now that our old friend, Rev. (Judge) H. C. Read, was a District Judge and later a member of the Supreme Court, and that Attorney W. A. Rantie and Attorney A.G.W. Sango were members of the Creek Council, and that Hon. J. Coody Johnson was a member of the House of Kings. (Mr. Johnson is today one of the wealthiest men in Oklahoma.)

The Negro citizens of the tribes intermarried with the Indians and all stood on an equal plain until Statehood came and then "L" broke loose. Among the first laws passed by the State legislature was one to *reverse* the Creator "God." They passed a law making the Indian a white man and then passed another law that the Negro and white should not marry. This was done to bar our boys from marriage with the Indian maidens and our girls from marriage with the braves, thus reserving the rich land of this country for their own boys and girls.

However, our group made hay when the making was good and prior to Statehood, many of them had married Indians and there are many dark skinned "Injun" babies who drew an allotment of 160 acres. Since Statehood, great numbers of our group following the example of the white man, have come from the different states, North and South, and have located in Oklahoma, bought homes, and are reaping wealth from the splendid resources of this Great State.

The K. K. K. came also, and seeing that our group was enjoying peace and prosperity, at once proceeded to bring about chaos and laid plans to drive Negroes from their homes. To their surprise and disgust, however, our brave men and women stood together as one, and when it was dangerous to oppose the Dragon, they served notice on the most cowardly set of scoundrels that ever snapped their fingers at justice and went unhung, that we were ready for the battle and that it should be to a finish, and then the sneaking cowards of the Invisible Empire took their pillow slips and sheets and skulked away. The Negroes of Muskogee have fought them at every stage of the game and on the 6th of April, 1926, we assisted the Christian white people of our city in driving the Cyclops and his minions from office, and immediately Muskogee took on new life. The day the K.K.K. was driven from power, a new bank was opened in our city and old nature came forward and joined the procession by giving us a new oil well of two-hundred barrel capacity, and many other good things are on the way.

Politically, our group in eastern Oklahoma is in a bad row of stumps, as many of our good men and women have been denied the right to register and to vote, but this year we are making herculean efforts to have all of our group registered and with our fifty thousand votes in the state, we can assist materially in bringing order out of chaos.

There have been a few lynchings in Oklahoma, but none in Muskogee. Our group has stood as a unit against this relic of barbarism. At one time the outlaws and the Hill Billies from Arkansas and Texas who had located here attempted to engage in their favorite pastime, lynching. Two Negroes, Willie Williams, and Homer Matthews, were lodged in the county jail and charged with the crime of murder. A crowd of five thousand gathered around the jail for a Lynching Bee. We begged the sheriff to disperse the crowd, but he could not do so. We then went to the best class of white citizens and begged and employed them to stop the gang of cut-throats from committing the crime of lynching, and they tried to do so but failed. The howling mob, thirsting for blood, attempted to storm the jail, and then a strange thing happened. Our group (including the writer), lost their religion, and suddenly from somewhere three hundred men with high powered rifles sprang forward and faced the cowards and served notice that a number of Free Tickets To Hell were to be given gratis, and the mob went hurriedly to their homes.

That is our antidote for mob violence. Later, a white man was brought to Muskogee from Wagoner County for safety (he was charged with murder and a mob from the county started for Muskogee to wreck their vengeance on the prisoner).

Our group served notice that they must not cross the Arkansas River, which is the division line between this and Wagoner County. We also stated that we are opposed to mob violence and no man, *white or black,* could be mobbed in this county. They took the hint and came not.

At the trial of John Welsh (Negro), charged with the murder of a white officer, when the K.K.K. was at the height of power and the presiding

Judge a Kluxer, and the sheriff and his force Kluxers, our colored lawyers, Carter W. Wesley, H. T. Walker and W. H. Twine, were the first lawyers in the United States to challenge a juror on account of his being a member of the K.K.K. and the first to ask the question, "Are you a member of the Ku Klux Klan?" They were over-ruled by the Court, the judgment was reversed on an appeal and now the question is being asked all over the Union. Our Oklahoma lawyers broke the ice.

In Oklahoma we have fought segregation and won a victory each time, but in Muskogee we have never fought it because our Group live all over the city and have business places in the very heart of the city. In spite of the many obstacles in our way, we are determined to stand by *our guns and stay in Oklahoma,* and continue to battle for our rights. We are determined not to sacrifice our property and seek other climes, but rather stand and fight the scoundrels who deny us our civil and political rights. If necessary, we will fight until the Plutonian regions are congealed and continue the battle on the ice. Our women, God bless them, have always been loyal and stood by us in every contest and have given valuable aid when the mob threatened. They have never faltered, but have stood out in the open ready and willing to die for the right. Pioneers? Yes, the best the world ever knew.

They say that the Garden of Eden is located at the confluence of three great rivers. Well, we have the Verdigris, the Arkansas and the Grand Rivers at our door; hence, we must be living in the Garden of Eden, Great Muskogee, the best town on earth.

ERNEST RICE MCKINNEY

Pennsylvania: A Tale of Two Cities

VOL. 5, NO. 5, MAY 1923

Born in Malden, West Virginia, in 1887 as the grandson of a slave, Ernest Rice McKinney was raised in an atmosphere of political activism. His parents were both schoolteachers, and in 1898 his father went to Washington to work with the Republican administration of William McKinley. McKinney attended Oberlin for four years without obtaining a degree, but while there he organized a branch of the NAACP with the help of W.E.B. Du Bois. He then lived in Denver and Pittsburgh until 1917, when he joined the American Expeditionary Forces to fight in France, when he was already thirty.

When McKinney was nine years old the Supreme Court gave its blessing to Jim Crow laws in the famous Plessy v. Ferguson case; he lived until Ronald Reagan was elected for a second term. Very few people saw as much of this century's progress and dishonor in race relations.

McKinney was one of the most radical journalists, alongside Eugene Gordon, who wrote for "These 'Colored' United States." He was a fairly established writer by the time he began work on this essay. His association with the African American press began with his work as a writer for the *Pittsburgh Courier* before the war. When he returned he began to write for and edit *The Pittsburgh American* and became a contributing editor at *The Messenger*. In 1929 McKinney published his own paper, a short-lived venture titled *This Month*.

In the 1930s his political career began to overshadow his journalistic aspirations. Like many of those inspired by the Russian Revolution, McKinney had joined the Communist party in 1920, but he withdrew in 1926 over political differences. In 1929 he helped organize the Conference for Progressive Labor Action, which later became the American Workers party (AWP). McKinney served on the National Committee for the AWP and in 1934 became trade union secretary of the Workers party, a new party formed by a merger of the Trotskyist Communist League with the AWP. When in turn the Workers party joined the Socialist party in 1936, McKinney became an organizer of African American steelworkers. When his Trotskyite faction was expelled from the Socialist party in 1937, he helped establish the Socialist Workers party. He continued work as a trade union activist and ran for Congress in 1946 as a Workers party candidate from Harlem. He lost, and his interest in the Workers party waned, leading him to withdraw from politics in 1950 and begin a career as an educator. McKinney taught labor and black history at Rutgers University and elsewhere, and he regularly ran courses to train and professionalize members of the United Federation of Teachers. He served as an advisor in his later years to the A. Philip Randolph Educational Fund, which conducted educational programs for African Americans and labor groups.

Always a proponent for action, in 1977 McKinney said in an interview in *Essence* that "we have to leave lamenting to the historians." It may seem, however, that McKinney was doing his own share of lamenting in this essay on Pennsylvania. "There is perhaps more ignorance per square foot in Pittsburgh than in any other large American City," he writes, and, even more emphatically, *"There is perhaps no city in the country that is more preacher-ridden than this city."* But his sometimes acidic pen always had a reform motive. As his *Essence* interviewer stated, even at the age of ninety, McKinney was still "shooting from the hip to dislodge some popular notions about what it means to be Black." McKinney died in 1984.

McKinney's attack upon the status quo in Pennsylvania begins with an opening rhetorical flourish in which he mocks the various options available to those who would easily sum up the state. His title segues into his argument: "Pennsylvania: A Tale of Two Cities. This is what any narrative or descriptive account of Pennsylvania means as far as colored people are concerned." From the outset, McKinney sets himself firmly in opposition to the easy assessments of Pennsylvania. To be an African American in Pennsylvania means that the "impersonal sort of epic" written to worship industrial power is simply not sufficient. Moreover, the other available choice, to hail the state's patriotic past, is not just "old fashioned" but "eclipsed" by current realities. To construct Pennsylvania as part of "These 'Colored' United States," McKinney finds it imperative to expose the industrial baron or mayor who could "stab unionism, annihilate free speech, declare a four hundred per cent stock divided, murder a miner's wife or rape his daughter, swear allegiance to the principles of Lincoln, steal elections, build play-grounds for the poor, and wave the flag all in the course of one day's work." McKinney's Pennsylvania is one in which the standard reporting techniques are not just inadequate but are morally questionable. An "endless hymn of praise" would not just avoid the African Americans upon whose shoulders the steel industry was built, it would insult and harm them by such omission.

McKinney's inclusion of African American contributions to the state of Pennsylvania goes well beyond the civic boosterism of some of the other contributors. He condemns the African American community in Pittsburgh for its anti-intellectualism, rails against the "rascality" of "venal and immoral" preachers and "feeble" attempts at political action. McKinney's essay seethes with the indignation and anger he was soon to channel more regularly into social activism, and it remains one of the most startling and complex readings in this series.

This is what any narrative or descriptive account of Pennsylvania means as far as colored people are concerned. These cities are of course Philadelphia and Pittsburgh. Philadelphia spread out on the banks of the Delaware across from the Victor Talking Machine Company and Campbells Soup; Pittsburgh squeezed in between the Allegheney and Monongehela Rivers and beginning again at the north bank of the Allegheney and the south bank of the Monongehela. Every school boy knows, of course, that the turgid waters of these two streams embrace at Pittsburgh and from this union the Ohio is born. Philadelphia, the "City of Brotherly Love," Pittsburgh, the "Gateway to the West."

When one thinks of Philadelphia one's thought rests, momentarily at least, on the Liberty Bell, Independence Hall, white marble steps and other symbols of an eclipsed old fashioned Americanism. But Pittsburgh, what is it but steel? Pennsylvania, State of Steel, and Pittsburgh is its heart. Of course there is coal at Pittsburgh too, coal in every hill, yet steel is king.

It is possible, absolutely possible, for one to write an endless hymn of praise to Pennsylvania, an impersonal sort of epic dealing only with her ship-yards, locomotive works, carpet factories, mills, mines, coke ovens, Stetsons, her mountains, Horseshoe Bend, the capitol at Harrisburg with memories of graft and lead chandeliers and numerous other pedestals to our advanced civilization.

However, if one is a patriot—as most Pennsylvanians are—one may dream and expostulate incessantly about the Sons and Daughters of the Revolution, the size of the crack in the Liberty Bell, Valley Forge, Gettysburg, the Block House at Pittsburgh, War Savings Stamps, Liberty Bonds and the Keystone State's full sized contribution of most excellent targets for the Germans in the great struggle for democracy, trade routes and African colonies.

The average Pennsylvania citizen is interested both in her industrial preeminence and her fine patriotic tradition. These two things go together and are inseparable in Pennsylvania. There is no finer patriot anywhere than the industrial baron or the major of a small steel town in western Pennsylvania. They can stab unionism, annihilate free speech, declare a four hundred per cent stock dividend, murder a miner's wife or rape his daughter, swear allegiance to the principles of Lincoln, steal elections, build play-grounds for the poor, and wave the flag all in the course of one day's work. It is a sort of dollar mark patriotism that has permeated the whole state. All who do not subscribe to it are in danger of the hell of fire and the state constabulary, affectionately known among the proletariat as "Pennsylvania Cossacks."

Pennsylvania is also a state from which no man can be elected to the presidency. It would be poor politics for either the Republican party or its twin sister the Democratic party to put forward one of our favored sons. The Republicans will not for the reason that this state is ferociously G.O.P. The Democrats would not for the reason that the Republicans would be sure to carry the state.

It has been said that even our Democrats are Republicans. This one party system permitted by the electorate has made it necessary for the dominant party to split into two factions. This is in order to make vote stealing, speech making and red fire parades really worth while.

But this series is not concerned so much with the general aspects of Pennsylvania as it is with Colored Pennsylvania. How about Pennsylvania Negroes? How do they compare with Negroes of the other states? Is there such a thing as a Pennsylvania Negro? What is their general status?

As early as 1790 there were as many as 9,000 Negroes in Pennsylvania, 3,000 of them slaves. That the number of slaves was not larger was probably due to the influence of the Quakers. The abolition of slavery began about 1780 and the further importation of slaves was forbidden the same year. The Negro population of the state is now around 300,000, over half of which is in the cities of Pittsburgh and Philadelphia.

The Pennsylvania Negro has a fine tradition behind him. Of course this is true only of the eastern part of the state. Through the decades the center of Negro culture, progress and attainment has been in Philadelphia. Pittsburgh has its "Old Pittsburghers," "O P's," but they have no such heritage and culture background as have the Philadelphians. This is a most natural state of affairs. Western Pennsylvania is a workshop, a place to sell one's muscle for money.

During the early days of the oil and steel industries, many adventurers—as well as solid, hard working pioneers—were attracted to the western end of the state. They came for wealth and they got it. These men were not interested in refinement and polish. They were looking for money. As the industries grew and expanded, workers were needed. High wages were offered. Men rushed in from the east and the south. Many of these were Negroes answering the call of high wages and the freedom offered at that time.

A very low value was placed on academic training. It is reported that old Bill Jones once told Andrew Carnegie that chemistry was going to ruin the steel business. Neither the owners of the industries nor the workers paid much attention to education for themselves or their children. Good wages were more attractive than the daily grind at books and test tubes. Consequently there developed in Pittsburgh a population lacking in culture and appreciation for the finer things of life in the same degree that one finds these things in other cities. Here in Pittsburgh we have a kind of wealthy proletariat.

This race for wealth affected Negroes just as it did the whites, only the situation is worse. The whites got the money but the Negroes remained poor. Here as elsewhere there is not as much opportunity for the ignorant, unqualified Negro as there is for the same type of white man. Due to the fact that western Pennsylvania is dominated by *millionaire "poor whites,"* there is not much encouragement given to educated and competent Negroes.

What the industries of our state needed was "hands," strong husky men who could carry heavy loads, work long hours, stand intense heat and multitudinous industrial hazards. The barons decided that the Negro and the Slav were just the men for this kind of occupation. Negroes must have felt the same way about it for they have and are still looking to Pittsburgh as a land of plenty. They were looking for work and they got it in the "Workshop of the World." They with their south European brothers came by thousands and furnished the strong arms and backs that produced millionaire on top of millionaire.

Good wages were not confined to the industries. Men who did personal service were also well paid. Thus not only was muscle drawn to this section, but also those who were looking for the easy luxurious life of butler, barber, waiter or messenger.

Now whereas the white industrial worker of the early days developed into the financial magnate, the upper strata of white society, nothing of a similar nature happened among the Negro workers. They went into the mills and factories as sons of toil, and sons of toil they are today. They are still the best paid group of manual workers but they have no social standing. They may rise to prominence in the church or the lodge—but not in "society."

Pittsburgh's society class is a heterogeneous mass of waiters, barbers, lawyers, doctors, house servants, post-office clerks, city and county employees, uniformed messengers and what-not.

Due to the fact that colored Pittsburghers have not burdened their minds to acquire education, one finds there a host of men and women who have assumed the role of leadership having no fundamental preparation or intelligent experience. The main leaders are of course the lawyers and preachers. These lawyers and preachers have not been highly successful in their efforts to show the people the way, the truth and the light. There is a tendency to distrust and repudiate the gentlemen of the bar and the cloth. The expression is often heard, "We don't want any profession man."

It is difficult however to make a clear and definite analysis of this situation. The man on the street says that he does not want the leadership of the lawyer and the preacher but he usually says it at the "big gate." In one way or another these two groups worm their way to the front, arm in arm, and carry off the glory. For one thing, the ordinary man does not make any distinction between *education* and *efficiency* and *education* and *rascality*. He makes a mistake in assuming that because he has had some impoverishing experiences with a few dishonest lawyers and preachers, that there is something wrong with education. One finds them prejudiced against the "professional man" as such. At a meeting in which the matter of candidates for the legislature was being discussed, one man rose and proclaimed—*"We don't need no man hump-back with degrees."* This is the way in which Pittsburgh gives encouragement and comfort to ignorance.

One Pittsburgher has characterized his home town as a city of "arrogant mediocrity." Comparing the "Smoky City" with other cities, this is a very charitable and evasive description. There is perhaps more ignorance per square foot in Pittsburgh than in any other large American city.

Philadelphia is somewhat different. The Negroes there got a better start. It is also true that they have slowed up considerably. But the travail and the turmoil of the anti-slavery struggle produced a rugged and intellectual type of Negro that persists to this day with a glory greatly dimmed. If Boston is the "Cradle of Liberty," in a national sense, Philadelphia is the Negroes' *"cradle of liberty."* Here was held the first Convention of Free Negroes in 1817, led by James Forten, a Negro abolitionist.

Philadelphians may also point with pride to a large and remarkable group of Negroes who worked hand in hand with the Quakers to beat back slavery and educate the slave and free Negro. There were William Whipper, capitalist; James Forten, abolitionist and friend of Garrison; Robert Purvis perhaps the most famous of them all; William Still, who published a book on the Underground Railroad; Mifflin Gibbs, lawyer; Richard Allen, Bishop; Absolom Jones, first Negro ordained to preach in the Protestant Episcopal Church; John Gloucester, first Negro Presbyterian minister; and many others editing papers, agitating and helping the Friends with anti-slavery propaganda. It was a Philadelphian, Bassett by name, who was the first Negro to receive an appointment from the federal government. It was in Philadelphia that the African Methodist Episcopal Church was formed.

Here is truly a great group of men for colored Philadelphians to tell their children about. Pittsburgh has produced one famous Negro, Henry O. Tanner. It is doubtful though that many Pittsburghers know that this man was born in their city or that he is a world famous painter.

Present day Philadelphians are by no means as extraordinary as their forbears. Perhaps the stimulus that comes from a great cause is lacking. Negroes are free now and are theoretically citizens with the right to aspire even to the presidency. After all is said and done, it is true that great men and women are not produced—in large numbers—in an age of plenty, ease and prosperity.

Another point is this. During slavery the mass of Negroes were forced into a state of like mindedness and fellow felling because they were all in the ditch together. Even though there were "cabin Negroes" and "big house Negroes" *they were all slaves!* The comparatively few Negroes suffered disabilities that no Negro faces today.

On the whole, the Negro in Pennsylvania is about the same as elsewhere. He is a consumer of goods manufactured by other races. Here he has the same sort of leadership as elsewhere. We have discussed the matter of preacher leadership in Pittsburgh. *There is perhaps no city in the country that is more preacher-ridden than this city.* But they are not confined to

Pittsburgh. They infest the cities, small towns and villages. Some have churches and are reputable christian gentlemen, while others are tramps and make their living begging from white business men. *The pity is that the worth while ministers allow the rascals to be members of the ministers' associations.* The writer once asked a minister why the high standing preachers allowed the rascals to belong to the ministerial associations. This preacher replied in effect that the *venal and immoral preachers were so numerous that they could outvote the decent ones.* It is a case of pure minded and intelligent men being submerged by a horde of long coated scallawags who cannot be trusted either with your money or the women in one's family.

In politics the Pennsylvania Negro is of course a stone-blind Republican. He is as conservative in politics as he is in religion. He believes in the politics and the faith once and for all delivered to him. The Republicans of Pennsylvania do not need the Negro's vote; consequently he gets very little out of state politics. There are two colored men in the legislature, both from Philadelphia. Pittsburgh tries feebly, every two years, to land a colored man in Harrisburg but always fails dismally. One candidate has run four times from a district thickly settled with Negroes, but the *Jews and the Irish always win!*

Our state is one of the few northern states having any distinctly colored schools. Such jim-crow schools are found in a few cities in the eastern part, notably Philadelphia. There is a group of Negroes in Pittsburgh—*led by a few fathers with daughters eligible to teach,* and *J. C. Austin a Baptist preacher,* who are attempting to bring in separate schools. This is the same J. C. Austin recently labeled as one of the smallest men in America by the Messenger. *He is a preacher-business man-politician.* He is a fanatic over glory, praise and applause. He jumped into the Garvey movement and rode down Broadway with Garvey at the last convention. When he discovered that there *was to be nothing in it for him,* he jumped out and looked for other worlds to conquer.

Finally it should be pointed out that our state has not been free from America's favorite sport—lynching. Since 1889 three Negroes have been lynched. But we have not been *partial* in this matter, since the same number of whites have been done to death by the mob. And so all in all we are like other people, lynching, murdering, running after money, playing politics and striving to be good 100 per cent Americans.

KELLY MILLER

South Carolina

VOL. 7, NO. 11, DECEMBER 1925

Kelly Miller was born to a poor family in Winnesboro, South Carolina, on July 18, 1863, but by the end of his spectacular career was one of the most widely recognized names in American education. He was the son of a slave and a freeman and attended a local school established during Reconstruction. His mathematical talent and general aptitude led first to his admission to Fairfield Academy and then to a scholarship at the Howard University preparatory department. He continued at Howard's college department from 1882 to 1886, where in addition to amassing a stellar academic record, he worked as a clerk in the U.S. Pension Office and saved enough money to purchase a farm for his parents.

Johns Hopkins University admitted him as their first African American student in 1887, and Miller stayed on to study graduate physics, mathematics, and astronomy. He taught mathematics at Howard University from 1890 to 1934. Miller became interested in social scientific methods and their policy ramifications and was responsible for having sociology added to the Howard curriculum. As head of the sociology department and the dean of the College of Arts and Sciences, Miller crusaded to broaden and increase the educational offerings and opportunities at Howard, spearheading an immensely successful recruitment campaign that quadrupled the size of the student body within his first four years as dean. Indeed, Miller's national profile grew to such a degree that Howard University was occasionally referred to as "Kelly Miller's university." His public profile was not without controversy, however; the president of Howard once called him a "contemptible puppy," and *The Crisis* was still discussing the incident six years later. Miller gained notoriety in the 1930s as an anticommunist, and by all reports never owned a watch or a fountain pen, trivial facts whose currency is a measure of the interest he generated as a person and public figure.

His own writing, as might be expected, ranged widely. A pamphlet he wrote in 1917 about the race riots in Miami and East St. Louis, titled *The Disgrace of Democracy: An Open Letter to President Woodrow Wilson,* caused a huge controversy and despite (or perhaps because of) various attempts to censor it, it sold over 250,000 copies. Besides *Race Adjustment* (1909), *The Appeal to Conscience* (1918), and *The Everlasting Stain* (1924), Miller also wrote a weekly column syndicated in over a hundred newspapers, both black and white. In addition, he regularly appeared in educational, social scientific, and general intellectual journals.

Miller's essay argues that South Carolina is a state full of contradictory ideals and impulses, and that it is necessary to understand these contradictions as precise manifestations of a kind of coherence. For instance, Miller suggests, look at the skewed trajectory of progress that was Reconstruction. An African American political machine briefly dominated the South Carolina state legislature during Reconstruction, only to be replaced by a disenfranchised and demoralized void: "The Negro now has been driven from every vestige of political power." And this has involved a quite literal rewriting of history, so that what he calls "the Negro regime" is talked about "as if there had been an inter regnum." But to understand South Carolina, both Negro power and Negro powerlessness need to be taken into account. This essay is obviously intended to create a more accurate history and a more inclusive sense of American historical identities.

One of the most intriguing aspects of Miller's essay is his move to define South Carolina, the "stormy petrel of the nation," not merely in comparison with other states, but via its expatriate or displaced population. He argues that the African American men who have left South Carolina are best able to illustrate what it is to be colored and South Carolinian. This migration was not limited solely to the massive economic migration north. After a virtual coup d'etat of the state legislature by whites in 1877, the important African American leaders of the state fled to "berths in the department service in Washington." Institutions such as the state universities were also emptied of African American professors. Miller describes being with one such professor, who could not only "stand at a distance and point out the room which he used to occupy." This figurative emphasis upon the often bitter clarity of distance is complemented by an equally powerful emphasis upon distance as a mitigating factor for many of South Carolina's faults and reminder of its virtues. Miller tells of the South Carolina Club at Howard University, for example, which protected a member accused of some transgression by saying, "No South Carolinian could be guilty of such unbecoming conduct." Expatriate loyalty, or at least expatriate identity, is present from his striking opening lines: "The writer was not born in the United States; he was born in South Carolina when that state was out of the Union."

Miller's essay, while devoid of the trenchant wit found in many of the other essays, nonetheless, in moments like these, exercises a subtle sarcasm. More to his purposes, though, he delineates the class and caste system of South Carolina with the eye of a social scientist and a sharp and moving prose style. He does not blink at the facts: he remains clear that South Carolina has a long and ongoing tradition of unbridled violence, as represented by Preston Brooks's brutal caning of Charles Sumner in the Senate and the 1822 slave uprising led by Denmark Vasey in Charleston. Miller was often accused of straddling fences in the important debates of his day, and he himself once declared that this was not shameful: "Effective horsemanship is accomplished by straddling." But this essay takes a clear, however complex, stand.

The writer was not born in the United States; he was born in South Carolina when that state was out of the Union. South Carolina is the stormy petrel of the nation. She arouses the nation's wrath, and rides upon the storm. There is not a dull period in her history. Calhoun threatened nullification; the iron resolution of Old Hickory nullified the threat. She was the first to secede from the Union, and the slowest to recede from the secession. Her fiery son, Preston Brooks, struck down Charles Sumner on the floor of the Senate; his defiant constituency returned him in triumph to his seat in the House of Representatives. She was forced to taste of the bitter cup of reconstruction; but was the first to wash the bitter taste out of her mouth. She sent Benjamin Tillman to the Senate, who boastfully denounced and defied the War Amendments to the Constitution; the North connived at his defiance. Governor Cole Blease, in conference of the governors, openly ejaculated, "To hell with the Constitution!"; he is sent to the Senate to enforce that document with the Eighteenth Amendment added. Truly the palmetto state has been a thorn in the flesh of the nation.

A glimpse at her origin will account for her temperament. She was planted as a colony for restless and dissatisfied spirits. The first successful colony was founded at Charleston, 1670. From the beginning it was a protestant proposition. Roundheads and cavaliers came from England, Huguenots came from France; dissatisfied Dutch came from New York; a restless group came from Barbadoes bringing their slaves, the first known to the colony; even a group of Congregationalists came down from New England. They were held together by but one common tie—the bond of protest. When freedom of conscience is carried to extremes, personal freedom counts for more than conscience. Protestantism means more protestants, until each individual follows his own personal philosophy. The Greek mind invented a scheme of democracy that ignored the bulk of the population with the status of the slave. It was wholly unaware of its ethical inconsistency. The South Carolina philosophy was a little more logical. Calhoun, the great apostle of the ideal of South Carolina, and of the South, never defended human slavery, but African slavery, on the ground that the African was not human. These are the words of William Simms Gilmore, the solitary singer whom South Carolina has inspired: "If it be admitted that the institution of Negro slavery is a wrong done the Negro, the question is at an end. No people can be justified for continuance in error and injustice.

In the South we think otherwise." Herein lay and lies the crux of the whole question. Abraham Lincoln said, "If slavery is not wrong, then nothing is wrong." South Carolina never developed a conscience on the moral evil of slavery. There was then no conscious moral inconsistency in the slaveholder proclaiming the fullest principles of religious freedom and personal liberty. An act to settle a maintenance upon a minister of the Church of England in Charleston in 1698 reads: "That he should enjoy the lands, houses, slaves, cattle and monies appointed to his use, and that a Negro man and woman and four cows and calves should be purchased for his use." All of this was not without complaisant benevolent intent. In a South Carolina publication in 1743, we read: "The Society for the propagation of the Gospel, having long at heart the propagation of the Gospel among the Negroes and Indian races, had resolved to purchase some country Negroes, causing them to be instructed to read the Bible, and in the chief precepts of the Christian religion, and thenceforth employing them as schoolmasters for the same instructions of Negroes and Indian children. It is thought and believed that they would receive instruction from teachers of their own race with more facility and willingness than from white teachers."

In 1746, thirty-five children and fifteen adults were instructed under these auspices. But the experiment was not continued after one of the two teachers died and the other turned profligate.

I am desirous to show that human conduct is that human conduct is the outcome of attitude. Conscience is a pliable faculty and is shaped to our dealings. How did it happen that South Carolina and Massachusetts, made up of the same moral stuff, assumed such diametrically opposite attitudes on the moral issue of African slavery? Let this historical analyst determine this. I am now chiefly concerned with the gradual approachments of the two attitudes at the present day. When these attitudes become consolidated on the lower level, the cause of the Negro will be hopeless. The nation as a whole does not now believe that the disfranchisement and segregation of the Negro is morally wrong. And therefore no serious attempt is made to remedy the grievances of which the colored race complains. The Negro has but one recourse, and that is to stimulate the conscience to the moral enormity of it all.

The story of the Negro in South Carolina, except as a negative, or rather a passive instrument of production, hinges about two centers, Charleston and Columbia. Early in the nineteenth century, Denmark Vesey, a West Indian Charleston slave, generalled an insurrection involving some nine thousand, as some estimates have it, in the city and surrounding communities. His generalship was superb and his courage unequalled. He failed because all such fatuous efforts were doomed to fail. Denmark Vesey with many of his followers were hanged. White men were fined and sentenced to prison for culpable complicity. The deathless legacy of that tragic episode are the last words of Peter, one of the culprits, to his partners in distress: "Do not open your lips. Die silent as you shall see me do." These are the dying, though deathless, words of a Charleston Negro in 1822.

Julius Caesar, in one of his sweeping generalizations, injected into the dry details of a military record, says, "All men love liberty and hate the condition of slavery." Denmark Vesey verifies the verdict of Caesar eighteen hundred years later.

The story of the free Negroes in Charleston is one that is full of interest and charm. In all of the older established cities there was a small band of free Negroes who lived in self-satisfied complacency in a little world below the whites and above the slaves. They enjoyed existence with a keenness of relish, which freedom has almost wholly destroyed. It is a glorious experience to have a mass of people below you, even if there are others above you. The free colored people had their own churches and schools, and enjoyed a certain area of recognized privileges which gave them an established place in the city's economy. They were assigned the bulk of the industrial and mechanical work as carpenters, painters, bricklayers, tailors and marketmen. The whites encouraged their social separateness from the slaves, as a means of ruling by division. The line of demarcation coincided almost wholly with the color line. As a result, there grew up between the two shades of color an almost impossible barrier. Many of the free Negroes were owners of slaves, and easily assumed the attitude and hauteur of the white master.

The emancipation proclamation, the reconstruction experiment and the opening of free public schools wiped out much of this conceit. In the earlier days of Howard University, two brilliant boys came from Charleston; one was brown and the other was white enough for anything. They were classmates and the most intimate of friends. In the interchange of intimacies, one day, the whiter of the twain said to his swarthier crony: "I am surely glad that we came to Howard University. I should never have been able to meet you in Charleston." The aristocratic conceit of the free Charleston Negroes, complicated with the color scheme, was deep-seated and hard to remove. I have seen the records of "The Brown Fellowship," a semi-social and literary organization of the Charleston elite that runs back over a hundred years. Charleston retained white teachers in the public schools longer than any other city in the union. It was only a few years ago that they were dislodged, and then this was against the earnest protest of many of the old-time aristocrats, who somehow felt the enchantment of white contact, if it be only to touch the hem of their garment. But the old order has practically passed away. The occupations once monopolized by the free blacks have been grasped by the whites. The Negro is left little to do except the outerskirts of the lower and menial pursuits. Many of the oldtimers have moved away. Many of the free colored people inherited not only the name but the blood of the original founders, along with their proud and dignified spirit. The Grimkés, the Cordozos, the Prioleaus, the Mouzons, the Mischeaus, the De Reefs, the Mazycks, and the rest remind one of the list of original settlers.

Speaking of the blood mixture of the races, South Carolina, especially

Charleston and the lower counties, is noted for the composite progeny. In the coastal cities, along the waterline, the old French system of two families, one of either race, was quite prevalent, so much so that one-eighth Negro blood was as high as they deemed it safe to fix the definition of a white man. Congressman Tillman, a relative of the more famous Senator Tillman, said in the Constitutional Convention, that to raise the limit to the artificial exactions of one-thirty-second, would cause a number of counties to be bathed in blood.

One of these days, the Society for the Study of Negro Life and History will undertake the study of the Free Negro in the several large cities of the South. It will prove to be an interesting and fascinating story when adequately and properly told. Charleston, New Orleans, Richmond, Savannah and the rest contain gold mines of rich and rare historical material.

Columbia next claims our attention. This is the capital of the state. Little need be said about the Negroes of this city until the days of reconstruction. In South Carolina and Louisiana, the Negroes actually held a majority of the legislatures. But the palmetto state had the advantage over its political rival in that it had a better basis of educated men to start with. Francis L. Cardoza had just finished his education in the universities of England and Scotland in time to corral the forces. He sent for the New York *Tribune* and had it distributed among all of the Negro members of the Constitutional Convention, which kept them well posted as to the best methods to pursue. Educated Negroes, like Elliot, came down from Massachusetts to swell the intellectual forces. Negroes filled all stations in the government, with the exception of governor, which was always accorded the white race. The Lieutenant Governor, Secretary of State, Treasurer, legislators and Congressmen were plentiful. As a boy, thirty miles away, my eyes and ears were just about beginning to be opened. I used to hear of the fabulous happenings going on in Columbia. I had relatives who went from Fairfield County as representatives and senators. They would tell me that Negroes often lit their cigars with five-dollar bills. Nowhere on earth did Negroes ever exercise so much political power as in Columbia. Nor did they ever revel so extravagantly in the excrescences of power. Every Negro boy in the state was dreaming of a political career. Had I been ten years older I would have been in the thickest of the fray. But the bubble must soon break. Babylon must needs fall. South Carolina is the only state that admitted Negroes to the State University. Of course, the whites left. Professor Richard T. Greener had the distinction of being the only Negro to be appointed professor in this famous institution. I was with him in Columbia many years later when he could only stand at a distance and point out the room which he used to occupy. After the overthrow of reconstruction, when the whites regained control, all records of the Negro regime were destroyed as if there had been an inter regnum.

Many of the Negroes cast down from the seats of power cut a sorry figure. As many as could sought berths in the department service in Washington.

When I was in Charleston last month I heard an eye witness tell of a former lieutenant governor becoming a street sweeper. Columbia dropped from the heights to the depths so far as the Negro was concerned. How did the the mighty fall? But South Carolina has had the experience, and that is worth something. After the downfall in seventy-six, some of the old-liners held on to a lingering hope. General Robert Small, Thomas Miller and George W. Murray were elected to Congress from the blackest district. But the rise of Tillman put an end to all of this. The Negro now has been driven from every vestige of political power. He makes no further effort, not even to function seriously in quadrennial election of Republican delegates.

The political experience gained in politics was quickly transferred to the several religious denominations and secret orders.

The Negro in South Carolina to-day is largely a farmer. The cotton manufacturing industry in the Piedmont section of the state is recruited mainly by white operatives. The only big chance now left the Negro in the state is on the farm, which he is prone to abandon for the allurements of the North.

The Negroes of my native state have had many ups and downs, but through it all they possess a courage and a determination to do worthwhile things. They possess a coherence and attachment for the old state that time and distance cannot destroy. After all, we love to be known as a South Carolinian. We have always had a large contingent of my fellow statesmen in Howard University. On an occasion some unworthy deed had been committed by a student, the South Carolina Club met to protect and defend the honor of its membership. The universal verdict was that "No South Carolinian could be guilty of such unbecoming conduct."

GEORGE W. LEE

Tennessee—the Last Stand of Justice in the Solid South

VOL. 7, NO. 7, JULY 1925

Born in Indianola, Mississippi, on January 4, 1894, George Washington Lee was raised by his mother, who worked as a sharecropper. He put himself through Alcorn A. & I. College in Mississippi by working as a bellhop in various hotels and graduated with a B.S. in 1917. By lying about his age, Lee was appointed one of Tennessee's representatives to train in the Negro Officer Training Camp in Fort Des Moines, Iowa, even though he was technically far too young to officially qualify. Before shipping out as an officer to France, Lee traveled in uniform to Vicksburg, Mississippi, where he was threatened with a lynching, an experience he was later to incorporate into his fiction. When he returned from the war he began what was to be a long career in politics and insurance, but he forever liked to be known as "Lieutenant Lee." He worked briefly in Mississippi and Georgia before moving to Tennessee as district manager for the Atlanta Life Insurance Company. Politically active, Lee served as the vice chairman of the Western Section of the Republican National Committee and was known as a moderate political leader in Memphis for many years, described by his biographer David Tucker as "the South's last black patronage boss until he went down in defeat at the Goldwater Republican Convention in 1964." He died in 1976 at the age of eighty-two.

His first work, *Beale Street: Where the Blues Began* (1934) garnered a great deal of attention when it was first published, and Lee became the first African American author to have his book advertised by the Book-of-the-Month Club. Although his book received praise for its vivid portraits of the steamy side of Memphis life, criticism also attacked Lee's "self imposed mission to catalogue the names and contributions of the street's businessmen, churches, schools, banks and of course insurance companies." Surprisingly, this is not a particular flaw in this essay, where the temptation to include a phone-book–style listing occasionally overwhelmed other contributors. Knighted the "Boswell of Beale Street" by a local paper, his literary fame was short-lived.

Lee's next work, a novel titled *River George* (1937), was about the lives of African American sharecroppers in Tennessee. It focused upon a young African American who upon returning from World War I is lynched by a mob in Mississippi. This second book did not cause much of a stir, although by 1948 critic Hugh Gloster hailed it as a work of "folk realism" and as "the first novel by a Negro to handle at length the exploits of a legendary racial hero." Lee's short-story collection, *Beale Street Sundown* (1942), fared somewhat better and, along with his first work, served to bring to national prominence what became known as one of the "main streets" of African American life.

Although "Tennessee—the Last Stand of Justice in the Solid South" is one of the more straightforward essays in the series, Lee does not skimp on the sarcasm. He writes, for example: "Due to the large number of White Republicans of Lily White extractions, the Negro has not had the meteoric career that his numbers warranted." When Lee excoriates "the so-called best Negro Leaders," he describes them as those who "will grasp the white man's point of view, especially when handed out on a platter of gold." Lee's tone is tempered elsewhere, however, as in his story of "Free Joe's Territory," a haven established by a local mulatto for the benefit of slaves and freemen alike. Carved out of a space that was not receptive to or even tolerant of such use, Free Joe managed not only to redefine his own land as an independent section of the South but also to redefine Tennessee itself. Although it was "a stone's throw of one of the largest slave markets in the South," Free Joe's Territory was part of Tennessee. Obdurate, stolid Tennessee, Lee showed, can be understood only as a place whose internal contradictions belie the apparent hegemony of the "Lily Whites," even as he reminds us not to forget the power of the hegemony that does exist.

The essay is not particularly well written, with such questionable uses of figurative language as "her mountains are the coal and iron pillars of the South flanked by rivers," and it was further marred by sloppy editing (much of which was corrected in this printing)—commas appeared in the wrong places or failed to appear where they should have, *petition* was rendered *partition,* agreement problems and the like were legion. It is also poorly organized. Though the two main sections are titled "Education" and "Politics," there is discussion of both topics elsewhere in the essay, and the politics section also includes discussion of business, labor, professions, and the race problem more generally. As a result it is hard to read too much into a particular arrangement of words. The last sentence, to take just one example, may be badly edited or may be more interesting than it first appears: it might be like a Nietzschean aphorism, for instance, in which the use of asymmetrical dashes demands serious interpretation based on the indeterminate relations of the various clauses in the sentence. Or it might be gobbledygook. And then again, it might be neither; it might just be badly punctuated: "This is a new day that calls for new deal—a white man with mental reservations that made his father master—the Negro with mental reservations that made his father the slave must be banished from the seats of thought control."

Way down in Tennessee is an expression that has been written and sung a thousand times over. It belongs to the vocabulary of Poets and Musicians. There is about this State a charm which these words do not express. The skies are clear; the temperature is mild. Spring comes early and lingers long into Summer. The Winters are not as a rule severe. Cotton, corn, wheat, tobacco, strawberries and melons grow in abundance. There is no scenery more picturesque than the fresh and sunny landscapes of the Cumberland Valley. Her mountains are the coal and iron pillars of the South flanked by rivers and lakes that furnish great opportunity for bathing, fishing, idling and dreaming.

Tennessee is the gateway of the mid south—the richest section of equal area in the world. The history of the state is in many respects similar to that of the United States. Tennessee was originally a part of North Carolina, but that part which is now Tennessee was by North Carolina ceded to the general Government. In June 1796, President Washington signed the Act of Congress that made Tennessee the Sixteenth State in the Union.

The original inhabitants were English, Scotch-Irish and Negroes. The Negro population is most numerous in the Western portion of the State. In the Eastern part live the Mountaineers—typical Appalachian Highlanders who have lived for generations in the mountain fastnesses and have partaken but little in the customs of the outside world. They are strongwilled people who have no fear but that of God—and who brook no interference of mere men as to their manners, beliefs and customs.

Tennessee is truly the last stand of Justice in the SOLID SOUTH. The last State to secede from the Union, with a preponderance of numbers in the Eastern Section decidedly in favor of the Union cause. When the Western Section of the State aligned with the cause of the South, the Eastern Section petitioned to the Legislature for the privilege of being allowed to form a separate State, and when the War crashed against her frontiers, thirty-thousand of her native sons enlisted in the Federal Army.

The first abolitionist paper ever published in the United States was in East Tennessee. It may be said as a whole that there was never any positive conviction in favor of nullification or disunion, even that portion of the State that rests on the borders of Mississippi offered potentious [sic] examples, in the section known as Free Joe's Territory. Free Joe was a Negro of mixed blood whose white father deeded him a large tract of land. He invited his people to dwell upon this land out of the reach of the bloody talons of their Southern Masters, where they enjoyed freedom in a stone's throw of one of the largest slave markets in the South. Here their children lived until this day as prosperous farmers. Their homes are modern, their lands are fertile, their churches are fine edifices around which might be seen on Sunday, fine horses and carriages and automobiles. The influence of Free Joe still lingers and there is to be found an independence among these people not to be found in any other rural section of the South.

There is something in the air of the middle and Western Sections of the

State that is of the substance of Southern narrowness, while not as rank in its prejudice against the Negro as Mississippi, not as open in its defiance of the Thirteenth Amendment as Florida, not as easily moved to mob violence as Georgia, yet there are definite measures employed to control the Negro's thought and progress to lessen his self respect and make secure the white superiority, which thus far has been maintained by money control, force and numbers.

The Negro's possession of the ballot in this section of the State offsets to an extent the Southern philosophy of keeping the Negro down by terror and hate—by subtle methods of physical slavery, yet, the fear of Negro progress and where it will lead to is as dominant in the Western section of the state as it is in other sections of the South. A leading white man of this section expressed it with unusual clearness when he said—"When we think of Negro Progress, we ask ourselves, will not this progress lead to a growing demand for Social Equality, and since we will never consent to Social Equality, why should we make our problem more difficult by aiding the progress which seems to lead to it?"

The whites of West Tennessee do not use shot gun methods to make the Negro docile and servile workmen. This method could hardly be employed as successfully as in other sections of the South. In order to control the Negro's thought and progress, the whites play upon the fundamental weaknesses of the Negro by elevating and holding up as examples—by listening to the suggestions of the so-called best Negro Leaders; by giving them jobs to parcel out so as to increase their importance in the eyes of other members of our race and by popularizing through the daily press the brand of Negro leadership that will compromise with the highest convictions of the race and consent to lead it to a life upon lower level; the kind of leadership that will grasp the white man's point of view, especially when handed out on a platter of gold. Of course there are exceptions. There are Negroes working in conjunction with whites that hold uppermost the advancement of the race.

The state has four large urban centers: Memphis, Chattanooga, Nashville and Knoxville. Two are known the country over. Memphis has managed to draw the interest of the world in its direction. It is here on Beale Street where the Blues were originated. W. C. Handy conceived the idea of putting to Music the songs of the rouster-bout and the section hand. And with his first productions—The Memphis Blues; The Beale Street Blues; The Saint Louis Blues gave jazz music a place in the sun and made the world shake a wicked shoulder. A man in Arkansas addressed a letter to the Devil in Hell. He sent it in care General Delivery, Memphis, Tennessee. Of course Memphis leads the cities of America in homicides—never-the-less, in Memphis is to be found one of the *greatest Negro Communities* in America.

Nashville is the great educational center of the South, the charm of its literary and intellectual atmosphere, the fame of Fisk, Meharry, Roger

Williams and State Normal gives it the undisputed title of "ATHENS OF THE SOUTH."

Knoxville is known as the most liberal city in the South. Here Negroes are to be found on the police force and many other departments of the city government.

"EDUCATION"

The first Industrial School ever established for Negroes in the United States was at Neshoba, Tennessee, in 1825. Fannie Wright, a white woman, purchased 1948 acres of land on which she erected suitable buildings and established a school for the education of Negroes. General Marquis de Lafayette and Robert Owens were members of the Trustee Board. Her idea was to prepare her pupils by a free moral, intellectual and industrial apprenticeship for the duties of free citizenship and offer to the people of Tennessee a practical plan of emancipation.

There are few localities in the State where the public school system for Negroes is good. A great deal of the discontentment is due to the realization of the poor Educational Facilities that the State offers Negro children. Nine dollars per year have been spent to educate a Negro child against twenty-four dollars for the education of the white child. Negro teachers and white teachers are not on the same scale of pay—the advantage being in favor of the whites.

The Colleges of Tennessee are among the best known in the land. Fisk University was founded in 1865. It takes its name from General Clinton B. Fisk, who fought in the Civil War and later devoted his time to Negro education. Fisk was the first institution in the country to collect and preserve Negro Music. The Fisk Jubilee Singers introduced it on an international stage and gave it rank with the music of the world.

Meharry College was organized in 1876 by the Meharry Brothers. One-half of the educated Negro Physicians in the South are graduates of this institution.

Roger Williams, Knoxville College, Lane College and the State Normal are all institutions of the first order, rendering great service to the state.

"POLITICS"

Tennessee is by no means a rock ribbed Democratic strong hold. The outcome of each election is based upon measures rather than parties. The Eastern part of the State has sent Republican Representatives to Congress in unbroken lines since the Civil War. Here the Negro may exercise the right of franchise without fear of violence, to person or property. There are two hundred thousand qualified Negro voters in the State. Due to the large number of White Republicans of Lily White extractions, the Negro has not had the meteoric career that his numbers warranted.

Under President Taft, J. C. Napier served as Register of the Treasury, with some distinction. The most unique character, past and present, in Tennessee politics is Robert R. Church. He is a dominant factor in the political life of the State and enjoys the confidence of both white and black. The Lily Whites hate him, but respect him. He has served along with A. W. Fite of Nashville on the State central committee for the past eight years. He has been a delegate to every National Convention since 1912. In the Harding Campaign he served on the Super-Committee as the National Director of Colored Vote. In 1922 Secretary of State Hughes appointed him as a representative of the Government on a Special Mission to Haiti. President Coolidge appointed him chairman of a Committee to study conditions in the Virgin Islands. He declined to accept both of these places. Time and time again he has fought the Lily Whites almost single handedly and oft-times lost, but his head was never bowed and even his enemies might point to him and say, he never compromised with his highest conviction. His first open break came with the Lily Whites in 1916, over the Republican Legislative Ticket. The White Republican leaders made a strong bid for the Solid Negro Vote. Church in turn demanded a mixed ticket that would be representative of all the people. The whites wanted the Negro vote without giving him representation. Church put an Out and Out Negro Legislative Ticket in the field, and candidate for Congress, Wayman Wilkerson, and threw his aggressive energy into the fight to prove to State and National Leaders, where the strength of the party was in the Western Section. It was in this legislative campaign that the question of an anti-lynching bill was first made an issue. 1924 was the acid test of his leadership. By a series of brilliant political maneuvers, he succeeded in capturing both the county and District Committees.

The State Convention composed of a thousand white delegates voted unanimously to give him control in the tenth district. When the district convention met to elect delegates to Cleveland, the Lily Whites found themselves without vote or voice sufficient to elect their delegates; they therefore resorted to force and led into the convention two hundred Ku Klux to drive out the Negroes and Whites. A bloody fight ensued, numbers were wounded. In the midst of it all Church stood to the front, his voice could be heard above flying chairs, crying "STAY WHERE YOU ARE." It required twenty armed deputies to restore order.

The State may well be proud of its business institutions; they arouse the keenest appreciation beyond its borders. There are four banks in the State—Solvent Savings Bank & Trust Company, Fraternal Savings Bank & Trust Company, Penny Savings Bank and Citizens Savings Bank. They take rank with the leading Negro Banks of the Country.

The largest casket Concern operated by Negroes in the world, Tri-State Casket & Coffin Company—One Insurance Company, the Universal Life, with home office in the State.

Preston Taylor's Amusement Park is the social center of the Middle Section.

The Baptist and Methodist publishing houses at Nashville and Jackson are national centers for those great churches. Negroes of the State control and operate every kind of business from the corner grocery to a coal mine.

There are six large weekly newspapers in the State. The East Tennessee News, edited by W. L. Porter, is the most militant.

The physicians and women are the best organized groups in the State. There are many large hospitals scattered throughout the State.

The Negro lawyers practice in the Courts of the State with a degree of freedom greater than any State west of the Ohio River.

Negro workmen have wormed their way into the very core of the industrial fabric—Negro mechanics in the railroad shops and firemen on the railroads.

Tennessee is the battle ground where the practical solution of the race problem will be fought out. It smacks of just enough Southern sentiment to be followed by the whole South with confidence and appreciation. It imbibes just enough Northern liberal thoughts to temper that program with justice. There is enough free thought in East Tennessee together with the free thinkers of the Middle and Western sections to neutralize West Tennessee positive conviction, and when East meets West to determine the future of the South and call the free and independent Negro Leadership of the self sacrificing type to join in the deliberations, a better understanding of the Negroe's aim, asperation and where his progress leads to will be obtained and the South, suffering from migration, will blossom like a rose.

This is a new day that calls for a new deal—a white man with mental reservations that made his father master—the Negro with mental reservations that made his father the slave must be banished from the seats of thought control.

CLIFTON F. RICHARDSON

Texas—the Lone Star State

VOL. 6, NO. 4, APRIL 1924

Clifton F. Richardson was born in Marshall, Texas, in 1891 and stayed in Marshall to study literature and journalism at Bishop College. Although *The Messenger* identifies Richardson as editor of the *Houston Informer,* he was in fact both publisher and editor of that paper (sometimes listed as the *Houston Defender*) for many years as well as a correspondent for several white newspapers. He was a prominent Texas businessman, serving as an officer for several companies, and was for some years director of the Houston Negro Chamber of Commerce. He also served as president of the Houston branch of the NAACP, director of the Colored Voters Division of the Republican party of Texas, secretary-treasurer of the Independent Colored Voter's League, and director of the Houston Community Chest, as well as other community organizations. He was a member of a number of fraternal orders (Knights of Pythias, Ancient Order of Pilgrims, etc.) and proudly listed himself as a "soloist" for the Bethel Baptist Church choir in *Who's Who of Colored America* of 1928.

Richardson's essay "Texas—the Lone Star State" is less imaginative than many of the others in the series, and from the first sentence ("The history of Texas . . . is singularly inspiring, interesting and illuminating, as well as unprecedented and unparalleled, compared with that of the other states"), we suspect that we are not in the hands of a great writer. But despite its lack of rhetorical or analytic sophistication, it provides interesting glimpses into African American life in Texas, as in the case of his starling statistics on fraternal organizations, pithy indictments of racist law enforcement officials, and an especially vivid picture of the variability of Jim Crow railway transport. Most of the essays in this series assume that the migration of African Americans in the 1920s is entirely to the northern cities. With its discussion of the immigration from other southern states to Texas, this essay is a significant exception. Richardson's list of colleges, organizations, and eminent individuals provide information that, however raw, is more detailed than that given by most of the other writers.

The most interesting section is that on the "great lodge people" of Texas. Richardson writes that the breadth and popularity of fraternal organizations among African Americans "prove the race's capacity for doing big things." The popularity of such activities, however, also indicates the willingness of African Americans to participate in the lodge lifestyle all the rage in white America.

Even more important, the widespread affection for such associations may indicate a desire to form codified and recognized social organizations that cumulatively might provide the power or clout denied individual African Americans in Texas. Richardson reports that the many African Americans in Texas were regularly terrorized by racism and suffered unduly under the "peonage" of sharecropping, the "evil, wicked, and inhuman institution of human bondage." His message here, as in the case of his validation of lodges, is that concerted and coordinated effort will be necessary to make the opportunities of Texas available to "all classes of people."

MR. RICHARDSON

The history of Texas (originally named after the Tezas Indians) is singularly inspiring, interesting and illuminating, as well as unprecedented and unparalleled, compared with that of the other states of the Union. Texas has the unique distinction of being the only state in the American commonwealth that possessed its own political autonomy prior to admission into statehood—being a republic in its early days, with a president, cabinet and coterie of officials. Texas fought its own wars and won its own independence from Mexico; the battle of San Jacinto, fought just below Houston, deciding the issue on April 21, 1836.

In area, Texas is the largest state in the Union, its length and breadth being nearly equal—around 800 miles—and comprising 262,398 square miles, of which 3,498 square miles are water surface. The state is rich in timber, minerals and natural resources and has a varied and fickle climate. The chief agricultural product is cotton, yet all kinds of products and vegetables are grown in the salubrious and luxurious soil of the state. Oil fields also abound in various sections of the state, some of the largest oil refineries in the world being located in the Lone Star State; while several colored Texans have become wealthy overnight due to location of oil on their holdings. Cattle raising and punching is one of the leading vocations of the state.

Not even a native-born Texan can even begin to comprehend the physical proportions of his state, which, during the days of its own political autonomy, was the rendezvous for the criminals fugitives from the "States"; with the result that in the early days of Texas the state attained an unenviable reputation for the six-shooter, wild and woolly life and utter disregard for human life—quite a number of these early settlers being descendants of these gunmen, trigger experts and desperadoes.

Although Texas won the pennant in the Lynching League of America during 1922, it was the only Southern state to show an increase in colored population during the last decade; this increase exceeding the 75,000 mark. This does not mean that colored Texans have not deserted their native state and migrated to other sections of the country (for they have and that in large numbers, especially from certain mob-ridden and klan-infested communities); but there has not been as large a movement of colored people from Texas as from several other Southern states, while on the other hand there has been, and still is, a steady and almost unbroken flow of race men and women, from adjacent Southern states, into Texas, Louisiana being the largest contributor to this new population. Despite this movement, farm holdings by colored people have increased 12 per cent during 1922 in Texas; while the state has a proportionately large number of colored property and land owners, some of whom own valuable buildings in the downtown area of any number of Texas towns and cities.

Texas is one of the two Southern states that provides fair educational facilities for its colored scholastics and gives colored schools, in the main, the same length of terms that the white children enjoy, and the same per capita appropriation, particularly in the cities and more populous centers; yet the physical equipment and buildings for colored children fall far below those for children of other races—all of whom (Mexicans, Italians and whatnots) attend the "white" (?) schools.

Texas, like her other Southern sisters, maintains the iniquitous "jim-crow" law and the accommodations provided on the railroads of the state for colored passengers, excepting two systems, are hardly fit for cattle and swine. On most of the Texas trains, men, women and children of the colored contingent are huddled and jammed into one small compartment of the day coach, with one toilet for both sexes; while their small section must generally be shared with the conductor, brakeman, butcher and porter. However, whenever there is a large or group movement of colored people to grand lodges or conventions, the railroads, in order to get that lump business, will provide the best accommodations, such as chair cars and even standard Pullmans and give a special train where 125 or more concentrate and leave a given place.

Through the "white man's primary" and its ramifications, colored citizens are, to all intents and purposes, disfranchised in Texas; yet most of the large cities, excepting Houston, have abolished the partisan municipal elections and operate a general election for city offices, with the result that all qualified voters (those who pay the poll tax or secure exemption certificate during a stipulated period) can cast a ballot for their choice. The so-called republican party in Texas is ultra-and-pro-"lily-white" and the colored brother is *persona non grata* in his erstwhile political stronghold.

Only a few Texas cities segregate colored residents per se; yet the districts or ghettos occupied by colored people are woefully lacking in those modern conveniences—such as electric lights, city water, sanitary connections, paved streets, drainage and rapid transit facilities—that are necessary for and indispensable to city dwellers.

The state maintains and supports Prairie View Normal and Industrial College for the education and training of colored teachers and leaders; while several other strong institutions of learning are supported by private organizations and denominations for the education of the colored youths, among which are: Bishop College and Wiley College, Marshall; Samuel Houston College and Tillotson College, Austin; Texas College and East Texas Academy, Tyler; Paul Quinn College and Central Texas College, Waco; Houston College, Houston; Jarvis Christian Institute, Hawkins; Kountze College, Kountze; Gaudalupe College, Seguin; Conroe College, Conroe; Mary Allen Seminary, Crockett; Farmers' Improvement Society College, Ladonia; Houston Normal and Industrial College, Huntsville; North Texas College, Denison.

Formerly the large number of colored people of the state were rural dwellers, but the trend seems city-ward today and thus the colored urban population is increasing by leaps and bounds with erstwhile tillers of the soil. Many things are responsible for this hegira from the farms to the city, among which may be mentioned low wages, Ku Klux Klan, poor living conditions, inadequate school facilities, lynch law and crop failures, the latter caused by floods, boll weevils and lack of crop diversification.

Next to Judge Lynch's court, the peace and constabulary officers of Texas are about the worst enemies to the colored people, the infamous and infernal "fee system" being largely responsible for their pernicious and damnable activities and depredations. Practically all inter-racial clashes and troubles are precipitated through and by these supposed minions of the law, who were formerly chosen by the notches on their guns and not by their fitness as custodians of the law.

Peonage exists on several farms and plantations in Texas, just like it does in several other Southern states, and the authorities, both county, state and national, seem to nod assent or wink at this evil, wicked and inhuman institution of human bondage, which the constitutional amendments expressly forbid and prohibit from the confines of the American republic.

Individually the colored race has done exceptionally well in the commercial and business world, but the race's best collective efforts have been demonstrated in their churches and fraternal organizations.

The Texas Negroes are great lodge people and their fraternal accumulations and wealth are staggering. The Colored Knights of Pythias and Court of Calanthe have assets and cash in excess of $600,000; Grand United Order of Odd Fellows and Household of Ruth around $410,000; United Brothers of Friendship and Sisters of the Mysterious Ten, $350,000; Ancient Order of Pilgrims, $165,000; Masons, Knights and Daughters of Tabor, Mosaics, American Mutual and other fraternities with an estimated aggregate of $300,000 to $450,000.

Most of these orders own or are buying buildings and real estate, viz: Pythians, magnificent temple at Dallas; Masons, handsome temple at Ft. Worth; U.B.F. and S.M.T., two (2) 2-story brick buildings in block next to City Hall in Houston; Taborians, 3-story brick building in business district of Houston and other holdings in Waco; Odd Fellows, two lots in business area of Houston, on which they plan to erect a $250,000 temple; Pilgrims, valuable real estate in Houston; to say nothing of halls and holdings of the various subordinate lodges of these and other colored orders. Their houses of worship, taken by and large, are a credit to any people and prove the race's capacity for doing big things.

Some Texas cities have colored men on their police and detective forces; while a large number of local postal carriers and railway mail clerks, even clerks-in-charge, are members of the colored race. Several colored men hold clerical and responsible administrative positions with some of the white firms and institutions in the state.

The Committee on Inter-Racial Co-operation, recently launched in Texas, is not functioning like similar bodies in other states; due largely to the fact that there appears to be a mistaken or misconceived idea on the part of the majority of white members as to the real scope and purpose of the organization.

Not only is Texas big in size and rich in fertility of the soil, but this state has produced some outstanding and conspicuous figures in the life of America and the world, among whom are Dr. Emmett Jay Scott of Washington; Dr. L. K. Williams, Colonel Franklin A. Dennison, Andrew ("Rube") Foster, John Arthur ("Jack") Johnson of Chicago; Drs. J. E. Perry and Joseph Dibble of Kansas City, Mo.; Wilford H. Smith, formerly of the New York City bar; Dr. J.R.E. Lee, New York City; William M. ("Gooseneck Bill") McDonald of Ft. Worth; W. S. Willis, R. D. Evans and Dr. A. S. Jackson of Waco; Dr. M. W. Dogan and W. F. Bledsoe of Marshall; Bishop I. B. Scott, Henry Allen Boyd and Dr. E.W.D. Isaacs of Nashville; Bishop John W. McKinney of Sherman; Dr. Sutton E. Griggs of Memphis; Heman E. Perry of Atlanta, Ga.; Dr. J. G. Osborne of Prairie View; and a galaxy of luminaries too numerous to mention here. Some of Texas' illustrious dead are Bishop M. F. Jamison of Leigh; Norris Wright Cuney of Galveston; W. E. King and Dr. A. R. Griggs of Dallas; F. W. Gross of Houston; M. M. Rodgers of Dallas; Dr. I. Toliver of Washington; A. W. Rosborough and Dr. R. H. Boyd of Nashville. S. H. Dudley, the well-known comedian, and Dr. W. J. King of Gammon are also Texas products.

The colored man has a very virgin and fertile field in Texas for working out his salvation—not without fear and trembling, however—especially along commercial, business and economic lines.

His justly due and inalienable political and civil rights and privileges will not be secured until he is willing to put up means and wage incessant legal battle for their acquisition and retention.

Texas has all kinds of climate and all classes of people; and, though conditions are far from ideal in this state for colored people on the whole, most of them are determined to stay in the Lone Star State and "fight it out along these lines, if it takes all summer."

WALLACE THURMAN

Quoth Brigham Young:—This Is the Place

VOL. 8, NO. 8, AUGUST 1926

Wallace Thurman was born in Salt Lake City, Utah, in 1902, and it seems to be a fact he was unable to forgive. He studied chemistry and pharmacy at the University of Utah from 1919 to 1920 and then abruptly moved to California, where he tried to establish a magazine *The Outlet,* for the New Negro Movement. Although the venture failed, he moved to New York in 1925 and drew upon his experience with *The Outlet* to obtain a position with another magazine, *The Looking Glass.* This magazine also failed, but Thurman was quick to make contacts and friends among the artists and hangers-on of the Harlem Renaissance. One of these was Theophilus Lewis, who assisted him in getting a job with *The Messenger.*

Thurman became a major force on *The Messenger,* even though he was only on staff for some months as editor. He was a regular contributor for two years and was responsible for bringing many of the Harlem Renaissance writers to publish there. Called the *"enfant terrible"* of the renaissance, Thurman not only oversaw the publication of Langston Hughes (who sent him his very first stories) and Zora Neale Hurston in *The Messenger* but in 1926 went on to found an experimental quarterly, *Fire!* with several other notable Harlem Renaissance figures, including Hughes, Hurston, and the painter Aaron Douglas. *Fire!* which was created as a forum for aspiring African American artists, did not meet with much success, and in 1928 Thurman went on to found *Harlem: A Forum of Negro Life,* yet another unsuccessful publishing venture. He continued to write unabated, however, and his caustic articles in these short-lived journals, as well as in *The New Republic, the Bookman,* and the *Independent,* gained him much notoriety.

By 1929 he found an editorial job with McFadden Publications, a publisher of popular books and journals on self-help, physical culture, and other faddish subjects. Thurman's erratic career encomposed ghost writing for *True Story* and playwriting. *Harlem,* which opened at New York's Apollo Theater in 1929, was a realistic drama co-written with a white writer, Jourdan Rapp. The play dealt with prejudice toward West Indian immigrants and the disillusionment faced by migrant blacks from the South. It was an immediate success, but Thurman is now best known for his two novels. His satiric, realistic novel *The Blacker the Berry* (1929) is about a young woman struggling between self-hatred and acceptance of the darkness of her skin. More highly acclaimed is his novel *Infants of the Spring* (1932), which chronicles the bohemian lifestyles of the increasingly elite world of the Harlem Renaissance artists. *Infants of the Spring* caused a sensation of sorts among the black intelligensia for its portrayal of characters obviously based on Zora Neale Hurston, Langston Hughes, Countee Cullen, Rudolph Fisher, and Carl Van Vechten. In this novel Thurman sought to debunk much of the mythology surrounding the Harlem Renaissance, even coining the term "Niggeratti" to refer to African Americans who were able to exploit the white craze for anything black. The novel ends with a powerful symbolic rendering of the end of the renaissance, when the stock market crash also ended the publishing boom that had fueled the artistic revolution. Thurman worked in Hollywood for a brief period and died in a charity hospital after a drinking bout in 1934.

In this essay on Utah, Thurman writes with an exile's scorn and none of an exile's wistfulness. After taking issue with the very idea of "These 'Colored' United States"—since no state has been vitally affected by its African American population in the way that city sections, such as Harlem, have—Thurman somewhat reluctantly agrees that the reciting of past and present achievements might help boost race pride and therefore might be valuable. But he then laments the accident of his birth in Utah: "I am sorry then that I have to write of the Utah Negro, for there has been and certainly is nothing about him to inspire anyone to do anything save perhaps drink gin with gusto, and develop new technique for the contravention of virginity." In such flourishes, Thurman reveals a talent for parodic deflation as prodigious as that of H. L. Mencken, who is a strong influence, most clearly when Thurman rails against the "booboisie" and the vegetablelike complacency of Utahans, black and white. Attached to his disdain, however, is an economic critique similar to that of the more radical writers in the series. African Americans are not only discriminated against economically, they are encouraged to congratulate themselves for it. "There are no Negro professional men. . . . There are no Negro business houses. There are no Negro stores. There are no Negro policemen, no Negro firemen, no Negro politicians. . . . Most of the Negroes in the state are employed . . . as porters and dining car waiters, . . . as janitors, hotel waiters, and red caps, thereby enabling themselves to buy property and become representative bourgeoisie." But after such criticism, he returns to Menckenesque, omnidirectional insult: "Thus is Utah burdened with dull and unprogressive Mormons, with more dull and speciously progressive Gentiles, with still more dull and not even speciously progressive Negroes."

Thurman lived fast and died young. He was only twenty-four when this essay on Utah was published, and only thirty-two when he died. For some time Thurman was considered a minor figure of the renaissance, but his novels have been getting more sustained attention in recent years. And as Mae Gwendolyn Henderson has written, "His significance . . . far exceeds the work he left behind. Not only was he tremendously influential upon the younger and perhaps more successful writers of the period, but his life itself became a symbol of the New Negro Movement."

I am fully aware of what Brigham Young had in mind when he uttered the above enthusiastic statement, yet try tho I may the most enthusiastic thing that I can find to say about my home state and its capital city is that it invariably furnishes me with material for conversation. It does not matter to whom I am talking, whether it be Jew or Gentile, black or white, Baptist or Episcopalian, thief or minister, when the conversation begins to lag I can always casually introduce the fact that I was born in Utah, and immediately become the centre of attraction, nonchalantly answering the resultant barrage of questions. I find that I can even play this trick on the same group of persons more than once, for it seems as if they never tire asking—Do Mormons still have more than one wife?—Do they look different from other people?—How many wives did Brigham Young have?—Are there any Negro Mormons?—Can one really stay afloat in the Great Salt Lake without sinking?—and thus they continue ad infinitum, and I might also add—ad nauseam. Nevertheless it is amusing at times, and, as I say, it is for this reason alone that Utah has one warm spot in my rather chilled heart, for whenever I stop to remember the many dull hours I spent there, and the many dull people I spent them with, even that aforementioned warm spot automatically begins to grow cold.

Utah was a wilderness composed of ore laden mountains, fertile valleys, and desert wastes frequented only by trappers and Indians when the Mormons, an outlaw religious sect believing in and practising polygamy, settled there. These Mormons had treked over half of the continent in search of a spot where they could found a settlement, earn their livelihood from the soil, and indulge in their religious peculiarities unmolested by their pernicious brethren in God who insisted that they practise other religious peculiarities. They had been run out of Illinois, they had been run out of Missouri and Kansas and they had forged their way over miles of Nebraska prairie land, miles of Wyoming sage brush hills, and miles of mountain trails before they finally stood on a peak overlooking the beautiful Salt Lake valley, surrounded by the Wasatch range of the Rocky Mountains, and cheered when their intrepid leader, Brigham Young, shouted: This is the place!

Once they had found this suitable site the Mormons, under expert leadership, founded their mundane Zion, named their townsite Salt Lake City after the great inland sea nearby, christened the crooked river than ran around the city's outskirts—the Jordon, cultivated the rich farm lands, carried on a profitable trade with the Indians, began to raise stock, and started the construction of their sacrosanct religious temple and tabernacle, which stand today as monuments to their super-achievement.

Things hummed in the new town. Cattle carts lumbered down rocky mountain trails carrying the big stones that were being used in building the temple. Gold rushers, bound for the coast, stopped and sometimes stayed if they felt like braving the arrogant hostility of the Mormon fathers. Square blocks of land were apportioned off to the various churchmen, who energetically erected primitive homes for themselves and their wives. The great tithing square on the site where the renowned Hotel Utah now stands teemed with people pouring in from the surrounding countryside to pay their tithes, while the public watering ground, where the Salt Lake City and county building was later built, was crowded with overland wagon trains, and Mormon visitors from nearby settlements, for Zion had soon over-flowed and mushroom towns appeared overnight in the immediate vicinity. Zion flourished, Zion grew wealthy, and Zion grew more holy per se.

However, all mundane paradises seem subject to an invasion by the devils forces, and the Mormon Zion was no exception, for the devil's forces soon came in the persons of non-Mormons, derisively called Gentiles. Like most gold seekers of their day (and are gold seekers ever any different?) they wanted only the chance to garner gold—damn how they got it or how they suffered meanwhile. So Zion was invaded, and Zion soon succumbed to a wave of prosperity, progress and prostitution, and the transcontinental railroad, which had its east-west junction near Ogden, was the most telling blow dealt by the Gentiles.

The result was pitiful. Thousands of easterners came pouring in to see whether or not these Mormons really had horns, and finding that they were not so endowed by nature decided to stay and break down the Mormon wall around the natural wealth of the state. The Mormons put up a brave battle while Brigham Young lived, but after his death there was a complete debacle. Utah was finally forced to come into the Union, and for coming in she had to abolish polygamy, and lose her individuality, for from that day on Utah was just another state, peopled by a horde of typical American booboisie with their bourgeoisie overloads, and today Utah is a good example of what Americanization and its attendant spores can accomplish.

I have as yet made no mention of the Negro, and this article is supposed to fit into the series called—"These Colored United States." For the moment I wish to quibble, and assert that there are no Colored United States, *id est,* no state in the Union where the Negro has been an individual or vital factor. As George S. Schuyler is so fond of saying, all Aframericans are merely lampblack whites steeped in American culture (?) and standardization. When it comes to such localities as Harlem, the south side black belt of Chicago, the Central Avenue district of Los Angeles, the Seventh Street district in Oakland, the North 24th Street district in Omaha, the Vine Street district in Kansas City, the Beale Street district in Memphis, and similar districts in Atlanta, Charleston, New Orleans, Houston, El Paso, Richmond, Birmingham, et cetera one might write of these as colored cities, for it is there that the Aframerican spirit manifests itself, achieving a certain individuality that is distinguishable from that achieved in similiar white districts despite all the fervent protests of Brother Schuyler to the contrary. What I am leading to is this, that to write of "These Colored United States" is to be trying to visualize a phantom, for in state lots the Negro, save in such southern localities where the population is greater than the white and even in these one can only pick out certain communities to dissect, is a negative factor contributing nothing politically, historically, or economically. He only contributes sociological problems.

The above paragraph is rather rash, and perhaps I should temper it somewhat, and confine myself to the north eastern and north western states, for I am not so sure that the Negro has not made some contribution at least economically in the southern states, but neither am I so sure that this has not been swallowed up beyond the point of recognition by the whites who most certainly hold the power. And now I find justification for having such a series of articles even if they are rather far-fetched, for Negroes need to be told of past achievements and present strivings. They need this trite reminder to stir them, and to urge them on to greater achievements. They must develop a race pride, and so they must be told of what they and their foreparents have achieved. I am sorry then that I have to write of the Utah Negro, for there has been and is certainly nothing about him to inspire anyone to do anything save perhaps drink gin with gusto, and develop new technique for the contravention of virginity.

There is little difference between the few Negroes in Utah and their middle class white brethren. The only difference is one of color, and those Aframericans who have been in the state longest have done everything in their power to abolish even this difference. Miscegenation was the common thing for years, and until a state law was passed prohibiting intermarriage the clerks at the county court house were kept busy signing up fair ladies with dusky men. Then when the prohibitive law was passed the roads to Wyoming and Montana were crowded until those commonwealths also passed anti-miscegenation laws. What is more it reached such proportions that even as late as 1915 there was in Salt Lake a club catering only to Negro men and white women, and, when I was last there, which was a year ago, there were three super-bawdy houses that I knew of, where white ladies of joy with itching palms cavorted for the pleasure of black men only.

This situation was of course not peculiar to Utah alone. It was also true of most western states, and the "Manassa" group of the middle-west was far more notorious than any like group Utah has produced. However, this happened only because the population of Utah was considerably less than that of some of her sister states. Statistics will readily prove, I believe, that comparatively speaking the intermixing of races was as great or greater in Utah than in any other western state.

But to get to another point—There were two Negroes in the first overland Mormon train, a man and his wife (he had only one, for Mormons did not believe that a Negro could ever enter into Heaven as an angel, and that since because of Ham's sin he was to be deprived of full privileges in Heaven, he was not entitled to enjoy the full privileges of a good Mormon on earth), who were servitors to Brigham Young. A little later other vagabond souls, eager to escape the terrors of both the pre and post civil war south, drifted in and remained if they found employment. Then still others were caught in the contemporary westward drift of American population, and entered into the "Bee" state as gamblers, gold-seekers, prostitutes, and home servants. And later, during the ascendancy of the Gentile regime, there was quite an influx of Pullman car porters, dining car men, hotel waiters plus more pimps and prostitutes. This population was for the most part transient, but a few of them accidently during drunken moments or temporary physical ecstasy settled there and commenced the raising of families, which families are now members of the Utah Negroes' *haute monde*.

Until the war had inspired the northern migration of southern colored people there were few of what is known as respectable Negroes in the whole state. These strived hard to cling together, and they generally did except upon the matter of religion, which I might boldly add herein, has done more to keep the American Negro at variance with himself than any other agency. Some folk were Methodists, some were Baptists. Then some Methodists would turn Baptists, and some Baptists would turn Methodists. Moreover some Methodists and some Baptists would grow discontented and there would be rumors of a split, and most times these rumors would develop into actualities. At the present time there are three Negro churches in Salt Lake City, which has a population of about 1,800 colored people. Only about 500 of these are of the church going variety, and imagine their strength divided as they are between two Baptist and one Methodist Churches.

Salt Lake City and Ogden have the largest Negro communities, and of these two Salt Lake has the greater population, but one would never believe this after walking thru the streets of the two cities, for one can walk for hours in Salt Lake without meeting a colored person, while in Ogden one will meet any number in the downtown district. This is due to the fact that the Negro population of Salt Lake has not become centralized, and there is no Negro ghetto, while in Ogden almost the entire Negro population is centered around the railroad yards and depot, because almost the entire Negro population of Ogden is engaged in fleecing the transient railroad porters and dining car waiters out of as much money as possible while these men are in the town. The only other place in Utah where there is an appreciable colored settlement is at Sunnyside, in the southern part of the state, where some two or three hundred men are employed in the coke ovens.

In the glorious state of Utah there are no representative Negro institutions of note save the deluxe gambling clubs, and whore houses in Salt Lake and Ogden. The churches are pitiful and impotent. There are no

Negro professional men. There are no Negro publications, not even a church bulletin. There are no Negro business houses. There are no Negro stores. There are no Negro policemen, no Negro firemen, no Negro politicians, save some petty bondsmen. There are a few Negro mail carriers, and the only Negro mail clerk in the state passes for Spanish or something else that he isn't in order to keep his position and not be forced to become a pack laden carrier. Most of the Negroes in the state are employed on the railroad as porters and dining car waiters, or else in the local railroad shops, or else earn their livelihood as janitors, hotel waiters, and red caps, thereby enabling themselves to buy property and become representative bourgeoisie.

Negroes are rigorously segregated in theaters, public amusement parks, soda fountains, and eating places. This too seems to be a result of the post world war migration of southern Negroes to the north which was accompanied by a post world war wave of Kluxism and bigotry. The earlier Negro settlers experienced little of these things. They were welcome in any of the public places, but as the Negro population grew, and as the Gentile population grew so did prejudice and racial discrimination until now the only thing that distinguishes Utah from Georgia is that it does not have jim-crow cars. Last year there was even a lynching—the second in the history of the state.

Add to this the general dullness and asininity of the place and the people, and you will understand why a writer (who was also born in Utah) in a recent issue of the *American Mercury* declared that there was not an artist in the entire state, and that if one was to stay there he would soon be liable to incarceration in the insane asylum at Provo, or else buried in one of the numerous Latter Day Saint cemeteries. I was there for a short time last summer, and sought to buy my regular quota of reading matter. I asked for a *New Republic* at every down town newsstand in Salt Lake City, and out of ten stands only one had ever heard of it. I made equally vain searches for *The Nation, The Living Age, The Bookman, The Mercury,* and *The Saturday Review of Literature.* At the only stand that had ever heard of these publications the proprietor advised me to pay him in advance and he would order them for me as he did for a few other of his customers who were crazy enough to read such junk. He capped it all by enquiring whether or not I was a Bolshevist.

Thus is Utah burdened with dull and unprogressive Mormons, with more dull and speciously progressive Gentiles, with still more dull and not even speciously progressive Negroes. Everyone in the state seems to be more or less of a vegetable, self satisfied and complacent. Yet I suppose that Utah is no worse than some of its nearby neighboring states, which being the case the fates were not so unkind after all—I might have been born in Texas, or Georgia, or Tennessee, or Nevada, or Idaho.

J. MILTON SAMPSON

Virginia

VOL. 5, NO. 7, JULY 1923

J. Milton Sampson was born on August 4, 1890, in Buckingham County, Virginia. He earned an A.B. from Virginia Union University in 1912 and an L.L.B. from Chicago's Kent College in 1925, while accumulating a number of credits from Columbia University's summer school programs in the Post-Graduate School of Philosophy. After nine years of teaching French and German at Virginia Union University (1912–21), Sampson moved to Chicago, where he was a research director for the Chicago Urban League from 1921 to 1923. He practiced law in Chicago from 1925 until 1935 and then moved back to Virginia, where he managed the Gilpin Court Housing Project for most of the 1940s. In *Who's Who in Colored America* for 1950, Sampson reports membership in Alpha Phi Alpha, the YMCA, and the Elks. That volume also notes that he was a Baptist and a Democrat, although up until the 1940s he listed himself as a Republican. Sampson was married to Sadie Mae Hilton in 1917 and had one child, Helen Brooks.

Aside from writing the occasional book review for *The Messenger,* little is known about Sampson's writing career. His essay on Virginia, although crafted with somewhat awkward prose, offers a vivid description of the role African Americans were allowed to play in the evangelical movements so popular during the 1920s. In keeping with Jim Crow, African Americans were "revived" only in certain galleries or on certain days and barred from playing the piano for hymns. Sampson recounts "the same sordid record" of discriminatory policies in the Methodist and Episcopal churches, in education, in politics, and in the labor movement. Appointing one African American to the executive board of the Virginia Federation of Labor, Sampson reports, led to the defection of dozens of unions, locals, and councils from the federation. The value of this essay is not found in its often stilted attempts at verbal flourishes ("There was politics in Virginia—there is not") or in any sophisticated sociologic analyses. Rather, Sampson sees the way in which petty humiliations or profoundly debasing experiences might inspire action in the future. As his last paragraph makes clear, past discrimination outlines future demands. Unraveling the textbook debates at Roanoke College, Sampson looks to a woman's spirited reply for hope. Her letter to a local paper fiercely claims, "It is time that southern papers should not shrink from telling the truth, if only to this generation." In keeping with this theme, Sampson uses this essay to tell the truth about injustice in the state in order to "[sum] up the wants of the Virginia Negro."

"It is years since a first-rate man has come out of it; it is years since an idea has come out of it. . . . a Washington or a Jefferson dumped there by some act of God would be denounced as a scoundrel and jailed over night."

Mencken, *Smart Set,* 1917.

Virginia is a State of 42,627 square miles, of which 2,000 are under water. Roughly speaking it has three main sections, the Tidewater, or seaboard section, the Piedmont, or valley section, and the Blue Ridge, or mountainous section. Like other states, it has inhabitants of varied colors. It has been blessed by Providence with a mean winter temperature of 39° and a mean summer temperature of 77°. It could be a far more wonderful state than it is. Many reasons have been assigned for its backwardness, but among them one could not mention a sparsity of natural resources either vegetable or animal, for it boasts of bituminous coal deposits, iron, manganese ore, pyrite, soapstone, slate, deer, hares, squirrels, chipmunk, opossum, wild turkey, partridge, sora, and plenty of fish, oysters, crabs and lobsters. The principal reasons why its prosperity has been retarded have been that its inhabitants have undervalued the need of education and have not awakened from the indolence of the slave regime, which believed in passing on the hard work, not to machines of iron and steel, but to human machines in bronze. These latter in an early period of the state's existence, say about 1740, outnumbered the whites.

In that early time the inhabitants of Virginia might be divided into three classes—the planters, the masses and the Negroes. This classification continued to be valid until the surrender of Lee. This early period furnishes many interesting facts and incidents concerning Negro life, as well as illustrates the changing attitude of Virginia toward the Negroes. It is historically fixed that slaves first landed in Virginia in 1619 or 1620, but no statutory recognition of slavery was given until 1661, when Negroes were said to be "incapable of making satisfaction for the time lost in running away by addition of time." By 1772 the State had passed no less than thirty acts looking toward prohibiting the importation of slaves. The preamble of the first constitution adopted in 1776 contains as one of the reasons for taking up arms against Great Britain, that "the King by the inhuman use of his negative refused permission to exclude by law the introduction of Negro slaves."

Virginia furnishes her example of Negroes of too proud spirit to submit to the indignities of slavery. Brawley's Social History of the American

Negro cites six instances of slave insurrections, started, if not completed—among them, the famous Nat Turner insurrection and Gabriel's ambitious attempt. It is common knowledge now that though slavery in its ordinarily accepted sense has been abolished, nevertheless it persists in the spirits of the people of Virginia, white and black alike. This may be illustrated in many ways, but probably most conspicuously in the failure of Virginia Negroes to take positive action to escape from oppression and in a constantly but very slowly decreasing fear of "white folks."

In business Virginia has been a pioneer, but unfortunately the most conspicuous examples of its success have been at once the most outstanding examples of failure. When fraternal insurance is mentioned, the order of the True Reformers and the bank which it conducted immediately come to mind. Regardless of the responsibility for the failure of this and other more recent enterprises, the reaction has affected the growth of Negro business, not only in Virginia, but in other sections of the country as well. Virginia, however, remains the mother among Negroes of fraternal insurance, and probably of banking throughout the country. There are larger insurance companies elsewhere; there are more powerful banks elsewhere, but the pioneers in each of these lines were in Virginia. At present it boasts 18 banks. A most lively insurance company is the Southern Aid, which is at the same time one of the finest examples of capitalistic enterprise within the colored group. On at least two occasions in the knowledge of the writer, this company has declared dividends of over 30 per cent. It engages over 500 persons and has an annual income of nearly a million.

In other lines, business is more or less sleepy. The church business is about the only other one that conspicuously flourishes. In the estimation of some, probably it is the most important business after all. Certainly there is more money invested in it than in any other kind. This business is both financial and spiritual, but there are many anomalies on the spiritual end. It is an unpardonable sin in many of them to dance and play cards or baseball, but one may lie with impunity. The day of shouting has not passed and the yearly revivals still bring itinerant evangelists who parcel out the gospel in periods of extreme emotion and who frighten sinners rather than win them into the fold. One interesting sidelight might be mentioned in this connection. Revivals are not limited to Negroes. Professional white revivalists also come to the Old Dominion and generally, out of a solicitude for their colored brethren and sisters, they set apart a day or a portion of the gallery for the edification of these latter. One particular instance, a day was set apart for colored people, but an official balked on allowing a colored girl to play the piano for the hymns.

It is a matter of common knowledge that the unification of the Methodist Church North and South has hung on the status of the colored brothers. One of the members of the Unification Committee, Bishop Collins Denny, of Richmond, illustrates this point of view very clearly in an article in the Richmond *News-Leader,* in which he says: "We are not called upon to consider whether a color line drawn at any point through the sphere of human relations be right and just and Christian. The sole question now before us is where an admittedly necessary color line shall be drawn." Recent press reports indicate that an agreement has been reached. Probably, therefore, they have discovered where that "admittedly necessary color line shall be drawn."

The Episcopal clergy also face discrimination within the portals of a Christian church. Again, the press reports that the colored clergy have partial enfranchisement in the diocese of Virginia and that a resolution was "passed" in 1922 to give them full representation. This resolution was to come up for final action in 1923, but when the council met, this year, it considered that the matter should be deferred another year, and this was done.

In education the same sordid record must be scanned. According to Professor Gandy, writing in August, 1922, there were only seven public high schools in the whole State open to Negroes. Of these, three were offering only three-year courses. The per capita cost for teachers' salaries was for Negroes $2.74; for whites $9.64. The school funds have not been apportioned according to need, but rather arbitrarily and the portion of the school funds which should normally and legally come to Negroes is constantly diverted toward the white with the result that the Negroes themselves, aided by Rosenwald's purse, have been responsible for the building of over seventy.

From another angle, the report of the Virginia Survey Commission shows conditions. The following facts are included in that survey: That less than two-thirds of the colored children of school age are enrolled; that the average daily attendance is about 37 per cent of the total colored school population, and that two-thirds of the teachers hold certificates indicating unsatisfactory qualifications, while only 3 per cent hold professional certificates. From the writer's knowledge, there is no school of higher than secondary grade supported by State funds for Negroes, unless the courses beginning at Virginia Normal and Industrial School and Hampton be considered of college grade. Education such as it is, is not sincere, for books are selected according to pre-conceived notions, and teachers are permitted to teach only what their masters regard as wise. If white people can be reprimanded for teaching what is obviously the truth, the conclusion is inescapable that a colored teacher would lose her position for doing the same thing.

One college—Roanoke College in Salem, Virginia, used Elson's History of the United States as a text book. This history had the following statements within its borders: "Too often an attractive slave woman was the prostitute to her master." "A sister of President Madison declared that though the southern ladies were complimented with the name of wife, they were only the mistresses of the seraglio."

A southern lady declared to Hamilton Martineau that the wife of many a planter was but the chief slave of the harem. Because of these passages, Confederate Camps and other organizations in the section and individuals took steps to condemn the use of the book in teaching southern students. Caustic letters were addressed to the heads of the college demanding that it be withdrawn from use and threatening that otherwise the students would be withdrawn from the college. A short while after that a Virginia woman wrote a letter to the *Times-Dispatch,* in which she made the following statement: "It is time that southern papers should not shrink from telling the truth, if only to this generation. Yet, as one of the generation, I know that it is always hidden. The older generation—the papers of the South, deny the truth about slavery because they are now ashamed of the blot on the country which tolerates the trade of human flesh and human misery." Thomas Jefferson himself said that the whole commerce between master and slave, "is a perpetual exercise of the most boisterous passions, the most unremitting despotism on one part and degradation and submission of the other . . . the man must be a prodigy who can retain his manners and morals undepraved by such circumstances." But in more modern times, the sort of state in which colored Virginians live, may be visualized in the case of Professor Kerlin of Virginia Military Institute, who protested against the railroading of the Elaine riot victims to death without a fair trial, and because of this, was summarily dismissed from his position at the school. Now the Supreme Court of the United States has vindicated his stand by holding that due process of law was denied those very victims for whom Professor Kerlin pleaded.

There was politics in Virginia—there is not. There is merely a slavish submission to the Republican party with a weak attempt by much talk, to make people believe that there is independent thought. Negroes will run against white people, but they will be voted for because they are Negro Republicans or voted against because—"I ain' go' vote for no nigger." Slemp was defeated in the Ninth Republican District of Virginia not because of the fact that he represents a certain trend of thought or political policy, but because of the fact that his anti-Negro acts put blood into the eyes of the voters of his district.

The Negroes have never recovered from the blow delivered by the last Constitution of Virginia, which provided an education clause as a prerequisite for eligibility to vote. It was easy under his clause to deny the right to vote to any person whose skin was black, by giving him some sections of the constitution that nobody other than a lawyer could understand, and then saying that his explanation was unsatisfactory. The application of this provision decimated the ranks of Negro voters in Virginia and though it was effective by its own provisions for only ten years, there are still in Virginia countless Negroes who believe that there is no use to try to register and vote for the reason that they would be unable to answer the questions asked.

As to race relations, Virginia is at the half-way point between the North and South. It has a well-defined system of segregation and discrimination going into most spheres of life, but it has few lynchings and outward expressions of race prejudice apart from those mentioned. A Negro property owner can live fairly well in Virginia so long as he stays within his own section. Of course, if a colored man gets into the courts on a charge of stealing ten apples, he may get a year in jail and a fine of $10. If a white man goes on the same charge, he may be dismissed upon restitution of the apples or paying for them. But such little things as this do not count in Virginia. They are the warp and woof of life. They are as common as the air which one breathes or the muddy water which comes from the James River, and which, perforce, he must drink.

On the other hand, there is a colored doctor in a certain town who has a large white practice. His name is not given for obvious reasons. Again when the influenza epidemic was on during the war period, colored people seemed to fare better than white with the result that many white people thought that Negro doctors had peculiar skill and many a Negro doctor was called to attend a white patient in extremity.

An action of a lodge of Elks in Richmond may be cited as showing the attitude of the Virginia Negro toward the conditions under which he lives. At the Elks convention, the Richmond Elks were making a manful effort to swing the convention for another year to Richmond. They made up a fine printed invitation booklet in which there were pictures of prominent men and their homes, statements as to Negro business, copies of the decision which dissolved an injunction prohibiting the Elks from using the emblem of the Elks of the World, in short, a strong appeal, a cordial invitation to the Negro Elks of the United States to have their convention in Richmond the following year. But in the meantime, one of the officers of a lodge in Richmond who realized what conditions were, protested against inviting his brother Elks to such a place, in a letter addressed to the committee in charge. The reasons stated were: That the places of interest in the city were for whites only; that they might be hampered in their deliberations by limitations of the police, as Monroe Trotter was molested in his speech at the City Auditorium. That they would have no security from assaults and insults; that white people would like colored people as long as they stayed in their places, and that if everything else were favorable, there were not accommodations in Richmond for 12,000 visitors. The indignation which resulted from this letter resulted in the ousting from office of the writer. So, we see a compound of satisfaction and dissatisfaction, of pride and the lack of it, of prejudice among whites and blacks.

The Virginia Negroes on the labor question straddle as they do on others. In Richmond, a city of over 55,000, there are not enough men of independent thought to support a Socialist local. The Virginia Federation of Labor will not follow the recommendations of the American Federation as to equality for the Negro. As an organization, the Virginia Federation did in 1919 elect a Negro—Page of Newport News—one of the five members of the

Executive Board. As result of this, before the month was out, the Retail Clerks Association, the Central Trades and Labor Council, the Metal Trades Council, the Allied Printing Trades Council, the Mechanics Lodge No. 696, the Mechanics Lodge No. 10, the Mechanics Helpers Lodge No. 100, the Iron Molders Union No. 128, the Painters and Paper Hangers Union No. 1018, the Plumbers and Steam Fitters Union No. 10, the Railway Clerks Lodge No. 253, the Typographical Union No. 90, the Carpenters and Joiners Union No. 398, all withdrew from the Virginia Federation as a result of this election. The same thing followed in different other cities. The writer has been unable to verify what the ultimate result of this has been. Whether the unions finally returned to the Federation or not is not known, but the fact is significant that these organizations should take such action because of the election of a brother laborer and unionist to a position in the Federation.

What of the future? Will Virginia ten years, twenty years, fifty years, from now be a land of the free? Do Virginia Negroes want to be in a land of the free? If the same Professor Gandy quoted above may be considered a spokesman for the Virginia Negroes, the following are the Negroe's wants: We want equal accommodations in public carriages; we want justice in the distribution of neighborhood advantages; we want equal wages for equal work; we want the same provisions made for our education as for that of others; and then he felt it necessary to add, we don't want social equality (whatever that means). From expressions throughout the State, it is fair to say that this about sums up the wants of the Virginia Negro.

ASHLEY L. TOTTEN

The Truth Neglected
in the Virgin Islands

VOL. 8, NO. 7, JULY 1926 (FIRST PART)

VOL. 8, NO. 8, AUGUST 1926 (SECOND PART)

The Messenger was founded as an official organ for the organization of the Brotherhood of Sleeping Car Workers, but few of the regular *Messenger* staff or contributors ever actually served as Pullman porters. Ashley Totten, however, who was born in 1884 in St. Croix, Danish West Indies, rose to prominence in the labor movement by working through the ranks of the porters' union. He attended high school in the West Indies and moved to the United States in 1905, becoming a naturalized citizen in 1911. He worked for the Pullman Company from 1915 until 1925, when he was discharged for feigning illness so he could attend a meeting of Chicago porters. A union activist for the rest of his life, Totten held a variety of positions in the brotherhood and was secretary-treasurer until shortly before his death in St. Croix in 1963.

Totten was a committed radical who once had to be discouraged by A. Philip Randolph from collecting weapons to use against strikebreakers. Despite a severe beating by strike breakers in 1929, from which he never fully recovered, he continued his civic activism and labor work. At various points in his career Totten was president of the American Virgin Islands Civic Association, served as a member of the American-China Policy Association, and was active in the Welfare Defense League. His article is one of the few in the series to assume the importance of labor history, both to the region itself and to its relations to other regions.

The inclusion of the two-part article "The Truth Neglected in the Virgin Islands" as part of "These 'Colored' United States" indicates an important aspect of the understanding of national identity held by African American intellectuals of the period. The article begins by asserting the incorporation of Virgin Islanders into the citizenry of the United States proper ("A peep into Virgin Island life as one sees it in New York and other neighboring Eastern cities."), but makes a case for separate identity as well by emphasizing the complex Danish and British influences that have altered a "national sensibility" and thus given the Virgin Islanders a unique, and problematic, heritage. The essay focuses more upon the role of the Virgin Islands in the national psyche than it does upon Virgin Islanders themselves. Thus, Totten's construction of regional identity immediately leaves behind state borders and relies instead upon dissecting questions of national and racial identity.

Totten conflates regional and national identity by balancing a description of people on the Islands with one of migrants from the Islands in the United States. As Totten discusses is his essay, there was much concern that the elaborate social caste system of the West Indies was threatening to transfer itself and infect the already-troubled African American communities of the United States. Totten argues that this is not at all the case, for as he ironically observes, once in the United States, dark skin is a great leveler. In New York the emigrated servant and mistress "both do the same menial work, and both are subject to the same condition." And, indeed, one of the mixed blessings Americanization bestowed upon the Islands was the simultaneous increase in legal freedoms and decrease in social freedoms. Totten writes: "And with American rule, Virgin Islanders are beginning to learn that under the American flag a Negro whether of light or dark hue is a Negro just the same, which condition has rendered havoc into the social make up in the islands." The Virgin Islands may not technically be part of the United States, but for all intents and purposes, the black man in the Virgin Islands was becoming an African American, subject to the same regime of racism. The identity of a people thus overruled the identity of a region. The Virgin Islands might not have been part of "These United States," but for African Americans of the 1920s, the Virgin Islands were one of "These 'Colored' United States."

It is not absolutely certain that this piece was part of the series. Essays were never consistently labeled, and as *The Messenger* changed its editors and editorial policies over the years, the magazine became increasingly unfocused and haphazardly constructed. The first part appeared in July 1926 and the second part in August 1926. An editorial note at the end of the second part mentions that "the third and last series of articles on the Virgin Islands will treat with native ability, their habits and customs and of the activities of Virgin Island organizations in New York." No such article ever appeared.

PART 1

A peep into Virgin Island life as one sees it in New York and other neighboring Eastern cities reveals the fact that there are ten thousand (more or less) expatriates who suffer from the dreaded disease of homesickness, a disease that is sadly in need of some specialist who can diagnose the case and find the cure.

The three Virgin Islands, St. Thomas, St. Jan, and St. Croix, became a part of the United States, March 31, 1917, after the exchange of ratifications for the sale from Denmark had been effected.

These islands are situated about 1,480 miles S.S.E. of New York, or 86 miles east of Porto Rico.

They have a most healthy climate with an even temperature of 65 to 90 degrees and a fertile soil rich enough to yield fruits and vegetables in abundance inclusive of the staple products sugar cane and cotton.

THE BEGINNING OF THE EXODUS!

Dating as far back as forty-five years ago the islands boasted of about forty thousand inhabitants who began to emigrate to the United States, Cuba, Porto Rico, Haiti, Santo Domingo, Panama, and to Central and South America.

It would not be a difficult task to find Virgin Islanders around Harlem, N.Y., who emigrated many years ago, that would gladly make a sacrifice so that they may be privileged to return once more to die in the land that gave them birth.

Many have toiled and labored in the struggle to accumulate enough to return and live, but few have made a success of this venture, and the truth is that hardly after they return, they find themselves hurrying back to New York. The reason for this is an economic one, plain and simple.

During the days of Danish rule, the natives enjoyed certain privileges which made them an indulgent people.

The Danish Colonial Government was a paternal one, of the kind that made the average citizen feel that he could always secure a government loan on good security.

Farmers, squatters and ranch owners who were victims of occasional droughts looked to the Government loan as a means of sustaining a loss in their crops and the thought of irrigation was never entertained during that period.

St. Thomas boasted of its beautiful harbor, where ships called for coal and water, and sailing crafts transported with their large warehouses goods consigned to South American trade.

The bay rum industry also helped to keep business alive, and St. Jan the lesser of the group provided the bay leaves from which the oil is obtained.

It might be said that the Danes allowed the islands to be used as a dumping ground for foreign exploiters who preyed upon the fat of the land.

There was a time when the penniless imposter could set up a home in the islands, thrive upon the hospitality of the natives and after years of cunning return to his country wealthy.

Those were the days of happiness when "work today and tomorrow will take care of itself" was the slogan.

Years of Danish rule saw laborers at St. Thomas laying around waiting for a steamship to put into port for coal while vast acres of land back of the hills lay idle, only to fall into the hands of lazy and non-progressive farmers, who raised cattle and hogs on the wild grass and fodder that grew there.

THE CONFLICT OF COLOR

The upper tens of Virgin Islanders had a very peculiar form of drawing the color line, which, happily, ceased to work out so very well under American rule.

First there was that element of pretense where many hardly a peg above a beggar conducted themselves in a manner to make the onlooker believe that they possessed wealth.

The Danes tolerated a social hob and nob which classified poor whites, and mulattoes with blacks who had money into the representative class of the islands.

The term Negro is still considered a gross insult to a mulatto, and a black man with money will resent it vigorously, but all who represent prominence whether they be mulattoes or blacks, nevertheless, lined up with the Danes to oppress the less fortunate, so that when a Dane called a field laborer "En Satan Neger" (A devilish Negro) their colored associates would do so too.

Virgin Island society has advanced several grades above cities like Washington in the education of the various shades and complexions and the quality of hair.

There are so many in whose homes the waters of poverty have crowded in, yet they are indeed too proud to dig a ditch for an honest dollar.

They must have servants, but the truth is that many who are thus employed are miserably underpaid, for their employers can hardly afford to pay them.

It is false pride on the one hand and chronic laziness on the other that accounts for the practice of servants in so many pauperized homes where only the bare necessities of life are in evidence.

In New York, where the mistress and the servant have emigrated, it will be found that both do the same menial work, and both are subject to the same condition.

And with American rule, Virgin Islanders are beginning to learn that under the American flag a Negro whether of light or dark hue is a Negro just the same, which condition has rendered havoc into the social make up in the islands.

The law of economics states that where wages are high, life is high, where wages are low, life is low.

With so many aristocrats, so few to cultivate the land and with European exploiters controlling the colonial government, a law was passed admitting immigrants to do contract labor.

Thus peonage started in the islands, with hundreds of British West Indian laborers pouring in daily, where they signed up a three year contract to work on the respective plantations for the mere pittance of twenty-

The Grand Hotel, St. Thomas, V.I., where Negroes of the better class had first taste of American race discrimination.

five cents a day, which gradually brought life to a very low economic level.

Hard times began to wend its way in many homes, native born mechanics and tradesmen suffered a slump in business and with the grip of oppression from the farmers, merchants, and those who represented prominence tightened closer, the exodus increased rapidly.

THE NEW NEGRO MOVEMENT

The economic condition grew from bad to worse: Denmark fell asleep on the job and entrusted the entire administration of the islands in the hands of a few haughty and ultra conservative Danes who were only concerned about their own personal welfare.

Shipping interests at St. Thomas were on the decline, and St. Croix depended only on the sugar cane industry, which yielded little on account of the German beet root sugar competition.

Besides, when the World War broke out in 1914, St. Thomas, depended wholly on German shipping trade for support; hence it is clear that as no German ship could go to the island ports, the inhabitants were actually face to face with famine.

St. Croix farmers, on the other hand, began to reap a harvest because of the rise in the price of sugar, but they still continued to oppress the laboring classes and never offered them an increase.

So the laborers organized and rapidly became a power in the island of St. Croix.

Now organization is an instrument which is good or bad according to the use with which it is put.

At the outset the movement started with brilliant leadership where, over seas of hardships, they forced rapid increases in wages until at one time laborers received two dollars per day.

But selfishness, egotism and bigotry creeped in, and it has since failed miserably.

The laborers had managed to set up a Union Bank and that failed. Property was bought by them and its value depreciated. Thousands of acres of fertile and well cultivated land fell into their hands, and they allowed it to become a mass of wilderness.

When agitation started in St. Croix the plantation owners called on the Danish Governor Helweg-Larsen at the time to use force and intimidation to stop it.

The gendarmes were called out and the Danish cruiser Valkyrien was dispatched to the scene of the so-called disorder, but even though the poor laboring classes had been driven off the farms because they had declared a strike, there was not a sign of disquietude at any time.

On one occasion while one of their leaders, Ralph Bough, was addressing the strikers the gendarmes under command of Capt. Fuglede made some sort of a cavalry charge on them, but Bough told the strikers to stand firm and show no resistance, and in the same instant he appealed to the Danish Crown for justice in their hour of need, waving the Danish flag as he did so. This cool-headedness amazed Capt. Fuglede, for he withdrew with his troops immediately.

It was clear to the governor that the sugar cane crop would become a total loss unless the laborers returned to work, so he called into conference a committee of labor leaders who were Ralph Bough, Charles Reubel and Ralph DeChabert to meet with the Planters Association.

The result of this conference ended in the first victory for labor in the islands.

The labor movement was also started in St. Thomas, and rapidly assumed large proportions.

Nature's forces in the form of a very severe hurricane visited the islands about the same time, devastated homes and villages, leaving the poor natives in a most frightful and pitiable condition.

In the meantime, Denmark, fearing that she could not defend her neutrality against Germany if she held those islands any longer, and feeling rather keenly the labor situation, secretly made negotiations for the transfer of the islands to the United States.

THE TRANSFER

A sad day it was indeed when the Danish flag (Danebrog) disappeared from view.

Home of a working man, Virgin Islands.

The Danish minister Herr Larsen in his prating words said: "Within these moments these islands shall pass into strange hands. Whatever mistakes we have made we ask that they be forgiven," and as tears streamed down the faces of many gathered there the Danish flag came slowly down the mast amid the booming of guns as the Star Spangled Banner hurriedly took its place.

A temporary form of government was set up under Rear Admiral Olliver, commandant of the Navel Station at St. Thomas and Civil Governor of the islands.

According to the explanation given me by Rear Admiral Omar, who was governor at the time I visited the islands (1920), the naval officers serve in the capacity of civil officials in order to save the municipality the expense of maintaining civilians.

The islands, said he, are not self-supporting and since the naval station would remain here just the same it is considered to the best advantage of the people that the naval personnel who receive their salary from the Navy be used free of any charges to serve in that capacity.

This form of government is perfectly alright from an economic viewpoint, but it does not meet the approval of the native inhabitants because it is believed that military or naval discipline is employed for some form of oppression upon a civil and law-abiding people.

Suppose we try to get to the root of this most contested point which has been the source of many unfriendly arguments among Virgin Islanders.

In the first place an American white man who is imbued with race hatred when in naval uniform is the same white man if dressed up in civilian clothes.

White men whether naval or civil do not necessarily oppress the natives because they are Negroes; the truth is that they know they have no power, they know that they are as separate as the fingers on one's hand.

Judge George Washington Williams, a civil judge, for instance is said to be a miserable race hating Cracker who could hardly measure up to any degree of prominence among the social elite in his southern home Baltimore.

But he finds in the Virgin Islands an opportunity to be a czar, because some Negroes there are trying to become his social pal on the one hand, and are too unscrupulous and disloyal to their own race on the other.

Now because a few Southern Crackers are taking advantage of the people in the islands is no reason to condemn the form of Government any more than it is fair to condemn the entire United States because Negroes are lynched in the South.

AMERICAN RULE VERSUS DANISH

It is generally known that the natives are enjoying more political rights under the present form of Government than they did under the Danish rule.

In the Judiciary Department we find a great contrast as compared with the days of Danish rule, when everything was at the mercy of a military judge who held the power to send a man to jail without a fair trial.

If he represented the laboring class he was trotted to town tied like a crab before two mounted gendarmes and when brought before the judge he would be greeted with "Hold mund Din forbandle Laat, Din sorte Svin" (Shut your mouth you detestable fool, you black pig).

Under the Danish law the ruling class had a voice in court, the underdog was at their mercy, but under the present administration they have an open court with jury trials, which has served at least to give all persons whether of high or low degree some measure of justice.

Natives are employed in the police force and in every governmental department, and this is indeed significant because during the Danish rule, these positions were only given persons of lighter hue, usually some retired Danish soldier or the son of a Danish official.

In the Department of Education we find children educated to an elementary grade and graduated to high school, which privilege they could not enjoy under the Danish rule unless their parents could afford to pay for their tuition.

In the Hospitals and Sanitary Department wonderful improvements have been made. Suffice it to say that the poor sick person is no longer dumped into a cart or carried in a hammock to the hospital, but an auto ambulance with a well uniformed native nurse answers the call instead.

Infant mortality, which at one time ran as high as ninety percent, has decreased considerably under American rule.

One word about the prisoners. They are no longer mistreated, and made to work on the public streets under the lash of the driver's cowhide, but they are given a chance to reform, they learn a trade and eat better food than the daily boiled cornmeal and raw pickled salt herring which they once received.

Improvements along political lines are needed however, in the form of suffrage.

Suffrage should be given to every man and woman in the islands provided they are native born or citizens of the United States.

In regulating this suffrage system, care should be taken not to include the large amount of British subjects who get by as Virgin Islanders but who find solace in their allegiance to Great Britain.

We have now reached to the point where one may make a study of the economic value of the islands, which is the underlying cause for the wave of discontent.

Whether the terrible economic condition is the fault of United States Government or whether it is due to the lack of ability on the part of the natives to help themselves will be the food for thought in the next issue.

PART 2

Among the ten thousand (more or less) Virgin Islanders to be found around Harlem, New York, there is a belief that American Negroes hold a dislike for them in consequence of which they never discuss any of their grievances with strangers.

But I find that they are in error. The intelligent American Negro admires the intelligent Virgin Islander, and is willing to take an active part in the struggle to bring prosperity to those islands.

It is the duty of Virgin Islands to realize and appreciate the fact that the twelve million Negroes on the mainland represent a great political and economic power despite the fact that they are disfranchised in some States.

Instead of placing the American Negro at such a terrible underestimate as some Virgin Islanders are doing, it would be better to remove the chip of conceitedness and solicit their aid.

No one will attempt to deny that the National Association for the Advancement of Colored People is a powerful organization.

The various fraternities and sororities cannot be overlooked.

If this serves as a bit of advice to Virgin Islanders, then let me add the various ministerial alliances all over this country who have not heard the message of the Virgin Island people and who know nothing of their aims and aspirations.

In other words the representatives of the Virgin Island cause owe a bit of courtesy to these agencies who are concerned about humanity, and whose endorsement will help to mould public opinion, which is more effective than all the red tape employed to gain a hearing at Washington.

Since the transfer of the islands there have been resolutions introduced in Congress and all kinds of investigations made, but the fact still remains that nothing will ever be done until public opinion gets busy to press the issue before the powers that be.

In the preceding article it was shown that the exodus started from the Virgin Islands before they became a part of the United States, and has since increased so rapidly that the remaining inhabitants are not Virgin Islanders at all.

The Tortolians at St. Thomas and Barbadians at St. Croix are decidedly loyal subjects of Great Britain, demanding equal political rights as native born Virgin Islanders, which privilege they did not enjoy when they lived in their native homes.

The Virgin Islanders argue that they are entitled to enjoy all the rights and privileges of every American citizen, and that it is the duty of the American Negro to aid them in their fight to realize these rights.

In other words they want the right of franchise, so that all foreigners regardless of their station in life be made to declare themselves citizens of the United States before they shall enjoy equal privileges with the native born.

Virgin Islanders should realize and appreciate the value of citizenship and the right to clamor for native born representation because they never enjoyed it before.

During the Danish regime the Legislature of St. Thomas and St. Jan, both classified into one municipality, was made up largely of foreigners. The municipality of St. Croix had but two native Negro representatives, and an American white man filled the dual position as chairman of the Danish Colonial Legislature and Vice-Consul General of the United States.

Local newspaper editors and labor leaders charge the American Government with suppressing their publications, and usurping their right to free speech under the law.

In some instances police officers were found to overstep their authority, while on the other hand it was lack of diplomacy on the part of the leaders themselves.

While it is true that a person may stand on the street corner and sharply criticise the Government of the United States, extreme care must be taken how to attack the President or any of the United States officials.

In an island like St. Thomas, where there are so many of the aristocrat and bourgeoisie type who are not concerned about the proletariat, it is no easy task for a radical to get a hearing and make converts.

In St. Croix the masses of Barbadian field laborers are exceedingly clannish, but too super-sensitive.

They will recognize leadership. It makes no difference whether such leadership is good or bad.

Though the islands have afforded them a free hospital where they find real happiness and comfort, they expect to dabble in its politics and still remain British subjects.

They set out to run the affairs of St. Croix, and were ably directed by a leader who despised any person of lighter hue than himself.

Instead of trying to educate his followers into a sense of race solidarity and race consciousness it is said that he started out with a reign of abuse attacking whites and mulattoes as a means of reprisals for their long drawn out caste distinction.

He made a sorry mess of his attempt to preach social equality, for the field laborers interpreted it to mean that they should refrain from the use of the term "yes, sir" and "no, sir" and paid absolutely no respect to persons of culture in authority.

This sudden change made many friends of labor to turn against them, for the poor misled creatures were too ignorant to see how much harm they were bringing to themselves.

They attempted to molest respectable persons with insulting remarks when they were seen on the streets, in consequence of which some of the landowners and capitalists began to look at St. Croix as a place of torment and left the island.

At Bethlehem, St. Croix, there is a Danish syndicate known as the Bethlehem Concern who operates and controls the largest sugar industry on the island.

Inclusive of this several thousand acres of the best soil adaptable for the cultivation of sugar cane fell in their hands before the transfer.

This syndicate it is said, desires to affect a monopoly on all lands in St. Croix, and some plantation owners charge that when illegal strikes were declared on their respective plantations followed by a series of fires of incendiary origin these were brought about at the direction of the labor leader at the time, who it is alleged received a handsome tip to help in the realization of the contemplated monopoly.

Dr. Longfield Smith, manager of the Agricultural Experimental Station, testified before the Kenyon Congressional Commission to the islands that the "Bethlehem Concern" made $425 for one hogshead of sugar, but the individual planter who sent his sugarcane to their factory only received $90 per hogshead.

It was also brought out in the investigations that they gave an annual bonus of from $500 to $1,000 to their managers, overseers, and clerical forces, but only paid 60 cents per day to their laborers and no income tax to the Government.

At St. Thomas a Danish syndicate owns, controls and operates the West India Dock and Engineering Co., a gigantic and magnificent wharf where seven large steamships may be moored at the same time.

The management at these docks as well as stevedores, shipping agents, and experts claim that ship captains refuse to call there for coal and water because prohibition is enforced in the islands.

They have quarantine, coast wise laws, and other peculiar American harbor restrictions which is applicable to all closed ports.

There is a doubt in the mind of the writer whether the natives would thrive on the coaling of steamships as a lucrative field for labor, if more ships called there. With the presence of a powerful crane on this wharf to fill the coal bunkers, the laborers are at the mercy of the dock owners, who may at any time dispense with the services of the three hundred coal passers, which is the number necessary to coal a ship: besides modern ships are burning oil, and it does not need much help to apply the hose through which the supply is furnished.

The aristocrats and bourgeoisie of St. Thomas are trying to hide behind a lame excuse, because of their failure to present an intelligent programme for the future welfare of the native inhabitants.

They were poor leaders when they were tolerated, but they have been tried and found wanting.

The new Negro movement started among poor ambitious young men and women who appreciate the fact that St. Thomas can no longer thrive on its harbor alone, and are prepared to prove that the land will produce enough in fruits and vegetables for export trade.

Where the soil is found not adaptable for cultivation they have suggested poultry farming, cattle and sheep raising.

Strange to say, the natives of the neighboring British Islands, Tortola, Annie Gorda, and Virgin Gorda supply the consumer at St. Thomas with charcoal, fruit, and vegetables, while the "Cha Cha"—a class of whites of French extraction—supply them with fish.

Mr. Lockhart, a native born Negro, is the "Rockefeller" of that island. He owns almost everything there, and has a monopoly on the baking industry.

One cannot eat bread in St. Thomas unless it is bought from Lockhart's Bakery, but the man himself is absolutely indifferent to the general welfare of St. Thomas.

There are the Lugos, Creques, Paiewonskies, Levins and other leading wholesale and commission merchants too numerous to mention, to whom the average St. Thomian will doff his hat in recognition of his supposed wealth, yet, put them all together, there is not enough "love of country" or business ability to do anything constructive in order to bring prosperity to St. Thomas. In that "Paradise of Idleness" the visitor finds bankers, bookkeepers, clerks, editors, merchants, mechanics, lawyers and laborers waiting for Uncle Sam to do something for them when in reality they are not putting forth their best energy toward doing something to help themselves. The only persons who never complain are the preachers and doctors.

In my feeble way I tried to explain in public addresses when I visited the islands (1920) that the secret to their success lies in cooperative action, that is to say let all the various factions unite into one cooperative movement of which the American and Virgin Islander resident in the United States should become a part.

At St. Croix, with its most fertile soil, there need be no hesitancy of the rapid success of a cooperative movement instituted there.

In a recent news item appearing in the New York *Times,* mention was made of a shipment of tomatoes and eggplant from St. Croix which the consignee said was absolutely the very best quality that the New York market had ever seen. St. Croix produces fruits and vegetables that are to be found only on the choicest tables on the mainland.

There are peas, beans, okras, yams, potatoes, various species of bananas, tannias, avocado pears, pumpkins and other vegetables too numerous to mention.

It is the home of mangoes, mesples, plums, sugar custard and bell apples, kinneps, cherries, and all other tropical fruits.

Native ability may be encouraged in the manufacture of jams, jellies, and marmalades made from the guava, cashew, cocoa plum and tamarind.

They are also noted for their ability to prepare delicious pickles out of limes which they call "assha," of their mutton cucumbers and peppers.

Guava berries, which have a striking resemblance to the blue berries of America, and the sorrel (a native herb) is usually picked from the trees during the Autumn and by adding just a little alcohol our anti-Volstead friends would be inclined to smack their lips ask for more.

The very first attempt to introduce Virgin Island products in New York was made by a Miss Isabel George, who started with little finance and proved conclusively that fruits and vegetables shipped to her at the time were without the least sign of decay.

Miss George is an active member of two leading Virgin Island Benevolent Organizations in New York, is connected with several other fraternities and is known as a most loyal worker among Americans and West Indians alike.

Another champion of cooperative action among Virgin Islanders is Mr. Andrew C. Pedro, who is perhaps the only person with an intelligent programme for the future welfare of the laboring classes of the islands.

A fair illustration of what the Virgin Islanders resident in New York could accomplish by cooperative action is shown by the fact that thousands of American and West Indian consumers patronize the fruit and vegetable vendors at the public market located on Eighth Avenue between 140th and 145th streets, but out of the vast amount of West Indian products on sale there, not a single shipment came from the Virgin Islands.

St. Croix has an area of eighty-four square miles. It is twenty-two miles long and six miles wide.

The soil is fertile, and at one time the whole island was under cultivation even to the top of the hills.

Land may be purchased for cultivation by the acre, but usually the owner sells the entire plantation inclusive of buildings stock, implements, etc., for a very reasonable price.

One hundred and fifty acres of land, thus equipped, is valued at about $20,000.

A number of distinguished visitors who were attracted by the remarkable size of the watermelons grown on a plantation called "Grange" came upon a monument with the inscription:

Rachael Fawcett Lavine
1736–1768

The guide in passing requested the visitors, who were all white Americans, to remove their hats as a mark of respect for the Negro mother of one of America's greatest statesmen, Alexander Hamilton.

Not very far from this spot is also a monument in memory of the Danish soldiers who lost their lives during the native uprising of 1878.

St. Croix has its boosters like St. Thomas. During winter months, tourists are escorted to motor buses carrying the advertisement "INDEED IT IS ALWAYS JUNE IN ST. CROIX," and the driver is usually more concerned about extending the hospitality of the island to strangers than he is about accepting a fee for his services.

Hon. George H. Woodson, Chairman of the Federal Commission to the Virgin Islands, declared in an address before the island legislature that St. Croix had the most beautiful scenery and St. Thomas the most beautiful harbor.

The three islands said he, are blessed with the finest climate he had ever been in since he was born.

T. GILLIS NUTTER

West Virginia

VOL. 6, NO. 2, FEBRUARY 1924

Like so many of the other contributors to this series, T. Gillis Nutter was the product of a hard-earned education. He was born to former slaves in Princess Anne, Maryland, on June 15, 1876, and began work at the age of nine, sawing a cord of wood a day to afford the luxury of attending school. He graduated from high school in 1896 and worked at a hotel to save money for Howard University Law School. He graduated from Howard in 1899 and then worked as a grade school principal in Maryland. He was admitted to the Marion County (Ind.) bar in November of 1901 but was unable to find work as a lawyer, so went back to working at hotels. In March of 1903 he responded to a call for help from a law school classmate and went to Charleston, West Virginia, to assist with the defense of an African American man accused of murder. Nutter's work with the case, which successfully reduced the offense to voluntary manslaughter, brought him prominence in the legal profession and a regular practice. He took to the Supreme Court of Appeals an unsuccessful motion for an injunction to ban showings of *The Birth of a Nation*. His work with African American defendants accused of rape and murder brought him into regular danger from mobs and lynchings, but Nutter continued undaunted to practice throughout the early twenties, after which little is known about his career.

Nutter provides some information about himself for his 1924 essay on West Virginia, and this information also speaks to Nutter's larger rhetorical project in the essay. We learn that he was secretary-treasurer of the Mutual Savings and Loan Bank of Charleston, the grand chancellor of the Knights of Pythias, the president of the NAACP branch of Charleston, and for two years a member of the West Virginia Legislature. (His blurb modestly does not mention that he served for three years as the grand exalted ruler of the Elks of the World.) His litany of accomplishments do more than establish his own credentials as an expert on West Virginia; they testify to the presence of a bourgeois and "respectable" class of which Nutter is a member.

The reader should not look in this dry and earnest piece for the irony or sarcasm that permeates many of these essays. By respectfully rather than ironically recounting geographic and commercial statistics, Nutter's essay demonstrates a commitment to portraying the African American in West Virginia as part of a fruitful and prospering society. He would play no part in disparaging his own people.

Flanked by solemn photographs of upstanding citizens of West Virginia, this essay is nevertheless focused largely upon the institutions of his state, the photographs intended to speak for the presence of African Americans as individuals and, most critically, as professionals. Nutter's interest in establishing in his reader's minds the prosperity of the bourgeois African American community in West Virginia leads him to discount the poverty of both white and black miners. Average miners, he writes, "set a splendid table and dress well." Accentuating the positive growth and promising future he believed West Virginia had before it, however Babbitlike it may sound to our ears, was hardly naive or foolish. As he points out, fifty years previous there had been no high schools for African American children; by 1924 there were over two hundred. He goes on to exhaustively enumerate the rooms in each school, but does effectively make his point that work has been accomplished. The twenty-eight photographs of prominent West Virginians that flank the essay are in the great tradition of uplift imagery and make of capitalism not an oppressive system, as do *The Messenger*'s more radical editorials, but a race goal. The African American population may still be oppressed, but it is not voiceless, and it is making strides. The presence of Nutter's conservative essay in the radical and controversial *Messenger* illustrates the broad editorial sweep of the magazine.

Nutter is a politician and manages to indirectly praise his own efforts to establish orphanages, old-age homes, asylums, and schools such as the Industrial Home for Colored Girls and the Deaf and Blind School for Colored People. These Jim Crow institutions, he argues, were necessary since separate institutions were already used. With the passage of Nutter's bills, African Americans took over the management and oversight of the institutions for "colored people," and thus Jim Crow is figured as a step toward self-determination. Nutter's self-congratulation is understandable in a politician, however silly the idea of West Virginia as the "garden spot of America for the Negro" might be.

James M. Cain's essay on West Virginia in *The Nation* focused on the "murder, dynamiting, arson, and insurrection" that were the "usual order of the day and night," and the lawlessness that resulted from the battle between labor and capital in the mines. Cain has the obligatory description of the mountain folk and corrupt politicians and ends doubting whether the state is "civilizable." In contrast to this stereotypical view, Nutter offers a sense of the multiple levels of development and culture that made West Virginia in the 1920s. Cain's dark view excludes even more, perhaps, than Nutter's over-rosy scenario.

Left: *Hon. T. G. Nutter, Charleston, W.Va.* Right: *John C. Norman, Prominent architect, Charleston, W.Va.*

West Virginia is rich in history and tradition. According to State history, the first and the last battles of the Revolutionary War were fought at Point Pleasant and Wheeling, October 10, 1774, and on September 11, 1782, respectively. The first boat propelled by steam was built in West Virginia by James Rumsey in 1784; the first electric railroad in the world, built as a commercial enterprise, was constructed between Huntington and Guyandotte; the first brick pavement laid in the world was laid in

Left: *Anderson H. Brown, Prominent realtor and capitalist, Charleston, W.Va.* Right: *C. H. James, Senior member of C. H. James & Son, wholesale fruit and produce co., Charleston, W.Va.*

Charleston in 1870, by Dr. J. P. Hale, at that time mayor of Charleston. He also introduced English sparrows into the United States about the same time.

West Virginia has an area of 24,022 square miles; the extreme length of the State is 225 miles; the extreme breadth, 200 miles, and it is divided into 55 counties.

The highest recorded temperature is 110 degrees Fahrenheit and the lowest, 37 degrees below zero. The rain fall ranges from 35 to 40 inches. The lowest point is 240 feet above sea level and the highest point 4,860 feet above sea level.

West Virginia is fifty miles from Washington on the east; extends twenty-five miles north of Pittsburgh; reaches beyond the middle of Ohio on the west; and is twenty-five miles south of Richmond, Virginia. It is referred to as the most northern of the southern states; the most southern of the northern states; the most eastern of the western states; and the most western of the eastern states.

It has a population of 1,463,701—native whites 1,315,329; foreign born, 61,906; Negroes, 86,345; Indians and others, 121.

West Virginia takes first rank as a coal producing state and has more unmined bituminous coal than any state in the Union. There is being produced about 80,000,000 tons annually and at that rate it will take 2,000 years to exhaust the supply. This state is the heart of the greatest coal field in the world, the Appalachian; ten thousand miles of her area are underlaid with coal, and twenty-nine seams are mined commercially. There are 1,287 bituminous mines, and 125,000 miners, 20,781 of whom are colored.

There are 27,363 petroleum and natural gas wells, producing 202,000,000,000 cubic feet of natural gas, and 230 natural gas plants. Timber products were valued in 1919 at $34,419,523.

The miners live in mining towns, which differ from other communities in that they are strictly industrial. The only reason for their existence is for the production of coal. The change from isolated mountainous condition to well regulated towns is phenomenal. The log cabin of one and two rooms has been replaced by comfortable homes of four, six and eight rooms that have modern conveniences; such as electricity, water, gas, fenced yards, and gardens. Social, educational and religious activities, and sanitation are superior to those found in the usual small town.

The average miner earns seven dollars and upwards daily. They set a splendid table and dress well. It is a common occurrence to see miners riding in their automobiles after work hours and on Sundays.

Prohibition has wrought a wonderful change in these sections. Miners who used to spend their money in riotous living are now buying homes and banking their money. Pay day used to be very much dreaded in mining camps when the saloon was in full swing, but since the passing of the saloons, pay day is just as quiet as any other, and law and order prevail as in other well regulated communities.

Left: *E. L. James, Junior member C. H. James & Son, wholesale fruit and produce commissioners, Charleston, W.Va.* Right: *C. E. Mitchell, C.P.A., Pres. Mutual Savings and Loan Bank, Bus. Mgr. W.Va. Coll. Inst., Member of Commission to Virgin Islands, Institute, W.Va.*

West Virginia is looked upon by many solely as a coal, oil, and gas section. While it is true these are her greatest wealth, yet she is rich in agriculture and manufactures. Her 87,289 farms are valued at $496,439,617, and the crops produced on these farms in 1919 were valued at $96,537,459. The same year there were 17,010,367 bushels of corn, 2,809,398 bushels of potatoes, 7,578,052 pounds of tobacco, 2,442,090 pounds of wool, poultry and eggs

Left: *E. T. Dumetz, Photographer, Charleston, W.Va.* Right: *Prof. J. Rupert Jefferson, Principal Summer High School, Parkersburg, W.Va.*

Left: *Rev. Geo. W. Fountain, D.D., Editor,* Fountain Digest, *Parkersburg, W.Va.*
Right: *O. L. Spaulding, Assistant City Health Physician and Physician of City Colored Schools, Charleston, W.Va.*

worth $12,728,178, dairy products $11,390,329. There are 5,554,731 fruit bearing apple trees and 2,049,867 fruit bearing peach trees. Some of the most delicious apples and peaches in this country are grown in the part of the state known as the Panhandle, where is found the largest peach orchard in the world and the only school for packing apples.

There are only 504 Negro farmers in the state. In some sections the Negro owns large tracts of land, but in most instances he does not produce enough on his farm to meet his needs. However, he is beginning to use better methods of cultivation and seed selection, and is rotating his crops.

The educational system of West Virginia has been of slow growth until recent years, when a more liberal attitude towards public school education has been quite manifest on the part of the law-making bodies of the state. The writer, as a member of the House of Delegates representing Kanawha County, assisted in piloting through the House the first million dollar appropriation for rural schools in the 1921 session. Fifty years ago there were only 431 public schools in the state taught by 387 teachers who received the munificent salary of $7,772.90. Today there are 7,419 schools with 12,869 teachers receiving salaries amounting to $22,209,813.

One is able to obtain some idea of the growth of the school system of this state when it is recalled that fifty years ago there was not a high school in West Virginia; while today there are 205 modern high schools, 1,441 high school teachers and 24,624 high school students.

The following brief summary indicates the facilities provided for the education of Negro youth: One room schools, 289; two rooms and up, 132; junior high schools, 24; first-class high schools, 7; second-class high

Left: *James Arthur Jackson, State Librarian of W.Va. for 3 years, Assistant Librarian 16 years, Assistant Clerk Supreme Court 4 years, Charleston, W.Va.* Right: *C. C. Barnett, Founder of Barnett Hospital, Huntington, W.Va.*

schools, 7; high schools below second class, 6. Normal school teachers, including presidents, 53; classified high school teachers, including principals, 84; elementary teachers, 641. The estimated number of pupils in high school grade is 1,350 and the number of pupils of college grade is 394. There are 23,880 Negro children in school, of which number 17,226 are in the first six grades.

Left: *T. Edward Hill, Director, State Bureau Negro Welfare and Statistics, Charleston, W.Va.* Right: *Prof. C. W. Boyd, Supervisor Colored Schools of Charleston, W.Va., Grand Keeper of Records of K.P. of W.Va.*

Left: *John W. Davis, President of the West Virginia Collegiate Institute, Institute, W.Va.* Right. *J.F.J. Clark, Principal Garnett High School, Charleston, W.Va.*

The salary paid elementary teachers in 1922 was $686,122.20 and that paid to high school teachers, $66,049.48. The average annual salary of teachers in normal schools, other than presidents, is $1,587.30.

W. W. Sanders, Supervisor of Rural Schools for Negroes, in speaking of the educational advantages offered to the Negro in West Virginia, makes this statement: "An item which indicates the increased educational sentiment of our state towards the Negro is that in one county boards of education have expended within the past two years $450,000 in the erection of school buildings for Negroes."

There are two state schools for colored youth offering normal training

Men's Bible Class, First Baptist Sunday School, Charleston, W.Va. Hon. T. G. Nutter, Teacher.

course, and one, the West Virginia Collegiate Institute, offers a normal and a collegiate course. The most expensive state building ever erected in West Virginia is now being built at this Institute; namely, the administration building, costing $380,000. Appropriations amounting to nearly $2,000,000 have been authorized by the last three legislatures for the Institute. It has a wonderful foundation for a great school.

Teachers of both races in the rural schools receive the same salary. Prof. William Davis, one of the pioneer teachers in West Virginia, was the first teacher to be granted a number one certificate in a uniform examination.

The Constitution of West Virginia provides that white and colored children shall be educated in separate schools. The spirit of this constitutional provision has been adhered to in all state and county institutions, with the possible exception of jails and the state penitentiary. The colored leaders, recognizing that to all intent and purpose separate institutions were being maintained for white and colored persons, but invariably under the control and management of white officials, have demanded the establishment of a number of state institutions to be under the control and management of colored citizens. As a consequence, we have a separate Orphans' Home, Old Folks' Home, and a Tuberculosis Sanitarium managed and controlled by colored men. The 1919 and 1921 sessions of the Legislature authorized the establishment of the West Virginia Insane Asylum for Colored People, Industrial School for Colored Boys, Industrial Home for Colored Girls, and a Deaf and Blind School for Colored People. The writer was author of the bills creating the Insane Asylum, the Industrial School for Boys and the Industrial Home for Girls; while Honorable Harry J. Capehart of McDowell County was author of the bill creating the Deaf and Blind School.

Politically, the Negro is the balance of power in the State, and this fact is recognized by the two great parties. As a consequence, in no other section of the country does the Negro wield the power and enjoy the political prestige of the colored voters as he does here. He sits in the councils of the party and helps to map out and dictate its policy. He holds more state offices than in any other state in the Union. He boasts of a State Librarian, State Supervisor of Rural Schools and a Director of the Bureau of Negro Welfare and Statistics. In 1919 there were three colored members in the House of Delegates; in 1921, two; and in 1923, one. There is at least one Negro on the payroll in each department of the government, filling responsible positions. There are three members of the Advisory Council to the State Board of Education. In different parts of the State are found Justices, Deputy Sheriffs, Constables and City Councilmen. A number of colored men are connected with the Federal Government, including postmasters and quite a number of mail carriers and mail clerks.

The Negro in this state is fast solving his economic condition by the acquisition of wealth, valuable real estate holdings, business institutions

Left: *Dr. R. L. Jones, Secretary State Medical Association, Charleston, W.Va.* Right: *J.H.G. Edwards, Contractor and capitalist, Morgantown, W.Va.*

and beautiful homes. There has been a marked change in that respect in the last ten years in every section of the state. He is fast learning that he must be a producer as well as a consumer and he is entering into every avenue of business.

This group is being greatly encouraged in this upward stride by the happy relation existing between the races, which is quite evident in the mining sections as well as other parts of the state. They work side by side and are

Left: *M.T. Whittier, Proprietor and Editor* McDowell Times, *Keystone, W.Va.* Right: *Hon. Harry J. Capehart, Third term member of W.Va. legislature, owner Capehart Hotel, Welch, W.Va.*

Left: *W. W. Sanders, Supervisor Colored Rural Schools, Chairman Advisory Council State Board of Education, Charleston, W.Va.* Right: *Ruth Stephenson, A.B., teacher of English, Charleston, W.Va.*

members of the same union. It frequently happens that colored men are presidents of the local unions and direct the policy of the union. They meet on a common level and fight for a common cause.

Charleston is possibly the most progressive section of the state—it being the capital and magnet around which gravitate all activities of the state. Here you find the Negro engaged in every walk of life. In this wide-awake city there are bankers, wholesale commission merchants, real estate men,

Left: *W. W. Sanders, Prin. Secretary to Supt. of Colored Rural Schools, Charleston, W.Va.* Right: *A. H. Brown, Auditor, Mutual Savings and Loan Co., Charleston, W.Va.*

Left: *Mrs. T. G. Nutter, Charleston, W.Va.* Right: *Maude Wanzer, Director Wanzer's School of Music and Musical Dept. of Garnett High School, Charleston, W.Va.*

merchants, contractors, carpenters, brick-masons, lawyers, doctors, preachers, and what not. Here one will find the best appointed Negro hotel in America, the Ferguson, owned and managed by Captain G. E. Ferguson, a veteran of the World War. Some of the most beautiful homes owned by Negroes in West Virginia are located in this city.

The idea of home ownership is spreading over the entire state, and magnificent homes are owned by our group in Huntington, Parkersburg,

Left: *F. H. Huskins, Field Agent State Board of Children's Guardians, Charleston, W.Va.* Right: *Hazel K. Lucas, Secretary Charleston Branch, N.A.A.C.P., secretary to Hon. T. G. Nutter, Charleston, W.Va.*

Wheeling, Bluefield, Keystone, Fairmont, Beckley, Morgantown and other sections. The social life of the people is of the highest order. In these cities you will find as progressive and enterprising a people as is found anywhere. It is truly stated, that "West Virginia is the garden spot of America for the Negro."

SUBJECT INDEX

ABOUT THE EDITORS

Tom Lutz is an associate professor of English at the University of Iowa and the author of *American Nervousness, 1903: An Anecdotal History* (Cornell University Press, 1991).

Susanna Ashton is an instructor of English at the University of Iowa.